INTELLECTUAL PROPERTY TITLES FROM WILEY LAW PUBLICATIONS

ELECTRONIC CONTRACTING, PUBLISHING, AND EDI LAW
Michael S. Baum and Henry H. Perritt, Jr.

HOW TO LICENSE TECHNOLOGY
Robert C. Megantz

INTELLECTUAL PROPERTY: LICENSING AND JOINT VENTURE PROFIT STRATEGIES
Gordon V. Smith and Russell L. Parr

INTELLECTUAL PROPERTY FOR THE INTERNET
Lewis C. Lee and J. Scott Davidson, Editors

INTELLECTUAL PROPERTY INFRINGEMENT DAMAGES: A LITIGATION SUPPORT HANDBOOK
Russell L. Parr

INTELLECTUAL PROPERTY LITIGATION: PRETRIAL PRACTICE GUIDE
Eric M. Dobrusin

LAW AND THE INFORMATION SUPERHIGHWAY: PRIVACY • ACCESS • INTELLECTUAL PROPERTY • COMMERCE • LIABILITY
Henry H. Perritt, Jr.

MANAGING INTELLECTUAL PROPERTY RIGHTS
Lewis C. Lee and J. Scott Davidson

MULTIMEDIA LEGAL HANDBOOK: A GUIDE FROM THE SOFTWARE PUBLISHERS ASSOCIATION
Thomas J. Smedinghoff

1997 WILEY INTELLECTUAL PROPERTY LAW UPDATE
Anthony B. Askew and Elizabeth C. Jacobs

PROTECTING TRADE DRESS
Robert C. Dorr and Christopher H. Munch

PROTECTING TRADE SECRETS, PATENTS, COPYRIGHTS, AND TRADEMARKS (SECOND EDITION)
Robert C. Dorr and Christopher H. Munch

SOFTWARE INDUSTRY ACCOUNTING
Joseph M. Morris

INTELLECTUAL PROPERTY
FOR THE INTERNET

SUBSCRIPTION NOTICE

This Wiley product is updated on a periodic basis with supplements to reflect important changes in the subject matter. If you purchased this product directly from John Wiley & Sons, Inc., we have already recorded your subscription for this update service.

If, however, you purchased this product from a bookstore and wish to receive (1) the current update at no additional charge, and (2) future updates and revised or related volumes billed separately with a 30-day examination review, please send your name, company name (if applicable), address and the title of the product to:

Supplement Department
John Wiley & Sons, Inc.
One Wiley Drive
Somerset, NJ 08875
1-800-225-5945

For customers outside the United States, please contact the Wiley office nearest you.

Professional and Reference Division
John Wiley & Sons Canada, Ltd.
22 Worcester Road
Rexdale, Ontario M9W 1L1
CANADA
(416) 675-3580
1-800-567-4797
FAX (416) 675-6599

John Wiley & Sons, Ltd.
Baffins Lane
Chichester
West Sussex, PO19 1UD
UNITED KINGDOM
(44) (243) 779777

Jacaranda Wiley Ltd.
PRT Division
P.O. Box 174
North Ryde, NSW 2113
AUSTRALIA
(02) 805-1100
FAX (02) 805-1597

John Wiley & Sons (SEA)
  Pte. Ltd.
2 Clementi Loop
#02-01 Jin Xing Distripark
SINGAPORE 0512
4632400
FAX 4634604

INTELLECTUAL PROPERTY FOR THE INTERNET

LEWIS C. LEE, EDITOR

Lee & Hayes, PLLC
Spokane, Washington

J. SCOTT DAVIDSON, EDITOR

Nixon & Vanderhye, PC
Arlington, Virginia

Wiley Law Publications

JOHN WILEY & SONS, INC.

New York · Chichester · Weinheim · Brisbane · Singapore · Toronto

Library of Congress Cataloging-in-Publication Data

ISBN 0-471-16703-7

Printed in the United States of America

10 9 8 7 6 5 4 3 2 1

To my wife, Sarah, and to my children, Jordan, Brendan, and Lindsay

L.C.L.

To my wife, Julie, and to my son, Samuel

J.S.D.

PREFACE

The Internet is one of the hottest topics in today's culture. E-mailing people across the world, banking on-line, strolling through Web pages, shopping by computer, and other marvels of the Internet have us fascinated with this new toy. The Internet has connected us to people and companies that we never knew before. But, as large as the Internet seems to those of us who use it, all of the technology underlying the Internet dwarfs what we actually see. Companies are racing to supply the enormous amounts of hardware and software required to operate this global network. With so much new technology evolving to support the network and its applications, company executives are obviously concerned about protecting their innovations from theft by competitors.

That's where intellectual property strategies come into play. A typical by-product of a rapidly evolving technological arena like the Internet is the increasing interest in protecting the ideas, concepts, names, and secrets emanating from that arena. Those ideas, concepts, names, and secrets are generically referred to as "intellectual property," since they can be claimed as property rights even though they are only intangible mental work products. The intellectual property currently being employed by Internet users is overwhelming. And by failing to adequately protect their property, some companies are just giving their rights away.

Our practice has shown us that many company managers and executives are well versed in their company's technology, but less experienced in how to protect the intellectual property they have created in it. Others, on the other hand, are more adept at the intellectual property protections than the technology being employed. Of course, in the ideal situation, each company engineer, manager, and executive would be acutely aware of both the technology and the property rights available to protect it. We, however, live in the real world where engineers, managers, and executives have too little time to become experts in all the fields associated with their company's business. But certainly each has time to grasp at least a general understanding of Internet technology, along with a framework for appropriately protecting the innovations of the company in this area. To do otherwise means to risk forfeiting valuable property rights.

We designed this book with the understanding that companies need, in easily understandable language, an outline of the intricacies of intellectual property protections in Internet technology. The book is designed to introduce engineers, technical managers, and attorneys to the intellectual property protections available within the framework of various Internet technologies. The chapters of the book have been broken down into the various technologies. In each chapter, a skilled intellectual property attorney has provided a look at the intellectual property protections that may have an impact on the technology discussed. The book has 10 chapters, the first eight of which focus primarily on U.S. intellectual property protections:

In **Chapters 1** through **3,** Lewis Lee and Scott Davidson present an overview of the Internet and an introduction to the various intellectual property protections. A general review is provided for patents, trademarks, copyrights, and trade secret protections. Then, intellectual property strategies are discussed for communication technologies and for encryption techniques on the Internet.

In **Chapter 4,** Dan Hayes discusses the hardware and software used to serve contents over the Internet—called "Servers"—and the intellectual property strategies for them.

In **Chapter 5,** Curt Rose presents a wonderfully entertaining discussion of the evolution of intellectual property protections for the user interfaces that enable human users to interact with the Internet.

In **Chapter 6,** Dan Laster examines copyright, trademark, and database issues that exist for the Internet. This chapter pays particular attention to copyright and trademark protections for these technologies.

In **Chapter 7,** Dan Crouse carefully guides the reader through the maze of standards that exist (or can exist) for Internet technologies.

In **Chapter 8,** Katie Sako provides an overview of litigation strategies that must be considered when analyzing intellectual property for the Internet.

Although the Internet originated in the United States, part of its luster is its boundless nature. The Internet now has an impact across the world. **Chapters 9** and **10** of this book are a special treat—they provide a look at intellectual property strategies for Internet technologies in foreign countries:

In **Chapter 9,** Heinz Goddar and Axel Nordemann take the reader through Internet protections available in Europe.

In **Chapter 10,** Joon Park explores intellectual property in Asia and its effect on Internet technologies there.

Because this book must cover two huge areas of information (the Internet *and* intellectual property)—each of which alone could consume several books of text—the present book is designed to review each technological area with an emphasis on the interrelationship between the technology and appropriate intellectual property protections. A book this size cannot purport to cover every conceivable aspect of the Internet technologies discussed, nor is it intended to provide specific legal advice to readers. This book does provide a much-needed look at the impact that intellectual property is having, and will have, on the wide range of Internet technologies being developed. Hopefully, reading it will help you understand where, in the world of Internet technology, intellectual properties are having their most significant impact and how your company can capitalize on them.

We hope you enjoy it.

February 1997

Lewis C. Lee
Spokane, Washington

J. Scott Davidson
Arlington, Virginia

ACKNOWLEDGMENTS

We would like to thank our contributors, whose thoughtful works have turned an idea into a reality. Our contributors are among the best minds in the Intellectual Property bar, but more importantly, they are genuinely great people. We would also like to thank Theresa Gaston for her tremendous assistance in coordinating this effort.

ABOUT THE EDITORS

Lewis C. Lee is a partner at Lee & Hayes, PLLC, an intellectual property law firm located in Spokane, Washington, that specializes in patent-related issues involving software and electronic technologies. He earned a B.S. degree in electrical engineering and a B.A. degree in business administration from Washington State University, and a J.D. degree from George Washington University. Lewis is a lecturer at the Center for Advanced Study and Research on Intellectual Property based at the University of Washington School of Law. He is admitted to practice in the state of Washington and before the U.S. Patent and Trademark Office. A member of Tau Beta Pi, the American Intellectual Property Law Association, and the Institute of Electronics and Electrical Engineers, Lewis co-authored *Managing Intellectual Property Rights* (John Wiley & Sons, Inc. 1993). He can be reached at
   lewis@leehay.attmail.com.

J. Scott Davidson is a partner in the intellectual property law firm of Nixon & Vanderhye, PC, in Arlington, Virginia. He earned a B.S. degree in electrical engineering from the University of South Florida and received a J.D. degree from the University of Florida. Admitted to practice law in Florida, Virginia, and the District of Columbia, he is also registered to practice before the U.S. Patent and Trademark Office as well as the Court of Appeals for the Federal Circuit. A member of Tau Beta Pi, Omicron Delta Kappa, the American Intellectual Property Law Association, and the Institute of Electronics and Electrical Engineers, Scott co-authored *Managing Intellectual Property Rights* (John Wiley & Sons, Inc. 1993). He can be reached at
   jsd@nixonvan.com.

ABOUT THE CONTRIBUTORS

Dan Crouse is a senior corporate attorney at Microsoft Corporation. Dan received his B.S. degree in electrical engineering from Iowa State University and a J.D. degree from the University of Iowa. Prior to joining Microsoft, he was a partner at Christensen, O'Connor, Johnson & Kindness, an intellectual property law firm in Seattle, Washington. Dan is a member of Tau Beta Pi, the Order of the Coif, and the American Intellectual Property Law Association (AIPLA). Dan is also on the Editorial Board of the *AIPLA Journal* and a lecturer at the Center for Advanced Study and Research on Intellectual Property based at the University of Washington School of Law. He is admitted to practice law in the state of Washington, and before the U.S. Patent and Trademark Office.

Heinz Goddar is a German and European patent attorney. He is a partner with Boehmert & Boehmert and Forrester & Boehmert, with offices at Alicante, Bremen, Düsseldorf, Kiel, Leipzig, Munich, Potsdam, Birmingham, and London. He has a Ph.D. in physics and physical chemistry. Before his career as a patent attorney, he was an assistant professor at the Physical Chemistry Department of the University of Mainz, Germany. Dr. Goddar is particularly responsible for international patent and licensing matters, including litigation and arbitration, with a special interest in EU (European Union) questions. An associate judge at the Senate for Patent Attorneys Matters at the German Federal Supreme Court, he is also a lecturer at the Center for Advanced Study and Research on Intellectual Property based at the University of Washington School of Law.

Daniel L. Hayes is a partner in the intellectual property law firm of Lee & Hayes, PLLC, in Spokane, Washington. Dan has a B.S. degree in electrical engineering from Washington State University and a J.D. degree from Gonzaga University, where he graduated summa cum laude. He is admitted to practice law in the state of Washington and is registered to practice before the U.S. Patent and Trademark Office and the Court of Appeals for the Federal Circuit. He is a member of the American Intellectual Property Law Association and the Institute of Electronics and Electrical Engineers. Dan can be reached at dan@leehay.attmail.com.

Daniel Laster is a senior corporate attorney at Microsoft Corporation, specializing in trademark and copyright matters. Dan received his B.A. degree from Pennsylvania State University and a J.D. degree from Harvard Law School and the University of Michigan. Prior to joining Microsoft, he was a senior lecturer at the University of Otage Faculty of Law in Dunedin, New Zealand. Dan is a member of Phi Beta Kappa, the Washington State Bar, and the Washington State Patent Law Association. He is admitted to practice law in the state of Washington.

Dr. Axel Nordemann Dr. jur., is an attorney at law and partner at Boehmert & Boehmert, a German law firm specializing in industrial and intellectual property. He is a former research fellow at the Max Planck Institute for Foreign and International Patent, Copyright, and Competition Law in Munich. Dr. Nordemann studied law in Göttingen and Munich and was admitted to the bar in 1992. He has published works on copyright protection for photography, unfair competition law, and trademark law. He can be reached at

boehmert.nordemann@t-online.de; postmaster@boehmert.de

Joon Kook Park is legal counsel for the Korean Commissioner of Patents and a partner at Shin & Kim, an intellectual property law firm. He received an LL.B. degree summa cum laude from Seoul National University College of Law, a J.D. degree from Wake Forest University School of Law, and an LL.M. degree in intellectual property law from the National Law Center at George Washington University. A former judicial clerk in the U.S. Court of International Trade, economic advisor at the U.S. Embassy in Korea, and manager in the Legal Affairs Department/Overseas Business Department of Hanhwa Business Group, Mr. Park is currently a lecturer at the International Intellectual Property Training Institute at Samsung Advanced Institute of Technology and an arbitrator at WIPO Arbitration Center. He is a member of the American Bar Association, American Intellectual Property Association, International Trademark Association, North Carolina State Bar, Washington, D.C. Bar, and the Court of Appeals for the Federal Circuit Bar. He is the author of *U.S. Patent Practice* (Hanbit Intellectual Property Center 1995). Mr. Park can be reached at

(Telephone): 822-3149-7810; (Fax): 822-3149-7839.

Curtis G. Rose is a senior regional attorney for the Hewlett-Packard Company in Corvallis, Oregon, where he manages the Intellectual Property Section of the Corvallis Legal Department and supports clients engaged in the research and development of HP's notebook personal computers, high-end graphics software, and diagnostic cardiology medical devices. He is an adjunct professor at the University of Oregon Law School. Before joining HP in 1993, Mr. Rose was a senior attorney for IBM at Rochester, Minnesota, supporting clients in the research and development of midrange computer software. Mr. Rose received a B.S. degree in electrical engineering and a B.A. degree in interpersonal public communications from Purdue University and earned a J.D. degree from George Washington University. Mr. Rose is licensed to practice before the U.S. Patent Trademark Office and in Minnesota and Oregon. He has had articles published in the *Journal of the Patent and Trademark Office Society* and the *Computer Lawyer.* He can be reached at

curt_rose@hp.com.

Katie Sako is a senior corporate attorney at Microsoft Corporation, responsible for the Internet Platform and Tools Division. Katie earned a B.S. degree in computer science and a J.D. degree from the University of Washington. Prior to joining Microsoft, she was associated with the intellectual property law firm of Christensen, O'Connor, Johnson & Kindness in Seattle, Washington. A former adjunct professor at the University of Washington School of Law, Ms. Sako is a lecturer at the Center for Advanced Study and Research on Intellectual Property based at the University of Washington School of Law. She is admitted to practice law in the state of Washington and before the U.S. Patent and Trademark Office. She is a member of the Washington State Bar, the U.S. Patent Bar, and the Washington State Patent Lawyer's Association.

SUMMARY CONTENTS

DETAILED CONTENTS

SHORT REFERENCE LIST

Short Reference	Full Reference
ACM	Association of Computing Machinery
ANSI	American National Standards Institute
ARPA	Advanced Research Projects Administration
ARPANET	Advanced Research Projects Administration Network
ASCII	American Standard Code for Information Interchange
ATM	Asynchronous Transfer Mode
BBS	bulletin board system
B-ISDN	Broadband Integrated Services Digital Network
BPS	Philippines Bureau of Product Standards
BSR	Board of Standards Review
CCIR	Consultative Committee International Radio
CCIT	Consultative Committee International Telegraph and Telephone
CDCC	Copyright Deliberation and Conciliation Committee
CDMA	Code Division Multiple Access
CD-I	compact disc, interactive
CEN	European Standards Committee
CEN/CENELEC	Joint European Standards Institution
CENELEC	European Electrotechnical Standards Committee
CERN	European Laboratory for Particle Physics

Short Reference	*Full Reference*
CONTU	Commission on New Technological Uses of Copyrighted Works
CPPA	Computer Program Protection Act
CSBTS	China State Bureau of Technical Supervision
CSK	Committee for Standardization of the Democratic People's Republic of Korea
DARPA	Defense Advanced Research Projects Agency
DDN	Defense Data Network
DES	Data Encryption Standard
DGIII	Directorate General III
DIS	Draft International Standard
DLL	dynamic-link library
DNS	Domain Name Service
DSM	Department of Standards of Malaysia
EBU	European Broadcasting Union
EC	European Council
EDI	electronic data interchange
EEPROM	electrically erasable and programmable read-only memory
ENs	European Standards
ENVs	European Pre-standards
EPIIS	European Information Infrastructure Standardization
ETSI	European Telecommunications Standards Institute
EU	European Union
FDDI	Fiber Distributed Data Interface
FDIS	Final Draft International Standard

Short Reference	*Full Reference*
FIRP	Federal Internetworking Requirements Panel
FTC	Federal Trade Commission (United States)
FTP	File Transfer Protocol
GIF	graphics interchange format
GII	Global Information Infrastructure
GIS	Global Information Society
GMS	Global System for Mobile Communications
GOSIP	Government OSI Profile
G7	"Group of Seven" (Canada, France, Germany, Italy, Japan, the United Kingdom, and the United States)
GUI	graphical user interface
HDs	Harmonization Documents
HLSG	High-Level Strategy Group
HTML	Hypertext Markup Language
IAB	Internet Architecture Board
IANA	Internet Assigned Numbers Authority
IC	integrated circuit
ICT	Information and Communications Technology
IEC	International Electrotechnical Commission
IEEE	Institute of Electrical & Electronics Engineers
IESG	Internet Engineering Steering Group
IETF	Internet Engineering Task Force
IFRB	International Frequency Registration Board
IISP	Information Infrastructure Standards Panel

Short Reference	*Full Reference*
INRIA	French National Information Processing/Automation Laboratory
INTAP	Interoperability Technology Association for Information Processing
InterNICs	Internet Network Information Centers
IP	intellectual property
IP	Internet protocol
IPO	initial public offering
IPR	intellectual property rights
IPSJ/ITSCJ	Information Processing Society of Japan/Information Technology Standards Commission of Japan
IRSG	Internet Research Steering Group
IRTF	Internet Research Task Force
IS	International Standard
ISDN	Integrated Services Digital Network
ISO	International Organization for Standardization
ISOC	Internet Society
ISP	International Standardized Profile
IT	information technology
ITTF	Information Technology Task Force
ITU	International Telecommunications Union
ITU-D	ITU Telecommunications Development Sector
ITU-R	ITU Radiocommunication Sector
ITU-T	ITU Telecommunication Standardization Sector
JASRAC	Japanese Society of Rights of Authors and Composers

Short Reference	Full Reference
JCA	Japanese Copyright Act
JDC	Japanese Digital Cellular
JEIDA	Japan Electronic Industry Development Association
JISC	Japanese Industrial Standards Committee
JPA	Japanese Patent Act
JPEG	Joint Photographic Experts Group
JPO	Japan Patent Office
JTC 1	ISO/IEC Joint Technical Committee
KCA	Korean Copyright Act
KIPO	Korean Industrial Property Office
KNITQ	Korean National Institute of Technology and Quality
KPA	Korean Patent Act
LAN	local area network
MCI	Ministry of Culture and Information (Korea)
MHEG	Multimedia and Hypermedia Experts Group
MIDI	musical instrument digital interface
MNISM	Mongolian National Institute for Standardization and Metrology
MPEG	Moving Picture Experts Group
MUX	multiplex
NCSA	National Center for Supercomputing Applications
NII	National Information Infrastructure
NIST	National Institute of Standards and Technology
NMF	Network Management Forum

Short Reference	*Full Reference*
NSI	Network Solutions, Inc.
OSF	Open Software Foundation
OSI	Open System Interconnection
PARC	Palo Alto Research Center
PAS	Publicly Available Specifications
PCT	Patent Cooperation Treaty
PCT	Private Communication Technology
PIN	Personal Identification Number
POPs	points of presence
POTS	Plain Old Telephone Service
PSB	Singapore Productivity and Standards Board
PTO	Patent and Trademark Office
RER	Referencing Explanatory Report
RFCs	Requests for Comment
ROM	read-only memory
RS	Referenced Specification
SAA	Standards Australia
SC	subcommittee
SGFS	Special Group on Functional Standardization
SGML	Standard Generalized Markup Language
SIMMs	Single In-line Memory Modules
SMTP	Simple Mail Transfer Protocol
SNMP	Simple Network Management Protocol

Short Reference	*Full Reference*
SNZ	Standards New Zealand
SSL	Secure Socket Layer
SWG	Special Working Group
TC	Technical Committee
TCOS	Telesec chipcard operating system
TCVN	Vietnam Directorate for Standards and Quality
TCP/IP	Transmission Control Protocol/Internet Protocol
TDMA	Time Division Multiple Access
TEDIS	Trade Electronic Data Interchange System
TIFF	tag image file format
TISI	Thai Industrial Standards Institute
TSAG	Telecommunications Standardization Advisory Group
TSB	Telecommunications Standards Bureau
TTC	Telecommunications Technology Committee
UCC	Universal Copyright Convention
UCPA	Unfair Competition Prevention Act
URL	Uniform Resource Locator
US TAG	United States Technical Advisory Group
UTSA	Uniform Trade Secrets Act
UWG	German Unfair Competition Act
VAG	VRML Architecture Group
VESA	Video Electronics Standards Association
VLSI	very large-scale integration

Short Reference	*Full Reference*
VRML	Virtual Reality Modeling Language
WAN	wide area network
WG	Working Group
W3C	World Wide Web Consortium
WWW	World Wide Web

CHAPTER 1

INTELLECTUAL PROPERTY AND THE INTERNET

Lewis C. Lee

J. Scott Davidson

§ 1.1   Introduction

This book explores two of the hottest topics of our day: the Internet and intellectual property. The Internet is experiencing unprecedented publicity and news coverage from both financial markets and technical circles. Record-shattering IPOs by Internet companies like Netscape, Yahoo!, and UUNet have underscored Wall Street's love affair with the Internet. For a time, the simple association between any company and the Internet made that company's stock an instant buy on most brokers' lists.

In the technical world, the trade magazines continually explore the vastness and usefulness of the Internet, often called simply "the Net." Is it really the Information Superhighway? Trade articles discuss the inevitable takeover of the Net as the primary distribution medium for information and knowledge. Pundits of all sorts ponder whether the Net is itself the computer of the future, with editorials and CEO interviews evangelizing small $500 network computers whose sole purpose is to provide access to the Internet. Strategic alliances among communications companies, computer companies, and software companies are being made and broken routinely.

To fuel the drama, several extraordinarily wealthy and technically sophisticated individuals, like Bill Gates,[1] Scott McNealy,[2] and Larry Ellison[3] to name a few, publicly banter and debate ideas regarding how the Internet will change the future. Oftentimes, it is impossible to determine from the articles themselves whether you are reading *Fortune, Wired,* or *PC Week.*

These are the times we live in—fast-paced, constantly evolving times. Our children are as comfortable with a computer mouse as they are with a baseball and bat. Surfing the Internet is becoming common, with seemingly every company, entity, Tom, Dick, and Susie having a Web page. We no longer send letters to one another, but e-mails. Acronyms like TCP/IP,[4] WWW,[5] HTML,[6] and URL[7] are becoming part of our normal dialog.

Other forms of media are capitalizing on the craze. A new 24-hour news network named MSNBC[8] began airing in July 1996 on traditional cable television to provide up-to-date news coverage, and it simultaneously went online over the Internet to provide the same, complementary, and often expanded news coverage.

The Internet is hot, but there is another IP that is equally as hot. This IP is not Internet protocol, but intellectual property. Companies that own intellectual property rights on their technologies will survive well into the twenty-first century, while those that do not own such rights will struggle against increasingly greater odds.

For many companies associated with the Internet, intellectual property is a foreign concept. These companies, which are predominately software companies, have forever been told that software is not patentable and copyright protection is the best that they can get. Because copyright protection for software is not very difficult to obtain, software companies have traditionally placed little

---

[1] CEO of Microsoft Corporation.

[2] CEO of Sun Microsystems Company.

[3] CEO of Oracle Corporation.

[4] Transmission Control Protocol/Internet Protocol.

[5] World Wide Web.

[6] Hypertext Markup Language.

[7] Uniform Resource Locator.

[8] MSNBC is a joint venture of Microsoft Corporation and the National Broadcasting Company.

emphasis on intellectual property. Rarely did pure software companies have in-house legal staffs specializing in the area of intellectual property.

However, times have changed. Software is patentable and the Patent and Trademark Office is issuing thousands of software patents a year. Software companies are taking note and developing intellectual property strategies in support of their business models. Software executives are beginning to recognize the value of intellectual property as a means for doing business in an immensely competitive global economy. To be able to participate effectively in the evolving marketplace, whether it be at a standards committee or a business alliance meeting or a technology licensing negotiation, a company needs to have its own set of intellectual property rights that can be used strategically.

§ 1.2   The Internet

Although the Internet has risen to national prominence only in the last few years, it was created over two decades ago by a group known as the Defense Advanced Research Projects Administration, or DARPA. The goal of DARPA was to create a way for widely separated computers to transfer information and data and to make these data communications as robust and reliable as possible.[9] Over time, the network evolved beyond defense-related projects, as universities and other government agencies were connected. The network became known as the ARPANET, for Advanced Research Projects Administration NETwork.

Today, the Internet interconnects computers from around the world. It is formed by the cooperative interconnection of computing networks, including local area networks (LANs) and wide area networks (WANs). The Internet connects existing and often incompatible technologies by employing common protocols that smoothly integrate the individual and diverse components.

The Internet has recently been popularized by the overwhelming and rapid success of the World Wide Web (WWW or Web). The Web links together various topics in a complex, nonsequential web of associations which permit a user to browse from one topic to another, regardless of the presented order of topics. A *Web browser,* such as Netscape's Navigator and Microsoft's Internet Explorer, is a graphical user interface (GUI—pronounced "gooey") which is executed on the user's computer to navigate or explore the Web. The Web browser allows a user to retrieve and render hypermedia content from the WWW, including text, sound, images, video, and other data.

Figure 1–1 is a pictorial representation of the Internet, and how expansive and diverse it can be. Traditionally, the Internet was used to link universities and government agencies. Today, however, there are many content providers ready to serve video, audio, multimedia, and other information over the Internet to home-based or corporate-based clients. Home users attach to the Internet

---

[9] Rick Stout, The World Wide Web Complete Reference, (1996).

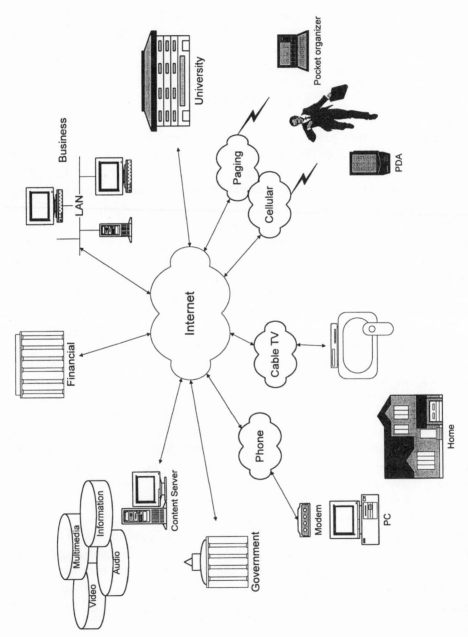

Figure 1–1. Illustration of the Internet.

through Internet service providers (ISPs) using modems and common telephone networks. Businesses provide access to the Internet from their LANs, using appropriate safeguards to prevent unauthorized access by outside parties to a company's internal network. Banks, brokerages, and other financial institutions are becoming connected. Merchants, vendors, and other commercial establishments support Web pages and enable buying and selling of goods over the Internet. It may soon be common for information delivered over the Internet to be delivered to users over traditional networks, such as cable television, cellular telephones, and paging networks.

Today, people can bank, buy stocks, order clothes, research limitless volumes of information from around the world, chat with others, send e-mail to the President of the United States, earn a college education, or simply have fun surfing the Web, all from the comfort of their own home computers.

§ 1.3 Protecting the Internet

The Internet involves a tremendous amount of technology. Because technology is fast becoming one of the most valuable assets a company can own, it follows that companies are seeking ways to protect their intellectual property rights in their technology. There are several ways that one can seek to protect intellectual property, but the most popular are patents, trademarks, copyrights, and trade secrets. Patents protect the technology itself by providing the right to exclude anyone from making, using, selling, offering to sell, or importing the technology. Patents are thus specific to the technology itself.

Trademarks are not specific to the technology but are instead specific to the source of the technology, that is, a particular company. Thus, a trademark protects the owner from a competitor's use of a confusingly similar name to identify similar goods or services. Copyrights protect the expressions of technology, such as printed materials and software written onto computer memory.

Trade secrets are intellectual property that, like patents, protect the technology itself. In the case of trade secret protection, a company can prevent someone from stealing company secrets.

This chapter provides a general overview of each of these intellectual property protections. The following chapters discuss the appropriateness of each protection for particular Internet technologies.

§ 1.4 Patents

A patent provides an ownership right in a new and useful technological innovation. It is perhaps best viewed as an agreement between the inventor and the federal government. The federal government awards the inventor exclusive ownership of an invention in exchange for disclosing the invention to the public. The benefit to the inventor is the right to prevent others from making, using, or selling the invention for a limited period of time. The benefit to the government is the technological advancement to society that is gained from public disclosure of the invention, whereby members of society are immediately able to study and learn from the technological innovation, even during the limited exclusive term of the patent. The patent may also be viewed as a reward for creative innovation and intellectual advancement. The exclusive right gives the inventor the incentive to innovate.

The United States Constitution empowers Congress to promote the progress of useful arts by securing for limited times to inventors the exclusive right to their discoveries.[10] Under this authority, Congress has enacted a patent statute, Title 35 of the United States Code. Patent law is governed exclusively by this federal statute. There is no state-governed patent law.

§ 1.5 —Subject Matter

A pressing question has been whether it is possible to patent Internet technologies. The answer is a resounding *yes*. The patent statute defines patentable subject matter as "any new and useful process, machine, manufacture, or composition of matter, or any new or useful improvement thereof."[11] This list might appear to be rather limited, or perhaps grossly outdated. There are stories of inventors who have patented such things as the hoola-hoop and genetically engineered mice, but no mice are mentioned in the definition of patentable subject matter. More importantly, the list does not mention modern-day computers, microprocessors, integrated circuit chips, modems, and networks, all of which are crucial for the Internet.

Fortunately, the classes of patentable subject matter are broadly interpreted. The class *machines,* for instance, covers mechanical things like ball-point pens, fire hydrants, and paper clips as well as electronic things like computers, calculators, integrated circuit chips, and networks. The class *processes* is defined to include any process, art, or method, as well as any new use of a known process, machine, manufacture, composition of matter, or material.[12] Methods for operating computers, sending data over a network, or displaying information on a screen are patentable subject matter under the *processes* class.

In fact, most of the Internet technologies can be included under the classes *processes* and *machines*. It is also important to remember that the statutory definition of patentable subject matter includes "any new or useful improvement" of a machine or process.

Thus, the realm of patentable subject matter is quite expansive. Indeed, to the excitement of the patent bar, the Supreme Court once pronounced that the

---

[10] U.S. Const. art. I, § 8, cl. 8.

[11] 35 U.S.C. § 101.

[12] *Id.* § 100.

congressional intent in defining patentable subject matter was to "include anything under the sun that is made by man."[13] Internet technologies are certainly
made by humans and often under the sun (except, perhaps, for those ideas
churned out by caffeine-guzzling Net-heads who work well into the night after
the sun has set peacefully over the horizon). Thus, Internet technologies must be
patentable, too.

§ 1.6   —Patent Requirements

Like other technologies, Internet technologies must satisfy the requirements
dictated by federal patent statute for obtaining patent protection. These requirements are:

1. Novelty
2. Nonobviousness
3. Utility
4. Enablement and best mode.

The patent statute requires that the subject matter be *novel* or new to receive
patent protection. The novelty requirement is defined in § 102 of the patent
statute.[14] Instead of defining what is novel, however, § 102 describes several
events that dictate when subject matter is not novel. Events like selling the
technology, or publicly using the technology, or describing the technology in a
printed publication more than one year before submitting a patent application
indicate that the invention is not new when the patent application is submitted to
the Patent and Trademark Office.

When one of these events occurs, patentability is prevented for lack of novelty. For this reason, the events described in § 102 are sometimes referred to in
the patent profession as the § 102 bars to patentability. If any one of the events
occurs, the event will bar or prevent patentability of the subject matter. Understanding how the § 102 bars operate is critical to understanding how otherwise
meritorious inventions can lose their opportunity for patentability.

An important aspect of the § 102 bars is that each bar is concerned with "the"
invention, so that the applicant is entitled to a patent unless "the invention" was
known, or "the invention" was on sale or offered for sale, or "the invention" was
described in a publication. This language leads to an important requirement of
§ 102. To bar patentability under § 102, the previously invented subject matter
must be identical to "the" claimed invention. In patent terminology, this means
that the previously invented subject matter must "anticipate" the applicant's
claimed invention. If your company's invention is not clearly anticipated by

---

[13] Diamond v. Chakrabarty, 447 U.S. 303, 206 U.S.P.Q. (BNA) 193 (1980).
[14] 35 U.S.C. § 102.

somebody else's invention, then § 102 will not bar patentability of your company's invention.

If novelty under § 102 were the only criterion for patentability under the patent statute, a patent applicant might be awarded a patent for each implementation that is not identical to prior art implementations. Under the patent statute, however, an invention surviving the novelty requirements of § 102 is not guaranteed patent protection.

Instead, § 103 of the patent statute[15] prevents the grant of a patent on an invention that is merely an *obvious* variation of known technology. Specifically, § 103 requires that, even though the claimed invention is novel under § 102, a patent will not be awarded if the difference between the claimed subject matter and the prior teaching is obvious to those of ordinary skill in the art to which the subject matter pertains at the time the applicant makes the invention. The procedure for determining nonobviousness includes:

1. Determining the differences between the claimed invention and the prior teaching
2. Determining what level of knowledge a hypothetical person having ordinary skill in the art would possess
3. Determining whether such a hypothetical person would consider the differences obvious.

In conducting the analysis, the hypothetical, ordinarily skilled person is really quite extraordinary, as this person is presumed to know all of the prior art in the field of endeavor, as though the references were hanging on the walls around the person.[16]

Another patent requirement is that the invention be new and useful.[17] Inventions that have no utility are not patentable. This requirement, however, is almost always satisfied. The classic example of an invention that does not satisfy this requirement is a perpetual motion machine.

The final patentability requirement is that the patent specification sufficiently describe in clear and complete terms how one of ordinary skill in the technological field would make and use the invention, including the best way to make and use the invention known to the inventor at the time of filing the patent application.[18] Because the goal of the patent process, at least with respect to the government, is to advance society's technological position through disclosure of new inventions, the government understandably requires that the specification teach others in sufficient detail how to best practice the invention.

---

[15] *Id.* § 103.

[16] Union Carbide Corp. v. American Can Co., 724 F.2d 1567, 220 U.S.P.Q. (BNA) 584 (Fed. Cir. 1984).

[17] 35 U.S.C. § 101.

[18] *Id.* § 112.

Technically, *enablement* and *best mode* are two separate requirements. They are designed to prevent inventors from obtaining patent protection for inventions without telling others the best way to practice their inventions. The requirements do not go to the merits of whether an invention is patentable. The requirements are more of a concern for corporate patent attorneys or counsel because they are typically responsible for writing enabling patent disclosures that disclose the best mode of practicing the invention. However, these requirements are mentioned here to point out that the patent law requires disclosure of the best way to implement the invention in a clear and enabling manner. If this requirement is not met by the inventor and counsel, the patent will be effectively invalid and unenforceable.

§ 1.7 Copyrights

A copyright is an exclusive ownership right in a form of expression. Copyright protection subsists in original works of authorship fixed in any tangible medium of expression, from which the works may be perceived, reproduced, or otherwise communicated.[19] For instance, words fixed to a page, voices fixed to a compact disc, and images fixed to a videotape are all eligible for copyright protection. It is important to note, however, that copyright protection does not extend to the ideas or concepts themselves, but only to the expression of ideas.

Patents and copyrights use different terms to describe the underlying subject matter. In patents, the patentable subject matter is referred to as an *invention*. In copyrights, the copyrightable subject matter is called a *work*.

The United States Constitution grants Congress the power to promote the progress of science by securing for limited times to authors, the exclusive right to their writings.[20] Under this power, Congress enacted a copyright statute, now Title 17 of the United States Code. Copyright law is governed exclusively by this federal statute. There is no state copyright law.

§ 1.8 —Subject Matter

The copyright statute defines copyrightable subject matter as including literary works, musical works, dramatic works, choreographic works, pictorial and sculptural works, motion pictures, sound recordings, and architectural works.[21] These categories are construed very broadly. For example, computer programs, both high-level software and low-level operational codes, are registrable as "literary works." In addition, copyright registration is available for compilations of data.

---

[19] 17 U.S.C. § 102(a).

[20] U.S. Const. art. I, § 8, cl. 8.

[21] 17 U.S.C. § 102(a).

Copyright protection does not extend to an idea, procedure, process, system, method of operation, concept, principle, or discovery, regardless of the form in which it is described.[22] Copyright protection extends only to the form of expression itself. Additionally, copyright protection does not cover titles, names, short phrases, and slogans (although this subject matter might be protectable under trademark law).

§ 1.9 —Copyright Requirements

If the subject matter is copyrightable, copyright protection involves two general requirements:

1. Original authorship
2. Fixation.

Subject matter eligible for copyright protection must be *original*. Works that consist entirely of information that is common property of the public and that do not contain original authorship are not eligible for copyright protection. For example, standard calendars, height and weight charts, tape measures and rulers, and lists or tables taken from public documents or other common sources are not capable of being copyrighted due to lack of originality.

All works must also be *fixed* in a tangible form of expression to be protected by copyright law.[23] This simply means that the subject matter must be expressed in some medium, such as paper, a computer disc, or a cassette tape. Copyright protection does not extend to "unfixed" works, such as a contemporaneous speech.

Copyright laws were historically very formalistic and contained rigid procedural requirements that, if not meticulously followed, could result in loss of copyright protection. Fortunately, a change to the copyright laws in 1988 greatly simplified the acquisition of copyright protection.[24] Today, copyright protection is secured automatically when a work is created and fixed in a tangible medium. As soon as the words in this sentence were written, the words received copyright protection. In addition, works no longer need to be registered with the Copyright Office to receive copyright protection.[25] Registration still remains desirable, however, because it provides proof that a valid copyright exists. Further, registration is required to bring an infringement action under the federal statute.[26]

---

[22] *Id.* § 103.

[23] 17 U.S.C. § 101.

[24] These changes arose out of the Berne Convention, which the United States entered in 1988.

[25] *Id.* § 408(a).

[26] *Id.* §§ 411, 412.

Copyright protection cannot be forfeited for failure to place a copyright notice (that is, the word "copyright" or the "©" copyright symbol, plus the year of publication or creation, plus the name of copyright owner) on the work. Notice is still recommended because it aids in the collection of damages in an infringement suit.[27] If the work carries a copyright notice, the defendant cannot legitimately claim that it innocently copied the work, not knowing that the work was intended to be protected. Therefore, prudence still dictates placing a copyright notice on all works.

§ 1.10   Trademarks

A trademark is any word, name, symbol, device, or combination of such elements used or intended to be used by a company to identify and distinguish its products from those manufactured and sold by others. The classic purpose of a trademark is to indicate the source of the marked products.[28]

Trademarks are governed principally under a dual system of state and federal laws.[29] The federal trademark laws are rooted in the commerce clause of the United States Constitution, which gives Congress the exclusive power to regulate interstate commerce.[30] From this power, Congress enacted a federal trademark statute known as the Lanham Act, or Title 15 of the United States Code.

To qualify for federal trademark protection, products or services must be traded in foreign commerce or across state lines. Because of current liberal interpretation of the term *interstate commerce* in other legal contexts, this is a fairly easy requirement for most companies to meet. Trademark protection under federal law extends throughout the United States.

In addition to federal registration, each state has a trademark registration process. Protection under state trademark law extends only to the state's territorial boundaries. Both federal and state protection may be obtained concurrently. In a clash between federal trademark law and state trademark law, federal trademark law preempts state trademark law.[31]

In the United States, rights in a trademark are established primarily through using the trademark. Some rights may be established in trademarks regardless of whether your company federally registers the mark with the Patent and Trademark Office or registers the mark in a particular state, but federal registration is

---

[27] *Id.* § 401(d).

[28] Lanham Act § 45, 15 U.S.C. § 1127 (1988).

[29] Federal or state registration of a trademark is not mandatory. Common law protects marks that are being publicly used. However, common law protection is geographically limited to the region of actual use.

[30] U.S. Const. art. I, § 8, cl. 3.

[31] Burger King, Inc. v. Hoots, 403 F.2d 904, 159 U.S.P.Q. (BNA) 706 (7th Cir. 1968).

far more desirable. Unregistered trademarks are termed *common law trademarks.* They are enforceable in the market area in which they are actually used.

Federal trademark protection is preferable over state trademark protection if a company intends to trade in interstate commerce, because federal trademark protection extends nationwide. Once a mark is federally registered, no other company can acquire any additional rights superior to those obtained by the federal trademark owner.[32] Additionally, federal registration may deter other companies from selecting a similar trademark. Other companies are more likely to search the federal trademark databases (as opposed to the databases of all 50 states) before selecting a trademark.

§ 1.11   —Subject Matter

Proper trademark subject matter includes fanciful words, some geographic terms and personal names, slogans, symbols, shapes, colors, scents, or visual appearances.

§ 1.12   —Trademark Requirements

Federal trademark protection involves five primary requirements:

1. Affixation
2. Use
3. Distinctiveness
4. Lack of similarity to other marks
5. Nonfunctionality.

The Lanham Act requires that the trademark be displayed on or *affixed* to the products or containers for the products so that the customers can view the marks in the marketplace. The *affixation* requirement makes sense because the purpose of a trademark is to assist the consumer in identifying and distinguishing one company's products from those of another company.

The Lanham Act requires that a company actually *use* the trademark in interstate commerce before registering for trademark protection, or at least have a bona fide *intent to use* the trademark within a period of time after filing for federal trademark protection. For registration based on an intent to use, the company must still eventually use the mark in interstate commerce to secure the requested registration.

Distinctiveness is another requirement for federal trademark protection. A distinctive mark is one that is unique or nonordinary when used with a particular

---

[32] *Id.*

type of goods. Some marks are inherently distinctive and are registrable immediately. Other marks are not distinctive and are not registrable immediately. For
federal registration, a trademark must either be distinctive at the time of registration or become distinctive over time.

The degree of distinctiveness among particular marks is often difficult to
determine. It is useful to think of distinctiveness as a spectrum ranging from
inherently distinctive marks to nondistinctive marks. This spectrum may be
segmented into five categories: fanciful, arbitrary, suggestive, descriptive, and
generic. Fanciful (for example, EXXON, KODAK), arbitrary (for example,
APPLE for computers), and suggestive (for example, COPPERTONE for sun-
tan lotion) marks are inherently distinctive and can be registered immediately
(assuming there is no confusion with another mark). Descriptive marks (for
example, *Yellow Pages* for phone directories) are not inherently distinctive, but
they can satisfy the distinctiveness requirement once they acquire secondary
meaning in the marketplace. A mark acquires secondary meaning when, over
time, consumers have grown to recognize the mark as identifying a particular
company's products. Marks that have been in exclusive and continuous use for
five years are generally considered to have attained secondary meaning and thus
are distinctive.[33]

Trademark protection will not be given to a mark that is likely to cause
confusion with another registered mark.[34] Permitting confusingly similar marks
in the marketplace would negate the purpose of trademarks, which is to assist
the consumer in identifying and distinguishing one company's products or services from those of another.

This *likelihood of confusion* standard necessarily requires inquiry as to whether
the two marks will be used in the same market and for related products or
services. The more similar the marks, products or services, and the market, the
less likely that trademark protection will be granted. On the other hand, trademarks on products that are very different from one another may indicate a small
likelihood of confusion. For example, the mark CADILLAC is registered by one
company for automobiles and by another company for dog food. Because automobiles and dog food are such different classes of goods, there is essentially no
confusion.

Factors that are considered in determining whether two marks are confusingly
similar include:

1. The similarity of the marks with respect to appearance, sound, connota-
    tion, and impression
2. The similarity and nature of the products or services
3. The similarity of established trade channels for the products or services
4. The conditions of the sale (impulse purchase versus sophisticated purchase)

---

[33] Lanham Act § 2(f), 15 U.S.C. § 1052(f) (1988).

[34] *Id.* § 2(d), 15 U.S.C. § 1052(d).

5. Fame of the prior mark
6. The number and nature of similar marks in use on similar products or services
7. The nature and extent of any actual confusion
8. The variety of products and services with which the mark is used.[35]

The final requirement—the *nonfunctionality* requirement—is a judicially created policy that considers whether a shape or feature has some utilitarian purpose or contributes to the ease or economy of manufacture. Trademark protection is typically not available for functional features. The rationale for this requirement is to avoid a clash with patent laws that are designed to protect functional aspects.

The fact that a product having a distinctive shape performs a utilitarian function does not necessarily prevent the shape from receiving trademark protection. For example, all bottles are functional in that they can hold liquid. However, some bottles can be designed with a distinctive shape that sets them apart from other bottles, such as the old Coca-Cola bottle, the Mrs. Butterworth syrup bottle, or the Listerine bottle. Each of these bottles might qualify for trademark protection even though they have a utilitarian purpose of holding liquid.

§ 1.13 Trade Secrets

The Uniform Trade Secrets Act (UTSA) defines a *trade secret* as follows:

> "Trade secret" means information, including a formula, pattern, compilation, program, device, method, technique, or process, that:
>
> (i) derives independent economic value, actual or potential, from not being generally known to, and not being readily ascertainable by proper means by other persons who can obtain economic value from its disclosure or use, and
>
> (ii) is subject of efforts that are reasonable under the circumstances to maintain its secrecy.[36]

In simpler words, a trade secret is confidential information that is valuable to a company by providing an advantage in the marketplace over those who do not know the secret.

Trade secrets are governed solely by state law. There is no federal trade secret law. The UTSA is one attempt to provide uniform treatment of trade secrets among the states, and it is an important source of legal guidance in trade secret matters. However, the states need not adopt the UTSA, and many states that have

---

[35] *In re* E.I. Du Pont de Nemours & Co., 476 F.2d 1357, 177 U.S.P.Q. (BNA) 563 (C.C.P.A. 1973).

[36] Unif. Trade Secrets Act § 1.

adopted it have made changes in its content. Thus, each state has slightly different trade secret laws.

§ 1.14 —Subject Matter

Trade secret protection has practically no subject matter requirements. The UTSA defines proper trade secret subject matter as information "including a formula, pattern, compilation, program, device, method, technique, or process."[37] The scope of subject matter that is protectable as a trade secret is considerably broader than, and includes, the subject matter protectable by patents, copyrights, and trademarks. Thus, trade secret protection includes patentable subject matter (such as machines, processes, articles of manufacture, and compositions of matter), copyrightable subject matter (such as company literature, compilations, and software), and subject matter registrable as a trademark (such as names for future products and future campaign slogans). Examples of subject matter that may be protected by trade secrets include:

1. Engineering blueprints and patterns
2. Drawings and data
3. Computer software
4. Market research studies
5. Operating and pricing policies
6. Processes
7. Customer lists
8. Sources for raw materials.

§ 1.15 —Trade Secret Requirements

Other than the subject matter requirement, the creation and maintenance of trade secrets include several legal requirements:

1. Secrecy
2. Value
3. Novelty
4. Affirmative steps.

Secrecy and affirmative steps are the more restrictive requirements. With respect to *secrecy,* the subject matter must be generally unknown in the industry.

---

[37] Unif. Trade Secrets Act § 1.

The UTSA requires that the subject matter not be "generally known" or "readily ascertainable by proper means."[38] Absolute secrecy is not required.

A company must take conscious, *affirmative steps* to keep the subject matter secret. The UTSA requires a company to make "efforts that are reasonable under the circumstances to maintain its secrecy."[39] However, the phrase *efforts reasonable under the circumstances* does not adequately impart the importance of acting positively to protect trade secrets. The descriptive phrase *affirmative steps* is more useful because it emphasizes that positive action should be taken to ensure secrecy.

Affirmative steps are defined as implementing extra precautions above and beyond normal operating procedures. Subject matter will not be deemed a trade secret if no affirmative steps are taken, even though the subject matter is secret to the rest of the world. Affirmative steps include restricting access to facilities, protecting confidential records, restricting access to proprietary documents, and forbidding employees from disclosing proprietary information.

In addition to secrecy and affirmative steps, another trade secret requirement is that the subject matter generate some independent economic *value* from the fact that it is not generally known to competitors. The subject matter is said to have value if competitors could obtain economic value from knowledge of it. Courts often require at least some minimum level of *novelty* before the subject matter is given trade secret protection. To satisfy the trade secret novelty requirement, subject matter must not be readily available in the industry. The level of trade secret novelty does not, however, rise to the level of novelty required by the patent laws.

---

[38] Unif. Trade Secrets Act § 1.

[39] *Id.*

CHAPTER 2

PROTECTING COMMUNICATIONS TECHNOLOGIES

J. Scott Davidson

§ 2.1   Introducing Communications Technologies

This chapter addresses how to protect network communications technologies. Although network communications can be a complicated technical area, this chapter is intended to appeal to a wider audience than just engineers.

One important tool that good patent attorneys have had to acquire (mostly through hard lessons) is the ability to communicate a technically complex subject in simple terms. For that reason, this discussion of protecting communications technologies begins with an illustration that can be referred to throughout the chapter. The illustration involves two people sitting around a large table. One person speaks only Japanese; the other speaks only English. With this scenario, it is clear that the two people can talk all day, but neither will understand what the other is saying.

If the illustration is changed to include a third person who knows how to translate Japanese to English and vice versa, the English speaker can then talk to the translator, who will translate the words into Japanese so they can be understood by the Japanese speaker.

This illustration has a direct analogy to communications technologies. Communications technology can be viewed in two different categories: *hardware* and *software*. In a communications network, the hardware consists of the tangible components that make up the physical computer network. In the illustration, the English speaker, the Japanese speaker, and the translator all correspond to network hardware since they are the things that are doing the talking.

The second category is the software, which corresponds to the knowledge that the people have and use to communicate with each other. That is, the English speaker knows how to speak English, so that speaker's "software" is that knowledge. Similarly, the Japanese speaker has the Japanese "software," and the translator has both English and Japanese "software." One might say that, based on prior language learning, the people are "programmed" to speak and understand only specific languages. So, too, the hardware boxes and components in a network are each programmed to speak and understand only specific languages. Those language programs are called software.

Now, if the knowledge of a language is analogous to software, then the actual language is analogous to a so-called communications protocol. The protocol is a set of rules that governs the way two objects speak to each other. The English language, in our analogy, is a protocol because it includes certain rules (defined alphabet, defined words, at least one vowel per word, each sentence started with a capital letter, and so forth) that cause it to be understandable to other readers. In the same way, the language that two pieces of hardware use to communicate with each other in a network is also a protocol.

It is clear why advancements in hardware, software, and protocol technologies are so valuable. For example, the illustration can be used to explain three factors:

1. How hardware characteristics affect the reliability of the communication
2. How software characteristics affect the quality and speed of communication
3. How protocol characteristics affect the quality, routing, and timing of communication.

In the example, the hardware is analogous to the people seated at the table who are trying to communicate with each other. The English speaker communicated with the Japanese speaker through an English-to-Japanese translator. Anyone who has experienced such a situation can attest to the communications problems that occur during the translation. Even when people speak directly to each other in the same language, words are sometimes misunderstood due to ambiguity, slurred speech, interrupted speech, background noise, and various other factors. When the translator is introduced to the scenario, the possibility arises that the translator will not have a good corresponding word or phrase for the translation or that the translator will simply err in translating. After an extended communication, the nature of the people themselves may ultimately introduce errors into the communication.

Two people speaking directly to each other in the same language is analogous to "peer-to-peer" communication. That is, for example, when one computer speaks directly to another computer, the computers are referred to as "peers" that speak in a "peer-to-peer" relationship. If, on the other hand, a computer speaks to other computers only through a network, the computer speaks not in a "peer-to-peer" relationship, but in a "client-to-server" relationship. That is, the network provides another piece of hardware (called a *server*) that assists the computers in speaking to each other. In the example, the English-Japanese translator who helps the English speaker and the Japanese speaker communicate is analogous to the server computer on the network.

Analogizing the translators to the network hardware points out that the hardware also can be a cause of reliability problems. For example, electrical components and the cables that connect them can introduce background noise, which prohibits the recipient components from understanding or receiving the data.

To further illustrate this, the translator scenario can be made more complicated by supposing that the English speaker and Japanese speaker are trying to communicate without the English-Japanese translator. Instead, suppose that an English-Spanish translator is available. The English speaker can now get the communication "protocol" from English to Spanish, but still cannot communicate with the Japanese speaker. Suppose further that a Spanish-to-French translator, a French-to-Korean translator, a Korean-to-Greek translator, a Greek-to-Braille translator, a Braille-to-German translator, and a German-to-Japanese translator are all available at the table, as shown in **Figure 2–1.**

In this case, the English person speaks in English, the statement is translated to Spanish by the English-Spanish translator, then to French by the Spanish-French translator, then to Korean by the French-Korean translator, then—in turn—to Greek, Braille, German, and Japanese. At that point, the Japanese speaker hears and understands the statement.

The potential for errors that can occur in this string of translations is significant. The hardware (in this illustration, the number of speakers and translators) becomes increasingly complex, and as a result the reliability of the system decreases. That is, the more hardware introduced, the less reliable the communication becomes. The same is generally true of a network; the more network hardware is added into a communication path, the less reliable the system becomes. The inescapable fact is that computer networking involves lots of hardware.

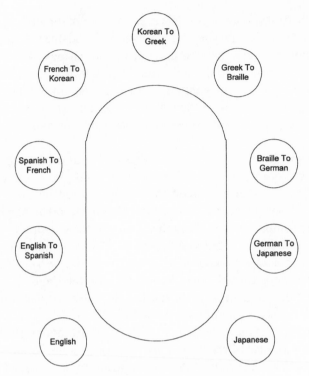

Figure 2–1. Illustration of translation chain.

In addition, the number of translators also affects the speed of communication. One of the translators in the series of translators will naturally be the slowest of the set, and that particular person will set the maximum speed of the ultimate communication. Further, the delays in passing the communication from one translator to another (propagation delays) also affect the speed of communication.

An obvious question is: Why would anyone want that many translators? The answer is that an increased number of translators, although adversely affecting the reliability of the system, adds to the flexibility of the system. For example, when the English person is speaking through the English-Japanese translator to the Japanese person, a Spanish speaker who then enters the room and sits down at the table will understand nothing of the conversation. However, if instead the string of translators are translating from one language to another, the Spanish speaker can "tap into" the translation by the English-Spanish translator to understand the message. Similarly, the number of translators present permits many other people to "tap into" the conversation using a variety of different languages. Although it may seem that the cost of creating so many translations is prohibitive compared to the possibility that someone will need to "tap into" one of the translations, the possibility that such situations will occur in the computer network environment is virtually absolute. The flexibility provided by the "tap in" capability is invaluable.

As noted in **Chapter 1,** the Internet is a network of components communicating with each other. The Internet actually rides on top of a telephone data network that has corresponding "translators" in its hardware as well. A typical (though somewhat simplified) computer telephone network is shown in **Figure 2–2.**

The communications network in **Figure 2–2** can be analogized to the translators and speakers from the illustration. Each block in **Figure 2–2** is a piece of hardware analogous to each translator. In the center is a long distance telephone network, sometimes referred to as a *backbone.* The backbone is an extraordinarily complex switching network that creates network information paths in a similar way that the telephone company connects your home voice telephone to anyone else's voice telephone. *Toll trunks* are connected to the backbone to send and receive computer information to and from the backbone (and to monitor the cost, or "toll," for doing so). The toll trunks are connected to *points of presence* (commonly referred to as POPs), which control the traffic of computer information to and from the toll trunk. One or two points of presence are usually found in major metropolitan areas to bring access to the backbone to the high traffic volumes in those areas. From a point of presence, local exchanges branch off to bring telephone access to more remote locations. That is, the local exchanges "tap into" the point of presence, just as the Spanish-speaking newcomer "tapped into" the string of translations in the earlier illustration.

Like the point of presence, the local exchanges control the flow of data traffic to points farther up and down the network route. From the local exchange, a router provides still further localized telephone presence. An Internet service provider (other than AT&T) could be providing nothing more than the router connected between a customer's house and the phone company's local exchange, and charging the customer (and being charged) a fee for the access. Other hardware, such as bridges, hubs, and gateways, may further control the flow of traffic around the network shown in **Figure 2–2.**

From the router, the hardware may become more familiar. Those who work on a computer in a company probably operate on a local area network (LAN) set up in their company to allow the company's computers to speak to each other. The top of **Figure 2–2** shows three LANs connected to a router, with one of the LANs expanded to show the LAN components in more detail. The LAN connects to the router by a network server. A server is like the translator at the table in the illustration in that it helps to translate one computer protocol (language) into another one. Here, the network server is translating the information from the many personal computers (PCs) into a language understood by the hardware components down the line. The LAN also includes a *file server,* which can be a local access point for company files.

To understand the complexity of the computer network, consider how a PC connected to the LAN at the top of **Figure 2–2** will communicate with the PC connected to the modem at the bottom right of **Figure 2–2.** Consider what communications have to occur in order for those two PCs to speak to each other. Start with the PC at the lower right of **Figure 2–2** and suppose that it is sending

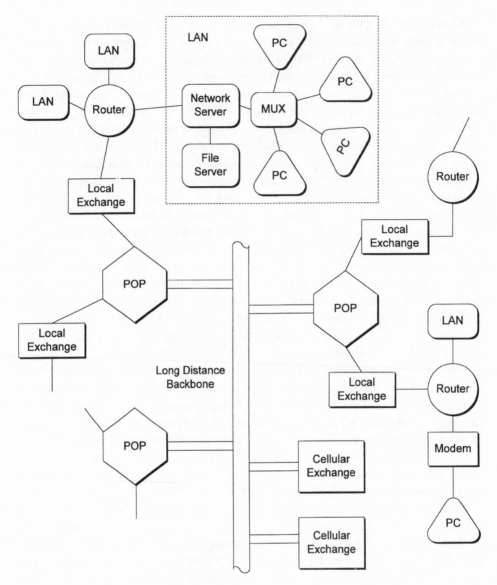

Figure 2–2. Computer telephone network.

an e-mail message to the PC at the top of **Figure 2–2.** First, the e-mail message is typed onto the PC. The communications protocol understood between the keyboard of the PC and the PC itself is called *ASCII text.*[1] The computer processes the ASCII text using an e-mail application (software) to convert it into a stream of data that can be recognized by another computer using the same application. The computer sends the data stream to the router using a standard protocol, the router accepts the data stream, modifies the data in order to merge it into all of the other data streams that it is receiving from other modems and LANs, and sends that full stream onto the local exchange. The local exchange adds that data stream to the many others it is receiving from other routers, and sends it onto the point of presence. The point of presence merges the data from many local exchanges and puts the merged stream onto the backbone via the toll trunk.

The data then travels long distance on the backbone (via a host computer) to the appropriate point of presence, which pulls the e-mail data stream from the huge volume of traffic traveling on the backbone. Of course, the point of presence is also pulling other data streams off the backbone that are destined for other points under its control as well. At this point, the e-mail data no longer looks like it did when the PC application created it. At the higher network levels, the data has been broken into small packets and transported down the network (most likely without its fellow e-mail data packets).

The e-mail message is sent to the local exchange, to the router, to the network server (then possibly to a *mail server*), and through the multiplexer, which sorts it to the destination PC. This example shows how analogous the translator illustration is. For the e-mail message to travel from one PC to another, the e-mail data is told, translated, retold, retranslated, and so on, over and over again before it reaches the destination PC.

It can also be seen that the different pieces of hardware must be operated at different speeds using different languages and different software in order to process the volumes of data. The amount of data volume processed by the PCs, for example, is minuscule compared to what the backbone is processing. Indeed, at each piece of hardware along the network path toward the backbone, the data volume increases, and thus the need for higher-speed communications protocols compounds.

In addition, the time needed for each piece of hardware to process the incoming data stream (just like the time needed by each translator to think through the translation) decreases the speed of the system. Just as translators from "easy" languages might be expected to translate faster than those for "harder" languages, so too can the complexity of communications protocols affect the speed of the transmission.

In summary, the network is a connected set of hardware using many different software protocols to transmit data from point to point. Increasing the amount of hardware in the network affects the reliability of the communication, but also provides flexibility. Thus, issues involving the intellectual property protection

---

[1] ASCII stands for American Standard Code for Information Interchange.

for advances in network hardware frequently arise as creative engineers develop faster, more flexible, and more reliable hardware components. Network software can also contain a gold mine of intellectual property since the way that the various pieces of hardware process data streams can affect the quality and speed of the transmission—a characteristic which is vitally important to a successful network. Finally, advances in communications protocols used by the hardware to speak to adjacent hardware can affect the speed of communication, the ability to control the quality of the communication, the routing of the communication, and the timing.

§ 2.2   Intellectual Property Concerns in Communications

Although some people guessed a decade ago that network communications technologies would be of critical importance as we moved into the twenty-first century, the lightning speed of advancement in network communications interconnections has surprised even some experts. Local area networks (LANs) and wide area networks (WANs) are being arranged with creative and new switching facilities. Even within the so-called Plain Old Telephone Service (POTS), new communications protocols speed data through the existing telephone infrastructure at higher rates with fewer data collisions.

The capability of communications conduits moved rapidly from kilobits per second (Kbps) through megabits per second (Mbps) rates and into the gigabits per second (Gbps) ranges with no end in sight. The need to pump more data faster through the existing communications conduits has become acute. Computer users who are accustomed to rapid data responses become impatient when their Mbps Internet connections take longer than a blink of an eye to return their requested information from across the continent.

One solution to the need for more advanced networks and faster throughputs was fiber optic cable installed in place of twisted copper pairs across the land. Fiber optic cables, with their higher bandwidth capabilities, were seen as the future of high-speed communications. Fiber optic cabling is still the fastest commercially viable communications conduit, but fiber optic service at each home and business in the United States is still beyond the foreseeable future. Hence, bandwidths have had to improve considerably using creative new compression schemes and communications protocols on existing twisted pair copper conduits.

Some of these new technologies can provide significant business opportunities for companies developing them.[2] For example, communications protocols

---

[2] For example, recent technological advances have placed communications onto copper power lines within our homes. New communications protocols have already been developed for accommodating these power-line communications. Radford, *Spread-Spectrum Data Leap Through ac Power Wiring,* Spectrum, Nov. 1996, at 48.

that provide magnitude leaps in bandwidth over existing protocols can create extremely high market power for the companies developing them. Unfortunately, in areas such as network communications, where technological advancements are moving extremely rapidly, the benefit of market power from a significant advancement can have an insignificant duration before the protocol is beaten by the next technological advancement. As a result, protecting intellectual property in communications protocols poses timing problems that are unique to rapidly advancing technological areas.

Patent Protection

Under new United States patent laws, patent protection extends for 20 years from the date of filing the patent application.[3] In a market arena such as network technology, however, the duration of the patent protection may be much less crucial than the time required to obtain the patent in the first place. In the network marketplace, the desire for faster and more advanced performance has expedited the demand for newer products. In such a rapidly expanding market, waiting on the issuance of a patent can be grueling while an inventor watches competitors openly using the invention pending the patent issuance. This can be especially painful if, by the time a patent issues, the competitors have moved on to newer technologies, and possibly ones that are not covered by the patent. In that case, the amount of time spent waiting for patent protection becomes much more critical than the amount of time that the patent is enforceable (over by-then obsolete technology).

The patent application examination process (from filing of the application to issuance of the patent) in the United States Patent and Trademark Office can now take anywhere from approximately one year up to (in rare cases) more than a decade. This duration has in the past caused some companies to forgo patent protection for product developments in markets, such as the current network market, that are driven by rapid technological advancements. The time delay before a patent issues is, of course, a consideration in deciding whether patent protection is a prudent investment. However, a blanket decision not to apply for patents to protect network technologies due to the momentum of product improvements can be a grave error.

Consider, for example, a company that has developed a router that improves by 10 percent the linking speed between a computer network server and the many personal computers connected to it. If the company estimates that the expected time in which the protocol will beat the newer developments is approximately one year, then the unique timing problems associated with seeking patent protection in the rapidly developing network area become acute. Suppose, for example, that the company files for patent protection and then begins selling the

---

[3] 35 U.S.C. § 154(a)(2). Pub. L. 103-465, § 534 changes the term for applications filed after June 8, 1995.

router on the market. One month later, the company notices that its closest competitors have begun selling identical routers. By the time the patent issues a year or more later and thus becomes enforceable against the competitors, the competitors have moved on to the more advanced products that the company expected would have arrived. If the patent is broad enough to cover the newer, improved routers, its value becomes very real. On the other hand, if the patent is not broad enough to enforce against the competitors' newer advancements, the speed of technology may make the patent obsolete before it issues. So, is trying to obtain patent protection in this situation in vain?

The answer is maybe yes, but maybe no. First, if the patent does not issue before the competitors move on to the next generation of technology, the company can still realize benefit from the patent application process. In that instance, even though the late-issuing patent did not specifically contemplate the next-generation technology, with a little skill and a little luck, the patent may nevertheless cover the next-generation technology if the claim language contained in the patent may be read broadly enough to include that later technology. This then would remove the problem of the competitors moving on to the next-generation technology before the patent issued since the patent would cover not only the original technology but the later technology as well.

Second, the patent application process can be continued in the Patent and Trademark Office for up to 20 years, thus permitting the company to view the later technology and decide whether claims can be written to cover it based on the original patent disclosure.[4] In this example, the company making the router would ensure that a continuation application remains in the Patent and Trademark Office even after the first patent issued. Then, when the competitors changed over to the next-generation routers, the company could attempt to write claims on the next-generation routers based on the disclosure given in the original patent application. If these new claims were issued as a patent, the competitors might have escaped the original patent only to be snared by the second.

A third way to realize benefit from filing patent applications in the rapidly moving network marketplace is to license the technology while the application is still pending—that is, before it issues into a patent. In this way, the speed of the network marketplace will not render technology obsolete before license revenue is realized. One might wonder why a competitor would care to pay for such a license, but several benefits exist to the competitor as well as to the potential patentee.

For example, a license to technology not yet patented can be cheaper than a similar license to the technology once patented. In many situations, it is reasonable for a competitor to insure against the uncertainty that exists about the scope a patent will have once issued by the Patent and Trademark Office. Although the competitor may not be concerned about narrow patent claims, that competitor cannot be assured that narrow claims are all that will issue from an application

---

[4] Some courts have held that such practices, in certain circumstances, can give rise to a defense of laches by an accused infringer.

that is still pending. The competitor always faces the possibility that the patent claims will be amended or added to a broader scope of invention—possibly one that covers not only the current generation of technology, but maybe a class of technology that includes next-generation technology as well. For this reason, some motivation exists for the competitor to agree to a cheaper patent license while the application is pending, rather than a potentially more expensive one down the road.

The competitor may also desire insurance against the possibility that the expected next generation of products is not realized or is not truly better. Alternatively, the competitor may agree to a license while the application is still pending as a result of extensive capital investment in the current technology that will extend its place in the competitor's product catalog long after the next generation of equipment comes about.

Good value can thus be gained by both the patent applicant and the potential licensees when the technology is licensed while the application is pending in the Patent and Trademark Office. Although the patent applicant may have to give concessions in the consideration provided for the license, the guarantee that revenue will be received before the technology is obsolete might be motivation enough to make such a concession.

Trademark Protection

Another method of protecting intellectual property in the rapidly evolving network field is by trademark protection. Unlike patents that must define the property right by carefully and specifically drafted claims to the products intended to be covered, trademark protection can be transferred from first-generation products to next-generation products, theoretically forever. Consider, for example, how the Crest brand of toothpaste has been used to identify the source of the original formula toothpaste as well as newer "gel" and "tartar control" brands. This intellectual property protection is called a *family of marks*. It offers the possibility of providing long-term protection for communications technologies that may be changing more rapidly than patent protection can keep up with.

For example, a communications protocol may have a market life of possibly only one year before it is expected to be updated and changed. Although patent protection to broad aspects of the protocol and its successors can be valuable, filing patent applications on many specific aspects of the protocols may not mature into issued patents in time to be useful in preventing competitors who have moved on to newer, possibly unpatented protocols. On the other hand, a trademark associated with the class of protocols can be carried over and applied to any new, successive protocols.

Of course, protocols protected only by trademark do not provide the potentially valuable opportunity to exclude a competitor from using, even copying, your unpatented communications technology. Rather, trademarks only preclude another from using a confusingly similar name for the technology. Accordingly, in a rapidly changing technological area such as communications technologies, the best protections are often a combination of patent applications to broad technological aspects, such as those that are expected to enjoy long useful market lives, together with trademark protection to permit consumers to associate the communications technologies with a particular source company despite rapid changes in the communications technologies.

Copyright Protection

Another source of protection that lends itself to rapidly evolving markets such as communications technologies is copyright protection. Copyrights have the characteristic of being instantaneously available. Once the copyrightable material is affixed in a medium, it is instantly copyrighted to the author.[5] Because virtually all communications technologies currently utilize software features for various purposes—for example, to control modulation, to control switching schemes, to modify data rates, to control data traffic, to impose security constraints, and so forth—these software features are instantaneously copyrighted to the author. Thus, without question, copyright protections can keep up in time with extremely rapid changes in communications technologies.

Summary

Communications technologies pose unique problems due to their rapid evolutions. Patent protection sometimes cannot be obtained quickly enough to provide meaningful value against competitors' rapidly changing communications protocols. However, when broad patent protection is available, it provides a powerful weapon against competitors. Trademark protection does not provide the same power to stop a competitor as patent protection provides, but it can be used equally well to motivate consumers to purchase one company's communications products instead of competing products while minimizing expenses needed to maintain the protection when newer developments are introduced. Finally, copyright protection provides the fastest method of obtaining some intellectual property protection for communications protocols, especially software aspects of those protocols.

§ 2.3   Protecting Communications Infrastructures

The introduction of the Internet, intranets, cellular communications, multimedia communications, and other high-volume data networks has produced volumes

---

[5] For copyright purposes, the *author* could be a corporation or other business entity in the case of a *work made for hire*. 17 U.S.C. §§ 101, 201.

of patents, trademarks, copyrights, and undoubtedly trade secrets in these technological areas. The number of separate hardware items used to transmit an e-mail message, for example, from a desktop PC to another desktop PC across the country is extraordinary. PCs, modems, servers, and encoders may handle the data at the local intranet. Routers, gateways, supercomputers, hubs, crossovers, switches, amplifiers, noise controllers, up-converters, and a host of other network hardware tools handle the data along its more lengthy journey. As one might expect, small improvements in the bottlenecks of these hardware components can give dramatic improvements in communication efficiency. These hardware components are thus being improved constantly to handle greater volumes of data on these networks at higher speeds. Of course, the value of improvements causes many different companies to pose many different types of solutions, leading to even greater numbers of components and greater amounts of disparity between communications protocols employed by each component.

The variety of components used in the communications stream poses its own unique problems. Just up-converting and down-converting to different data speeds along the way is significant. Data traveling on such a path can be analogized to a car traveling from Los Angeles to New York. Sometimes it travels slowly with large groups of cars on narrow two-lane roads, sometimes it travels alone on interstate highways at a faster pace, but by merging and moving from traffic flow to traffic flow, it can arrive at its destination. Like the different highways, the various hardware components of an network can be viewed as a set of layers of highways that connect with bigger and smaller highways to move varying degrees of data.

A typical intranet connected to the Internet can have PCs with Plain Old Telephone data links communicating with local servers at 30 kilobits per second (Kbps). Servers communicating internally can communicate at tens of megabits per second (Mbps) on local bus lines. Internet servers can communicate with routers at hundreds of Kbps. Backbones then can communicate between switching networks and host computers at up to hundreds of Mbps. The amount of hardware that must compatibly and reliably communicate with other hardware involved in the trafficking of data is overwhelming. Just a simple intranet communicating on an external Internet can utilize V.34 modems, ISDN[6] lines, T1 lines, B-ISDN lines, Ethernets, and FDDI[7] networks, all operating at different speeds using potentially different protocols. More and more hardware is being introduced to process the newer and faster data protocols, and every time a new protocol is introduced, hardware changes to accommodate it up and down the communications paths.

All network hardware can be viewed as moving data at different rates and in some instances, in different multiplexed formats. The Internet can be viewed

---

[6] Integrated Services Digital Network.

[7] Fiber Distributed Data Interface.

from a macroscopic standpoint as a set of hardware and software layers that move data at such varying levels. This perspective can become an important starting point for determining how intellectual property can be best tailored to cover advances in the hardware and software components.

§ 2.4 —Wireline Networks

Networks can be divided into wireline and wireless networks. Wireline networks, which include all networks that are hardwired (connected by wires), are discussed in this section. Wireless networks, such as microwave, cellular, and satellite networks, are discussed in § 2.5.

Prominent wireline networks include intracompany local area networks (LANs), analog telephone networks, and the Internet. The original LAN may have been the Ethernet developed at the Xerox Palo Alto Research Center (PARC) complex in California. The Ethernet connected a number of Xerox Alto computers to a data wire (called a *bus*) that was shared by all of the computers. Each of the computers could send information at any time onto the bus with destination addresses telling the computers which of the several computers connected to the bus should accept the data. One or more of the computers hosted the bus by keeping a table of addresses for each of the connected computers and communicating that table to the connected computers. A number of significant protocol issues were addressed by the PARC employees, including data addressing, changes in connected computers, data collision effects, and the like. Surprisingly, the now-famous decision by Xerox that the personal computer had no marketing future left it without significant patent protection on the Ethernet hardware.

Today, the Ethernet or a variation of it is used by many LANs. The LAN is characterized as a "geographically close" system, meaning that all of that hardware in the network is connected close together, such as within a single building. LANs have low noise problems, suffer from little signal echoes on the wire lines, and typically have few transmission errors (such as collisions). Since LANs are geographically limited, they usually can be designed and used without governmental regulation, or compliance with particular technical standards, although voluntarily complying with standards permits the LAN to connect more easily to external wide area networks (WANs) such as the Internet.

Because LANs are usually confined to a particular company, trade secret protection can be available for propriety connections and components used in a company's LAN, provided the company identifies the connections or components as trade secrets and takes affirmative steps to maintain them in secret.

As illustrated in **Figure 2–2,** the Internet infrastructure is actually a telephone data network. In essence, the Internet amounts to a designated group of supercomputers scattered around the world that are connected to each other by backbones for communication. More remote computers tap into the supercomputers via an array of hardware. So, how does one decide on what intellectual property law can protect such an overwhelming array of hardware? One way to make the job easier is to break down the newly presented technology into the respective layers that it occupies in the array of hardware or software. The technology can then be claimed as intellectual property based on the technology as it exists in the layered structure, as well as any appropriate extensions of that layer into greater or lesser networked layers. Some examples of how this can be viewed are discussed in § 2.9.

§ 2.5   —Wireless Networks

Today, the most significant wireless network is the cellular telephone network. Here, constraints in the areas of bandwidth, spectrum allocation, and error rates are areas most commonly discussed in improving the technology.

Time Division Multiple Access (TDMA) is currently a standard format for cellular telephone communications. Essentially, TDMA breaks a data stream into data packets and broadcasts the packets across a data channel. Code Division Multiple Access (CDMA), which is a newer variation on TDMA, also breaks data into packets but then attempts to broadcast them in different communications channels. Europeans currently use another data communications standard, called Global System for Mobile Communications (GMS), and Japan uses its own standard, called Japanese Digital Cellular (JDC).

All of this means that data must increasingly change from one standard to another as it travels from one system to another. Such bridging techniques are becoming increasingly important not only between countries, but also within countries between competing hardware tools. This extra level of complexity, however, can be viewed as simply another level of communication conversion that occurs during the data transportation. As such, it provides more, not less, opportunity to claim intellectual property in new network hardware. As before, one should ask how does the new technology affect communication at every level above and below its operational level. With newer and better communication conversion tools adding new levels of communication traffic control, the new technology can be relevant to (and claimed as) part of all affected communication conversion layers as well.

Another way that data is being bridged from one standard to another is between wireline and wireless conversions. For example, a POTS telephone communicating with a cellular phone sends data in one format (analog telephone) to a phone that responds only to a different format (for example, TDMA). One such layer is shown in **Figure 2–2** in which a *cellular server* and a *foreign server* are used to convert data streams received on the backbone into cellular or foreign formatted data. Thus, bridging wireline and wireless technology is another layer that one may consider potentially affected by new network hardware.

Consider how one can protect new network technologies, such as a new switch, a new router, and the like. In such a case, one should consider not only claiming ownership of the hardware apparatus per se, but also the apparatus as part of a system of gradually increasing levels of complexity. First, the apparatus should be viewed as a system including only proximate hardware, with special emphasis on how the apparatus will communicate with the proximate hardware. Next, increasing levels of complexity should be considered, such as how the new apparatus may affect wireless-to-wireline bridging, code conversion techniques, and so on.

Although this discussion is not intended to cover every conceivable aspect of claiming specific apparatus types, it can be seen that an apparatus in a network is a part of a complex set of intercommunicating layers that should each be considered when deciding how to claim the apparatus. Viewing the new apparatus only as a specific hardware component ignores the very nature of the network as a system of intercommunicating components. Simply begin by asking the question, "How does this apparatus affect, if at all, the next successive layers of communication?"

§ 2.6   Protecting Communications Switching Technology

Imagine yourself at a dinner table with 20 guests when, after a short period of silence, each of the guests spontaneously begins talking. Who would you understand? Which person would you respond to? Our human conversations are (usually) governed by informal rules of priority. Thus, once one person talks, the rest do not interrupt. Also, when two people speak at the same time, possibly the elder gets priority. A network environment also must employ rules of priority to determine which hardware can speak and when. The technology that controls the timing and priority of communication consists of *switching circuits*.

Some readers may be old enough to recall telephone operators who "put you through" to another person by physically connecting a cable between a plug corresponding to your telephone and a plug corresponding to the other person's telephone. By plugging the cable between the two plugs, the circuit was completed and the two people could speak. Today, with the huge volumes of data and voice traffic that span our country and world, humans could not come close to physically making all of the connections necessary to complete each voice and data telephone call. Instead, complex banks of electronic switches route data from telephone line to telephone line.

Even outside of the telephone switching systems, the data within a computer network such as a company's LAN is switching many times before reaching a particular employee's desk. One classic example is the "MUX" shown in the LAN of **Figure 2–2**. A MUX (multiplexer) is a gate that controls the flow of data through it. The MUX can recognize which data is destined for the respective PCs and can send the data to the appropriate places.

Switching technology is really dependent on the type of routing necessary for a given computer network. **Figure 2–3** illustrates various computer networks that require switched data.

As shown in **Figure 2–3,** a computer network consisting of various pieces of hardware can be configured in a variety of different schemes. Of course, the networks shown above are greatly simplified in the amount and complexity of the hardware. This discussion deals with the three network structures shown above, the Ring, the Multipoint, and the Star. Each of the structures in effect connects the four pieces of hardware together by communications lines.

Before the discussion turns to how data is switched through these various structures, the idea of addressing data should be introduced. The discussion in § 2.1 illustrated how an e-mail message traveled from one PC, through the network, to a second PC. The message itself did not know which way to go, but the hardware along the way did. The technology used to switch (or *route*) messages along the network usually uses addresses to identify where data is going. In a very simplified sense, a data stream includes not only the data itself, but also an address included at the beginning of the data in a field called the *header.*

The header is analogous to the information written on an envelope that is put into the United States mail. The envelope is read by a postal worker (the "hardware") and sorted ("switched") a number of times until it is delivered to the recipient. The letter inside is analogous to the data itself, since it is the information that will ultimately be processed by the recipient. It is important to note that the various people who handle the mail along the way do not read the data (the letter) itself, they read only the address and sort the data along its way based on a reading of the address. The only "hardware" that reads the data is the ultimate recipient.

Now, it is time to look at the various network structures. In the Ring network structure, the four hardware pieces are connected by a communication ring. With this Ring configuration, when Hardware 1 wants to send a message to Hardware 3, it must do so by passing either Hardware 2 or Hardware 4. For the ring to work, each data stream includes an address that is read by each hardware item. If the data is addressed to a particular hardware item, it will read the data upon receipt. If not, then the hardware item will pass the data on to the next hardware item along the ring, which in turn reads the address and either passes the data or accepts it. This structure is flexible but inefficient since each hardware item must include switching technology to read the address and time must be allotted for each hardware item to do so along the data path.

The Ring configuration is sometimes employed with a Token Ring technology, named for the passing of a "token" around the ring. Each hardware item takes the imaginary "token" for a period of time during which it can put as much or as little data onto the ring (destined for other computers) as desired. After the time elapses, the token passes to the next computer, which is allowed its time to send its data onto the ring. Each hardware item can internally process data without holding the token, but can transmit data only when its turn arrives. For

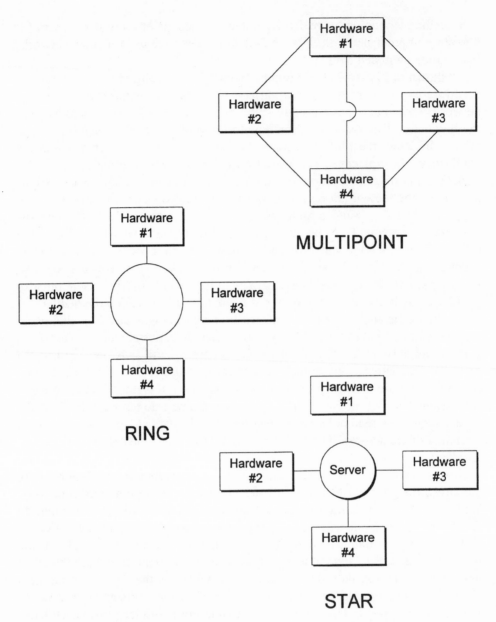

Figure 2–3. Types of computer networks.

this reason, the token ring switching technology can been criticized for being inefficient in giving "air time" (or, better stated, "ring time") to computers that may not need it, while denying ring time to those that do.

Vast improvements have been introduced that keep the token ring system viable, such as switches within the hardware that permit intelligent reallocation of time among the computers during the transmission, sophisticated interrupt schemes, and other methods. The intellectual property in these improvements can be protected in a variety of ways. The software employed by intelligent switches can be copyrighted. The switches and their method steps for reallocating time or interrupting conversation can be patented. Also, the ring systems as a whole, with improved time allocation, interrupt, and other switching technology, can be protected by patents. In a few instances, such as switching technology that is kept within a private LAN or maintained in a confidential environment, the switching technology may also be protectable as a trade secret.

The Ring configuration is not the only available method of connecting networks. An alternative configuration is the Multipoint system shown in **Figure 2–3,** in which every hardware item is directly connected to every other hardware item in the network. This situation is ideal for improving speed and reliability of communications, but it is usually cost-prohibitive. Instead, Star configurations are typically employed (shown in **Figure 2–3**), in which the hardware items are commonly connected to a single server that routes data from hardware items to other hardware items based on data addresses. The Star configuration is helpful in increasing the speed of communication between the respective hardware items over the Ring configuration without requiring the hardwire connections demanded by the Multipoint system.

As might be expected, network connections usually employ a hybrid system in which more than one of the configurations described here are employed together. That is, one of the "hardware" items attached to the Star server could be a Ring or Multipoint network. Thus, when thinking about intellectual property protections for a new switching technology within the realm of any one of the above systems, one should consider whether the new switching technology will dictate changes or additions to the network where transitions occur to alternative network configurations. For example, one might consider patenting a new addressing scheme for the Ring system, but fail to recognize that the same addressing scheme might need to be readable and usable by a Star server as well. Thus, patent claims can be directed not only to the addressing scheme within the context of a Ring system, but also within the context of a hybrid Ring/Star system along with its associated data transition requirements.

In considering intellectual property protection for switching technologies, one should recognize that the switches are being used for particular network configurations and thus may have both specific and broad advantages within the context of the network. Intellectual property in a new switching system can include the specific hardware switch, the software running the switch, the use of the switch in a specific design configuration, and the use of the switch in a larger hybrid system context. At least patent and copyright protections, and possibly trade secret and trademark protections, should be employed to cover a wide range of applications from the most specifically designed feature to the broader use of the switch in a wide network of configurations.

§ 2.7 Protecting Communications Protocols

As telecommunications and computing functions increasingly converge upon one another, the languages that one employs to transport data from one place to another becomes increasingly important. For example, the number of applications for network bandwidth is increasing, but the various communications protocol layers in advance of the application on the network cause only a relatively small percentage of allocable bandwidth to be usable by any given application. This can be shown by viewing the way two pieces of hardware communicate. See **Figure 2–4.**

In this protocol, the *hardware* layer covers the physical connection between the two user stations. The *link* layer controls the sequencing of data frames (packets of information) to the network layer and detects frame errors. The *network* layer sets up the communications path between the user stations by identifying addresses for all connection entities between the two users. The *transport* layer is the median layer that converts transport connections at the user station to transport connections at the network level, so that the data is network independent as it travels to the higher levels. The *session* layer organizes the data into data frames for the particular application. The *presentation* layer adds further structural support. The *application* layer provides the final communication access characteristics, such as the identification of communications users and any handshaking procedures (in software, a means of specifying an agreed protocol between two devices) between them.[8]

Because each of the layers can be viewed as taking the data from its preceding layer and adding to it a header or other control characteristic peculiar to its layer's function, the processing requirements by the hardware, link, network, transport, session, and presentation layers rob the application layer of communication bandwidth. When viewed this way, one sees that improvements in one protocol layer has obvious implications on other protocol layers. As a result, intellectual property claims for communications protocols should focus not only on the specific protocol improvement, but also on the system of protocol layers having a collectively improved performance.

One can also think of each protocol layer as involving sublayers that can be considered in ascertaining the full scope of intellectual property in a protocol improvement. The networks themselves can be viewed in several levels, and thus also the protocols used by those network levels. As a basic example, the network between peers is different from the network between a client and a

---

[8] B. Marsden, Communication Network Protocols (1992).

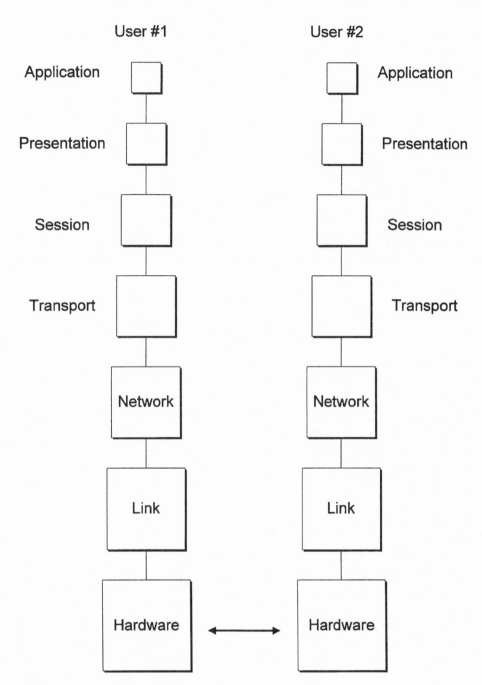

Figure 2–4. Communications protocol.

server. By the same token, a WAN is different from a company LAN. The corresponding protocol layer specifics will be correspondingly different. Thus, one should consider when drafting patent claims whether improvements in a communications protocol layer will have an impact on different network types.

As an example, the hardwire connection of two personal computers is a network and may use a communications protocol, such as a "V dot" standard. On another level, the more permanent connection of several personal computers to a server is a higher level of networking, as is used, for example, in a LAN that may use ISDN or T1 communications protocols. Networks can also span states or countries using, for example, WANs that may include satellite or microwave protocols. Any one of these types of networks, together with their specific protocols, could take an entire chapter to describe thoroughly. For our purpose, to maximize intellectual property in the protocol, one must look not only to the protocol itself, but also to its interaction with protocols at remote areas of the network.

§ 2.8 —Overview of Protection Strategies

The first issue one must address in analyzing protection strategies for communications technology is which intellectual property protections are available. One common method of protecting communications protocols is by trade secret. Although this method can provide some protection, it suffers from some serious drawbacks. First, communications protocols, by their very nature, are usually more valuable when they are publicly known. That is, if one manufacturer's modem uses a secret, proprietary communications protocol, it may be unable to communicate with other modems that do not recognize that protocol. In addition, the "secretiveness" of a communications protocol that is being used, for example, on an Internet or WAN can be questioned, thus subjecting the trade secret status to some level of doubt.

The upside of using trade secret status as a protection for communications protocol technology is that it is not costly and can be used effectively at least up to (and possibly beyond) its introduction into the commercial environment. If value can be realized through licensing, market positioning, and the like prior to the commercial introduction, the trade secret status can prove to be of worth, alone or in addition to other forms of protection. Of course, a company should be careful in defining the communications protocol that is protected by trade secret so a court can see that affirmative steps were taken by the company to maintain the protocol as a secret for the relevant time period.

A more favored alternative is patent protection for the communications protocol. Patents can provide protection beyond the commercial introduction of the communications protocol and provide the opportunity to obtain injunctive relief from continued infringement. Thus, a modem manufacturer, for example, can prevent an infringer from continuing to use a patented communications protocol

for the lifetime of the patent. However, at least two significant business considerations should be analyzed before seeking patent protection on a communications
protocol.

A first business issue is whether the communications protocol is most effective
only when it is available to a wide selection of a company's and its competitors'
end-users. Consider, for example, an Internet communications protocol, such as
HTML.[9] If HTML had been unavailable to all users of the Internet as a standard
protocol, would it have been incorporated by some of the commercial Internet
providers even though such incorporation may have meant that other competing users would have been unable to communicate with them? The answer, of
course, is that it depends. One could argue that HTML carries with it sufficient
demand to compel providers to use it—thus suggesting that patent protection is
desirable. On the other hand, one might argue that protocols could be introduced
to make HTML compatible with other protocols—thus suggesting that money
spent on patent protection may be better spent on a rapid market entry. This type
of decision involves weighing risks and rewards and is one that business managers are familiar with making.

Another business decision with respect to patenting communications protocols
versus holding them as trade secrets is the opportunity for mandatory licensing
through standardization procedures. Several technological organizations gather
groups of competing businesses to set up standard communications protocols for
particular network technologies. Thus, for example, the V.34 standard is used in
personal computer POTS modem technologies. Having a company's technology
accepted as part of an industry standard generally involves an agreement of
some sort providing mandatory licensing of patented aspects of the protocols.
Broader, more powerful patent portfolios can capture more attention at such
standardization sessions and thus become a useful tool for obtaining mandatory
licensing income—or at least for reducing mandatory licensing expenses under
your competitors' portfolios.

One must also recognize the legal and psychological effect of a broad patent
portfolio for communications technologies. Even if a company never intends to
use a portfolio offensively to prevent competitors from using its patented technology, a company is wise to obtain patent protection for at least the broader
aspects of its communications protocols, in order to have a defense against a
competitor's claim for license revenues under their patent portfolios.

In addition to patent and trade secret protection, trademark protection can also
be envisioned for protecting intellectual property in communications protocols.
One example of how trademarks can be used is in a combination of protections
sometimes seen for certain communications protocols: trade secret protection
prior to public commercialization of the protocol, with trademark and patent
protection thereafter. The trade secret protection curbs unscrupulous employees
or thieves from bringing the protocol to market before you. The trademark

---

[9] Hypertext Markup Language.

protection provides quick intellectual property assets to provide an advantageous distinction between your machines running the protocol and those of your competitors. The patent protection provides a subsequent property right with stronger power to stop a competitor.

Finally, copyright protection can be envisioned for protecting communications protocols. When a communications protocol is based on computer software (as virtually all protocols are), copyright protection is available to prevent copying of the software. Copyright protection is cheap (copyrights can automatically exist upon affixation of the code in memory), but it carries with it a greater degree of legal risk. Some courts have been criticized for creating legal standards that preclude effective, enforceable copyright protection for computer software. The criticism may not be altogether justified since the courts are usually faced with the arduous task of determining whether software code that is close but not identical to copyrighted code was, by circumstantial evidence of their similarity, copied from the copyrighted code.[10] Even many highly trained engineers try to avoid reading software object or source code, and thus a court's reluctance to do so—although maybe not excusable—is at least understandable. Thus, the practical limitations of the judicial system mitigate against relying exclusively on copyrights as a good protection for communications protocol software, although their extremely inexpensive status argues in favor of a company claiming those copyrights to which it is entitled.

§ 2.9 —A New Way of Viewing Intellectual Property in Protocols

The first step in describing the options for protecting the intellectual property in computer network protocols should be first to identify the relevant levels of communication that are applicable to the protocol. For example, from a macroscopic standpoint, communications protocols can be viewed differently between different levels of hardware, as shown in **Figures 2–2** and **2–4**.

Thus, one can first look at the level of communication between the user and an interface terminal. The communications protocols at this level are typically ASCII or related protocols. Bandwidth may not be an issue since the constraining factor at this level of data input is speed of the user, rather than the speed of the communication devices. Nevertheless, improvements are being made to increase the speed by which users can communicate to interface terminals—such as through voice recognition circuitry, graphic interfaces, and the like. Devising a protection strategy for improvements in communications protocols should not ignore the potential application of the protocol in any user-to-terminal data transportation.

---

[10] See § **2.15.**

The next communications level may be a software coupler that converts the communications protocol at the user level to a recognizable communications protocol within a network of terminals. Then, the protocol used at the interface between one terminal and another terminal (peer-to-peer) or between one terminal and a server (client-to-server) can be viewed as another hardware level.

As can be seen from **Figures 2–2** and **2–4,** moving up the levels (toward increased networking) causes increases in needed bandwidth in order to accommodate the increases in passing data traffic at higher aggregate nodes (junctions), coming from the multitudes of terminals, servers, and the like pyramiding upwardly into these higher networking levels. Remember that every aggressive new communications protocol at a low level of communication further strains the bandwidth limitations of every level of communication above it. Thus, for example, doubling personal computer modem protocol speeds causes telephone switching networks to process a higher volume of data. Obviously, these networks can do so by reducing speed, maintaining speed, or increasing speed, ultimately resulting in differences in bandwidth at this higher level. A higher bandwidth may dictate a different protocol at the telephone switch, and hence a coupling software (usually an application) to convert the new modem protocol data into the new switching protocol. Patent claims recognizing these structural and operational differences when the new modem protocol data is used might insure that broad patent protection is ultimately obtained.

A good protection analysis for communications protocols will take into account the viability of the protocol in various levels of communications hardware. For example, patent claims that are carefully tailored to one particular hardware level might in certain circumstances be a key to avoiding infringement of prior art protocols that occur at different hardware levels.

Protection strategies should also take into account how a new communications protocol will affect the structure, method, or operation of the hardware needed to communicate the data using the protocol. A new protocol may affect not only the software loaded in the modem ROM,[11] but also the hardware used by the modem to process the protocol.

Once data is converted from a user level to the terminal-to-terminal or terminal-to-server level, it is then in a form to be sent onto the telecommunications infrastructure, thus involving another communications hardware level worth considering. This infrastructure level may implicate new switching technologies in order to accommodate the new communications protocols. For example, progressing from a POTS to an ISDN to a T1 protocol dictates new switching, router, and processing structures not only at the user inputs, but also higher up the line into the telecommunications infrastructures. When a company recognizes that a new communications protocol used by peer-to-peer or client-to-server interfaces will employ new switching, router, data processors, or other infrastructures, claims

---

[11] Read-only memory.

should be made not only to the new communications protocol, but also to the switches, routers, and processors that will specially employ them.

Once a protection strategy is considered in light of the various levels of hardware and software used to support the new protocol, it can be seen that interactions will undoubtedly occur between existing standard protocols and the newer one. For example, one might ask how communications switches will handle different incoming protocols, such as a company's newly developed protocol and existing time-division multiplexing, frequency-division multiplexing, or wave-division multiplexing schemes. The methods in which a newly developed protocol can be easily synthesized into existing streams should also be considered in analyzing protectable features.

Because constantly emerging hardware and software improvements change the type and operation of the many levels of communication that occur in LANs and WANs, one should first model existing network structures to determine where a newly developed communications protocol can have significant effects on existing (and, with some degree of foresight, future) network communications topologies. In a simple case, for example, one might envision an Ethernet ring of terminals communicating in turn on a hyperchannel, which communicates on a fiber optic cable backbone. A new communications protocol used in this application may affect each or only some of the switching structures and operations in this scheme. The scope of desired intellectual property protection can then be creatively developed by considering the structures and operations needed to make the new protocol merge with—or replace one of—the existing protocol layers.

§ 2.10   —Patent Protection

The first issue that one must deal with in claiming patent protection for a communications protocol is whether the claim being made is subject matter that is capable of patent protection. Algorithms are not patentable[12] and one might argue that communications protocols per se are algorithms. The Court of Appeals for the Federal Circuit has recently struggled with the issues of when computer programs are algorithms and when they are not. In *In re Lowry,*[13] the court permitted a patent applicant to claim a "memory" containing a "data structure." Clearly, communications protocols can be viewed similarly as "data structures" which reside in a computer "memory." Although the propriety of such a claim is

---

[12] *In re* Wamerdam, 33 F.3d 1354, 1359 (Fed. Cir. 1994):

> One notion that emerged and has been invoked in the computer related cases is that a patent cannot be obtained for a "mathematical algorithm." . . . The difficulty is that there is no clear agreement as to what is a "mathematical algorithm," which makes rather dicey the determination of whether the claim as a whole is no more than that.

[13] 32 F.3d 1579 (Fed. Cir. 1994).

not absolute, the *Lowry* case certainly gives a foundation for arguing that such a claim is appropriate.[14]

Given the current state of the law, one would also be wise to consider the real-world application of a communications protocol when drafting patent claims attempting to cover it. Thus, in addition to drafting *Lowry*-type claims that cover a memory storing the communications protocol, it is important to consider how, for example, the protocol will interact with existing infrastructures. Claims can be drafted to include hardware such as a PC, a modem, a router, a gateway, a switching circuit, and the like to cover the protocol in its real-world application. It should be determined whether the protocol will have application in peer-to-peer communication, as opposed to client-to-server communications. Claims can be drafted toward use of the protocol in both types of systems. Consider whether telecommunications infrastructures will need to change or adapt in order to accommodate the new protocol; if so, the patent application should claim large-scale switching networks employing the protocol.

Some protocols are application-blind, meaning that all of the routing hardware does not necessarily know what type of data (facsimile, movie, audio, document, e-mail, and so forth) is being sent. One such protocol is Asynchronous Transfer Mode (ATM). ATM is a protocol specifically designed to transport diverse data types and can be used to couple large bandwidth hardware with smaller bandwidth hardware. For such protocols, the scope of network hardware that can be claimed to include or use the protocol is virtually endless. Nevertheless, when significant application-blind protocols are developed, they should be claimed in a wide variety of generic and specific hardware items so that the sweep of the resultant patent will be wide enough to maximize the exclusivity provided by the patent rights.

Finally, one should recognize when developing an intellectual property protection strategy for a communications protocol that some protocols can be expected to have relatively little market power given the barriers to breaking an established protocol from a position of market dominance. Consider, for example, the Internet File Transfer Protocol (FTP) that is used by all computers connected to the Internet to transfer files from one place to another on the Internet. The FTP specifies that files are transferred in one of two formats: ASCII or Binary. Certainly protocols exist that can more effectively transfer data, but trying to replace FTP as the standard would be met with considerable market resistance.

Considering such market pressures, careful consideration should be given to whether expensive patent protections are appropriate for new protocols, or whether less expensive copyright or trade secret protections can be employed. For a discussion of the appropriateness of copyright and trade secret protections for computer protocols, see §§ **2.14** and **2.15**.

---

[14] **Section 2.11** examines the United States Patent and Trademark Office's response to these cases, and possible ways to claim protocols per se.

§ 2.11 —Communications Protocols Claimed as Algorithms

In light of the several new cases grappling with the issue of algorithms in patent claims, the United States Patent and Trademark Office recently revised its own internal guidelines for examining applications containing algorithms.[15] The guidelines seek to distinguish between subject matter that has a "practical application or use" from subject matter that is simply an abstract idea.[16] To do this, the Patent and Trademark Office distinguishes between "non-functional descriptive material" (such as literary works) which are not patentable subject matter even if stored in a computer and "functional descriptive material" (such as computer applications) which can only be patentable subject matter if recorded on a computer-readable medium. In the latter case, according to the Patent and Trademark Office, the computer program "becomes structurally and functionally interrelated to the medium and will be statutory in most cases."[17]

For now, the Patent and Trademark Office appears to permit patent claims for communications protocols in the form of computer programs when they are claimed as part of a computer-readable medium such as a memory. Thus, claims such as the following example should be patentable:

> A memory for storing a communications protocol including:
>
> a data header field defining . . . ;
>
> a data field defining . . . ;
>
> a control field defining . . . .

However, the Patent and Trademark Office apparently will continue to reject a claim like this one if it fails to include—in substance—the first four words ("A memory for storing") or something similar.

In summary, under *Lowry*[18] and the new Patent and Trademark Office guidelines, it is possible that patents will soon be issued on claims to communications protocols as they exist on floppy disks, ROM cartridges, or removable hard drives.

§ 2.12 —Compression Schemes

Compression schemes have become increasingly important as the bandwidth limits of established data conduits are continually reached. An established data pipeline will accept only a particular bit rate, meaning that the amount of data and the speed that the data moves will vary inversely relative to each other.

---

[15] Manual of Patent Examining Procedure § 2106 (July 1996).

[16] *Id.* § IV, A.

[17] *Id.* § IV, B, 1.

[18] *In re* Lowry, 32 F.3d 1579 (Fed. Cir. 1994), discussed in § **2.10.**

Imagine, for example, water pouring through a garden hose. If you want more water, you can turn up the pressure, but at some point, you maximize the water output. From there on, you just have to wait if you want more water. The same is true of data in that only a certain amount of data can be expected to come through a data pipeline at any given period of time. With data, however, even if more data volume cannot pass through a pipeline, more data content can go through it. Data—unlike water—can be compressed, and this characteristic can be used to reduce the amount of data necessary per application, thus permitting more data content to be driven through a pipeline using the same bandwidth.

One of the first data compression schemes was the elimination of streams of redundant numbers. A string of 10,000 zeroes, for example, can be stated as "000000 . . . 000," or it can be stated as "0 (10,000 times)." The latter requires significantly less data volume to communicate the same information, thus saving bandwidth during the communication.

Later compression methods involve fractal analysis, in which the computer is told that a particular code represents a certain pattern. If the pattern recurs, the sending computer transmits the representative code rather than the pattern and the application on the receiving computer knows to substitute the pattern for the code. Consider, for example, a picture of a tree which has been digitized into a giant string of data describing it pixel by pixel. Such a data string can be enormous (as those who have tried to transmit graphics on the Internet can attest). However, if the computer is told to represent a leaf by a code describing the leaf identity, its position, and its appearance, the transmitting computer can pull apart the tree leaf-by-leaf, assign codes to each leaf, and transmit the code rather than the pixel data to the receiving computer. The receiving computer can then reconstruct the tree, leaf-by-leaf, at the receiving end.

Compression schemes are most easily protected by patent and copyright protections. Because the compression schemes must be understandable at both the sending and receiving ends, trade secret protections are difficult (though not impossible) to maintain for compression schemes. As in the case of communications protocols, one should attempt to patent compression schemes as programs on a computer-readable medium.[19] Then, additional protections should be sought for application of the compression scheme between communicating computers, routers, modems, and the like.

§ 2.13 —Creative Patent Protection

For the patent practitioner, deciding on the best way to write a claim for communications protocols can be tricky. Quite a few options for broadly and narrowly claiming protocols can be envisioned. A few of the possible claim structures are described in this section.

---

[19] *See In re* Lowry, 32 F.3d 1579 (Fed. Cir. 1994), discussed in § **2.10.**

Method Claims

Method claims are permissible ways to claim patent protection.[20] Method claims (sometimes referred to as process claims) claim an invention as a set of steps. For example, a communications protocol might be claimed as:

> A method of communicating data from one computer memory to another computer memory, comprising the steps of:
>
> 1) reading data from one computer memory in an original format;
> 2) converting the data into a data packet format in which each data packet has a header field and a data field;
>
> *   *   *
>
> 7) receiving the data;
> 8) converting the data back into the original format; and
> 9) storing the data in the other computer memory.

System Claims

System claims may be the most overlooked patent claims for communications protocols. Unfortunately, patent practitioners think of patent claims in terms of their "broadest" possible scope (meaning the least number of limitations possible), yet forget to claim them with more limiting scopes such as part of a full system. These more limiting claims potentially provide added protection against invalidity of the claims over prior art,[21] and they also can provide a basis for claiming infringement damages on a larger product group (that is, the "system" as a whole, rather than a computer, or even a ROM with a protocol).

Some system claims are easily crafted once the "protocol on a ROM" claims are prepared. For example:

> A network system, comprising:
>
> a plurality of computers;
>
> a server in electrical communication with the plurality of computers to control communication between the computers, the server including a memory having a communications protocol in which . . . .

The practitioner is well advised, however, to draft additional, even more specific claims that focus on those aspects of the system which will be affected by implementation of the protocol. For example, if the computers require a high-speed shift register to keep up with the flow of data coming to it from the server, system claims can be drafted to include that feature. For example:

---

[20] 35 U.S.C. §§ 100(b), 101.

[21] For a discussion of how claims can be found invalid over prior art, see Lewis C. Lee & J. Scott Davidson, *Managing Intellectual Property Rights* (John Wiley & Sons 1993).

A network system, comprising:

a plurality of computers, each having high-speed shift registers;

a server in electrical communication with the plurality of computers to control communication between the computers via the high-speed shift registers, the server including a memory having a communications protocol in which . . . .

Although the concept of a high-speed shift register may seem minuscule compared to the value of the communications protocol, it is impossible to predict all of the prior art that may be found during litigation, and a limitation like "high-speed shift registers" may be just what is needed to save a patent from invalidity.

Transceiver Claims

The most common method of analyzing and claiming such intellectual property in network communications protocols is to visualize them in terms of the hardware receivers and transmitters that use the protocols. Thus, for example, a modem within one PC that communicates with a second modem in a second PC can be regarded as a transmitter and a receiver of the data being communicated. The modem uses a particular protocol to make the necessary communication. Thus, the modem may be viewed as a transmitter/receiver using a protocol. Claiming it as such may look like this:

A transceiver, comprising:

an input for receiving a data stream to be transmitted;

an encoder for modifying the data stream in accordance with a protocol in which . . . .

Codec Claims

The transmitter/receiver claims can be changed slightly to cover only the electrical components in the transmitters and receivers that convert the data into a data stream conforming with the established protocol. Usually, these electrical components are called Codecs (coder-decoders). A Codec claim can avoid potential problems with the "transmission" or "reception" language of a transceiver claim by claiming the protocol as simply the "encoder" or "decoder" used by either broadcasting or hardwired boxes that use a particular protocol. Thus, one might claim the protocol in its practical application in a Codec as: "An encoder for encoding a data stream in accordance with a protocol in which . . . ."

Processor Claims

As noted in § 2.2, communications protocols are usually employed by software. Where there is software, there is usually a "processor" to perform the software functions on an incoming data stream. Accordingly, communications protocols can be claimed based on standard "processor" hardware as follows:

> A communications system, comprising:
>
> a memory for storing an incoming data stream;
>
> a processor, connected to the memory, for modulating the incoming data stream in accordance with a communications protocol in which . . . .

Memory Usage Claim

The *Lowry* case[22] implies that a permissible claim format might be: "A memory storing a communications protocol in which . . . ." Accordingly, such a claim may be one of the broadest formats in which a communications protocol can be claimed. However, an extension of that claim format can be envisioned in which the memory is described in terms of its actual usage. If the characteristics of a communications protocol dictate certain memory allocation at certain times— for example, during encoding—the memory may be claimed in terms of those allocations and usage in addition to the generic "protocol on a memory" claim.

Signal Interaction Claims

A communications protocol involves two pieces of hardware communicating with each other according to a set of rules and regulations. One way to claim the protocol is to claim the interaction between the two pieces of hardware. For example, the basis of a patent claim might be the way that a protocol detects errors in transmission, such as by using data block counts, parity bits, polynomial checks, acknowledgments, timers, automatic retransmissions, or some other novel method. The patent claim can be in the form of a "protocol on a memory" with the particular interaction rules and regulations specifically claimed, or it can be in the form of a host hardware and a guest hardware that communicate according to the specifically described interactive rules.

§ 2.14 —Trade Secret Protection

Trade secret protection requires a communications protocol to satisfy a few criteria. The protocol must be used in business, must offer the owner an opportunity for a competitive advantage over competitors, must be secret, and must be the subject of affirmative steps taken by the owner to maintain it as a trade secret. Communications protocols can be problematic when it comes to trade secret protection due to their probable use by third parties. Although some communications protocols are used only internally at a company and therefore

---

[22] *In re* Lowry, 32 F.3d 1579 (Fed. Cir. 1994), discussed in **§ 2.10.**

their secrecy can be controlled, when the communications protocol must be given out to third parties in order to be effective, its secrecy can be lost.

A communications protocol, however, is not necessarily incapable of trade secret protection. For example, in *Telerate Systems, Inc. v. Caro,*[23] a provider of computer financial information used a proprietary network protocol that permitted external PCs to connect directly to the plaintiff's computer network. The plaintiff supplied each customer with a computer disk to load on a PC in order to permit the customer's computer to communicate in accordance with the protocol. The defendant obtained the protocol during some consulting work for the plaintiff, then offered it to its own customers to use in connecting to the plaintiff's network. When the plaintiff contended that the defendant had misappropriated its trade secret, the defendant claimed that the protocol was not "secret enough" since it could have been reproduced through reverse engineering. The court disagreed, stating that the fact that a protocol "could have been discovered" does not negate the existence of a trade secret. "The possibility of [as opposed to the actual] discovery by 'fair and honest methods' does not preclude the finding of a trade secret."

The *Telerate* case can be interpreted to permit trade secret protection to exist for communications protocols even when those protocols are publicly disseminated, provided there remains "difficulty in acquiring the information" from the distributed disk.[24]

§ 2.15 —Copyright Protection

In general, copyright protection is available for communications protocols. In the most common example, the communications protocol existing in computer software can be copyrightable software. Courts have held that software can be copyrighted and that an infringing copy of the work occurs whenever the copyrighted work is loaded onto a permanent memory storage.[25] Indeed, one court has held that copying amounting to infringement can occur when the program is transferred from a computer's hard drive to the computer's RAM.[26]

In that case, the software copyright owner allowed its customers to use the software on their own computers, but disallowed uses by third parties such as the defendant. The defendant contended that its use of the computer software did not amount to infringement since it never copied the software. The court held otherwise, stating that the defendant's "loading of copyrighted software into RAM creates a 'copy' of the software in violation of the Copyright Act."[27]

---

[23] 689 F. Supp. 221 (S.D.N.Y. 1988).

[24] *Id.* at 232.

[25] MAI Sys. Corp. v. Peak Computer, Inc., 991 F.2d 511, 518 (9th Cir. 1993).

[26] *Id.*

[27] *Id.* But note that the *MAI Systems* case is binding only in the Ninth Circuit and may or may not be followed in other jurisdictions.

Whether a communications protocol in software is copyrightable can be a complicated decision. One court attempted to separate the protectable expressions from the unprotectable program ideas and processes by developing an "abstract-filtration" test. This test involves dividing a computer program into various levels of abstraction and then categorizing each level as either an expression or an idea. Ideas are those that are necessary to the program, required by characteristics external to the program, or taken from the public domain. The court filters out all of the ideas, leaving the expressions to be compared to the accused "copy."[28]

The courts have certainly left open the possibility that communications protocol software can include expressions (as opposed to program ideas and processes) that are protectable under copyright. In addition, the copyrights on those expressions may be infringed simply by loading the software into a computer's RAM.

§ 2.16 Summary

Intellectual property protections for network communications technology involve hardware, software, and protocol considerations. In general, patent protection is usually the best place to look for good protection for each of these three categories of technology. If, however, time or cost constraints dictate quicker or cheaper avenues of protection, one can consider copyright, trademark, and trade secret protections in lieu of or in addition to patent protection.

Patent protection is available for hardware apparatus and should be considered on both specific hardware being improved as well as hardware on higher and lower levels of the communications network system. In addition, clarifications by the courts and changes in the Patent and Trademark Office procedures have eliminated any doubt that patent protection is available for computer software in practical applications, such as in communications protocols. Now, patent practitioners can begin creatively claiming communications protocols to provide broad and narrow patent claim coverage.

---

[28] Computer Assocs. Int'l Inc. v. Altai, Inc., 23 U.S.P.Q.2d (BNA) 1241 (2d Cir. 1992).

CHAPTER 3

SECURITY TECHNOLOGIES

Lewis C. Lee

§ 3.1   Introduction

For the Internet (the Net) to blossom fully into a supernetwork supporting such activities as communication, entertainment, commerce, and education, the Net must offer some form of data security. Although some transactions or communications over the Internet might require little or no security, other transactions or communications will require, and indeed demand, high to near-absolute security. For this latter category, the security should at a minimum ensure that only authorized individuals are involved in the transaction and that the communication between them is safe from eavesdroppers.

Authenticity, document integrity, and confidentiality are among the principal requirements of an effective network security system. Unfortunately, several problems arise when attempting to satisfy these requirements. Participants to a transaction might be impersonated, signatures on messages might be forged, and the messages themselves might be undetectably altered. Standardized rules and practices exist in the nonelectronic, paper-based world to minimize the risks of such problems. Personal face-to-face verification, notary signatures, and hand delivery are conventional practices to ensure the authenticity, integrity, and confidentiality of a communication.

Although such standards may be fine for the nonelectronic world, the Internet presents a whole new universe—a virtually endless public network formed by the cooperative interconnection of computing networks from around the world. Messages originated at a single computer can be irretrievably beamed to thousands of computers all over the globe simultaneously in less time than it takes to read this sentence. Authenticity, integrity, and confidentiality take on a whole different meaning for the Internet. Whoever solves the Internet security problem will revolutionize the way the world communicates and transacts business. A secured Internet will enable the ultimate marketplace, where a buyer in Brazil can use her home PC to shop for dresses from Paris or Beverly Hills, trade stocks on the New York or Tokyo stock exchanges, send personal e-mail messages to friends in Amsterdam and Moscow, or book travel arrangements for a trip to Barbados.

Intellectual property protection strategies must be adaptable to protect the evolving security technologies which will fertilize the explosive growth of the Internet. This chapter examines different types and levels of network-related security technologies. Broadly speaking, Internet security technologies can be divided into two general categories: party verification and secure communication. *Party verification* concerns technologies which attempt to identify and provide network access to legitimate authorized users only, while simultaneously prohibiting network access by unauthorized users. *Secure communication* involves protecting the data being exchanged between legitimate parties from an eavesdropper as the data is communicated over an otherwise unsecured network.

§ 3.2 Party Verification

When a user attempts to access a network, be it a corporate LAN (local area network), a bank ATM (automatic teller machine) network, or the Internet, security procedures are often in place to identify the user and to ensure that the user is authorized for access to the network or to selected resources on the network. The practice of attempting to identify and grant or deny access based on this identification is known as *party verification.*

Party verification has arisen as a critical component in the network realm due to the impersonal nature of electronic transactions. An illustration can help explain. In Old Town, USA, Consumer Joe shops for clothes at the local clothier Fred's Fashions. Joe and Fred have been friends for many years, and Fred seems to have a knack for picking just the right seersucker suits for Joe. After fitting and tailoring, Joe pays Fred for the new suit with a personal check. Fred recognizes Joe and knows that Joe's credit with Old Town Bank down the street is good. Hence, Fred gladly accepts the check and sends Joe on his way with the new suit.

Hidden beneath this friendly exchange is the practice of party verification. During the face-to-face encounter, Fred identified the buyer as his friend Joe and authorized the sale based on his personal experience that Joe is a valued customer.

The complexity of party verification increases dramatically when moved from the point-of-purchase context like Fred and Joe, to a network context between remotely located parties who typically have no history of interaction. Consider a modern-day shopping experience on the Internet between Buyer Blade, the neighborhood's coolest in-line skater, and Wheels Inc., a supplier of skate wear with a Web site. Late one evening while surfing the Net, Blade hits the Web site for Wheels. Tickled by the radical bit map of a new light-weight ultra-comfortable pair of burgundy skates, Blade downloads pricing and order information. From his PC, Blade fills out an electronic purchase order identifying the skates and listing his name and address, and authorizes payment for the skates by using his credit card or other payment instructions. The purchase order and payment instructions are zipped across the Net to the sales division at Wheels, Inc. An employee at Wheels processes the order electronically and sends a confirmation back to Blade. Within a few business days, Wheels ships the new burgundy skates to Blade.

In this scenario, Blade and the Wheels employee have no personal contact. Instead, the whole transaction occurs in the electronic domain, where digital code names built by bits of "1"s and "0"s are used to identify the parties. This impersonal dealing raises a number of questions.

1. From Blade's perspective, is Wheels a legitimate place of business?
2. From Wheel's perspective, is Blade a bona fide purchaser, and are his payment instructions legitimate?
3. Did Blade and Wheels really communicate with each other on the Net, or was an impostor intercepting the communication to one of the parties?

These issues are the concern of party verification. The separate issues of whether Blade's confidential account numbers are protected over the open Net is the venue of secure communications, which is described in §§ **3.8** through **3.13**. General technologies used today for party verification are described in §§ **3.3** through **3.7**.

§ 3.3 —Verification Classes

Party verification in the electronic arena can be segmented into two broad classes: human-to-machine and machine-to-machine. A human-to-machine interface occurs at points of access to a network, such as workstations of a LAN or ATMs of a bank network. The party verification issue surrounding the human-to-machine interface concerns assuring that the person requesting access to the machine is indeed that person and not an impostor. A machine-to-machine interface occurs between two computing devices without human intervention. The party verification issue surrounding the machine-to-machine interface concerns assuring that the two computing units are legitimate and that neither one is an impostor or tampered machine. As an example, banking computers verify each other's identity prior to exchanging financially critical data over the network.

Both the human-to-machine and the machine-to-machine party verifications can be performed online or offline. Online verification involves interaction between a human or machine and a point-of-access computer which is actively tied into a network. In such situations, the identification information submitted by the person or computer requesting access is passed from the point-of-access computer to a verifying computing unit elsewhere on the network. An offline verification occurs between a human or machine and a standalone or point-of-access computer which is occasionally offline from the network. Offline verification is handled locally by the standalone or point-of-access computer.

A familiar exercise performed by many employees each day is remotely logging onto their employer's LAN. The logon process often routes the employee through several different levels of access. For instance, the employee might first enter a password simply to gain access to her own portable computer. She might then enter another password to gain access to the operating system, as well as other passwords for e-mail, personal scheduling applications, and so forth. This logon ritual is exemplary of human-to-machine offline verification.

After gaining access to local resources, the employee dials up the employer network using a modem. Another password is required to access the company LAN, and possibly other passwords for accessing resources on the LAN. These passwords are often verified at the remote access server. These logon procedures are typical of human-to-machine online verification.

The portable computer and server might also verify their own identities, apart from the identity of the employee, to assure each computer that it is communicating with a legitimate and authorized computer. This form of verification typifies a machine-to-machine class of verification.

Protection strategies can vary slightly depending on whether a new security technology involves a human-to-machine interface or a machine-to-machine interface. In the patent context, for example, it may be desirable to avoid claiming activities performed by the human in a human-to-machine verification because such claims may be difficult to enforce under a charge of direct infringement. Rather, the patent owner may be limited to a theory of contributory or inducement to infringement because the infringing product does not perform the human based steps recited in the claims, but only a user performs those steps.

§ 3.4 —Passwords

Passwords are commonly used as a low-level security measure for party verification in the human-to-machine interface. A password is a string of characters or numbers, or both, unique to the user. Personal Identification Numbers (PINs) are a special case of passwords. Password protocols require a user to enter his unique password. The password is compared to a stored version or list of authorized passwords. If the entered password matches a stored password, the user is presumed to be legitimate and access is granted. The password protocol provides no protection against an impostor who illicitly obtained the user's password.

§ 3.5 —Credentials

Credentials are widely used in the network setting for party verification in the machine-to-machine interface. A credential is an electronically generated packet of digital information which helps uniquely identify a participant in a network transaction. Participants to a network transaction submit registrations with a certified issuing authority that is trusted by all participants and whose authenticity is without question. The issuing authority validates the registration information and the fact that the participant is a bona fide entity seeking to participate in the network transactions. If the participant is authentic, the issuing authority issues a credential to that participant.

The credentials themselves contain unique identification information pertaining to the participant, dates specifying the duration of the credential, information on the issuing authority, and any other information determined in advance by the participants. The issuing authority signs the credential in a way that enables every participant to identify whether or not a credential is issued by the certified issuing authority.

During a network transaction, the participants exchange credentials as a form of introduction and to aid in further communication. The participants independently verify the authenticity of the other's credential using the signature of the issuing authority. In this manner, the credentials provide an initial form of party verification.

§ 3.6 —Automated Callback

Automated modem callback is an Internet security measure used for party verification. This security protocol requires a user to register with a service provider on the Internet. The registration includes the user's modem phone number and is stored at the Internet service provider. When the user dials up to access the service, the automated callback security protocol terminates the original connection and immediately dials the user's modem at the registered number. If the user is legitimate, his modem answers the callback and access is granted. An impostor, on the other hand, is presumed not to be present at the registered callback number. Hence, access is denied to the impostor since the callback will not reach the impostor.

§ 3.7 —Personal Identification Tokens

Personal identification tokens have risen in popularity as a means to facilitate party verification. Tokens act as authorization keys which a user employs to gain access to a piece of hardware, such as a PC or ATM. The most common forms of tokens are magnetic-stripe memory cards, magnetic-lined keys, and smart cards.

A token is uniquely assigned to each user by a token administrator. The user submits personal identification information (for example, a photo driver's license) to the token administrator which takes appropriate steps to verify the authenticity of the registering user. If the user is deemed authentic, the token administrator issues a token which typically stores unique information about the user. In some company settings, the employer-issued token is the sole means for gaining access to the corporate resources. The employee uses the token to access her PC, enter a building, or make photocopies.

In other cases, the token is an added level of security which can be coordinated with other security forms, such as passwords, to provide a tiered security system. In the banking environment, a bank acts as a token administrator for issuing magnetic-stripe bank cards to participating members for use in accessing ATMs. The bank issues the bank card with certain identification information stored on it, such as the member's name, account number, the issuing branch, card serial number, and the member's PIN.

After issuance, the member uses the card as her pocket credential to gain access to the banking ATMs. The member inserts the bank card into the ATM and enters the multidigit PIN. The entered PIN is compared to the PIN stored on the bank card, with a match authenticating for the ATM that the person standing at the ATM is the member who owns the inserted band card. Once the member's PIN is verified, the bank card passes the member information to the ATM to use for processing the banking transaction.

§ 3.8 Secure Communication

Verifying the parties is only one prong of a network security challenge. The other prong involves protecting the communication between the authenticated parties as it is transmitted over a network. Integrity, confidentiality, and authenticity are among the principal requirements of securing communication over a network.

In general, there are two ways to secure communications over a network. The first approach is to physically secure the communication channel itself. This is accomplished by erecting proprietary networks that are closed to the general public and by maintaining high-security protocols on the proprietary networks. Conventional banking networks are an example of closed proprietary networks.

These proprietary networks handle the requirements of integrity, confidentiality, and authenticity almost by definition. Participants are authenticated by the very fact that they have physical access to the proprietary networks, messages are automatically authenticated, explicit signing is not required, and the integrity of the information and value are preserved within the confines of the closed system. The approach of physically securing the communications channel itself cannot be transported to the Internet, which by definition is open to the public. Internet users must communicate over unsecured public networks which are open to eavesdroppers and impostors. Simply securing the network, and every point of access to it, is not an option.

Accordingly, a second approach to providing secure communication is to secure the data being transmitted over the network. This process involves the topic of cryptography.

§ 3.9 —Cryptography

Cryptography is the art and science of keeping messages secure. In the electronic realm, cryptography involves the use of mathematical algorithms or ciphers. Messages are encrypted by the cryptographic cipher from their original text to an encrypted state. The messages are transferred over the network from an originator to a recipient in the encrypted state. The recipient decrypts the encrypted message back to the original text. The security depends solely on how difficult it is for an unauthorized eavesdropper to intercept and recover the original text from the encrypted state.

All modern cryptographic ciphers employ at least one *key*. The key is typically a large number. The cipher used to encode the original message is a mathematical function of the key and message.

Cryptographic ciphers used in electronic networks are generally based on one-way functions. A one-way function is a mathematical function that is relatively easy to compute in one direction, but computationally infeasible to undo. With many functions, one can determine the input value from knowledge of the output value and the function being used. One-way functions are distinguishable in that the original input value cannot be easily determined by merely computing the inverse function on the output value. With one-way functions, forming an encrypted text from the original text is mathematically easy, but deciphering the encrypted text to recover the original text is computationally infeasible without knowing a secret.

The security of cryptographic ciphers is rooted in the mathematical strength and ability of the one-way function to withstand computational brute force in attempting to undo a function. One example of a mathematical function used in cryptographic ciphers is an exponential function, whereby the security is based on the difficulty of calculating discrete logarithms.

§ 3.10 —Symmetric versus Asymmetric Ciphers

There are two general types of cryptographic key-based ciphers: symmetric and asymmetric. In a *symmetric* cipher, the key used for both encryption and decryption can be calculated from one another. In many cases, the encryption key and the decryption key are the same. The symmetric key must be known to both the sender and receiver, but otherwise kept secret. Once the symmetric key is divulged, any party can encrypt or decrypt messages. Example symmetric ciphers are the Data Encryption Standard (DES) encryption algorithm and the RC4 algorithm. Encryption and decryption using a symmetric cipher are represented mathematically as follows:

$$E[\text{Message}]_{Ksym} = \text{Encrypted Message}$$
$$D[\text{Encrypted Message}]_{Ksym} = \text{Message}$$

where "E" is the encryption cipher using the symmetric key "Ksym," and "D" is the decryption cipher using the same key.

An *asymmetric* cryptographic key pair consists of two separate keys, a first key to manipulate data to an altered form and a second key to convert the altered data back to its original form. The keys are based on a mathematical relationship in which one key cannot be calculated (at least, not in any reasonable amount of time) from the other key. Cryptographic key pairs are used for different functions, including encryption, decryption, digital signing, signature verification, and authentication. As an example, encryption and decryption using an asymmetric key pair can be represented as follows:

$$E[\text{Message}]_{K1} = \text{Encrypted Message}$$
$$D[\text{Encrypted Message}]_{K2} = \text{Message}$$

where "E" is an encryption function using the first key "K1," and "D" is a decryption function using the second key "K2." The inverse is also true in that a message can be encrypted using the second key and decrypted using the first key. An example asymmetric cipher is the RSA cryptographic algorithm named for the creators Rivest, Shamir, and Adleman.

§ 3.11   —Digital Signatures

Digital signatures are used in the paperless world of computer networks and electronic data exchange in the same manner that handwritten signatures are used in a paper society. Like handwritten signatures, digital signatures act as proof that the sender deliberately signed a particular message and that the message has not been altered since its signature.

The digital signing operation is a special case of the encryption process and involves an asymmetric key algorithm. One key is used to encrypt or "sign" a message or representation of the message, yielding a digital signature. A second key is used to decrypt or "unsign" the encrypted message to authenticate the sender. When a large message needs to be signed, the message might first be passed through a hash function to translate the message into a cryptographic digest or hash. A *hash function* is a mathematical function that converts an input data stream into a fixed-sized, often smaller, output data stream that is representative of the input data stream. The digital signature is then created upon encryption of the cryptographic digest. A signing operation is represented as follows:

$$E[\text{Message or Digest}]_{K1} = \text{Digital Signature}$$

The digital signature is attached with the encrypted message and sent to the recipient. The recipient is equipped to decrypt the digital signature. If the decryption yields intelligible text, the signature is presumed to be authentic; otherwise, the message has been forged or altered after being legitimately signed.

§ 3.12 —Private versus Public Key Systems

Cryptographic systems employed on the Internet can be categorized into two classes: private key systems and public key systems. A private key system employs symmetric key ciphers. Both participants to any communication must be in possession of a secret key used to encrypt and decrypt their messages. The secret keys must be delivered by some mechanism other than the Internet so that they remain confidential, such as hand delivery. Once the secret keys are safely distributed, the participants can exchange messages using symmetric encryption ciphers.

A public key system is built on an asymmetric key cipher. Each participant generates a pair of asymmetric keys. One of the keys, known as the *public key*, is freely distributed to other participants and can be listed in public books or posted on bulletin boards. The other key, known as the *private key*, is maintained in confidence by the participant.

The public and private keys ensure two results. First, only the holder of the private key can decrypt a message that is encrypted with the corresponding public key. Second, if another party decrypts a message using the public key, that party can be assured that the message was encrypted by the private key and thus originated with a holder (presumably, the authorized holder) of the private key.

§ 3.13 —Example of Public Key System with Digital Signatures

The combination of encryption and digital signing provide the foundation for a secure exchange over the Internet. To illustrate a public key cryptography system, recall from § 3.2 the story of Blade, the cool in-line skating dude, and Wheels Inc., a supplier of hip skates. Assume that a general public key protocol is applied to a purchase order sent from Blade over the Internet to Wheels.

Software executing on Blade's PC generates a purchase order for new burgundy skates. The purchase order is passed through a hashing algorithm HASH(x) to produce a cryptographic digest of the order, as follows:

$$\text{HASH(Order)} = \text{Order Digest}$$

Blade's PC software digitally signs the cryptographic digest on behalf of Blade by encrypting the digest using Blade's private signing key of an asymmetric key pair, as follows:

$$\text{E[Order Digest]}_{\text{Blade's private key}} = \text{Blade's Digital Signature}$$

The digital signature (that is, signed digest) is attached to the purchase order to form a packet. Blade's PC software encrypts the packet using the Wheels public key, which is freely available on the Internet, to produce the following.

E[order + Blade's signature]$_{\text{Wheels' public key}}$ = Encrypted Signed Order

The encrypted order is then transmitted from Blade's computer over the Internet to Wheels' computer. Since the Internet is unsecured, any eavesdropper can intercept the packet. By using Wheels' public key, however, Blade is assured that only Wheels, the bona fide holder of the corresponding private key, can decrypt the purchase order which is encrypted with its public key. The eavesdropper does not have the private key. Due to the inherent nature of one-way functions, the eavesdropper is unable to unscramble the encrypted order into any intelligible meaning.

Software executing on Wheels' computer begins by decrypting the encrypted order using its own private key, as follows:

D[Encrypted Signed Order]$_{\text{Wheels' private key}}$ = order + Blade's signature

This decryption yields an intelligible purchase order from a person named Blade for a pair of burgundy in-line skates. To authenticate that the purchase order truly came from Blade, and not an impostor, Wheels' PC software verifies Blade's signature by decrypting the order digest. The decryption algorithm uses Blade's public key which is readily available on the Internet or, more likely, was sent by Blade's computer as part of the purchase order packet.

D[Blade's Digital Signature]$_{\text{Blade's public key}}$ = Order Digest

Wheels' software also independently computes a hash of the decrypted order it received from Blade. If the signature decryption yields a result that compares bit-for-bit with the independently, locally computed hash of the order, Wheels is assured that the packet came from Blade and was not subsequently altered. This assurance is grounded in the fact that only Blade is presumed to be in possession of the corresponding private key used to produce the digital signature.

Accordingly, message encryption coupled with digital signatures form a formidable security protocol for protecting data transmitted over the public Internet.[1]

§ 3.14 Protection Strategies

The security technologies described in §§ 3.2 through 3.13 can be protected as various forms of intellectual property. Chief among the available protections are patent protection and copyright protection. Additionally, because private keys used in public key cryptography are by their very nature intended to be kept private, it is relevant to consider trade secret protection of these valuable trade

---

[1] For more information on cryptography, see Bruce Schneier, Applied Cryptography: Protocols, Algorithms, and Source Code in C (2d ed., John Wiley & Sons 1996). This text is very readable and explains in great detail and ease the intricate details of most modern-day ciphers.

secrets. The remainder of this chapter focuses on intellectual property protection strategies for Internet security technologies, beginning with patent protection.

§ 3.15 Patent Protection

Security technologies are, of course, patentable. The patent statute defines patent subject matter as "any new and useful process, machine, manufacture, or composition of matter, or any new or useful improvement thereof."[2] This list does not specifically mention security technologies, or even allude to computers, microprocessors, integrated circuit chips, modems, and networks, which are all important for the Internet.

As noted in **Chapter 1,** the classes of patentable subject matter are broadly interpreted. The class *machines,* for instance, covers both mechanical and electronic things. The class *processes* is defined to include any process, art, or method, as well as any new use of a known process, machine, manufacture, composition of matter, or material.[3] Methods for operating computers, sending data over a network, or displaying information on a screen are patentable subject matter under the *processes* class. In fact, most of the Internet technologies can be included under the classes *processes* and *machines,* and the statutory definition of patentable subject matter also includes "any new or useful improvement" of a machine or process. The realm of patentable subject matter is quite expansive. Thus, security technologies are patentable subject matter.

§ 3.16 —Hardware Components

The straightforward hardware side of the security technologies can be addressed before moving onto the more interesting cryptography aspects discussed in **§§ 3.17** through **3.23.** This discussion of hardware security technologies deals primarily with the use of personal identification tokens, such as magnetic-stripe memory cards, magnetic-lined keys, and smart cards. These tokens are used to grant or deny access at a network terminal, long before the user actually accesses the network itself.

For instance, corporate employees are often asked to carry about smart cards or magnetic-stripe cards which have been uniquely assigned to them. The workstations, photocopiers, and other machines are equipped with card readers. The employees are requested to insert their cards into the readers, which might be connected to a larger verification system. The readers determine whether the card is valid, hence verifying the authenticity of the card holder (which is

---

[2] 35 U.S.C. § 101.

[3] *Id.* § 100.

presumed to be the card owner). If everything checks out, the user is permitted to log on to the computer or operate the photocopy machine.

Apart from card-based authentication systems, other hardware technologies that make possible the Internet security protocols include encryption integrated circuit (IC) chips, modems, routers, and the like. These hardware systems and devices are clearly patentable subject matter. The only remaining questions, then, are whether the system or device is new and whether the system or device is nonobvious. Patent protection is available if both of these questions can be answered in the affirmative.

§ 3.17 —Patenting Cryptographic-Based Technologies

Cryptography presents an interesting patent situation because at the heart of cryptography are mathematical algorithms. In public key systems, there is an encryption algorithm and a decryption algorithm, which both rely on mathematically derived keys.

Consider one famous and widely used public key system, known as RSA, which employs a public key and a private key. The public key consists of two values, a value "n" which is the product of two prime numbers p and q (which are kept secret) and a value "e" which is relatively prime to $(p-1) \times (q-1)$. The private key consists of a single value "d" which is derived using Euclid's algorithm to be according to the following formula:

$$d = e^{-1} (mod(p-1) \times (q-1))$$

To encrypt a message "m," the encryption algorithm is simply:

$$c = m^e (mod\ n)$$

where "c" is the encrypted message.[4] To decrypt the encrypted message "c" and recover the original message, the decryption algorithm is stated:

$$m = c^d (mod\ n)$$

---

[4] The notation "X mod(M)" represents a common arithmetic operation performed by a computer in large integer arithmetic known as the "modular reduction" operation, or simply "modulo" operation. The modulo operation is an arithmetic operation whose result is the remainder of a division operation. In the expression "X mod(M)," X is a number written in some base and M is the "modulus." The result of the operation "X mod(M)" is the remainder of the number X divided by the modulus M. As a simple example, the modulo operation 17 mod 3 yields a result of 2, because 17 divided by 3 yields a remainder 2. Because it produces a remainder, the modulo operation is often alternatively referred to as the "division remainder" operation.

Although this section may seem like a math lecture, the above formulas are included to explain an important point. Cryptography is rooted in mathematical algorithms. However, algorithms per se are not patentable. Algorithms are just math, something that exists in nature, something to be discovered like raw materials, and no one can patent oil, gold, Einstein's theory, or algorithms. This raises a question as to whether the RSA algorithm is freely available for sending secure messages over a company's network without obligation to the people who invented it. Although the algorithm itself is not patented and is available for use by anyone, a user risks receiving a scathing infringement letter if the user attempts to implement the RSA algorithm in the computing and communications environment, because the RSA cryptographic system is patented.[5]

§ 3.18 —Patenting Nonpatentable Algorithms

DISCLAIMER: The discussion in § **3.17** is not intended to state, imply, or otherwise mislead one to believe that a cryptographic algorithm is patentable. The fact is that *algorithms are not patentable*. This mantra is beaten into every patent attorney's head, and with good reason.

Mathematical algorithms are typically found in the statutory list of nonpatentable subject matter,[6] which also includes methods of doing business, natural phenomena, and laws of nature. In 1972, the Supreme Court held that a method for converting binary-coded decimal numerals into pure binary numerals was not eligible for patent protection.[7] In 1989, the Federal Circuit agreed with this position that an algorithm is not statutory subject matter and hence cannot be patented.[8] In fact, most patent treatises and digests plainly state that algorithms are not patentable subject matter.

It may seem contradictory that the law says algorithms are not patentable, and yet the RSA-based cryptographic system is patented, raising the question of whether it is in fact possible to patent cryptography solutions. The answer is both *no* and *yes*. (Do I sound like a lawyer? It took me years to learn such answers.) After pronouncing that algorithms are not patentable in and of themselves, the same 1989 Federal Circuit opinion that pronounced algorithms as nonstatutory subject matter also noted that the mere recital of an algorithm within a patent claim which is otherwise statutory does not automatically render the claim nonstatutory.

Thus, clever patent attorneys will never say that an algorithm can be patented. However, those same attorneys will unabashedly declare that a cryptographic

---

[5] U.S. Patent No. 4,405,829, "Cryptographic Communications System and Method," issued Sept. 20, 1993, to Rivest, Shamir, and Adleman.

[6] 35 U.S.C. § 101.

[7] Gottschalk v. Benson, 409 U.S. 63, 175 U.S.P.Q. (BNA) 673 (1972).

[8] *In re* Grams, 888 F.2d 835, 12 U.S.P.Q.2d (BNA) 1824 (Fed. Cir. 1989).

system or method or protocol or the like can be patented, as long as the word "algorithm" is cleverly omitted.

§ 3.19 —Claim Drafting: Form over Substance

The trick to obtaining patent protection for cryptographic security systems is to claim them in a real computing context, and not in the theoretical mathematical realm. That is, the key is to draft claims which dress the nonstatutory algorithm in statutory clothing.[9]

Consider the RSA algorithm described in § **3.17.** A competent patent attorney would never draft a claim as follows:

> 1. A mathematical function comprising:
>
> an encryption function $c = m^e$ (mod n), where "m" is a message, "c" is a digital message, and "e" is a key which is relatively prime to $(p-1) \times (q-1)$ where "p" and "q" are both prime numbers, and "n" is the product of "p" and "q"; and
>
> a decryption function $m = c^d$ (mod n), where "d" is a Euclidean function of "e."

This claim would be thrown out of the Patent and Trademark Office as failing to recite statutory subject matter because the claim simply recites a naked algorithm. Nevertheless, the algorithm can be stated in statutory language. The following is claim 1 of the RSA patent:[10]

> 1. A cryptographic communications system comprising:
>
> A. a communications channel,
>
> B. an encoding means coupled to said channel and adapted for transforming a transmit message word signal M to a ciphertext word signal C and for transmitting C on said channel, where M corresponds to a number representative of a message and $0 \leq M \leq n-1$ where n is a composite number of the form $n = p \times q$ where p and q are prime numbers, and where C corresponds to a number representative of an enciphered form of said message and corresponds to
>
> $C \equiv M^e$ (mod n)
>
> where e is a number relatively prime to 1 cm(p–1, q–1), and
>
> C. a decoding means coupled to said channel and adapted for receiving C from said channel and for transforming C to receive message word signal M' where M' corresponds to a number representative of a deciphered form of C and corresponds to

---

[9] *Claims* are those numerated sentences listed at the back of a patent. Claims are akin to a land deed, which stipulates the property boundaries of physical land, in that claims stipulate the bounds of the intellectual property rights afforded by patent. A discussion of claims and how to read them is provided in Lewis C. Lee & J. Scott Davidson, Managing Intellectual Property Rights (John Wiley & Sons 1993).

[10] U.S. Patent No. 4,405,829.

$$C \equiv M^e \pmod{n}$$

where d is a multiplicative inverse of e(mod(1 cm((p–1),(q–1)))).

Compare the fictitious claim 1 and the RSA patent claim 1. The algorithm is the same, but the claim language is entirely different. Notice that the fictitious claim defines a "mathematical function," whereas the RSA patent claim defines a "cryptographic communications system." Notice also that the RSA patent claim requires a "communications channel," an "encoding means," and a "decoding means." These elements are physical, electronic, and, in short, statutory things. Thus, in the land of claiming algorithms, the following equation applies:

Algorithm + Statutory Subject Matter = Patentable

§ 3.20   —Common Claim Formats

There are many claim formats that can be used to cover security technologies. One common claim format is a *system* format. System claims define the entire security technology from a systemwide perspective. For cryptography technologies, for example, a system claim format recites the sender, the receiver, and perhaps the communications channel between them. The cryptography aspects are then woven into the claim as functions or tasks performed by the sender and receiver.

The patent claim recited in § 3.19 is an example of a system format in which the RSA algorithm is claimed as part of a system. The RSA patent claim defines "a cryptographic communications system" having "a communications channel," "an encoding means" which encodes messages using the RSA algorithm and transmits them over the communications channel, and "a decoding means" which receives the encoded message from the communications channel and decodes the encoded messages using the RSA algorithm.

Another common claim format is a *machine* or *apparatus* format. An apparatus claim defines the invention as a single device. These claims are appropriate for defining a standalone product or an individual component of an overall system. In the cryptography context, for instance, an apparatus claim might be directed only to the encoder, or only to the decoder, of the cryptography system. An apparatus claim recites specific elements of the device. A fictitious example of an apparatus claim for a cryptographic encoding device might be as follows:

1. An encoder for encoding a message M, comprising:

a first buffer to hold the message M;

a second buffer; and

a computing unit connected to the first buffer to receive the message M, the computing unit coverting the message M to a ciphertext C, where C=f(M), the computing unit being further connected to the second buffer to store the ciphertext C in the second buffer.

Another common claim format is a *method* format. Method claims define the invention as one or more steps in a process. A fictitious example of a method claim for a cryptography technology is outlined below:

1. A method for securely transmitting a message over a network, comprising the following steps:

encrypting a message M into a ciphertext C, where C=f(M);

transmitting the ciphertext C over a network;

receiving the ciphertext C; and

decrypting the ciphertext C into the message M, where M=f(C).

§ 3.21 —The Rise and Fall of "Means Plus Function" Claims

Patent claims are intricate creatures, involving precise language that weaves legal phraseology together with technical definitions. This is particularly true of software and algorithm-based claims. Oftentimes it is difficult to precisely define the components in such claims, without describing each intricate detail of the component. Yet, those same components can often be described simply in terms of their functions.

The patent statute contains a provision which allows an invention to be expressed in terms of the component and its function. The statute stipulates:

An element in a claim for a combination may be expressed as a means or step for performing a specified function without the recital of structure, material, or acts in support thereof, and such claim shall be construed to cover the corresponding structure, material, or acts described in the specification and equivalents thereof.[11]

The statutory provision lays the foundation for a particular claim format known as "means plus function." According to this format, each element in the claim is recited as a component or "means" in combination with a corresponding function performed by that means. A few examples of means plus function elements are:

input means for entry of data . . .

calculation means for computing a function . . .

transmission means for carrying a signal . . .

---

[11] 35 U.S.C. § 112, ¶ 6.

dinner bell means for calling children to dinner . . .

TV means for depicting mind-numbing programming . . .

The last two items show how almost anything can be described in this manner. To a patent attorney, drafting means plus function claims is comparatively easier than drafting other types of claims. The attorney simply defines the invention in terms of the various functions that the components perform, without having to recite the structure, material, or acts in support of the components. The means plus function claims do not require intricate detail, thereby avoiding potential limitations that might be adversely construed to narrow the scope of the patent.

Means plus function claims became widely used by patent attorneys. These claims were particularly popular for electronic, software, and algorithm-based claims. The RSA claim quoted in § **3.19,** for example, contains elements that are drafted in the means plus function format, including *"encoding means . . . for transforming* a transmit message word signal M to a ciphertext word signal C and *for transmitting* C on said channel," and *"decoding means . . . for receiving* C from said channel and *for transforming* C to receive message word signal M'." (Emphasis added.)

According to long-standing practice, the Patent and Trademark Office (PTO) had always interpreted a means plus function claim element by giving it the "broadest reasonable interpretation," interpreting the element as reading on any prior art that was equivalent to the corresponding structure, material, or acts described in the specification.[12] With this broad interpretation, the examiners could cite essentially any prior art device which performed the recited function as a basis for rejecting the claims. However, the PTO's practice was out of line with the statute and the way courts interpreted means plus function claims. When a patent holder enforced a means plus function claim, the courts construed the claim element to cover the corresponding structure or material described in the specification and equivalents thereof, as expressly prescribed in the patent statute. The claims were not given their "broadest reasonable interpretation." The statutory provision afforded a more restrictive scope of protection, as allegedly infringing products might be able to escape being found to constitute infringement if they contained elements that were not equivalent to the embodiments described in the patent specification.

As a result, a perplexing dichotomy evolved. Means plus functions claims were being examined in the PTO using one standard—the "broadest reasonable interpretation" standard—which permitted the examiners to introduce essentially any prior art that satisfied the function, and the claims were being enforced in court according to a second standard—the statutorily prescribed standard—which was more restrictive and more difficult to apply to allegedly infringing products.

---

[12] Manual of Patent Examining Procedure § 2181 (July 1996).

In 1994, the Federal Circuit handed down the *Donaldson* decision,[13] an *en banc* decision which ended the dichotomy and the PTO's examination practice as it related to means plus function elements. The *Donaldson* decision required the PTO examiners to interpret means plus function claim elements as limited to the corresponding structure, materials, or acts described in the specifications or equivalents thereof, as is expressly stipulated in the patent statute.

In view of this ruling, the patent bar became increasingly nervous about exclusively relying on means plus function claims, as such claims might now be interpreted more narrowly than before. The courts might decide to take a more restrictive view of what "equivalents" should be accorded to the structures mentioned in the specification. This raises interesting questions, such as whether a patent attorney should list every conceivable "equivalent" in the specification, or whether the attorney should risk leaving it to the courts to interpret. As a result, many patent attorneys have steered away from sole use of means plus function claims, except perhaps in certain circumstances where the subject matter is particularly difficult to define.

Thus, although the means plus function format remains a viable and often useful approach, the present trend is away from exclusive use of such claims.

§ 3.22   —New and Evolving Claim Formats

In addition to the classic claim formats described in §§ 3.20 and 3.21—system, method, apparatus, means plus function—other claim formats are evolving which are particularly applicable to software-related inventions. The new claim formats have arisen as a result of recent cases before the Federal Circuit. Two notable cases are *In re Lowry*[14] and *In re Beauregard.*[15] The results of both cases are that software objects, data structures, or computer-executable instructions embodied on a storage medium are statutory subject matter.

In the *Lowry* case, the invention involved an object-oriented data structure that defined functional relationships between computer memory elements. One of the claims presented in *Lowry* recited a "memory for storing data for access by an application program being executed on a data processing system" comprising "a data structure stored in said memory." The claim went on to list various data objects included in the data structure and their relation to one another. The Federal Circuit concluded that the claim satisfied the statutory subject matter requirements and, hence, is a viable claim format.

The *Lowry* decision provides patent holders with another weapon in their infringement arsenal. Patent claims can be directed to cover a data structure

---

[13] *In re* Donaldson Co., 16 F.3d 1189, 29 U.S.P.Q.2d (BNA) 1845 (Fed. Cir. 1994) (en banc).

[14] 32 F.3d 1579, 32 U.S.P.Q.2d (BNA) 1908 (Fed. Cir. 1994).

[15] 35 U.S.P.Q.2d (BNA) 1383 (Fed. Cir. 1995).

stored on a computer disk or other memory device (such as the shrink-wrapped program sold by the manufacturer) or a data structure created in memory during or as a result of some computer process.

In the security technologies context, this offers some interesting possibilities. For instance, suppose a new cryptography technology enciphers messages into a ciphertext which has a specific data structure for transmission over a network. If this data structure is new and nonobvious, a patent attorney may consider drafting claims directed to the data structure itself (embodied, of course, in a storage medium), in addition to system, method, means plus function, and other potentially viable claims to the cryptography solution.

The *Beauregard* case involved an algorithm for filling in a polygon on a computer monitor. One of the claims recited an "article of manufacture" comprising a "computer usable medium having computer readable program code means embodied therein for causing a polygon having a boundary definable by a plurality of selectable pels on a graphics display to be filled." The claim then defined the various functions performed by the computer-readable program code means to accomplish the filling operation. The PTO had originally rejected this claim as nonstatutory subject matter, but later withdrew its conclusion in view of the *Lowry* decision.

As a result, the *Beauregard* case offers another new claim format that the PTO is willing to accept. In a *Beauregard* claim format, the software code is claimed in conjunction with the storage medium on which the software code is stored as an article of manufacture. This is similar to the *Lowry* case, except that rather than a data structure, the program instructions themselves are claimed in conjunction with the storage medium. The reasoning is that the otherwise generic storage medium is converted by the inscribed computer-executable instructions into a unique and patentable article of manufacture.

The *Beauregard* claim format can be recited in terms of structure in which the claim recites a memory and then computer code means stored on the memory to do something. Consider the following example:

> 1. A computer usable medium having computer-readable program code means for encrypting a message, the computer-readable program code means comprising:
> computer program code means for encrypting the message M . . . .

The *Beauregard* claim format can be equally presented as steps in a process. The second approach is perhaps best thought of as a hybrid apparatus and method claim. The claim recites a storage medium in the preamble of the claim, and then defines the steps performed by the computer-executable instructions of the software stored on the storage medium. A fictitious example of the storage medium format in the cryptography context is:

> 1. A computer-readable memory used to direct a computer to perform the following steps:
> encrypting a message M . . . .

The *Beauregard* claim format is very useful for pure software inventions, such as cryptographic-laden applications. The claim format affords patent protection of software embodied in a storage medium, such as common shrink-wrapped products in which software is sold on a floppy disk or CD-ROM, or computer-implemented software in which software is loaded into a computer memory (for example, RAM, ROM, or disk memory).

Another benefit of this claim format is that it gives the patent holder a firmer ground on which to file infringement charges against an infringing party. With the storage medium format, a party now directly infringes the patent claims simply by selling software embodied in a storage medium that would direct a computer to perform the steps recited in the claims.

§ 3.23   —Use All Claim Formats

All claim formats are available for use. From a business perspective, the prudent approach is to pursue patent protection using as many patent claim formats as the business circumstances dictate. If the company plans to sell security technologies implemented in software, the primary emphasis of a patent claim strategy should be placed in *Beauregard* and method claim formats, with lesser reliance on system and apparatus claim formats. For companies planning to sell hardware devices that perform security functions, claim emphasis may alternatively be placed on apparatus and method claims. Accordingly, a prudent business manager should sit down with patent counsel and describe the business model envisioned by the business manager for selling the product. With this knowledge, the patent counsel can tailor the claim strategy to best protect the products within that business model.

§ 3.24   Copyright Protection

The issue presented in this section is whether copyright protection is viable for security technologies, particularly cryptography technologies. Copyright protection covers original works of authorship which are fixed in any tangible medium of expression, from which the works may be perceived, reproduced, or otherwise communicated.[16] Quite simply, software is copyrightable. Similarly, the content of memory embedded in firmware, an application-specific integrated circuit (ASIC), or other device is likewise copyrightable. Hence, software programs containing cryptography algorithms, subroutines containing code defining an algorithm, and cryptographic code embedded in semiconductor devices are all protectable under copyright.

---

[16] 17 U.S.C. § 102(a) (1990).

A more interesting question, however, is whether messages which are encrypted and sent over the Internet are somehow protectable under copyright law. An argument could be made that an illegitimate eavesdropper who intercepts a communication between two parties in an attempt to decipher the communication is liable for copyright infringement, assuming the message contents are themselves copyrightable. In such a situation, the eavesdropper has effectively reproduced or copied the communication into a memory or temporary buffer at the electronic listening device during interception of the communication. This illegitimate copy arguably triggers a violation of the copyright owner's exclusive rights to reproduce the message or to make a derivative of the message.[17] It is unlikely that the eavesdropper could claim "fair use" of the message.[18]

A scenario in which a sender multicasts encrypted copyrightable messages over the Internet to many users who are given appropriate decryption means beforehand might play out differently for the eavesdropper. This multicast situation is akin to a television station that scrambles a satellite feed for broadcast over a satellite network to many subscribers who have purchased the licensed descrambler. In this context, eavesdroppers to the multicast address, like non-subscribers to the satellite feed, might legitimately receive the messages without risk of copyright infringement because they are merely listening to a publicly accessible multicast address. An eavesdropper might then be free to try to decipher the multicast and obtain the keying material for future messages.

These issues are very interesting and, for the most part, untested in court. It is impossible to predict with certainty which way the courts will proceed when addressing such issues. This author's belief (and that is all it is) is that the courts will try, in the interest of public policy, to promote and preserve free access to content and resources available on the Internet. Downloading data from the Internet for personal use, even by an unauthorized or unregistered party, might very well be labeled a fair use of the content in the copyright realm. The "fair use" doctrine allows unauthorized use of copyrightable works without permission from the owner for certain limited purposes as long as the use does not adversely affect the value of the copyrighted work.[19] Essentially, the fair use doctrine means that a copyright owner's exclusive rights are technically violated, but other circumstances justify the violation.

The famous *Sony* case[20] may offer a clue as to how the Supreme Court will handle this issue. In *Sony,* the Court held that a viewer could legitimately record a broadcasted television program by using a VCR, even though such copying seemingly violates the copyright owner's exclusive rights. The Supreme Court found that such copying fell into the category of "fair use."

---

[17] *Id.* § 106.

[18] *See id.* § 107 on the fair use doctrine.

[19] *Id.* § 107.

[20] Sony Corp. of Am. v. Universal City Studios, Inc., 464 U.S. 417 (1984).

§ 3.25   Trade Secret Protection

The question addressed in this section is whether trade secret protection is available for security technologies. A trade secret is confidential information that is valuable to a company by affording an advantage in the marketplace over those who do not know the secret. More specifically, the Uniform Trade Secrets Act defines a *trade secret* as follows:

> "Trade Secret" means information, including formula, pattern, compilation, program, device, method, technique, or process, that:
>
> (i) derives independent economic value, actual or potential, from not being generally known to, and not being readily ascertainable by proper means by other persons who can obtain economic value from its disclosure or use, and
>
> (ii) is subject of efforts that are reasonable under the circumstances to maintain its secrecy.[21]

There are many aspects of the security realm that are conducive to trade secret protection. In a public key cryptography system, for example, the private key held secretly by the key holder can qualify for trade secret protection. The private key derives economic value by not being generally known to others, and the key holder typically takes affirmative steps to keep the key secret. The cryptography algorithm itself may well qualify for trade secret protection in a similar manner, assuming the algorithm cannot be readily ascertained by others.

The problem with applying trade secret protection to cryptography technologies is that it affords protection only against those who acquire the trade secret through improper means.[22] Trade secret protection ends when a competitor discovers the trade secret through proper means. Note that the trade secret definition above requires that the trade secret "not being readily ascertainable *by proper means* by other persons." (Emphasis added.)

In the Internet context, the encrypted communication is passed over a public network. Unintended recipients of encrypted messages who are able to discover the sender's private key or algorithm through reverse engineering or other proper techniques might well put an abrupt end to the trade secret protection of these aspects. An argument might be made that the very act of intercepting a message addressed to another amounts to the use of improper means to discover the message content or encryption keys, but this argument has not been addressed.

Thus, although trade secret protection might be available for security technologies, it might be readily lost and practically difficult to enforce.

---

[21] Unif. Trade Secrets Act § 1.

[22] *Improper means* includes (1) unlawful conduct and (2) otherwise lawful conduct that is improper under the circumstances.

§ 3.26 Summary

This chapter touched on various types of security technologies which provide secure access to, and secure communication over, the Internet. The security technologies include both hardware and software solutions. The following list summarizes the important points:

1. Patent protection is available for security technologies that are new and nonobvious.

2. Patent protection is available to algorithm-based cryptographic solutions, as long as patent counsel uses the proper claim formats to present the concepts.

3. There are many different ways to claim security technology, each giving rise to different business and market practicalities as well as enforcement issues. It is prudent to invest in a variety of claims written in many different formats.

4. Copyright protection is available for security technologies implemented in software and firmware, such as password protocols and cryptography solutions.

5. Trade secret protection is available for certain aspects of security technologies, such as protection of secret keys used for cryptography purposes. It is unclear whether trade secret protection will protect communication and encryption keying information against an eavesdropper who intercepts the encrypted communication sent over the public Internet.

CHAPTER 4

SERVER-RELATED ISSUES

Daniel L. Hayes

§ 4.1   Introduction

Internet entities can be generally categorized as servers or clients. Generally, servers are providers of services and information, while clients are consumers of the services and information. This chapter deals with the intellectual property aspects of "server-related" technology and content. More generally, this chapter deals with intellectual property issues that are of concern to anyone attempting to provide server-related functions over the Internet. Note that these issues apply to nearly anyone who is trying to actively exploit the Internet by providing online services or information. They also potentially apply to anyone providing

elements of hardware or software in the communications network between network entities. This includes anyone from the local service provider, who is
mainly concerned with the mechanics of information transfer, to the content
publisher, who is responsible for the actual information that is being transferred.
The topic of intellectual property aspects of "client-related" technology is taken
up in **Chapter 5.**

The goal of this chapter is to give a few examples of how the different areas
of intellectual property law apply to different aspects of providing services and
information over the Internet.

It is helpful to think in terms of two different objectives when providing
Internet services and information. One objective is to respect other parties'
intellectual property rights. From a business standpoint, this is a purely practical
consideration that is independent of anyone's feelings of what is "right" or
"fair." Intellectual property laws set out legal requirements that do not always
coincide with an individual's understanding of morality and fair play.

Apart from purely business considerations, however, business people should
also consider their personal standards regarding the rights of others. Quite often,
the law defines only the minimum standards of behavior; behavior that is *legal* is
not always *right.* There is nothing to stop anyone from setting a higher standard
than set by the law.

The other objective when providing Internet services and information is to
protect your own intellectual property rights. You should not expect others to be
as scrupulous as you, and you may at some time need help from the legal system.
When this time comes, your position will be much stronger if you have already
taken the necessary steps to formalize your intellectual property ownership.

§ 4.2   Technological and Historical Background

The Internet is a loosely knit organization of regional networks, service providers, and local area networks, connected by communications paths of different
types. A variety of hardware and software is used in implementing these elements. In addition, there are numerous protocols and formats that have been
defined for transferring information over the communications paths. Finally,
there is content itself that is transferred between different individuals and organizations using the hardware, software, protocols, and formats of the Internet.

Internet entities can be classified either as content and service providers
(servers), or as end users (clients). World Wide Web browsers get a lot of
publicity because they are the only part of the Internet visible to end users.
However, these browsers are only a small part of the overall technology of the
Internet. The real work takes place before the information even gets to the
browsers, although this is changing somewhat with the advent of embedded
scripts, applets, and controls in Web documents.

In the past, the Internet was used mainly for educational and research purposes, particularly with regard to computer technology. In those years, the Internet formed a small and neighborly "community" whose members rarely thought in terms of intellectual property.

Now, however, the Internet is being viewed primarily as a business opportunity. Although not inevitable, it is conceivable that the Internet could eventually become a dominant means of doing business—not only for communicating but for buying and delivering goods and services. Note that some goods (such as software, books, and music) and many services (travel assistance and reservations, bill-paying, stock information, and news) can currently be delivered via the Internet, in many cases more efficiently than using traditional means. Many other goods and services can be ordered over the Internet. There is some possibility that even traditional television content and viewing will become intertwined with the Internet.

Logically, modern Internet players are taking a more businesslike attitude than their research-oriented predecessors, and they are seeking whatever legal protection is available for their original works and innovations. Indeed, the components that make up the Internet—hardware, software, protocols, formats, and content—are all potentially protectable by copyrights or patents.

§ 4.3 Copyrights

Copyright laws apply on the Internet just as they do in any other environment. That is, a person cannot copy and distribute the materials of others without the owners' permission. This general concept of copyright law applies (with exceptions) even though the materials have been posted on the Internet by others or sent in e-mail. Likewise, this concept applies even though Internet distribution of the materials technically involves only the transmission of binary data. "Copying" under the copyright law occurs simply by transferring copyrightable content from one digital storage device to another. Thus, copying occurs when someone downloads a graphics file and stores it on a computer's hard disk. It occurs again when the file is loaded in graphics memory. Even browsing a Web page on the Internet involves making at least one copy.

Computers, the widespread digitization of almost every type of information, and the communications capabilities of the Internet have made large-scale copyright infringement possible with only the slightest of efforts. A single mouse click can produce a copy of an entire book or possibly an entire collection of books.

It has been argued that copyright law does not make sense in this environment. As support for this argument, some point to the ease of copying and the great difficulty of detecting infringement on the Internet. Others point out that even the most routine Internet functions such as forwarding e-mail and browsing

Web pages are technical infringements under the copyright law—even though most people would not consider those activities to be wrong. Regardless of whether it makes sense, however, rest assured that information providers on the Internet are and will continue to be subject to copyright laws.

Sections 4.4 through **4.13** outline the various types of Internet materials that are protected by copyright, as well as other important issues relating to the subject of copyright. The focus is primarily on avoiding infringement, because that is the most challenging task. Obtaining copyright protection for materials requires very little effort.

§ 4.4 —Computer Programs

Software is protected under copyright law as a literary work.[1] Both source code and object code are protected by copyright. Copyright law covers traditional programs written in conventional programming languages, as well as any other operating instructions such as "macros" that are "expressed in words, numbers, or other verbal or numerical symbols or indicia . . . ."[2] Thus, copying a program and giving it to a single friend constitutes copyright infringement. Distributing a program without permission to countless Internet users would be considered a very flagrant example of copyright infringement.

In most cases, no time should be spent speculating whether a particular program is copyrighted, because it almost certainly is. As discussed in **Chapter 1,** no formalities are required for authors to have copyrights in their works. Unless a person has the permission of the copyright owner, that person cannot legally distribute copies of a program over the Internet.

Even shareware is usually protected by copyright. Here, however, the copyright owner has explicitly agreed to and even encouraged unlimited distribution of a program under a very specific license. End users are licensed to use the program for a limited time, but they are required to pay for the program if they use it beyond that time. Generally, a user is free to distribute shareware from the user's Internet site. However, before doing so, the user should read and comply with any restrictions the author has placed on the distribution of the software.

Recently, some software companies have begun distributing free versions of software, either to gain market acceptance or to test "beta" versions of the software. Even these free copies are copyrighted. They are generally distributed under a license agreement that the user is required to accept before using the program. Redistribution may or may not be permitted under the terms of the license agreement. Again, it is important to read the license agreement carefully before allowing users to download a program from your Internet site.

---

[1] 17 U.S.C. §§ 101 (definition of "literary works") and 117. *See* Computer Assocs. Int'l Inc. v. Altai, Inc., 982 F.2d 693 (2d Cir. 1992) ("it is now well settled that the literal elements of computer programs, i.e., the source and object codes, are the subject of copyright protection").

[2] 17 U.S.C. § 101 (definition of "literary works").

§ 4.5 —Multimedia

Multimedia content contains text, graphics, sound, and perhaps other types of materials. Copyrights cover most if not all of such multimedia content. The copyright statute expressly encompasses "literary works," "musical works," "pictorial" and "graphic" works, "motion pictures and other audio visual works," and "sound recordings."[3] These works are covered even though they are stored in digital form. The term *literary works* encompasses primarily textual content such as books, articles, poems, and even everyday e-mail content. It also covers various textual materials posted on Web sites and discussion groups.

Musical works include words, tunes, and arrangements of songs. MIDI[4] files (which are essentially keystroke lists comparable to player piano rolls) are thus protected by copyright. *Sound recordings* include digitized audio files.

Pictorial and *graphic* works include practically any graphical content that a user may find or wish to distribute on the Internet. These works are most often distributed on the Internet as digital files in GIF,[5] JPEG,[6] or some other format. It is important also to remember that copyright law continues to protect photographs that originate as printed matter. A user cannot freely digitize and distribute magazine photographs, for example. Simply scanning a photograph constitutes copyright infringement, as does downloading the scanned photograph from an Internet source, unless the copyright owner has given permission.

Motion pictures and other audio visual works include typical video data and files, whether stored on compact disc, magnetic hard disc, or other media, and whether viewed using a conventional film projector or on a computer monitor.

§ 4.6 —Data

Pure data is not protected by copyright. Data is considered to be facts, which cannot be taken from the public domain. Thus, a user is generally free to copy such things as telephone numbers, addresses, names, dates, and the like.[7]

Wholesale copying of even facts, however, is often an invitation for trouble—especially when those facts have been gathered only at great expense. Before 1991, copyright protection for databases could often be based on a "sweat of the brow" theory, under which protection was available even for facts or raw data if significant work was involved in obtaining and documenting the facts. In 1991, however, the Supreme Court eliminated the sweat of the brow theory, emphasizing instead that copyright availability relies primarily on "originality." The

---

[3] 17 U.S.C. § 102(a).

[4] Musical instrument digital interface.

[5] Graphics interchange format.

[6] Joint Photographic Experts Group.

[7] Feist Publications Inc. v. Rural Tel. Serv. Co., 499 U.S. 340, 18 U.S.P.Q.2d (BNA) 1275 (1991).

Supreme Court found that there was not enough originality in telephone white pages listings to merit copyright protection.

Unfortunately, not all situations are as clear as the one before the Supreme Court, and it is often quite difficult to decide whether certain "data-like" information is protected by copyright. Consider, for example, the used car valuation guide often referred to as the "Red Book."[8] The Red Book sets forth editors' projections of used car values for different geographic regions. Are these "facts"? Can they be copied and sold? CCC Information Services, Inc., decided to explore this issue in some depth by loading major portions of the Red Book onto its computer network and republishing Red Book information in various forms to its customers. CCC's contention was that the information constituted "facts" which were unprotected by copyright.

An initial court agreed with CCC and found no infringement liability, holding, among other things that "the Red Book employed no originality or creativity in the selection, coordination or arrangement of data" and therefore did not constitute a protected "original work of authorship," and that "the Red Book valuations were facts, or interpretations of facts, and were, therefore, not protected by copyright."[9]

On appeal, however, the lower court was reversed. The appeals court emphasized that although originality is certainly required, a very small amount suffices. The court said:

> The district court was simply mistaken in its conclusion that the Red Book valuations were, like the telephone numbers in Feist, pre-existing facts that had merely been discovered by the Red Book editors. To the contrary, Maclean's evidence demonstrated without rebuttal that its valuations were neither reports of historical prices nor mechanical derivations of historical prices or other data. Rather, they represented predictions by the Red Book editors of future prices estimated to cover specified geographic regions. According to Maclean's evidence, these predictions were based not only on a multitude of data sources, but also on professional judgment and expertise. The testimony of one of Maclean's deposition witnesses indicated that fifteen considerations are weighed; among the considerations, for example, is a prediction as to how traditional competitor vehicles, as defined by Maclean, will fare against one another in the marketplace in the coming period. . . . The valuations themselves are original creations of Maclean.[10]

CCC was thus found guilty of copyright infringement.

This case illustrates the difficulty of determining whether particular information constitutes unprotected facts. More importantly, perhaps, it illustrates the fact that legal decisions often hinge on a court's sense of fairness, rather than

---

[8] The actual title is *Automobile Red Book—Official Used Car Valuations,* published by Maclean Hunter Market Reports, Inc.

[9] CCC Info. Servs. Inc. v. Maclean Hunter Mkt. Reports Inc., 33 U.S.P.Q.2d (BNA) 1183, 1186 (2d Cir. 1994).

[10] *Id.* at 1188.

upon a formulaic application of the law. Indeed, in this case, CCC had additional, more complex arguments that the appeals court found difficult to overcome. Nevertheless, the court seemed determined to rule against CCC, finally resorting to a "policy judgment."[11] It is apparent that the court simply did not want to let CCC reap the rewards of someone else's extensive labors.

The discussions in §§ **4.7** and **4.9** regarding compilations and shrink-wrap licenses provide additional examples of how a court might find liability even for copying what might appear to be bare facts.

§ 4.7 —Compilations

Even facts and raw data might have some degree of copyright protection if they are included in a compilation. A *compilation* is "a work formed by the collection and assembling of preexisting materials or of data that are selected, coordinated or arranged in such a way that the resulting work as a whole constitutes an original work of authorship."[12]

Compilations as a whole are protected by copyright. However, any underlying elements that are not protected by copyright do not become protected because they are included in a compilation. Accordingly, individual elements of raw data can still be copied. In the case of a telephone book, anyone can copy individual listings. In addition, anyone is free to copy the alphabetized arrangement; alphabetizing the listings does not involve enough originality to merit copyright protection.

However, it is not always clear how much editorial input and arrangement is required before the resulting work becomes protected by copyright. In the Red Book case discussed in § **4.6,** the appeals court based its judgment in part on the argument that the Red Book was protected as a compilation.

> Recognizing that "[o]riginality may also be found in the selection and ordering of particular facts or elements," the [lower] court concluded that none had been shown. . . . This was because the Red Book's selection and arrangement of data represents "a logical response to the needs of the vehicle valuation market." . . . In reaching this conclusion, the district court applied the wrong standard. The fact that an arrangement of data responds logically to the needs of the market for which the compilation was prepared does not negate originality. To the contrary, the use of logic to solve the problems of how best to present the information being compiled is independent creation. . . .
>
> We find that the selection and arrangement of data in the Red Book displayed amply sufficient originality to pass the low threshold requirement to earn copyright protection. This originality was expressed, for example, in Maclean's division of the national used car market into several regions, with independent predicted

---

[11] *Id.* at 1190.

[12] 17 U.S.C. § 101 (definition of "compilation").

valuations for each region depending on conditions there found. A car model does not command the same value throughout a large geographic sector of the United States; used car values are responsive to local conditions and vary from place to place. A 1989 Dodge Caravan will not command the same price in San Diego as in Seattle. In furnishing a single number to cover vast regions that undoubtedly contain innumerable variations, the Red Book expresses a loose judgment that values are likely to group together with greater consistency within a defined region than without. The number produced is necessarily both approximate and original. Several other aspects of the Red Book listings also embody sufficient originality to pass Feist's low threshold. These include: (1) the selection and manner of presentation of optional features for inclusion; (2) the adjustment for mileage by 5,000 mile increments (as opposed to using some other breakpoint and interval); (3) the use of the abstract concept of the "average" vehicle in each category as the subject of the valuation; and (4) the selection of the number of years' models to be included in the compilation.[13]

It is clear from these statements that very little in the way of editorial input is required to make something into a compilation that is protected by copyright.

Consider another example. Suppose that you want to create a business directory, containing telephone listings, on your Internet site. Wishing to conserve your energies and finances, you want to use listings from an existing printed yellow pages directory. As already noted earlier in this section, copyright law does not prevent you from copying individual listings. But how far can you go? Can you copy all the listings from a particular existing directory? Can you copy category headings?

In a similar case, an infringement defendant copied a significant number of yellow pages listings and included them in a new business directory.[14] The new directory did not, however, use the same categorization scheme as the preexisting directory. Rather, it used a much simpler scheme, with significantly fewer categories. The court found that the categorization schemes were not even "remotely" similar. Nevertheless, three categories in the new directory were duplications of the preexisting directory, and similar listings were found in similar categories in the two directories.

The court analyzed the case in terms of two issues: (1) whether the preexisting directory was protected by copyright; and (2) whether the new directory infringed any existing copyright in the preexisting directory.[15]

The court held that the preexisting yellow pages directory was protected as a compilation under copyright law. The "original" elements affording copyrightability were "first, the arrangement of over 260 categories under which businesses are catalogued and, second, the selection of the 9000 businesses so categorized."[16]

---

[13] CCC Info. Servs. Inc. v. Maclean Hunter Mkt. Reports Inc., 33 U.S.P.Q.2d (BNA) 1183, 1188–89 (2d Cir. 1994).

[14] Key Publications Inc. v. Chinatown Today Publishing Enters. Inc., 20 U.S.P.Q.2d (BNA) 1122 (2d Cir. 1991).

[15] *Id.* at 1125.

[16] *Id.* at 1127.

The court noted that the categories had not been copied wholesale from other, preexisting yellow pages directories.

However, the court held that there had been no infringement. Infringement would have required copying the original elements of the preexisting directory: the category arrangement and the listing selections. The court found that this had not taken place. First, the defendant used a different category arrangement. Second, the defendant had not copied the particular selection of listings; only about 17 percent of the listings of the preexisting directory were present in the new directory.[17]

Even though there was no infringement in this particular case, it is apparent from the court's opinion that wholesale copying of the business directory would have constituted infringement, because the directory as a whole was a protectable compilation. Copying just the categorizations might also have been an infringement. It might also have been an infringement to have simply published the particular listings from the directory, even apart from their categorizations (because the selection of listings for inclusion in the directory was an "original" activity).

On the Internet, a similar situation exists with URLs. A "related links" Web page, listing URLs of selected Web pages, is similar to a telephone directory. Although the URLs alone are not protected by copyright, a Web page listing such URLs may be copyrightable because of the originality used in selecting or categorizing them.

§ 4.8 —Public Domain

Although it is safest to assume that most content is protected by copyright, there are many works in the public domain that can be freely copied.

One way that a work can enter the public domain is through the expiration of its copyright. The duration of copyrights has changed through the years. Generally, the maximum copyright duration for things created prior to January 1, 1978, is 75 years (although many of these copyrights might have expired, or might expire, after 28 years).[18] For works created after January 1, 1978, copyright protection lasts for the life of the author plus 50 years. If a work created after January 1, 1978, was created as a work made for hire, the copyright lasts for 75 years after publication or 100 years after initial creation of the work, whichever comes first.[19]

---

[17] *Id.*

[18] Copyrights under prior copyright law were divided into two terms: an original term of 28 years and a renewal term of 47 years. The author of the work must take affirmative steps to renew the copyright during the final year of the initial 28-year term in order to protect the work for the renewal term. This two-term structure was eliminated when the entire copyright statute was replaced in 1976, with an effective date of January 1, 1978.

[19] 17 U.S.C. § 302.

Works created by the federal government are also in the public domain.[20] Thus, anyone can generally copy government-created materials from the Internet. However, this rule does not apply to everything *published* by the government. Specifically, it does not apply to materials created by and obtained from nongovernment sources. Those materials do not lose their copyright protection by virtue of being republished by the government. In addition, this rule does not apply to materials generated by state or local governments.

§ 4.9 —Licenses

Anyone who wants to copy something that has not entered the public domain must first obtain a license to do so. In many cases, a person can obtain an express license, under which the copyright owner explicitly gives a licensee permission to copy the copyright owner's materials. This can be done in a negotiated contract. In other cases, copyright owners might distribute statements with their materials that give permission to copy. Keep in mind, however, that such statements often include restrictions.

In many cases, the copyright owner might have intentionally or unintentionally created an implied license. An *implied license* is created as a result of specific conduct by the copyright owner, apart from any explicit permission, by which the owner seems to "invite" copying. This type of conduct is prevalent on the Internet. For example, why would a copyright owner create a Web page unless he or she intended for the page to be copied and displayed on a user's computer? In this case, the copyright owner can be presumed to have implied at least a limited license to take the steps that are necessary to view the page. Be aware, however, that such an implied license may not include a license to copy elements of the page to your own page.

So-called shrink-wrap licenses are also commonplace. A shrink-wrap license is an agreement that is printed on or inside a software package. In many cases, the purchaser cannot read the license until buying and opening the package. In other cases, the license is presented on the user's monitor during a program's installation process, perhaps after the user has downloaded the program from an Internet site. Although there are legal arguments against the validity of shrink-wrap licenses, they have been upheld in certain cases by the courts.

One example in particular, *ProCD Inc. v. Zeidenberg,*[21] illustrates the incredible value of shrink-wrap licenses. In this case, a manufacturer (ProCD) had assembled a CD-ROM containing telephone listings from over 3000 telephone directories. The data on the CD-ROM cost more than $10 million to compile, required continuing efforts to maintain, and was sold to the general public for $150 under the trademark "SelectPhoneTM."

---

[20] *Id.* § 105.

[21] 39 U.S.P.Q.2d (BNA) 1161 (7th Cir. 1996).

As noted in §§ **4.6** and **4.7,** copyright law does not protect bare telephone listings. It is possible that ProCD itself could have copied the listings without permission from the owners of the telephone directories, relying on the fact that such listings (as "facts") are not protected by copyright.

Matthew Zeidenberg bought a single copy of SelectPhoneTM and formed a company to resell the phone listings on the Internet. ProCD successfully sued Zeidenberg, even though the data was not protected by copyright, because of a shrink-wrap license included in the ProCD package. The license in this case limited the user of the CD-ROM to noncommercial purposes. A United States Court of Appeals held that this shrink-wrap license created an enforceable contract between the manufacturer and the purchaser. Zeidenberg lost the case and was presumably forced to pay damages to ProCD. Without the shrink-wrap license, it is unlikely that ProCD would have been able to stop Zeidenberg.

§ 4.10 —Works Made by Employees and Others

Generally, an author owns the copyrights in things created by the author. Not surprisingly, an employer is considered to be the author of materials created by its employees, and thus owns the copyright in materials created by its employees.[22] However, this applies only to materials created within the employee's scope of employment.

What about the case of an independent contractor—a consultant hired to create a Web page for you or your company? Who owns the copyright in the original materials (such as text, graphics, and the like) that the consultant creates for your Web page? Many people expect that they would own any copyrights that result from a paid consultant's work, but this is simply not the case. If a consultant creates original material for a Web page, the consultant owns the copyrights in the material.

This result is not always disastrous; in most cases, you will at least have an implied license to use the paid consultant's work in your Web page. However, there are potential problems when someone else owns the copyright in "your" materials. As an example, suppose you want to use original artwork, originally provided by a consultant as an integral part of a particular Web page, in a new and improved Web page designed by another consultant? Would that use be part of the implied license? As another example, what if the artwork you commissioned subsequently shows up on other Web pages designed by the same consultant? Since the consultant owns the copyright, would you have any right to stop him or her from using the artwork in this way?

These issues can be avoided simply by having a written agreement with your consultant, before work begins, in which the consultant assigns all potential copyrights to you. In some cases, the written agreement can state that both

---

[22] 17 U.S.C. § 201. *See also id.* § 101 (definition of *work made for hire*).

parties consider all materials to be "works made for hire." In these cases, the agreement is referred to as a "work-for-hire" agreement. It must be signed by both parties. The result of a work-for-hire agreement is that the party for whom the work is performed will be considered the author of the work, and will own any copyrights.

Note that the commissioned product must fall into one of the following categories before it can be validly considered a work made for hire:

1. A contribution to a collective work (such as a book or magazine that includes independent articles by different authors)
2. A part of a motion picture or other audiovisual work
3. A translation
4. A supplementary work (such as forewords, illustrations, appendixes, and other similar materials)
5. A compilation
6. An instructional text
7. A test
8. Answer material for a test
9. An atlas.[23]

It is possible to cover all bases by using a work-for-hire agreement that also contains an assignment. The agreement can be phrased so that the work-for-hire part of the agreement applies as long as the work falls within one of the above categories, and the assignment steps in if it is eventually determined that the work does not fall into one of the categories. Remember that both parties need to sign the agreement.

Be aware that you cannot turn a consultant or independent contractor into an employee by simply calling him or her an "employee." The courts have developed fairly restrictive and fact-based rules for settling this issue. If you have any doubt at all, get a written agreement.

§ 4.11   —Fair Use

The copyright statute specifically allows "fair use" of copyrighted materials without permission from the copyright owner. *Fair use* is defined as being for "purposes such as criticism, comment, news reporting, teaching (including multiple copies for classroom use), scholarship, or research."[24] The statute lists four factors that must be considered in determining whether a particular case involves fair use:

---

[23] *Id.* § 101 (definition of *work made for hire*).

[24] 17 U.S.C. § 107.

1. The purpose and character of the use, including whether such use is of a commercial nature or is for nonprofit educational purposes;
2. The nature of the copyrighted work;
3. The amount and substantiality of the portion used in relation to the copyrighted work as a whole; and
4. The effect of the use upon the potential market for or value of the copyrighted work.[25]

For practical purposes, the first and last of these factors are often the most important. A copyright holder is much more likely to sue if the user is profiting from the use of the copyrighted works or if the use deprives the owner of profit.

The second factor, the nature of the copyrighted work, refers to whether the copyrighted work tends toward factual subjects or more fictional and "creative" subjects. A copying is more likely to be considered fair use if the copied material is largely factual. The third factor indicates that copying an entire book is less likely to be considered fair use than copying a paragraph or two.

§ 4.12 —Liability for Distribution of Uploaded Works

It is common for Internet service providers to allow customers to store materials and to make those materials available to the world through the Internet. If the materials have been wrongly copied, the service providers can in some cases be considered guilty of copyright infringement.

A recent case illustrates the difficulty of applying copyright law to Internet cases.[26] In this case, an individual used the services of a small service provider to post allegedly infringing materials on the Internet. The small service provider in turn accessed the Internet through a much larger Internet service provider called Netcom On-Line Communications, Inc. At issue was whether Netcom could be held liable for infringing Usenet postings or, as stated by the court, "whether possessors of computers are liable for incidental copies automatically made on their computers using their software as part of a process initiated by a third party."[27]

The court ruled that Netcom was not liable for infringement until the time at which it became aware of the infringing postings. The court reasoned that to hold Netcom liable for infringement absent some element of volition or causation would go too far, and would subject perhaps thousands of newsgroup servers to liability. Such a result, the court reasoned, was not necessary and not desirable.

---

[25] *Id.*

[26] Religious Technology Ctr. v. Netcom On-Line Communication Servs. Inc., 37 U.S.P.Q.2d (BNA) 1545 (N.D. Cal. 1995).

[27] *Id.* at 1551.

This case seems to indicate a fairly clear rule for service providers. They are not liable for copyright infringement where their system operated automatically to make infringing copies posted by customers and where they were not aware that posted materials were infringing. On the other hand, the case indicates that there may be a duty for a service provider to remove infringing materials once a charge of infringement has been made known to the service provider.

It remains to be seen whether other courts will follow this reasoning. Critics have argued that the result sends the wrong message to service providers. Specifically, the case encourages service providers to remain ignorant of their customers' activities, because they can be liable only if they become aware of infringing activities. These critics argue that service providers should take a more active role in policing copyright infringement.

§ 4.13   —Registration and Notice

The mechanics of copyright registration are discussed in **Chapter 1.** For purposes of this chapter, there are three important issues. First, the lack of a copyright notice on certain materials does not mean that others are free to copy those materials. The materials can be copyrighted even in the absence of a copyright notice. Second, the lack of copyright registration does not mean that others are free to copy the materials. Copyright protection does not depend on registration. Third, both copyright notice and registration are important to protect the copyright holder's own rights. Including a copyright notice with materials is an effective warning to others against copying the materials. Furthermore, whether or not a copyright is registered will often make the practical difference in whether a copyright plaintiff can succeed financially in a lawsuit. If the copyright in the materials has been previously registered, the copyright holder will have the option of seeking attorneys' fees and "statutory damages" from an infringer. Statutory damages can be set somewhat arbitrarily by a judge without requiring the copyright owner to prove actual loss. In many cases, proving actual loss is difficult and costly, so avoiding this requirement is an important practical benefit.

§ 4.14   Patents

Sections 4.15 through **4.17** discuss how patent law is applicable to server-related technologies. Server-related technologies can sometimes be difficult to identify with sufficient precision to comply with patent laws, so § **4.15** discusses how to identify inventions. Then, § **4.16** discusses the issues related to filing for patent protection for such technologies. Finally, § **4.17** discusses infringement issues particular to servers.

§ 4.15   —Identifying Inventions

Patents are fundamentally different from copyrights in many ways, as described in **Chapter 1.** One very practical difference is that it is harder to know when you have created something that is patentable than it is to know when you have created something that is copyrightable. A drawing, for example, is copyrightable by the person who created it. It is not evaluated against other drawings to determine whether you have created something unique. A particular circuit, however, is patentable only if it is new and nonobvious when compared to previously existing circuits. Because an inventor usually cannot know about all prior circuits, it is difficult to know whether something is patentable. This is particularly true in the software industry, in which innovations are occurring at an incredible rate.

Another practical difference is that it is harder (and more costly) to obtain a valid patent than to obtain a valid copyright—especially in areas relating to computers, software, and the Internet. Obtaining a copyright registration is a simple matter of filling out a one- or two-page application and sending it to the Copyright Office with a small fee and samples of the work that is to be copyrighted. There is only a cursory inspection of the application, and a copyright is usually issued as a matter of course. A patent application, on the other hand, is a long document that must be drafted with great care. High fees must be paid to a patent attorney for drafting the application, and to the Patent and Trademark Office for processing the application. Furthermore, the Patent and Trademark Office examines patent applications rigorously, and rarely issues a patent without a fight (and corresponding additional attorneys' fees).

Once the decision is made to dedicate some amount of resources to obtaining patents, it is important to have some idea of the kinds of things that might be patentable.

It is a fairly safe assumption that anything that actually does something is potentially patentable if it is new and nonobvious. Forget the arguments about whether programs, software, databases, floppy disks, and so forth are "patentable subject matter." The fact is that most inventions can be patented in some form if they are new and nonobvious, and if they have not been publicly disclosed for more than a year before filing a patent application. Most of the disputes about patentable subject matter regard the format of patent claims. Although these disputes might have consequences regarding the coverage of a particular patent, they should not be of particular concern to someone trying to identify patentable inventions. There are acceptable ways of claiming almost anything that accomplishes some useful result, *including software.* In fact, there are a great number of ways to claim software.

Computer technology in general, and Internet technology specifically, is so new that it is often overlooked when thinking about patents. Furthermore, some software inventors have a distinct dislike of patents; others are under the mistaken impression that software and other computer-related technology are not patent-able. Because of this, it is useful for inventors to have some examples of specific things that can be patented. It is also useful for inventors to have some familiar-ity with claims and their objectives. This section is intended to meet this need.

Direct versus Indirect Infringement

Before proceeding, it is useful to understand the difference between "direct" and "indirect" patent infringement. Having a patent means that the holder of a patent can exclude others from making, using, and selling the invention as it is defined by the patent claims.[28] "Direct" infringement results when an unauthorized party makes, uses, or sells something that is described by at least one of a patent's claims. If a particular claim recites four elements, and the party implements only three of those elements, there is no direct infringement. This is true even if one of the three elements is considered to be the "key" to the invention.

The problem is that in many cases the identity of a direct infringer can make enforcement impractical. For example, suppose you patent a software-implemented process for quickly decompressing bitmap images, using a previously unknown "rotating" step. Suppose your patent has method claims such as this:

1.   A method of decompressing a bitmap image comprising the following steps:

(a) reading data elements from a compressed data file representing a bitmap image;

(b) rotating the data elements as they are read from the compressed data file;

(c) expanding the data elements after rotating them to produce an uncompressed bitmap image.

These steps are performed only on end users' computers, making the end users the only direct infringers. However, you would not want to deal with every individual user as a potential infringer. Rather, you would like to deal with whoever sells programs incorporating your patented method—or disks contain-ing those programs. But the disks themselves do not infringe, because by them-selves they do not perform your patented steps. They merely contain instructions that cause an end user's computer to perform your patented steps.

There are two solutions to the problem. The first and most desirable solution is to put claims in your patent that directly cover the activities of those who would be the most likely target of a lawsuit or injunction. The examples given later in this section show how this can be done.

The second solution is to rely on "indirect" infringement. The law defines two types of indirect infringement: contributory infringement and inducement of infringement. *Contributory infringement* is defined as follows:

---

[28] 35 U.S.C. § 271(a).

Whoever sells a component of a patented machine, manufacture, combination or composition, or a material or apparatus for use in practicing a patented process, constituting a material part of the invention, knowing the same to be especially made or especially adapted for use in an infringement of such patent, and not a staple article or commodity of commerce suitable for substantial noninfringing use, shall be liable as a contributory infringer.[29]

Inducement of infringement is defined rather briefly as: "Whoever actively induces infringement of a patent shall be liable as an infringer."[30]

In the example, we would hope that manufacturers and distributors would be liable as indirect infringers for selling disks containing instructions that cause computers to infringe the patent claim. Unfortunately, making a case of indirect infringement can be complicated because the statutory definitions leave a lot to judicial interpretation. Suffice it to say that a lawsuit for indirect infringement requires the patent owner to address issues that would not otherwise be relevant (knowledge of infringement or intent, for example), thus increasing the cost and uncertainty of the lawsuit.

Because of the difficulties in pressing charges of indirect infringement, attorneys tend to be concerned about whether their patent claims can be used in cases of direct infringement. Following are several examples of server-related technological areas and of patent strategies for protecting such areas. The examples are of course not exhaustive, since there are almost endless categories of technologies used in connection with the Internet. Rather, the examples are designed to broaden your thinking about patents—to point out that almost any innovation should be considered for patent protection. The examples also discuss different claim formats and strategies used by patent attorneys.

Server Hardware

Strangely, hardware is often the most transparent element of the Internet. To most users, the Internet is represented at their own locations only by telephone or network jacks. "Soft" components, such as programs, data, protocols, and so forth completely dominate the users' experience. However, upstream of individual users, the Internet is supported by a great variety of hardware: telecommunications lines and routing equipment, server computers, modems, routers, power supplies, cables, disk storage media, microprocessors, electronic memory, and a host of other systems and components. These are all things that are traditionally covered by patents. Although they are not as visible and perhaps not as glamorous as other Internet components, their candidacy for patent protection certainly should not be overlooked.

---

[29] *Id.* § 271(c).

[30] *Id.* § 271(b).

Hardware can be claimed in conventional ways, one of which is illustrated by the following claim:

2. A system for communicating from a first location to a second location, comprising:

a digital data transmitter at a first location;

a digital data receiver at a second location;

a communications cable connected to communicate data from the digital data transmitter to the digital data receiver;

wherein the communications cable is coiled along at least part of its length.

A hardware system such as this can also be claimed as a method:

3. A method of communicating from a first location to a second location, comprising:

connecting a communications cable from a digital data transmitter at a the first location to a digital data receiver at a second location;

coiling the communications cable along at least part of its length;

transmitting digital data from the digital data transmitter to the digital data receiver through the communications cable.

Both of these claims illustrate the challenge of drafting claims so that they cover the activities of the appropriate parties. Assuming that the coiled cable is the feature that makes the above invention new, the claims ought to be drafted so that they would directly cover cable manufacturers that make and sell coiled cables. However, a cable manufacturer could manufacture a coiled cable without directly infringing either of the above claims. The manufacturer would not infringe claim 1 because it would not manufacture a system including a transmitter and a receiver at respective locations. The manufacturer would not infringe claim 2 because the manufacturer itself would not perform the step of connecting a communications cable from a data transmitter to a data receiver. What is really needed is a claim as follows:

4. A communications cable that is coiled along at least part of its length.

In many cases, it will be possible to obtain a claim such as this that specifically targets the novel feature of the invention. In some cases, however, a claim like this might not define anything patentable. Suppose, hypothetically, that coiled cables have been used for decades to transmit analog communications signals. Thus, the novelty of the invention might lie only in the use of the coiled cable for digital data. In this case, the claims will have to include something that refers to digital data.

Software

Software is patentable if it does something new and nonobvious, just like anything else. In its purest form, a software invention might involve only a particular sequence of instructions, removed from any physical components. An example might be a sequence of steps to calculate an optimum value based on a set of input values. In a case like this, a patent applicant might run into objections from the Patent and Trademark Office on the ground that the invention is a mathematical algorithm. Bare mathematical algorithms are not patentable. In the vast majority of software inventions, however, software interacts with actual physical components and stimuli such as memory, display devices, communications devices, user inputs, and the like. Furthermore, the software must be executed by something physical such as a computer, and stored on something physical such as a floppy disk. When these elements are considered and included in patent claims, software inventions easily become more than mathematical algorithms and as such are patentable. In many cases, the problem of mathematical algorithms in the patent realm is simply a claim drafting problem.

In the Internet environment, software controls everything. Software runs server computers, network routers, and even telecommunications switches. In many cases, it is desirable to frame mechanical or electrical processes in terms of both software and hardware. For example, consider a hypothetical invention involving a router. Suppose that the router is novel in that it uses an EEPROM (electrically erasable and programmable read-only memory) for storing routing tables. There are several ways to draft claims for the router. For example:

5.   A router comprising:

first and second data ports for connection to first and second networks;

an EEPROM containing routing tables;

a controller that is responsive to the routing tables to selectively route data packets between the first and second networks.

Claim 5 directly covers the manufacturer of the router, but gives little opportunity to elaborate on the software steps.

6.   A method of routing data packets between first and second networks, comprising:

storing routing information in an EEPROM;

receiving data packets from the first and second networks;

reading the EEPROM to determine routing information for the received data packets;

routing the received data packets in response to the routing information read from the EEPROM.

Claim 6 is arguably a "software" claim because it recites the steps performed by software. Although this claim format makes it more convenient to recite detailed software steps, there is no direct infringement until the router is turned on and used by an end user. Thus, a router manufacturer infringes claim 6 only indirectly.

Hybrid claims are also possible:

7. A router comprising:

first and second data ports for connection to first and second networks;

an EEPROM containing routing tables;

a data processor programmed to perform the following steps:

storing routing information in the EEPROM;

receiving data packets from the first and second networks;

reading the EEPROM to determine routing information for the received data packets;

routing the received data packets in response to the routing information read from the EEPROM.

Claim 7 is useful because it allows recitation of detailed software steps, while remaining an apparatus claim that could be directly infringed by a router manufacturer.

Now suppose that the router has or might someday have upgradeable software. For example, suppose the router can be updated by replacing a ROM (read-only memory). In this case, a claim needs to focus on the ROM:

8. A computer-readable storage medium having instructions for routing data packets between first and second networks, the instructions being executable to perform steps comprising:

storing routing information in an EEPROM;

receiving data packets from the first and second networks;

reading the EEPROM to determine routing information for the received data packets;

routing the received data packets in response to the routing information read from the EEPROM.

With this kind of claim, which has only recently been permitted by the Patent and Trademark Office, direct infringement results from the manufacture or distribution of a CD-ROM or floppy disk having instructions for performing the recited steps. This is a very valuable claim format for software publishers.

To take this example just a little further, suppose that the software might be upgradeable by modem or over an Internet connection. Now, there is no physical item (like a CD-ROM or floppy disk) used to transfer the software. However, the provider of the software will have probably stored a copy of the program on some "computer-readable medium," making the provider a direct infringer in at least one instance. In addition, it has been suggested that the physical transmission lines themselves, such as telephone lines, might form the "computer-readable storage medium" of claim 8. Whether this argument would succeed is debatable. Even if it would, who would the patent holder sue for infringement? The phone company? It would probably make more sense to sue a more culpable party—the party providing the software—and rely, if required, on theories of indirect infringement.

An interesting aspect of many Internet-related inventions is that they involve software executing at a server and other software executing at a client or user's computer. In these cases, it is often good to separate inventions into functions that are performed by the server and functions that are performed by the client, and to claim each set of functions separately. In that way, both the server and the client infringe directly. A system claim, reciting elements performed by both the server and the client, may leave the patent holder with no single direct infringer.

It is, however, becoming more and more difficult to separate server and client functions. In practice, the divisions of responsibility between server and client can be made quite arbitrarily. With new browser technologies, viewing an Internet page might include downloading an *applet* or *control,* which is essentially a small program that executes on the client machine without the user even being aware of it. The applet can be made to perform many of the functions that would otherwise be performed by a server. To illustrate, consider an Internet page that allows a user to search a database. The user specifies some sort of search criteria and a formal query is generated. The results are formatted and displayed for the user.

There are at least two different ways this could be implemented. First, the client software could act simply to display preformatted information to the user and to relay user keystrokes back to the server. In this case, the server would formulate the formal query and format the search results. Another way would be for the server to download an intelligent applet to the client. The client would execute the applet, which would request a search criteria from the user and in response formulate the formal query, send it to the server, accept raw results from the server, format the raw results, and display the formatted results to the user. In more complicated applications, there could be dozens of possible divisions of responsibility.

Because of this, it can be prudent to construct patent claims that avoid specifying any particular division of responsibilities. A traditional way to handle this problem is to claim the invention as a method, without tying specific steps to the server or to the client. Another approach is to claim the invention as a computer-readable medium having instructions for performing the necessary steps—again, without tying any particular step to either the server or the client. It is also possible to claim a system having a server and a client that are programmed, in combination, to perform the inventive steps.

Protocols and File Formats

The Internet is largely defined by its protocols. Without protocols, communication of any type would be impossible. Accordingly, there is some debate on whether it makes sense to patent communications protocols. Whether or not it is appropriate, it is definitely possible. Hayes Microcomputer Products, Inc., for instance, successfully patented and profited from its well-known Hayes-compatible modem handshaking protocol. Here is an actual claim from the Hayes patent:

> [9]. In a modem including a data input port for connecting said modem to a utilization device, and a telephone port for connecting said modem to a telephone line, said modem being of the type having two distinct modes of operation:
>
> (a) a transparent mode of operation for which said modem provides modulated signals to said telephone port in response to data signals provided to said data input port; and
>
> (b) a command mode of operation for which said modem responds to said data signals provided to said data input port as instructions to said modem;
>
> said modem including means defining a predetermined sequence of said data signals as an escape character; the improvement comprising:
>
> timing means for detecting each occurrence of a passage of a predetermined period of time after provision of one of said data signals to said data input port; and
>
> means, operative when said modem is in said transparent mode of operation, for detecting provision of said predetermined sequence of said data signals, and for causing said modem to switch to said command mode of operation, if and only if said predetermined sequence of data signals occurs contiguous in time with at least one said occurrence of said passage of said predetermined period of time during which none of said data signals are provided to said data input port.[31]

This claim illustrates another method of claiming software, using "means" clauses. Using this method, each programmed function is recited as "means for [performing a function]." Although means-type claims are currently somewhat out of favor, they have worked for Hayes Microcomputer Products, Inc.

Data structures are now also recognized as the proper subject of patent protection, again assuming that the structures are new and nonobvious. This is another area where Internet-related businesses might expect to develop patentable inventions. Many compression techniques, for instance, result in data structures or file formats that can be explicitly claimed in patent applications. Particular arrangements of data that facilitate efficient retrieval might similarly be patented in terms of a file or data format.

Here is an example of an allowable claim format for a data structure:

> [10]. A memory for storing data for access by an application program being executed on a data processing system, comprising:

---

[31] U.S. Patent No. 4,549,302.

a data structure stored in said memory, said data structure including information resident in a database used by said application program and including:

a plurality of attribute data objects stored in said memory, each of said attribute data objects containing different information from said database;

a single holder attribute data object for each of said attribute data objects, each of said holder attribute data objects being one of said plurality of attribute data . . . .[32]

The claim goes on to list additional objects contained in the data structure.

Data compression techniques are similarly patentable. Unisys, for example, holds a patent that it believes covers the widely used GIF (graphics interchange format) and TIFF (tag image file format) standards.[33]

§ 4.16 —Filing Patent Applications

After identifying patentable ideas (an ongoing process), it will be necessary to decide which inventions merit the expenses of the patent process. An initial screening mechanism should be to evaluate the relative commercial value of obtaining patents on the various ideas that have been identified. Obtaining a patent is expensive, and it is important to make sure that the benefits to be derived from the patent justify the expenses of obtaining it. For instance, it is necessary to evaluate the potential revenue from the patented feature, whether it might be possible to license the invention to other companies, whether it would be possible to detect infringement if it happened, the cost for a competitor to design around a patent, and so forth.[34]

In many cases, at least a cursory patentability search should be considered. Patentability searches may help avoid the filing of patent applications for inventions that have only a small chance of being allowed by the Patent and Trademark Office, and thereby focus resources on patent applications having the highest possibilities of success.

§ 4.17 —Avoiding Infringement

Another difference between patents and copyrights is that it is usually harder to know when you are infringing a patent than to know when you are infringing a copyright. When you copy something, you can usually assume that you are infringing a copyright (subject to fairly well-defined exceptions). If you create something yourself, without copying from something else, you can be assured that you are not infringing a copyright. This is not the case with patents. It is entirely possible to spend years developing a product, with features that you

---

[32] *In re* Lowry, 32 U.S.P.Q.2d (BNA) 1031 (Fed. Cir. 1994).

[33] U.S. Patent No. 4,558,302.

[34] *See* Lewis C. Lee & J. Scott Davidson, Managing Intellectual Property Rights ch. 8 (John Wiley & Sons 1993).

believe are completely original, and to find that you are infringing someone else's patent. You might even have obtained your own patents, and still find that you are infringing someone else's patent.

In many cases, it is impossible to rule out infringement even if you try. In some instances, businesses rely on receiving notice from patent holders when the patent holders believe there has been infringement. Once notice is given, the allegedly infringing company decides how to respond, usually based on the advice of an attorney in light of his or her thorough analysis of the patent.

Note that this is not a completely safe practice. Burying your head in the sand and waiting for an infringement notice will not protect you from liability. You can be found liable for patent infringement even if your infringement was completely innocent. However, it is better to be an innocent infringer than a *willful* infringer, because a finding of willful infringement allows a court to triple the liability of the infringer.

The alternative to a reactive strategy is a proactive strategy in which a company conducts an infringement search in the Patent and Trademark Office and an independent analysis of the search results. This is not, however, the common practice, for a variety of reasons. The most obvious reason is the simple enormity of the task. There can be a great number of potentially patented features in a single product, requiring the examination of perhaps thousands of patents.

Even more significant, however, is the amount of effort required to properly analyze patents found in a search. Suppose, for example, that it is possible to narrow the scope of an infringement search by selecting two or three features that you think are the most likely to be patented by someone else. You could engage a professional searcher, who would return anywhere from 20 to perhaps over 100 patents as being relevant to your product.

Now, you would be faced with evaluating each *claim* of each of those patents. Reading a patent is not particularly entertaining. The claims, especially, are usually written in what appears to be a different language. Most patents have more than one claim; it is not uncommon for a single patent to have 20 or more claims. Even a preliminary analysis of a single patent might take several hours.

Nevertheless, suppose that you are able to eliminate half the patents from consideration by spending only a few hours with each one. Now you have to get serious. The courts have said that patent claims can be properly interpreted only in light of (a) the description that precedes the claims and (b) all the correspondence between the patent applicant and the Patent and Trademark Office during the pendency of the patent. It can take days to evaluate the claims of even a single patent.

Furthermore, once you find a patent, you have exposed yourself to the risk of becoming liable for willful infringement and the associated risk of liability for triple damages. You can often avoid willful infringement by relying on an attorney's opinion that you do not infringe. However, it is not enough for your attorney to casually evaluate the patents found in your search. Rather, he or she must prepare a formal noninfringement opinion. The courts have stated that such an opinion must be comprehensive and well-reasoned. This process can be very expensive.

For the reasons given above, many companies opt not to perform routine infringement searches. However, there are some situations where infringement studies are certainly warranted. The first and most obvious situation arises when you have been given notice of a patent and of the allegation that your product infringes the patent. In this situation, you have little choice other than to analyze the patent and develop some sort of strategy for responding to the patent holder, whether by denying infringement or trying to work out a licensing arrangement.

In other situations, you may actually be aware of one or two patents relating to a product of yours that is still under development. For example, you might become aware of a patent because a competitor's product or advertising has been marked with the patent's number. It makes sense to study these patents as you develop your product in order to avoid infringement. Designing around a patent is generally viewed favorably by the courts. However, you should ensure that you have a very thorough understanding of a patent and its claim scope before attempting this.

In still other cases, you may have heard vague rumors that a certain competitor has patented a particular technology. In these cases, it is probably best to perform a limited search for patents that have issued to that competitor.

CHAPTER 5

PROTECTING THE INTERNET USER INTERFACE

Curtis G. Rose

§ 5.1   Disclaimer

What follows is a nice little story I hope will brighten your day and bring you great joy and happiness. It is not legal advice to you or anyone else. I don't even know who you are, and cannot possibly know what your specific legal issues are unless my crystal ball was working, which it isn't. I do know that intellectual property law is a bizarrely complex subject you should not try to comprehend alone, so go forth and seek the advice of a competent intellectual property attorney before you do anything you will later regret.

I should also mention that all of the opinions expressed in this chapter are mine alone and do not in any way, shape, or manner reflect the opinions of my employer, the Hewlett-Packard Company.

§ 5.2   Introduction

The year is 1968. Where were you? Are you an "Xer" who wasn't even born yet? Were you in Vietnam? Or were you avoiding Vietnam by getting an advanced degree in a namby pamby, prestigious East Coast institution of higher learning? Maybe you were even already learning how to be a business executive, or maybe even, God forbid, a lawyer. Did you have a main squeeze? Do you remember his or her name? Did you even know you were a boomer? Or were you, like me, a 'tweener, bemused and confused as you watched the boomers get beat up by the cops in Chicago? Did you have a cause? Did you groove to the Airplane? Did you inhale?

Do you even remember 1968?

OK, probably not. But that's cool, we can make up for lost time now.

For our purposes, the most significant event in 1968 was not the Vietnam War, or the election of Richard Nixon, or the Democratic convention in Chicago. It was the day a piece of paper arrived at the desk of Frank Heart, a manager of Bolt Beranek and Newman, a high-tech consulting firm in Cambridge, Massachusetts.[1] The paper was a simple request from the Department of Defense: design a network that would allow computers from across the country, regardless of manufacturer, to talk to each other.

What a stupid idea. But if the government is stupid enough to pay for it, we will build it. So thought Bolt Beranek and Newman.

From the ashes of stupidity a creature of genius emerged. The Internet was born.

§ 5.3   Development of the Internet User Interface

Born, but completely useless. Like a small child, the Internet took 25 years of incremental growth and development under the watchful eyes of its "parents" to become what it is today—a young adult who has lots of potential but needs to mature. Here's a brief look at the Internet baby book.

§ 5.4   —ARPANET

The Department of Defense's Advanced Research Project Administration, better known by the government acronym ARPA, commissioned the project that would become known as ARPANET.[2] ARPANET initially linked up four universities with vastly different computer systems: UCLA, the University of California–Santa Barbara, the Stanford Research Institute, and the University of Utah. By November 21, 1969, UCLA and Stanford were up and running. A handful of people witnessed a very historic event: two computers hundreds of miles away actually talked to each other.

Nobody paid enough attention to remember what the computers said. But everyone remembers one thing: the connection worked.[3]

Over the next 10 years, the number of computers on the Internet grew from 2, to 20, to 200.

But how did these computers talk to each other back then? Crudely. The 70s was the era of the punch cards, and, if you were really lucky, a teletype machine that allowed you to type in not more than 80 characters before you had to hit

---

[1] *The History of the Future,* Computerworld, Oct. 3, 1994, at 101.

[2] *The Birth of the Internet,* Newsweek, Aug. 8, 1994, at 56–58 [hereinafter *The Birth of the Internet*].

[3] *Id.* at 57.

the enter key to send your trained-to-be-truncated thoughts elsewhere. Color?
Mice? Graphical User Interfaces? Naaa ... our computer pioneers learned to
communicate the *hard* way, performing the equivalent of walking five miles to
and from school uphill through the snow through the bad part of town—both
ways, every day.[4] It wasn't pleasant, but somehow they got the job done.

§ 5.5 —Gopher

It wasn't until 1991 that an improved user interface stormed onto the scene.
Developed at the University of Minnesota, Gopher blasted through the line
mode, 80-character barrier to present the Internet user with the radical concept
of a menu—a screen chock full of characters capable of free navigation via the
up, down, left, and right cursor control keys. Computers running Gopher could
be linked together, and for the first time a user could actually browse through
a data space without really knowing—or caring—which computer he was
talking to.[5]

§ 5.6 —World Wide Web

Shortly after Gopher blasted onto the Internet scene, the World Wide Web was
born. Originally just a line mode browser, the World Wide Web added the radical
concept of *hyperlinks*—the ability to go to another computer for information by
merely selecting a highlighted word or phrase. Even today, the concept of hyperlinks and hypertext is probably the most fundamental part of the Internet, as it
allows a user to travel the world's information space without posteriorily exit-
ing the seating means.

But even by 1992, the Internet was the domain of the nerds—the savvy
computer users who knew how to find their way around cyberspace without a
map.

§ 5.7 —Graphical Browsers

In 1993, a college student named Marc Andreessen gave the world a map. While
killing time as a college student at the University of Illinois, Andreessen wrote
a software program that would soon be known as Mosaic. Mosaic brought the
Internet to the masses by providing a graphical user interface to the Internet.
Revolutionary computing navigational aids such as "color," "pictures," and "mice,"
known to Apple-wonks for nearly a decade, found its way onto the Internet via
Marc Andreessen. Given away for free, thousands of ahead-of-the-curve users
downloaded Andreessen's bits of genius and tuned in to the Internet.

---

[4] My dad says he did this, even though he lived in Hollywood, Cal. Hmmm . . . .

[5] Understanding the Internet, PBS Documentary (1995).

Much as we try to deny it, college is never forever—not even for a genius like Marc Andreessen. When he graduated from the University of Illinois, he knew he had to find a real job. So he did what any good old boy from the Midwest would do—he started his own company. On April 4, 1994, Andreessen and Jim Clark founded Netscape Communications.[6] Andreessen and Clark got right to work, and Mosaic metamorphosed from its humble collegiate roots to the first world-class Internet browser—Netscape Navigator.

Navigator 1.0 was darned impressive. Now anyone with a PC and a stout modem, including those not even twinkled-in-the-eye-of in 1968, could use Navigator to surf the net with the greatest of ease. The world was within the reach of anyone who could move a mouse and depress the index finger of the right hand a few millimeters. Best of all, Navigator was available for free to anyone with the wherewithal to know an FTP from a hole in the ground.

Netscape Navigator was the undisputed king of the hill until a skinny guy with glasses in Redmond, Washington, woke up on October 6, 1994. By the time Bill Gates of Microsoft informed his troops about the "sea change" the Internet was creating, the Internet had already grown from 2 computers in 1968 to 21,700, and stodgy sticks-in-the-mud like IBM, GE, and even Tupperware had home pages.[7] Microsoft clearly had a lot of catching up to do, but it mobilized its vast resources to begin working on an Internet browser to compete with Netscape.

The market was perhaps a bit more clued in to the future than Bill Gates. On August 8, 1995, Netscape sold its stock in an initial public offering, and saw it skyrocket from an initial offering price of 28, all the way up to 75 before settling at 58—in a single day.[8] Way cool for Netscape and its new shareholders, but heaped upon angst for a paranoid-prone Pacific Northwest powerhouse. The pace in Redmond quickened even before Netscape's star-studded IPO day, and workdays turned into worknights, complete with sleeping bags and espresso.[9] By August 24, 1995, Bill's boys and girls had delivered Microsoft Internet Explorer, a bona fide competitor to Netscape Navigator. The race was now on, as Netscape and Microsoft outdueled each other with rapidly released revisions that gave (yes, gave) an eager, hungry public more and more cool ways to navigate—or explore, depending on your loyalties—around the exploding net.

§ 5.8   Definition of the Internet User Interface

Are you, dear reader, jazzed to read on? Isn't this a great story? Over 1,300 words so far in this chapter,[10] and not even a hoot of a mention of anything smacking of intellectual property, the reason you bought (well, at least are reading)

---

[6] *Inside Microsoft,* Bus. Wk., July 15, 1996, at 56–70 [hereinafter *Inside Microsoft*].

[7] *Id.* at 62.

[8] *Id.* at 63.

[9] *Id.* at 56.

[10] So sayeth Microsoft Word 7.0, a truly awesome word processor. Luddites can start counting and walk over to my house to tell me how many there *really* are.

this book. Fearlessly secure thy pants, for we are rapidly converging on such a discussion. But first, we need to define a term: the *Internet User Interface,* and all synch up as to what this means. Let's be expeditious and not fritter away the preceding 1,300 words: the "Internet User Interface" includes the graphical browsers we just talked about: Netscape Navigator and Microsoft Internet Explorer.[11]

But it is more and, in some ways, less than this. Let's sweep in home pages—the wonderfully democratic tool that puts mighty IBM on the same footing as the 13-year-old kid who lives two houses away from you. While we are at it, let's include *intranets*—private TCP/IP networks run by companies, both large and small, and secured from the nasty real world by one-way mirrors called firewalls.[12] Let's also be forward thinking and add in any Web-enabled operating systems and application programs. By the time you read this, the functional aspects of today's browser programs will probably be present in Microsoft's operating systems and application programs.[13] Other operating system and application developers are likely to follow suit. Or the opposite might be true: Netscape Navigator could become the dominant operating system for the rest of the twentieth century and beyond. In either event, it is critical to include Web-enabled operating systems and application programs into our definition of Internet User Interface.

But this chapter is only supposed to be 20 to 30 pages long, so let's start chopping away some stuff so I can go to the beach with my kids. For starters, Internet *content*—the text, images, audio, and video that make up the real reason people spend the wee hours of the morning basking in the phosphorous glow of their computer screen—is *not* part of the Internet User Interface. Neither is the underlying source and object code that makes up the graphical browsers, home pages, intranets, and Web-enabled operating systems and application programs we just talked about. Between the two tangible worlds of code and content is a fine line of delicious intangibility we will call the Internet User Interface. For most Internet users, this fine line is their window into the Internet—the framework that they experience as they explore the magical words, sights, and sounds of the world through their computer.

The question we are faced with today is how those who spend their creativity, talent, energy, and money investing in and enhancing the Internet User Interface can protect their investment from slimy, no-good, rotten thieves who shamelessly steal from their foreparents[14] and propagate their ill-gotten booty to the masses for their own unjust enrichment.[15] Have no fear—our forefathers[16] anticipated this very event 'way back in the late 1700s, and came up with a two-word

---

[11] Yeah, yeah, and a handful of others that won't be around by the time this book goes to print.

[12] *Here Comes the Intranet,* Bus. Wk., Feb. 26, 1996, at 76–84.

[13] *Netscape: Sitting Pretty—Or Sitting Duck?,* Bus. Wk., July 15, 1996, at 67.

[14] John Wiley and Sons told me to write this chapter in a gender-neutral manner, and I think I'm doing quite well so far! Right, men?

[15] First legal term. Much more still to come.

[16] Uh, John and kids, I checked—no women signed the Constitution.

solution—"intellectual property." After a brief yet important philosophical diversion, we will spend the remaining part of the chapter discussing the various and sundry forms of possible intellectual property protection for our Internet User Interface.

§ 5.9 No Protection for the Internet User Interface?

In retrospect, a large reason Microsoft was late to the Internet dance had more to do with the inherent nature of the fabric of the Internet than the lack of foresight in what may be America's greatest corporate success story. Katie Hafner, an author of a book on the ARPANET, perhaps described the weave of this fabric best when she described the ARPANET as "a very democratic spirit. The spirit in which the network was built you can still see in the network today."[17]

Was, and is, the Internet "democratic"? Bill Gates saw it differently. As late as April 1994, Gates's view was that since the Internet was "free," there was no money to be made there, and the business, by definition, was "uninteresting." Even after Microsoft committed to be a presence on the Internet, the word "democratic" was not on the lips of the Microsoft leaders. When Benjamin Slivka, a Microsoft project leader for the Internet Explorer, proposed to Gates that Microsoft give away Explorer for free, Gates reportedly called Slivka "a communist."[18]

So, what gives? Is the Internet an exercise in the purest form of democracy, or the reincarnation of the communist experiment? Or is it some of both? Is the Internet free enterprise, or socialism? Will Ms. Hafner look at the vestiges of the Internet in 2005 and still see the democratic spirit of the ARPANET? These are difficult questions to answer, but one thing is clear: the Internet has already transformed from the seeds of its intellectual purity to something either more grown-up or sinister, depending on your point of view. Although much of the Internet remains "free," commercial advertising threatens to overwhelm its humble, ivy-covered origins. Already, a supported copy of the previously free Navigator will set you back $49.95. And does anyone really think Microsoft assigned 2,500 of its best programmers to a public works project out of the warmness of its corporate heart? Do you truly believe that Bill Gates is going to see the error of his capitalistic ways and donate his $35-million Pacific Northwest version of Xanadu to the state of Washington?

Paul Evan Peters, Executive Director of the Coalition for Networked Information, states that both the Internet and its emerging replacement, the National Information Infrastructure, must support both "free" and "commercial" uses.[19] If he is right that at least part of the Internet will remain "free" and uncontaminated by the pedestrian vice of capitalism, this "free" part of the Internet is subject to

---

[17] *The Birth of the Internet* at 58.

[18] *Inside Microsoft* at 63.

[19] *Virtual Estate in Cyberspace,* 29 Educom Rev. 68 (Mar./Apr. 1994).

the following basic maxim: there is no form of intellectual property law that can, or should, protect something that is truly free.

Stated another way, a combination of the words "free" and "protect," in an intellectual property context, is an oxymoron. Imagine, for a moment, the utter senselessness of spending millions of dollars suing someone who infringed something that was free. Why would you care? Why would the courts care? Who is harmed by this egregious act?

Sure, maybe "free" doesn't mean "truly free." Maybe there would be enough strings attached to "free" that infringement would be possible, and enough harm could occur for the "owner" of the "free" thing to consider it worthwhile to run to the courts to seek redress of this horrific act. Maybe "free" to some doesn't mean "free" to all. Or maybe "free" today is a subterfuge for "definitely not free" tomorrow. But as a practical matter, the portions of the Internet User Interface that are truly "free" are not subject to the various forms of intellectual property protection we will soon discuss. For these portions, "no protection" is the correct answer. But because the unmistakable trend is to commercialize an increasingly larger share of the Internet, including the Internet User Interface, we need to become aware of possible forms of intellectual property protection for our Internet User Interface.

§ 5.10   Trade Secret Protection of the Internet User Interface

One possible form of intellectual property protection for the Internet User Interface is trade secret law. Possible, at least, in the sense that Arnold Schwartzenegger could *really* get pregnant.

Trade secret law protects valuable, non-public ideas. But once the idea is discovered by legal means, it is lost forever. Trade secret protection is a useful concept when discussing the formula of a new soft drink, a carefully guarded manufacturing technique, or even the source code of an operating system. But it is not a useful concept when discussing protection options for the Internet User Interface, as we have defined it above. Why? By definition, the Internet User Interface is what people see. If they see it, it is discovered, and is not eligible for trade secret protection. Therefore, trade secret protection is not a viable option for our Internet User Interface.

§ 5.11   Trade Dress Protection of the Internet User Interface

Because trade secret protection of the Internet User Interface was a nonstarter, we now move on to a *slightly* more feasible form of intellectual property protection for the Internet User Interface—trade dress. Trade dress protection is an offshoot of trademark law and seeks to protect the visual appearance of a product from being copied by another. Trade dress protection finds its legal home in § 43(a) of the Lanham Act,[20] which states, in a very long sentence that makes up § 43(a)(1), that:

> Any person who, on or in connection with any goods or services, or any container for goods, uses in commerce any word, term, name, symbol, or device, or any combination thereof, or any false designation of origin, false or misleading description of fact, or false or misleading representation of fact, which—
>
> (A) is likely to cause confusion, or to cause mistake, or to deceive as to the affiliation, connection, or association of such person with another person, or as to the origin, sponsorship, or approval of his or her goods, services, or commercial activities by another person, or
>
> (B) in commercial advertising or promotion, misrepresents the nature, characteristics, qualities, or geographic origin of his or her or another person's goods, services, or commercial activities,
>
> shall be liable in a civil action by any person who believes that he or she is likely to be damaged by such act.

Whew! So what does this mean for trade dress? If we carefully select words and phrases out of the above, we can construct a reasonably coherent (and much shorter) sentence that says:

> Any person who uses any symbol or device on any goods or container for goods in commerce which is likely to deceive another person shall be liable.

Better. But one question still remains: So what does this mean for trade dress? Well, stated hyper-simply, it means what the courts say it means. What have the courts said? The courts have said that the red and white label on Campbell's soup cans is protectable as trade dress.[21] Fine—it makes sense that Joe Blow's Soup Company cannot confuse people into buying his soup by making its labels look like Campbell's. But how far can we take this concept? The term *trade dress* originally referred to the "patterns, color, and other design markings that appear on a product's packaging or displays, which could come to be associated with a particular producer."[22] But it would be so boring to stop there, and the courts have held that the net of trade dress protection could be cast over a wide range of things beyond soup cans, from the design of a tennis shoe[23] to, as the Supreme Court held recently, the decor of a restaurant.[24]

---

[20] Officially known (to almost no one) as 15 U.S.C. § 1125(a).

[21] Mitchell Zimmerman, *Trade Dress Protection for User Interfaces Revisited and Interred?*, 13 Computer Law. 4–9 (Feb. 1996) [hereinafter Zimmerman].

[22] *Id.* at 4.

[23] Payless Shoesource, Inc. v. Reebok Int'l Ltd., 998 F.2d 985 (Fed. Cir. 1993).

[24] Two Pesos, Inc. v. Taco Cabana, Inc., 505 U.S. 763 (1992).

§ 5.12   —Elements of a Trade Dress Infringement Claim

So could trade dress be used to protect our Internet User Interface? Superficially, it seems like the answer could be yes—*if* (pause for effect) the three elements of a trade dress infringement case can be established:

1. **Distinctiveness**
2. **Nonfunctionality**
3. **Likelihood of confusion.**[25]

§ 5.13   —Distinctiveness

Distinctiveness means that the feature claimed as trade dress must be able to identify the source of the product. Red and White soup can? Campbell's!

Distinctiveness can either be deemed "inherent," or established via "secondary meaning." In *Two Pesos v. Taco Cabana,*[26] the Supreme Court held that the decor of the Taco Cabana restaurant, including Mexican artifacts, bright awnings, umbrellas, murals, and an exterior painted in a festive and vivid color scheme using top border paint and neon stripes was enough to be "inherent."[27] If the court agrees that the distinctiveness is inherent, the plaintiff does not have to prove secondary meaning by showing that the relevant consuming public views the trade dress as an indication of the source of the product. If the trade dress is not inherently distinctive, the plaintiff attempts to prove secondary meaning by submitting evidence of consumer surveys, advertising, sales figures, and so forth. This can be a difficult and expensive task, especially for startup companies.

But how likely is it that our Internet User Interface will be distinctive—that is, identify the source of a product as being a particular manufacturer? Computer user interfaces of the heady and tumultuous times of the 1980s were arguably much more distinctive than they are today. Operating systems from Apple, IBM, Microsoft, and others were different—and looked different. Application programs that ran on these operating systems usually took on a completely different look as well. Today, Microsoft Windows 95 has a "user interface" widely considered in the technical community to be closely related to the user interface of the Apple Macintosh of a decade earlier. And nearly all application programs that run under Windows 95, including Netscape Navigator and Internet Explorer, have a similar appearance. Why?

---

[25] Gilson, Trademark Protection and Practice § 7.02[7][c] [hereinafter Gilson].

[26] 505 U.S. 763 (1992).

[27] Gilson at § 7.02[7][c].

The glib answer is that computer users want it this way.[28] Learning the operation of a computer program is a difficult endeavor. If all computer programs operate in basically the same manner, the time spent on the learning curve can be leveraged against multiple computer programs. For example, once a user learns how to perform a cut and paste operation, it is likely that this knowledge can be used across a wide variety of computer programs.

Stated simply, the opposite of "distinctive" is "standard." Once a user interface becomes "standard," it cannot be "distinctive," and therefore cannot become the basis for a trade dress infringement claim.[29]

§ 5.14 —Nonfunctionality

If the plaintiff is able to clear the difficult hurdle of distinctiveness, the next hurdle is showing that the trade dress is nonfunctional. Stated more clearly the other way, if a trade dress is functional, it is not protectable. Courts look at the entire design of the product, not its individual elements, in determining if it is functional or not.[30] In other words, the courts don't look just at a trash can icon to see if it is functional or not—they look at the entire user interface, of which the trash can icon might be a part.

So what is "functional"? Courts differ in defining what is functional, based on competing policy grounds. Some courts consider a product feature to be functional if "it is essential to the use or purpose of the article or affects the cost or quality or is the actual benefit for which purchasers obtain the product."[31] Other courts take a broader view and consider useful features to be nonfunctional as long as competition is not unduly burdened.[32]

So what does this mean for our Internet User Interface? Is it functional or not? Interestingly, two scholarly articles that have analyzed this issue for computer user interfaces arrived at diametrically opposite conclusions: nonfunctionality is either (1) an easy hurdle to overcome in the computer user interface context,[33] or (2) a very uncertain but extremely difficult hurdle to overcome in the computer user interface context.[34]

For our purposes, let's assume that the nonfunctionality prong of this test is easy to overcome for our Internet User Interface. Because all three prongs must

---

[28] For a contrary (but perhaps outdated) position, see Jonathan Grudin, *The Case Against User Interface Consistency,* 32 Communications of ACM 1164 (1989).

[29] Lauren Fisher Kellner, *Trade Dress Protection for Computer User Interface "Look and Feel,"* 61 Univ. Chicago L. Rev. 1011 [hereinafter Kellner].

[30] Kellner at 1027.

[31] Zimmerman at 7.

[32] *Id.*

[33] Kellner at 1027.

[34] Zimmerman at 7.

be met, the inherent difficulty in meeting the other two prongs makes this prong largely irrelevant.

§ 5.15 —Likelihood of Confusion

The third and final hurdle of the trade dress infringement claim is the showing that there is a likelihood of confusion. Likelihood of confusion occurs if a large number of consumers are likely to be misled or confused as to the source of the goods in question.[35] Evidence of intentional copying is a "most compelling factor" showing likelihood of confusion.[36]

Use of this "most compelling factor" could theoretically be quite powerful in clearing this hurdle in the computer user interface context, where interfaces are commonly intentionally copied. But if the purpose of copying this interface is to comply with a *de facto* or *de jure* standard, this purpose would seem to be much less compelling. Stated another way, the whole point of this third element, and indeed trade dress and trademark law in general, is to assure that the plaintiff loses if their customers aren't confused. If the user interface is truly a standard, it does not serve as an identifier of plaintiff's product, and cannot form a basis for confusion.

§ 5.16 —Summary

If you were smart enough to cut to the chase by skipping directly to this section, move to the head of the class.[37] Here's the scoop about trade dress protection for our Internet User Interface:

1. As of this writing, no court case has ever held a user interface to be protectable as trade dress.[38]

2. The increasing standardization of all computer user interfaces, including Internet User Interfaces, makes it extremely unlikely that a court will find a user interface protected by trade dress, since standardized interfaces cannot be distinctive interfaces, and distinctiveness is a required element in establishing a trade dress infringement claim.

3. Trade dress protection flies in the face of a judicially recognized (and socially encouraged) right to copy goods that are not protected by copyright or patent.[39]

---

[35] Gilson § 7.02[7][c].

[36] *Id.*

[37] Winner, sentence with the most mixed movement metaphors (3).

[38] Zimmerman at 4.

[39] *Id.* at 5.

In other words, trade dress protection for our Internet User Interface looks like a loser. So lets get back up off the floor, dust off our collective rears, and see if copyright protection looks more promising.

§ 5.17 Copyright Protection of the Internet User Interface

OK. So where are we? "No protection" is the answer for the (probably diminishing) "free" portions of our Internet User Interface. Trade secret protection was a no-show, and we just called trade dress protection a loser. How about something that is actually in the constitution: Copyright law?

Article 1, § 8 of the Constitution states: "Congress shall have the power . . . To promote the progress of the sciences and useful arts, by securing for limited times to authors and inventors the exclusive rights to their respective writings and discoveries."

But what does this mean? For starters, this clause was a merger of two separate proposals, one by James Madison and one by Charles Pinckney, to cover both patents and copyrights.[40] Surprisingly, the term "sciences" refers to copyright, and "useful arts" refers to patents. So what part of our author's "science" does the copyright law protect?

The seminal[41] case of *Baker v. Selden*[42] held that copyright protects the *expression* of ideas, but not the ideas themselves. Therefore, as in *Baker,* a book describing a new bookkeeping system is not infringed by another book that expressed similar ideas differently.

Section 102(b) of the Copyright Act codifies *Baker v. Selden* by stating: "In no case does copyright protection for an original work of authorship extend to any idea, procedure, process, system, method of operation, concept, principle, or discovery, regardless of the form in which it is described, explained, illustrated, or embodied in such work."[43]

Because § 102(b) is worded so strongly, doubt was expressed in some legal circles whether computer software was protectable at all. This was despite very clear legislative history in the 1976 Copyright Act that "the expression adopted by the programmer is the copyrightable element of a computer program."[44] It took a special commission to clear up some of the confusion. The National Commission on New Technological Uses of Copyrighted Works (CONTU) provided clarification to the copyright law in 1980 that computer programs were

---

[40] P.J. Federico, Commentary on the New Patent Law, 35 U.S.C.A. §§ 1–110, at 3 (1954) [hereinafter Federico].

[41] Legalese for a golden oldie.

[42] 101 U.S. 99 (1880).

[43] 17 U.S.C. § 102(b).

[44] Pamela Samuelson, *Computer Programs, User Interfaces, and Section 102(b) of the Copyright Act of 1976: A Critique of* Lotus v. Paperback, 55 Law & Contemp. Probs. 311 (1992).

indeed copyrightable. Although it was pretty well settled that the source and object code of a computer program was "protectable expression" under the copyright law, it remained unclear if this "protectable expression" extended beyond the source and object code to so-called non-literal elements of a computer program, such as its structure and its user interface. A review of the legislative history of CONTU shows that no consideration was given to the protectability of a computer user interface under the copyright law.[45] As we will now see, the courts have struggled with this issue ever since.

§ 5.18 —The Copyright User Interface Blues: Condensed Version

If this book was a thorough, musty, dusty old legal treatise, this next section would perform an in-depth analysis of a litany of convoluted cases in excruciatingly painful detail. Fortunately for all of us, it is not such a book, thereby giving us literary license to traverse this ground without conjuring up thoughts of dental instruments. Still, readers are encouraged to buckle their seatbelts and hang on for a pretty convoluted ride.

§ 5.19   —*Whelan v. Jaslow*

Still there? Didn't scare you off yet? You are an inspirational person destined for greatness.

The first computer software case that rocked the legal landscape was *Whelan v. Jaslow.*[46] Here's the skinny: Whelan wrote a program.[47] Jaslow agreed to market the program. Jaslow saw that the program could be way cooler if it could be written in a different language to run on a different computer. Jaslow decided to do this way cooler thing all by himself, without troubling Whelan. Jaslow's program acted almost exactly like Whelan's, but did so with completely different source and object code.

The Third Circuit decided in 1986 that Jaslow had infringed Whelan's copyright despite the fact that he didn't copy Whelan's source or object code. The court reasoned that Jaslow did copy the "sequence, structure, and organization" of Whelan's program, and that was just as bad. The court went back to the idea/expression dichotomy of *Baker v. Selden*[48] and defined *idea* narrowly as

---

[45] Richard A. Forsten, *It Walks and Talks Like My Duck, So How Come It's Not Infringement? The Case Against "Look-and-Feel" Protection for Computer Programs,* J. Pat. & Trademark Off. Soc'y 639–65 (Oct. 1988).

[46] Whelan Assocs., Inc. v. Jaslow Dental Lab, Inc., 797 F.2d 1222 (3d Cir. 1986).

[47] Actually, to perform bookkeeping tasks for, arrgh, a dentist's laboratory!

[48] 101 U.S. 99 (1880), discussed in § **5.17.**

being the "purpose or function of a utilitarian work." Everything else, the court reasoned, was protectable expression.

Intellectual property attorneys all over the country started walking around muttering "sequence, structure, and organization" (quickly shortened to an easier-to-remember "SSO") to anyone who would listen. Spouses, children, and innocent used car dealers screamed in horror as the SSO-obsessed intellectual property attorneys headed their way.

Whelan was clearly a watershed event that generated a lot of controversy and commentary. Although practitioners split on whether this case was a positive development or not, it was clear to most that copyright was emerging as a potentially strong form of protection of computer software. Unfortunately, it was also clear that the bright line between "idea" and "expression," established by *Baker v. Selden* over 100 years before, was now quite fuzzy.

§ 5.20   *—Lotus v. Paperback Software*

For the next six years, most district courts and circuit courts followed the *Whelan* decision,[49] and even expanded it into the user interface arena.[50] Noteworthy of the cases in the 1986 through 1992 timeframe was *Lotus v. Paperback Software.*[51] The facts are easy: Lotus developed a spreadsheet program called 1-2-3. Paperback developed a work-alike clone of 1-2-3 called VP-Planner. Like Jaslow's program, VP-Planner had completely different source and object code from 1-2-3. What VP-Planner did do was use the same user interface as the 1-2-3 user interface. In 1990, Judge Keeton of the United States District Court for the District of Massachusetts relied on *Whelan* to hold that Paperback had violated Lotus's copyright in 1-2-3.

§ 5.21   *—Computer Associates International v. Altai*

Whelan[52] and its progeny like *Lotus v. Paperback*[53] clearly stated the unofficial law of the computer user interface land until 1992. But this heady, cocky world of ever-increasing copyright protection for computer software came crashing

---

[49] Whelan Assocs., Inc. v. Jaslow Dental Lab, Inc., 797 F.2d 1222 (3d Cir. 1986), discussed in **§ 5.19.**

[50] Manny D. Pokotilow, *Supreme Court Deadlock Leaves Decision That Lotus Menu Commands Are not Copyrightable,* Bull. of L./Sci. & Tech., ABA Sec. Sci. & Tech. 5–8 (June 1996) [hereinafter Pokotilow].

[51] 740 F. Supp. 37 (D. Mass. 1990).

[52] Whelan Assocs., Inc. v. Jaslow Dental Lab, Inc., 797 F.2d 1222 (3d Cir. 1986), discussed in **§ 5.19.**

[53] Lotus v. Paperback Software, 740 F. Supp. 37 (D. Mass. 1990), discussed in **§ 5.20.**

back to reality when the Second Circuit decided *Computer Associates International v. Altai.*[54] The Second Circuit did something unprecedented, but widely expected: it criticized, and refused to follow, *Whelan v. Jaslow.* Gone, at least in the Second Circuit, was the concept of "sequence, structure, and organization." In its place was a new, and to many a better reasoned but equally Byzantine, concept: the "abstraction, filtration, and comparison" tripartite test.

Arrgh!! What the blazes is "abstraction, filtration, and comparison"? The used car dealers dove for cover again, trembling with fear. Take a deep, cleansing breath, and let's give this a shot.

"Abstraction" is just the recognition that computer software does not contain one idea, but several. As a court-appointed expert pointed out in *Computer Associates,* a computer program contains many different programs and sub-programs, each of which contains at least one idea. It is possible to arrange all of these ideas on a continuum, from the most specific, least general ideas (object code) to the least specific, most general ideas ("general outline" of the program).[55]

After all of these ideas have been arranged on this continuum, the "filtration" step filters out those ideas deemed to be not protectable by copyright law. Such ideas include:

1. Broad ideas
2. Elements dictated by logic and efficiency
3. Elements dictated by external considerations
4. Industry standards
5. Elements in the public domain.[56]

After all the nonprotectable stuff is filtered out by the "filtration" step, the "comparison" step looks to see if what is left is "substantially similar" to the copyrighted program. If so, there is copyright infringement. If not, there is no copyright infringement.

Whew! It sure feels good to have this all cleared up, doesn't it? Hello? Still there?

§ 5.22 —*Apple Computer v. Microsoft*

The Ninth Circuit decided to follow *Computer Associates*[57] by applying the "abstraction, filtration, and comparison" test in what is widely perceived to be the computer software copyright case with the most profound implications to date: *Apple Computer v. Microsoft.*[58]

---

[54] 982 F.2d 693 (2d Cir. 1992).

[55] Morgan Chu & Andre Brunel, *Post-Altai Computer Copyright and Trade Secret Decisions,* 11 Computer Law. 1 (Jan. 1994) [hereinafter Chu & Brunel].

[56] Pokotilow at 7.

[57] Computer Assocs. Int'l v. Altai, 982 F.2d 693 (2d Cir. 1992), discussed in § **5.21.**

[58] 32 U.S.P.Q.2d (BNA) 1086 (9th Cir. 1994).

Apple sued both Microsoft and Hewlett-Packard for infringing its "Lisa" and Macintosh graphical user interface through Microsoft's Windows user interface and HP's NewWave user interface. The court first discarded those portions of Windows and NewWave that Apple had previously licensed. Then it used the "abstraction, filtration, and comparison" test to filter out even more portions of Windows and NewWave that were unprotectable. What was left? Very little, it turned out, and the court said that although Apple theoretically had copyright protection in what was left, it raised the bar for determining whether this small portion was infringed from "substantially similar" to "virtually identical" and found no infringement. Thus, the net effect of the *Apple* decision was to grant a weak (but basically worthless) copyright in the user interface of a computer software program.

It is interesting to compare the result of the *Apple* decision with an article written over 10 years ago by Jack Russo and Douglas Derwin.[59] This article, written shortly after the district court decision but before the Third Circuit decision in *Whelan*,[60] analyzed the protectability of "look and feel" of computer software in detail and concluded that the computer user interface was entitled to weak copyright protection to protect against "close copying of the look and feel."

Sound familiar?

§ 5.23   —*Lotus v. Borland*

Pumped from its litigation success against Paperback Software,[61] Lotus rolled the dice again and took on Borland, claiming that, like VP-Planner, Borland's Quattro-Pro program copied 1-2-3's menu tree, or user interface. Once again, the source or object code of 1-2-3 was not copied, just the user interface. Once again, Judge Keeton of the United States District Court for the District of Massachusetts heard the case. And once again, he held that Lotus's copyright in 1-2-3 had been infringed.[62]

But it is at this point that the similarities between *Lotus v. Borland* and *Lotus v. Paperback Software* end. For although the *Paperback* suit was settled and not appealed, Borland appealed Judge Keeton's decision to the First Circuit. Borland admitted that Quattro and Quattro-Pro contained "a virtually identical copy of the entire 1-2-3 menu tree," but it claimed that this was not copyrightable under § 102(b) of the Copyright Act, because it was "a system, method of operation, process, or procedure." The First Circuit agreed with Borland, and

---

[59] Jack Russo & Douglas K. Derwin, *Copyright in the "Look and Feel" of Computer Software,* 2 Computer Law. 1 (Feb. 1985).

[60] Whelan Assocs., Inc. v. Jaslow Dental Lab, Inc., 797 F.2d 1222 (3d Cir. 1986), discussed in **§ 5.19.**

[61] Lotus v. Paperback Software, 740 F. Supp. 37 (D. Mass. 1990), discussed in **§ 5.20.**

[62] Lotus Dev. Corp. v. Borland Int'l, 799 F. Supp. 203 (D. Mass. 1992).

reversed the district court. It held that "the Lotus menu command hierarchy is an uncopyrightable 'method of operation'" under § 102(b).[63]

Zowie!! In three short years the computer user interface has gone from maximum protection (*Whelan,*[64] *Lotus v. Paperback*), to minimal protection (*Computer Associates,*[65] *Apple,*[66] *Lotus v. Borland*). The various circuit courts have whiplashed around, first following *Whelan,* now embracing *Computer Associates.*[67]

What could possibly happen next to make this any more confusing than it already is?

I know—just for fun, let's say that Lotus is so mad at losing in the First Circuit, they decide to appeal the case to, hmmm, the Supreme Court! The Supreme Court usually does its best to avoid intellectual property cases like the plague, but let's say they can't avoid this one, because it appears there is a definite split among the circuits on this issue. So they agree to take the case. Just to make it more interesting, let's say that one justice—hmmm, let's pick an old one like Justice Stevens—decides to sit this one out. OK, now we're down to eight justices. Hmmm . . . what else can we do? I know—let's have a *blizzard* during oral argument! Yeah, that's the ticket!! If you've ever been in D.C. during a blizzard, you know what fun that can create! So . . . let's say that the eight remaining justices brave the elements at great personal risk and peril yet heroically make it to the Supreme Court in time to hear the arguments. They are in a collective foul mood, but, gosh darnit, they are consummate professionals and patiently listen to the attorneys from Lotus and Borland bicker at each other. Their mood gets fouler. Now the eight remaining justices (Justice Stevens gloating in abstentia at his good fortune) have to decide the case. More bickering. Let's say this goes on for eight days before they can't stand it any more. Out of exasperation, they announce they are deadlocked 4–4, and therefore let stand the First Circuit opinion without comment!

Wouldn't this be a great way to heap even more confusion on this issue? I'm a pretty creative guy to have come up with this wild tale, aren't I?

Guess what? It's all true.

§ 5.24 —Summary

Are you learning yet? Did you skip all the dreck above and go right to this section? If not, don't you wish you had? Can't you see by now that I could have

---

[63] Lotus Dev. Corp. v. Borland Int'l, 49 F.3d 815 (1st Cir. 1995).

[64] Whelan Assocs., Inc. v. Jaslow Dental Lab, Inc., 797 F.2d 1222 (3d Cir. 1986), discussed in **§ 5.19.**

[65] Computer Assocs. Int'l v. Altai, 982 F.2d 693 (2d Cir. 1992), discussed in **§ 5.21.**

[66] Apple Computer v. Microsoft, 32 U.S.P.Q.2d (BNA) 1086 (9th Cir. 1994), discussed in **§ 5.22.**

[67] Chu & Brunel at 1.

made this chapter a lot shorter, but for the fact that I promised it would be at least 10,000 words long?[68]

Here's the scoop about copyright protection for our Internet User Interface:

1. The courts have swung wildly on this issue for the last 10+ years. If you live in Pennsylvania, your Internet User Interface might be protectable via copyright law. If you live in New York or California, or just about any place else, your Internet User Interface is probably not protectable, or just minimally protectable, via copyright law.

2. The Justices on the Supreme Court are probably so mad at themselves for taking the *Lotus v. Borland* case they will go into total denial about this issue and not accept another software copyright case for a long, long time, leaving the issue unsettled.[69]

3. The clear trend is towards less and less copyright protection for user interfaces. If there is a consensus on the state of the law today, it is that expressed by the Ninth Circuit in *Apple v. Microsoft:*[70] User Interfaces are entitled to a weak copyright to protect against "virtually identical" copying.

In sum, don't depend on copyright law to protect your Internet User Interface. It's time to move on to a vast, largely unexplored frontier—the land of patent protection for the software user interface.

§ 5.25 Patent Protection of the Internet User Interface

Let's review where we've been. No protection works if it is truly free. Trade secret doesn't work. Trade dress protection is unlikely to work. Nobody has a clue whether copyright protection works or not, but it doesn't look good. There is only one option left—patenting the Internet User Interface.

Patenting a user interface? Are you serious? Aren't patents supposed to be for *real things,* like machines, and circuits, and chemicals and stuff? True. But let's keep an open mind, step through the patent story for software, and see where we end up, OK?

As we have already discussed in **§ 5.17,** both the patent law and the copyright law find a home in the same place: Article 1, § 8 of the Constitution: "The

---

[68] 7,138 down, 2,862 to go!

[69] In the alternative, they will rise to the occasion and deliver the most insightful, thought-provoking, well-reasoned opinion to come out of the judiciary since Learned Hand. Or something in between. Or they'll all quit and join the Washington Redskins. The point is, nobody knows for sure what the Supreme Court will do next.

[70] Apple Computer v. Microsoft, 32 U.S.P.Q.2d (BNA) 1086 (9th Cir. 1994), discussed in **§ 5.22.**

Congress shall have the power . . . To promote the progress of the sciences and useful arts, by securing for limited times to authors and inventors the exclusive rights to their respective writings and discoveries."

As we have said, this clause is a merger of two separate proposals by James Madison and Charles Pinckney to cover both patents and copyrights, and "useful arts" is the patent part.

The first patent law was enacted on April 10, 1790.[71] Patents were granted by a high-powered board consisting of the Secretary of State, the Attorney General, and the Secretary of War. The Secretary of State was someone named Thomas Jefferson, who was an inventor/tinkerer and was deeply interested in the patent law. He is widely considered to be this country's first patent examiner.

Thomas Jefferson soon found out that being the Secretary of State and future president for a fledgling nation ate too heavily into his duties of being a patent examiner, so something had to give. So in 1793, the patent law was changed to make granting of patents a clerical function. Anyone who paid the fee and filed the right papers got a patent.

This worked fine for a few years, but eventually the public became dissatisfied with the process of granting patents without any examination as to whether anyone else had done this before. So in 1836, the Patent Office was created, and a commissioner was given the authority to examine patent applications and refuse to grant patents that were not novel (that is, new).

In 1870, all the statutes of the United States were revised and consolidated, including the patent statutes. In 1954, the patent statutes were revised again and codified into Title 35 of the United States Code. The most significant addition to patent law in the 1952 Act[72] was the codification of the judicial doctrine of obviousness, which says that a patent application will be rejected if one skilled in the art would consider the advancement to be obvious over what was already known.

Several amendments have been made to the patent statutes since 1954, but the statute today is very similar to what was passed in 1954. The most significant changes occurred in 1994 with the ratification of the GATT treaty—most notably the change of the patent term from 17 years from issuance to 20 years from filing.

§ 5.26 —Is Software Patentable Subject Matter?

With this background in place, it is time to fine tune our analysis and examine the history of software protection in the United States.

The fundamental question we need to address is whether software is patentable. You may be surprised to learn that this relatively straightforward question has generated a great deal of controversy over the last 30 years.

---

[71] Federico at 3.

[72] Passed in 1954. Hey, these things take time!

OK—the question is, "Is software patentable?" Let's rephrase the question in slightly more legalistic terminology: "Does software fall within the statutory class of patentable subject matter under the patent law?" To answer this question, we need to look at what the statutory class of patentable subject matter is.

Section 101 of the Patent Act says: "Whoever invents or discovers any new or useful process, machine, manufacture, or composition of matter, or any new and useful improvement thereof, may obtain a patent therefor, subject to the conditions and requirements of this title."[73]

It is significant that with all the changes in the patent law over the last 200 years, and with all the changes in technology over these 200 years, our definition of what is patentable is basically unchanged from Thomas Jefferson's definition in 1793: "any new and useful art [eighteenth-century term for process], machine, manufacture, or composition of matter, or any new or useful improvement [thereof]."[74]

There is one other item of significance worthy of mention at this time. The legislative history of the 1952 Act makes it clear that Congress intended statutory subject matter to "include anything under the sun that is made by man."[75]

Isn't our Internet User Interface something "under the sun that is made by man?" Hmmm, maybe we are on to something here! But hold on for yet another rocky ride.

§ 5.27 —The Pre-*Benson* Era

In 1965, IBM Vice President J.W. Birkenstock chaired a presidential commission that investigated whether software should be patentable. The commission concluded that it should not be patentable, largely because the patent office was not equipped to handle the increase in work that would result if it was patentable.[76]

Think about this for a moment. Deny patent protection to a new technology just because it will be a lot of work? Hunh??

Skeptics have observed that IBM had 80 percent of the computer market at that time, was estopped from aggressively enforcing its patents due to antitrust concerns, and had much more to lose than it had to gain in having strong patent protection for software (or anything computer related, for that matter).[77]

This IBM-led 1965 policy would haunt the computer industry, including IBM, for nearly three decades to come.

---

[73] 35 U.S.C. § 101.

[74] U.S. Patent & Trademark Office, *Legal Analysis to Support Proposed Examination Guidelines for Computer-Implemented Inventions,* Pat., Copyright, & Trademark J., Oct. 5, 1995, at 661.

[75] Diamond v. Diehr, 209 U.S.P.Q. (BNA) 1 (1981).

[76] Paul Heckel, *Debunking the Myths About Software Patents,* Communications of ACM 5 (June 1992) (draft copy circulated by Abraham Lincoln Patent Holders Association).

[77] *Id.*

§ 5.28   —*Gottschalk v. Benson*

Gottschalk v. Benson[78] was the first Supreme Court case to address the issue of the patentability of software.

In this 1972 case, the Supreme Court held that a method for converting binary coded decimal (BCD) numbers into binary numbers was unpatentable. Stated more globally, the Court held that mathematical algorithms cannot be patented, no matter how new and useful.

The court's rationale seems to be based on a policy issue. Whose policy? Well, three paragraphs of the IBM-led 1965 policy found its way into this relatively short decision. Hmmm . . . .

Professor Donald Chisum, a well-known and respected expert in patent law, said the following about *Benson:*

> The continuing confusion over the patentability of computer programming ideas can be laid on the doorsteps of a single Supreme Court decision—*Gottschalk v. Benson* . . . . A careful analysis of that decision shows the holding is not supported by any of the authorities on which it relied, that the Court misunderstood the nature of the subject matter before it, and that the Court failed to offer any viable policy justification for excluding by judicial fiat mathematical algorithms from the patent system.[79]

Kinda makes you want to go back and read the copyright section again, doesn't it?

§ 5.29   —*Parker v. Flook*

The Supreme Court got another shot at the patentability of software in 1978, with *Parker v. Flook.*[80] The patent application in question in *Flook* covered a method of updating an alarm limit in a chemical process, based on the current state of process variables such as temperature and pressure.

The Court held that these claims were also not patentable. They assumed that the mathematical expression was known, and then examined the claim to see if it was still patentable. Thus, the Court mixed concepts of statutory subject matter and novelty together. The dissent pointed out that this mixing was impermissible. The majority denied the mixing occurred.

The Court said:

> The plain language of § 101 does not answer the question [of patentability]. It is true, as respondent argues, that his method is a "process" in the ordinary sense of the word. But that was also true of the algorithm . . . that was involved in

---

[78] 175 U.S.P.Q. (BNA) 673 (1972).

[79] Chisum, *The Patentability of Algorithms,* 47 U. Pitt. L. Rev. 959, 971 (1986).

[80] 198 U.S.P.Q. (BNA) 193 (1978).

Gottschalk v. Benson. The holding that the discovery of that method could not be patented as a "process" forecloses a purely literal reading of § 101.[81]

It is interesting—and awe inspiring—to note that the Court in *Parker v. Flook* identified the error in *Benson,*[82] but said they were duty bound to repeat it.

Out of exasperation and frustration, the Court stated that it was not the proper entity to resolve the question of whether software per se is patentable, and that it should not expand patent rights absent a clear and certain signal from Congress.[83]

As we will see, this reasoning is exactly backwards from Thomas Jefferson's intent—that "ingenuity should receive a liberal encouragement,"[84] and that new technologies are patentable absent a clear indication from Congress that they are not.

After all, isn't this the whole point??

§ 5.30   —*Diamond v. Diehr*

The count is 0-2. In 1981, the Supreme Court took one last swing at deciding the patentability of software. In *Diamond v. Diehr,*[85] the Court finally got it mostly right.

Diehr involved a patent application for curing rubber using a digital computer. This time, the Court held that the claims were patentable under 35 U.S.C. § 101. In a 5–4 decision, the Court shifted direction 180 degrees and said that "courts should not read into the patent laws limitations and conditions which a legislature has not expressed."[86] It then reiterated the legislative history of the 1952 Act: "Congress intended statutory subject matter to include anything under the sun that is made by man."[87]

Unfortunately, the *Diehr* court did not expressly overrule *Benson*[88] and *Flook,*[89] even though the policy grounds on which both of those decisions were based had been gutted. It instead performed some revisionist history on *Benson* and *Flook* and said that what these cases really meant to say was that computer software was patentable, but that algorithms were not.[90]

---

[81] *Id.* at 196–97.

[82] Gottschalk v. Benson, 409 U.S. 63, 175 U.S.P.Q. (BNA) 673 (1972), discussed in **§ 5.28.**

[83] 198 U.S.P.Q. (BNA) at 199–200.

[84] PTO at 661.

[85] 450 U.S. 175, 209 U.S.P.Q. (BNA) 1 (1981).

[86] 209 U.S.P.Q. at 6.

[87] *Id.*

[88] Gottschalk v. Benson, 409 U.S. 63, 175 U.S.P.Q. (BNA) 673 (1972), discussed in **§ 5.28.**

[89] Parker v. Flook, 437 U.S. 584, 198 U.S.P.Q. (BNA) 193 (1978), discussed in **§ 5.29.**

[90] 209 U.S.P.Q. (BNA) at 7.

So what's the difference between computer software and an algorithm? Is this not a technical discussion? From a purely technical point of view, there is no difference.

This was the last time the Supreme Court has heard a software patent case.

The Court of Appeals for the Federal Circuit was established in 1982. The stated rationale of establishing this court was to bring continuity to the patent law. A slightly skeptical translation of this rationale is that the other circuit courts and the Supreme Court didn't like patent cases, didn't understand patent cases, and didn't do a very good job in deciding them. They were giving up, and wanted a court staffed with specially skilled judges to decide these cases from now on.

§ 5.31 —The Software Sky Is Falling and I Can't Get Up

For the rest of the 1980s, patent attorneys, the Patent and Trademark Office, and the courts were generally satisfied with the notion that this matter had been decided, and that software was patentable. But like leaving Saddam Hussein and Darth Vader alone to fight another battle, the fact that *Benson*[91] and *Flook*[92] were still on the books as good law would come back to haunt us.

The uneasy peace came crashing down in 1990. Richard Stallman, founder of the League of Programming Freedom and recipient of a MacArthur Foundation scholarship, picked up the anti-software patent cause that IBM had abandoned years before. Stallman wrote several articles in the trade presses explaining why software patents were evil.[93] His general approach was to make broad, nonlegalistic characterizations of a selected group of software patents, cavalierly dismiss such patents as disclosing concepts so simple no one even bothered to write them down, tell his followers that these patents will doom the software industry to extinction, and conclude that software patents should be abolished.

Mr. Stallman got a lot of attention for his efforts. Several of his followers wrote similar "the sky is falling" articles.[94] The mainstream press, especially the *New York Times,* picked up the story. Congress got involved. They started asking the Patent Commissioner questions. The Patent Commissioner got involved. He started asking the group director in charge of the group that examines software applications questions.

The group director got involved. He did what any self-respecting government official would do. He wrote a memo.

---

[91] Gottschalk v. Benson, 409 U.S. 63, 175 U.S.P.Q. (BNA) 673 (1972), discussed in § **5.28.**

[92] Parker v. Flook, 437 U.S. 584, 198 U.S.P.Q. (BNA) 193 (1978), discussed in § **5.29.**

[93] *See, e.g.,* League of Programming Freedom, *Viewpoint: Against Software Patents,* Communications of ACM 17–22 (Jan. 1992).

[94] *See, e.g.,* Paul W. Abrahams, *Software Patents: An Example of the Threat,* 27 ACM SIGPLAN Notices, No. 8, at 87–88 (Aug. 1992).

§ 5.32 —Director Goldberg's Total Quality Management Memo

But not just any memo. Here's an excerpt of the memo the group director sent out to all his examiners in August 1990:

> The office, and our group have come "under fire" for allowing applications that are perceived as being either well known or claiming non-statutory subject matter. It is in the Office's best interest, and that of the public as well, that we issue valid patents. How you as examiners view applications and, most importantly, the claims is therefore of utmost importance.

> To issue a "quality" patent we need to implement a "conservative", vigorous approach to claim interpretation. Many of the complaints we have heard would be eliminated if claim language were more strictly construed.

> Claims that deal with "computer programs", equations or mathematical calculations . . . need to be carefully analyzed. If the claim is the least bit suspect regarding the 101 question—make the rejection. At least the record in the application will be clear that we considered this question.

> The whole "software" question is very sensitive. Congress and many members of the public are and will be watching what we do. If too many patents are issued that are borderline or are perceived as being borderline the unfriendly publicity could adversely affect us.

Dear reader, you have just read how a relatively low-level bureaucrat in an administrative agency can overrule the United States Supreme Court.

As you might suspect, this memo had a chilling effect on the issuance of software applications in the Patent and Trademark Office (PTO). All of a sudden, the examiners started rejecting software cases on doctrines that were killed off by the courts 20 years ago. Patent practitioners argued the state of the law largely in vain—the examiners were too afraid of their own careers to be persuaded to follow the law or the agency's own published rules.

Patent attorneys who were lucky enough to have clients that could afford to regularly appeal such rejections out of the software examining group[95] and into the PTO's Board of Patent Appeals and Interferences were usually successful. But appeals are costly, and the backlog of cases under appeal grew substantially, to the point where a wait of three or four years to have an appeal heard was not uncommon.

It was a very dark and stormy time for software patents.

§ 5.33 —*Alappat*

One case stands out as representing the trials and tribulations of this time between 1990 and 1995: *Alappat. Alappat* involved an invention on a rasterizer

---

[95] PTO Art Group Unit 2300. The "cluster" that now examines software is Groups 2300, 2400, and 2600.

for a digital oscilloscope. The rasterizer determines how the waveform will be displayed on the oscilloscope. Alappat's rasterizer was software that improved the appearance of the waveform over previously known techniques.

The PTO rejected the claims of the application as being directed to nonstatutory subject matter. Alappat appealed, and the three-person Board of Patent Appeals and Interferences reversed the examiner. Then an extremely interesting thing happened. The examiner who was reversed requested reconsideration of the board's decision under an internal procedural rule. The commissioner agreed to the reconsideration request, and went a step further. He expanded the original appellate board from three members to eight members. The additional five members were the commissioner, the deputy commissioner, the assistant commissioner, the board chairman, and the board vice-chairman.

The expanded panel reconsidered the case. They voted 5–3 (surprise, surprise) to overturn the original board decision and affirm the examiner in rejecting the claims.[96]

The original panel cried foul. They, along with most of the other examiners on the Board of Patent Appeals and Interferences, sent what amounted to a "Declaration of Independence" to the commissioner.[97] The commissioner responded by basically saying "Tough. You work for me, and I can do anything I want."[98]

This attitude extended not only to the employees of the PTO, but to the Federal Circuit itself. When the Federal Circuit came down with a case the PTO didn't like, they ignored it. A particularly pointed Federal Circuit decision[99] was summarily dismissed by the PTO as being irrelevant, because, in their view, a panel decision of the Federal Circuit could not overrule a decision of its predecessor court, the Court of Customs and Patent Appeals (CCPA).[100]

Can you feel the drama? Can you sense the intrigue? Do you think the Federal Circuit is really, really, *angry* at the PTO right about now?

Is this a great story, or what??

Alappat appealed the decision to the Federal Circuit. He also asked for an en banc ruling. The Federal Circuit granted the request.

The practitioners waited for the Federal Circuit to hand down their decision. And waited. And waited. Finally, on July 29, 1994, the Federal Circuit spoke.[101] The voice the court spoke through was none other than Giles Rich. The Giles Rich that has been deciding patent cases for the CCPA and the Federal Circuit for nearly 50 years.

Giles Rich was 90 years old when he wrote the *Alappat* opinion. His opinion is a study in elegant simplicity. We could all be so fortunate to be so thoughtful at age 90. Or 40. Or 25.

---

[96] 23 U.S.P.Q.2d 1340 (PTO Bd. of Pat. Appeals & Interferences, 1992).

[97] Pat., Trademark, & Copyright J., May 14, 1992, at 33.

[98] *Id.*

[99] *In re* Bond, 15 U.S.P.Q.2d (BNA) 1566 (Fed. Cir. 1990).

[100] *PTO Notice on Application of 35 U.S.C. 112, Paragraph 6,* Pat., Trademark, & Copyright J., Dec. 19, 1991, at 161–67.

[101] *In re* Alappat, 31 U.S.P.Q.2d (BNA) 1545 (Fed. Cir. 1994) (en banc).

Judge Rich held that the Alappat invention was patentable under 35 U.S.C. § 101. He reiterated the view in *Diehr*[102] that Congress intended § 101 to extend to anything under the sun made by man, including software. He scolded the reconstructed board, stating that under their reasoning, "a general purpose computer could never be viewed as patentable subject matter under § 101. This reasoning is without basis in the law."[103] Stating perhaps the obvious, he concluded by saying that "A computer, like a rasterizer, is apparatus, not mathematics."[104]

§ 5.34 —PTO Draft Guidelines on Patentability of Software

Once again, the patent attorneys thought the issue of the patentability of software had been resolved. Or re-resolved. Now it was the job of the PTO to come up with guidelines to instruct their examiners to follow *Alappat*.[105] The PTO got to work, and presented their proposed guidelines to the Electronic and Computer Law Committee of the American Intellectual Property Law Association meeting in February 1995.

The patent attorneys on the committee all waited anxiously for Steve Kunin, Assistant Commissioner of Patents, to speak. He distributed the draft guidelines. He started explaining them to the 75 or so patent attorneys in the audience.

The proposed guidelines largely ignored *Alappat*.

The audience gasped in horror. The normally genteel, calm, even-tempered group of the nicest attorneys on this planet were ready to group-kill poor Mr. Kunin. "Revolting!" "Shocking!" "What dragon are you trying to slay here?" "Are you above the law?" "Are you out of your mind?" "I find your analysis, quite frankly, to be appalling!"

Mr. Kunin escaped and went back to the drawing board. Those proposed guidelines were never adopted.

§ 5.35 —In re Beauregard

What happened next was equally as shocking. Three months later, the same committee met again in Seattle. The PTO was again scheduled to present its proposed post-*Alappat* guidelines. But before it arrived, a sidebar discussion took place between an attorney for IBM and Nancy Linck, the new PTO solicitor. They were discussing the next case to go to the Federal Circuit—*In re Beauregard*.[106]

---

[102] Diamond v. Diehr, 450 U.S. 175, 209 U.S.P.Q. (BNA) 1 (1981), discussed in § **5.30.**

[103] 31 U.S.P.Q.2d at 1558.

[104] *Id.*

[105] *In re* Alappat, 31 U.S.P.Q.2d (BNA) 1545 (Fed. Cir. 1994) (en banc), discussed in § **5.33.**

[106] 35 U.S.P.Q.2d (BNA) 1382 (Fed. Cir. 1995).

Beauregard was an IBM patent application that had claims that would later become known as "program product" claims—basically, claiming bits of software on a disk—without a computer being part of the claim. The Board of Patent Appeals and Interferences rejected the claims as being nonstatutory. The Federal Circuit was poised to hear the case. Everybody was bracing for the next fight.

Then the PTO solicitor told the IBM attorney that the PTO had changed its mind. The PTO now agreed with IBM that program product claims were patentable. The PTO would move to dismiss the case as being moot. *Beauregard* was the straw that broke this stubborn camel's back.

§ 5.36 —Published Examination Guidelines for Computer-Related Inventions

The PTO published its "Examination Guidelines for Computer-Related Inventions" in January 1996. The new guidelines reflected the PTO's recent change in heart. The "anything under the sun made by man" language of the 1952 Act, the *Diehr* case,[107] and the *Alappat* case[108] was firmly embraced. The legal analysis even quoted Thomas Jefferson and referred approvingly to the statutory language of the 1793 Act.[109]

The new line of what was OK and what was not was drawn at the demarcation between what is traditionally protected exclusively by copyright. A new song wouldn't be patentable just because it was a new song—it was the copyright law's job to protect expression. But patents protect ideas. If the software contained an idea that was useful, it was going to be statutory under 35 U.S.C. § 101.

§ 5.37 —User Interface Patents Are Here!

The Examination Guidelines clearly left the door wide open for strong patent protection for user interfaces. Although none of the above key software cases involved user interface technologies, user interface patents have existed for years, with surprisingly little fanfare. In fact, several PTO subclasses in newly created class 395 are specifically set aside for user interface patents.

One software user interface patent that did receive some attention in 1995 is U.S. Patent No. 5,386,564, issued to Wanda Shearer and Barbara Holden of

---

[107] Diamond v. Diehr, 450 U.S. 175, 209 U.S.P.Q. (BNA) 1 (1981), discussed in § **5.30.**

[108] *In re* Alappat, 31 U.S.P.Q.2d (BNA) 1545 (Fed. Cir. 1994) (en banc), discussed in § **5.33.**

[109] U.S. Patent & Trademark Office, *Legal Analysis to Support Proposed Examination Guidelines for Computer-Implemented Inventions,* Pat. Copyright, & Trademark J., Oct. 5, 1995, at 661.

Hewlett-Packard, titled "Conversion of Data and Objects Across Classes in an Object Management System." Claim 1 reads as follows:

1. A computer implemented method within an operating system process comprising the step of:

(a) in response to a user pasting data within a clipboard to a window controlled by the operating system process, performing the following substeps:

(a.1) creating, by the operating system process, a new data file for the data;

(a.2) placing the data within the new data file; and,

(a.3) displaying, by the operating system process, an icon for the new data file.

Gregory Aharonian, self-proclaimed editor of the *Internet Patent News Service,* awarded this patent (along with a user interface patent from IBM—U.S. Patent No. 5,388,993) his "Worst Software Patent of the Decade" award,[110] largely due to their breadth and relevance to the computer industry. It is interesting to note that the two patents Aharonian felt had the most potential to have a significant impact on the computer industry were both user interface patents.

§ 5.38 —Summary

Is the third time the charm, dear reader? Did you skip right to this section? Way to go! So nice to see that you are a highly trainable life form. This time, though, we threw a little curve ball at you, so you might want to go back and skim some of the stuff in §§ **5.25** through **5.37** to see how we got here. Here's the surprising whiz-bang on patent protection for our Internet User Interface:

1. Patents are a viable way to obtain strong protection of our Internet User Interface.

§ 5.39 Conclusion

We've covered a lot of territory in the last 11,670 words. I hope you have found the ride to be an interesting and enlightening expedition through the wild and wacky world of intellectual property protection in the software user interface arena. For those of you underachievers who haven't read *any* of these 11,670 words (except, of course, the disclaimer section)—not even the strategically

---

[110] PATNEWS, *Worst Software Patents of the Decade Awarded to HP and IBM,* to subscribers via the Internet (Mar. 7, 1995).

placed three summary sections—you will be happy to know that I share your lack of pain. Here's all you need to know to obtain glib understanding of the protection options for the Internet User Interface:

1. The Internet User Interface is the human-perceptible thin line between (a) the code that makes the browsers, home pages, intranets, Web-enabled operating systems, and Web-enabled application programs tick; and (b) the content that is the real reason people are so jazzed about the Internet right now.

2. "No protection" is appropriate for the truly free portions of the Internet User Interface.

3. Trade secret protection is inappropriate for the Internet User Interface.

4. Trade dress protection is theoretically possible but practically a long shot for the Internet User Interface.

5. Copyright protection is a real crap shoot for the Internet User Interface; the odds of winning are pretty low and getting worse.

6. Patent protection for the Internet User Interface is strong, relatively stable, and viable.

7. Trade dress, copyright, and patent protection are not mutually exclusive, so all three should be considered for the Internet User Interface.

CHAPTER 6

COPYRIGHT, TRADEMARK, AND DATABASE ISSUES

Daniel Laster

§ 6.1   Introduction

The online world presents particular challenges with respect to trademarks, copyrights, and databases. A brief surf of the Internet reveals that on any particular site there may be layers of the above interests. For example, the name of the site may be functioning as either a trademark or service mark, copyrighted graphics are likely to appear on the page, the particular nonfunctional appearance of the site might come to be associated as distinctive of the site and thus constitute protectable trade dress, and there may be some collection of data on the site. In terms of determining what and how particular content from a site may be used, as well as how a Web site's owner may protect the various elements of its site, the purpose of this chapter is to provide a brief overview of the law concerning copyright, trademark, and database protection.[1] As a practical matter, one should conduct a review of all elements on the site (names, logos, graphics, text, layout, audio, audiovisual) to assess whether protectable interests of third parties may be implicated. It should be noted that there are a host of additional considerations which must be assessed in connection with setting up a Web site which are beyond the scope of this chapter—defamation, data privacy, publicity rights, obscenity regulations, and contest rules, to name a few.

§ 6.2   Copyright

Copyright protects a variety of creative expressions: literary works, musical works (both lyrics and compositions), dramatic works, pantomimes and choreographic works, pictorial, graphic, and sculptural works, motion pictures and other audiovisual works, sound recordings, and architectural works.[2] Computer programs and computer databases are protected as literary works.[3] Not surprisingly, any given Web site may combine any number of these types of works.

---

[1] The views expressed in this chapter are solely those of the author and may reflect positions not subscribed to by the editors. In addition, many of the issues are in flux. Accordingly, before counseling clients, the reader is strongly encouraged to obtain and independently assess up-to-date source materials.

[2] 17 U.S.C. § 102(a).

[3] *Id.* § 101.

§ 6.3 —Rights of Copyright Owner

The copyright owner has several exclusive rights:

1. Making copies
2. Making derivative works
3. Distributing copies
4. Publicly performing or displaying a work
5. Importing copies of a work.[4]

In the case of computer programs and sound recordings, the distribution right includes the right to control distribution in the form of rental of the work.[5] Not surprisingly, the online context raises a host of issues concerning most of the copyright rights.

§ 6.4 —The Reproduction Right

The following acts were all identified in the United States government's 1995 White Paper on the National Information Infrastructure as involving reproduction of copies:

• When a work is placed into a computer, whether on a disk, diskette, ROM, or other storage device or in RAM for more than a very brief period, a copy is made.

• When a printed work is "scanned" into a digital file, a copy—the digital file itself—is made.

• When other works—including photographs, motion pictures, or sound recordings—are digitized, copies are made.

• Whenever a digitized file is "uploaded" from a user's computer to a bulletin board system (BBS) or other server, a copy is made.

• Whenever a digitized file is "downloaded" from a BBS or other server, a copy is made.

• When a file is transferred from one computer network user to another, multiple copies generally are made.

• Under current technology, when an end-user's computer is employed as a "dumb" terminal to access a file resident on another computer such as a BBS or Internet host, a copy of at least the portion viewed is made in the user's computer. Without such copying into the RAM or buffer of the user's computer, no screen display would be possible.[6]

---

[4] The first four rights are provided by 17 U.S.C. § 106. The exclusive right to control importation of copies or phonorecords is covered by 17 U.S.C. § 602(a).

[5] 17 U.S.C. § 109(b).

[6] The Report of the Working Group on Intellectual Property Rights, Intellectual Property and the National Information Infrastructure 65–66 (1995) [hereinafter White Paper].

Accordingly, there are multiple ways in which the reproduction right may be implicated in the online context. As discussed in §§ **6.10** and **6.11,** one of the biggest challenges is determining who is liable for any given act of reproduction.

§ 6.5   —The Right to Make Derivative Works

Any time a party modifies, adapts, translates, revises, or edits a substantial part of a work, the exclusive right to make derivative works is implicated. Whether the part used is "substantial" is measured qualitatively. This right is most likely implicated where a site builder includes some adaptation of a copyrighted work on a Web site without the permission of the underlying copyright owner.

§ 6.6   —The Distribution Right

The Copyright Act provides that the copyright owner has the exclusive right "to distribute copies or phonorecords of the copyrighted work to the public by sale or other transfer of ownership, or by rental, lease, or lending."[7]

Whether electronic transmission is within the distribution right is unclear.[8] One federal district court has held that the unauthorized uploading and subsequent downloading of digitized photographs by BBS subscribers "implicated" the right of distribution in an action against the BBS operator.[9] Although there are reasonable arguments that it does fall within that right, the recent White Paper proposal includes a recommended revision to the definition of *distribution* to confirm or clarify the point.[10]

§ 6.7   —The Public Display and Performance Rights

The definition of *public performance* or *public display* under the Copyright Act readily accommodates the online context.

---

[7] 17 U.S.C. § 106(3).

[8] "Distribution" is not a defined term in the Copyright Act. Interestingly, "transmit" is defined in § 101 of the Copyright Act and is used in the definition relating to "publicly" displaying or performing a work. The term "transmit" does not appear in the sections dealing with the distribution right.

[9] Playboy Enters. Inc. v. Frena, 839 F. Supp. 1552 (M.D. Fla. 1993). *See also* Sega Enters. Ltd. v. MAPHIA, 857 F. Supp. 679 (N.D. Cal. 1994) (unauthorized copying and distribution were included in court's factual findings, but infringement of distribution right was not expressly reached in conclusions of law).

[10] White Paper at 213–17.

To perform or display a work "publicly" means—

(1) to perform or display it at a place open to the public or at any place where a substantial number of persons outside of a normal circle of a family and its social acquaintances is gathered; or

(2) to transmit or otherwise communicate a performance or display of the work to a place specified by clause (1) or to the public, by means of any device or process, whether the members of the public capable of receiving the performance or display receive it in the same place or in separate places and at the same time or at different times.[11]

As such, the posting of graphics on a Web site would appear to implicate the public display right since such posting is a transmission which enables "display of the work to ... [members of] the public ... whether [they are] capable of receiving ... it in the same place or in separate places and at the same time or at different times." One federal district court has held the display right was violated where copyrighted photographs were posted on a BBS.[12]

Although at first blush this analysis would seem to apply categorically to public display and public performance, this right raises some interesting issues which require careful consideration of the particular technology by which material is transmitted. When an audio file is posted and may be downloaded for subsequent playback,[13] there are substantial questions about what rights are implicated. Although the reproduction right would appear to be implicated, it is less clear if a distribution is occurring or if a public performance is involved. Arguably the better view is that a distribution has occurred, but not a public performance. This view is supported by the White Paper.

> A distinction must be made between transmissions of *copies* of works and transmissions of *performances* or *displays* of works. When a copy of a work is transmitted over wires, fiber optics, satellite signals or other modes in digital form so that it may be captured in a user's computer, without the capability of simultaneous "rendering" or "showing," it has rather clearly not been performed. Thus, for example, a file comprising the digitized version of a motion picture might be transferred from a copyright owner to an end user via the Internet without the public performance right being implicated. When, however, the motion picture is "rendered"—by showing its images in sequence—so that users with the requisite hardware and software might watch it with or without copying the performance, then, under the current law, a "performance" has occurred.[14]

---

[11] 17 U.S.C. § 101.

[12] Playboy Enters. Inc. v. Frena, 839 F. Supp. 1552 (M.D. Fla. 1993).

[13] The same issue concerning public display arises when material is contained in a file and the file is posted for download—that is, the material is not readily viewable on the Web site, but rather a file on the site may be downloaded. In such case, reproduction and distribution rights may be implicated, rather than public display.

[14] White Paper at 71 (footnotes omitted).

Thus, when an audio file is transmitted, a distribution may occur, but not a public performance. In contrast, where audio is streamed (and is capable of "simultaneous 'rendering' or 'showing'"), public performance more aptly tracks the context.[15]

§ 6.8 —The Importation Right

The online environment also raises challenges concerning application of the importation right. For example, is the transmission or downloading of a file from a Web site operated on a server outside the United States to an individual in the United States an infringement of the importation right? There is no definitive answer to this question, but there are serious doubts about whether the current importation prohibition in the Copyright Act covers transmissions. The White Paper states:

> The applicability of the importation provisions to the transmission of works into the United States via the NII (or GII) may be debated. Nevertheless, the importation right is an outgrowth of the distribution right, both of which refer to "copies or phonorecords." A data stream can contain a copyrighted work in the form of electronic impulses, but those impulses do not fall within the definition of "copies" or "phonorecords." Therefore, it may be argued that the transmission of a reproduction of a copyrighted work via international communication links fails to constitute an "importation" under the current law, just as it is less than clear that a domestic transmission of a reproduction of a work constitutes a distribution of a copy under a literal reading of the Copyright Act.[16]

The White Paper includes a recommendation to amend the language in § 602 of the Copyright Act to clarify or confirm that importation by transmission is proscribed.[17]

§ 6.9 —Digital Transmission of Sound Recordings

Effective February 1, 1996, the copyright owner of a sound recording has the right to control digital transmissions pursuant to the Digital Performance Right in Sound Recordings Act of 1995.[18] Prior to that date, the public performance right did not attach to sound recordings. The significance of this new law is that prior to making a digital transmission of a sound recording a party needs to

---

[15] One should note that performing rights societies may seek to characterize either scenario as falling within the public performance right.

[16] White Paper at 108–09.

[17] *Id.* at 221.

[18] Pub. L. No. 104-39 (1995).

consider both the record company's rights in the recording as well as the under-lying music publisher's public performance or distribution right. The Act distinguishes among three types of digital performances: subscription transmissions, nonsubscription transmissions, and transmissions by interactive services.[19] In the case of interactive service use, individual licenses must be negotiated, whereas certain noninteractive transmissions may qualify for statutory licensing. The statutory license rates and terms will be determined either by industry negotiations or by a Copyright Arbitration Royalty Panel.

§ 6.10   —Theories of Liability

Two forms of liability exist under copyright law: direct infringement and indirect infringement. A claim for *direct infringement* exists against the party who directly exercises one of the exclusive rights noted in §§ 6.3 through 6.8 without the permission of the copyright owner or as authorized by law.[20] *Indirect infringement* stems from use of the phrase "to authorize" in § 106 of the Copyright Act. Two forms of indirect infringement have been recognized by the courts: contributory infringement and vicarious liability.

Contributory infringement occurs when a third party materially contributes, causes, or induces the direct infringer to commit the infringing conduct. Constructive or actual knowledge is an element of contributory infringement.

Vicarious liability exists in the traditional context of respondeat superior, such as the employer-employee situation. In addition, there is a line of cases—known as the "dance hall" cases—in which the courts have recognized that a dance hall proprietor is accountable for the conduct of a party using the premises even if the operator does not know that particular music is being performed without a license.[21] The test which has evolved in these cases is that two conditions must be met for liability to attach: (1) a party must have the ability to control the conduct of the direct infringer; and (2) a party must obtain a direct financial benefit from the conduct of the direct infringer.[22] It remains unclear whether this theory will apply in the online context. Arguably the differences between the online environment and the dance hall scenario support a different outcome—that is, the test should not categorically be extended to the Internet.

---

[19] The Act defines *interactive services* as "one that enables a member of the public to receive, on request, a transmission of a particular sound recording chosen by or on behalf of the recipient."

[20] The Copyright Act includes a number of exceptions to a claim: these exceptions appear in 17 U.S.C. §§ 107–113. The most significant exception is fair use, discussed in § 6.12.

[21] *See* Dreamland Ball Room, Inc. v. Shapiro, Bernstein & Co., 36 F.2d 354 (7th Cir. 1929). *See also* Shapiro, Bernstein & Co. v. H.L. Green Co., 316 F.2d 304, 307 (2d Cir. 1963), for a summary of the law and cites to numerous cases.

[22] Shapiro, Bernstein & Co. v. H.L. Green Co., 316 F.2d 304, 307 (2d Cir. 1963).

§ 6.11 —Liability of Transmission Intermediaries

One of the most significant unresolved issues regarding potential copyright infringement in Internet transmissions concerns the scope of responsibility of various parties involved in the transmission chain. For example, does an Internet access provider or online service provider commit direct infringement when it incidentally stores a copy of material on its server in the course of transmitting material posted by an individual? In *Religious Technology Center v. Netcom On-Line Communication Services, Inc.,*[23] the district court held that such intermediate copying was not direct infringement. In addition, the court rejected a vicarious liability theory but held that contributory infringement might lie. The court adopted a fairly high threshold for notice before liability would attach, particularly in cases of possible fair use.

> Although a mere unsupported allegation of infringement by a copyright owner may not automatically put a defendant on notice of infringing activity, Netcom's position that liability must be unequivocal is unsupportable. While perhaps the typical infringing activities of BBSs will involve copying software, where BBS operators are better equipped to judge infringement, the fact that this involves written works should not distinguish it. Where works contain copyright notices within them, as here, it is difficult to argue that a defendant did not know that the works were copyrighted. To require proof of valid registrations would be impractical and would perhaps take too long to verify, making it impossible for a copyright holder to protect his or her works in some cases, as works are automatically deleted less than two weeks after they are posted. The court is more persuaded by the argument that it is beyond the ability of a BBS operator to quickly and fairly determine when a use is not infringement where there is at least a colorable claim of fair use. *Where a BBS operator cannot reasonably verify a claim of infringement, either because of a possible fair use defense, the lack of copyright notices on the copies, or the copyright holder's failure to provide the necessary documentation to show that there is a likely infringement, the operator's lack of knowledge will be found reasonable and there will be no liability for contributory infringement for allowing the continued distribution of the works on its system.*[24]

If other courts adopt the *Netcom* standard,[25] parties who are not directly posting material, but rather are acting in some fashion as a transmission intermediary, may seek to adopt procedures along the lines of those now adopted by Netcom.[26]

---

[23] 907 F. Supp. 1361 (N.D. Cal. 1995).

[24] *Id.* at 1374 (emphasis added).

[25] It should be noted that at least one court has held a BBS operator directly liable for postings by members of the BBS. Playboy Enters. Inc. v. Frena, 839 F. Supp. 1552 (M.D. Fla. 1993). Although the defendant claimed to have had no notice of the alleged infringement, the facts in the case would have provided ample support for a finding of constructive knowledge under a contributory liability theory, and the author submits that such a finding would have constituted a better rationale for the court's conclusion.

[26] Netcom's procedures appear on its home page. The specific terms on Netcom's home page are a result of its settlement of the lawsuit, but they are nonetheless instructive from a practical perspective in terms of how to address alleged copyright complaints.

§ 6.12   —Fair Use

Even when there is a prima facie claim of infringement, a fair use defense may lie. Section 107 of the Copyright Act provides:

> Notwithstanding the provisions of sections 106 and 106A, the fair use of a copyrighted work, including such use by reproduction in copies or phonorecords or by any other means specified by that section, for purposes such as criticism, comment, news reporting, teaching (including multiple copies for classroom use), scholarship, or research, is not an infringement of copyright. In determining whether the use made of a work in any particular case is a fair use the factors to be considered shall include—
>
> (1)   the purpose and character of the use, including whether such use is of a commercial nature or is for nonprofit educational purposes;
>
> (2)   the nature of the copyrighted work;
>
> (3)   the amount and substantiality of the portion used in relation to the copyrighted work as a whole; and
>
> (4)   the effect of the use upon the potential market for or value of the copyrighted work.[27]

Several comments are in order about fair use. First, the list of purposes outlined in § 107 is not exhaustive, and accordingly there may be instances where a fair use defense could succeed in circumstance not expressly stated in the section.[28] Second, the fact that a use is specifically mentioned in § 107 does not create a presumption that a use is permissible.[29] Third, the Supreme Court in *Sony Corporation v. Universal City Studios, Inc.,*[30] stated a presumption that all commercial uses are presumptively unfair.[31] However, in *Campbell v. Acuff-Rose Music, Inc.,*[32] the Supreme Court stated that this presumption, although not dispositive, is most difficult to overcome in instances of "mere duplication." The Court recognized that the presumption can be most readily overcome if the defendant's use is transformative. Fourth, the courts have consistently found the fourth factor—the effect of the use on the market value for the original—to be the most important factor.[33]

One interesting issue is how to analyze any copies of material on a Web site which may reside in a user's hard drive as a consequence of the ordinary use of browser software. Although no court has addressed the issue, it would seem reasonable to characterize such a copy as a permissible fair use which occurred in the ordinary course of viewing a site. Perhaps a more interesting question is

---

[27] 17 U.S.C. § 107.

[28] Harper & Row, Publishers, Inc. v. Nation Enters., 471 U.S. 539, 561 (1985).

[29] *Id.*

[30] 464 U.S. 417 (1984).

[31] *Id.* at 451.

[32] 114 S. Ct. 1164, 1177 (1994).

[33] *See, e.g.,* Harper & Row, 471 U.S. 539.

whether replication of a site on another server for purposes of expediting transmission could likewise be viewed as a fair use. The only case to date which touches on this issue is *Netcom.*[34] In *Netcom,* the court recognized that intermediate copies of material were made by Netcom in the course of transmitting material. The court held that such copying in the course of transmission was not a direct infringement, but rather should be viewed as contributory infringement.

> Accepting that copies were made [on Netcom's servers], Netcom argues that Erlich, and not Netcom, is directly liable for the copying. *MAI [Systems Corporation v. Peak Computer, Inc.*[35]] did not address the question raised in this case: whether possessors of computers are liable for incidental copies automatically made on their computers using their software as part of a process initiated by a third party. Netcom correctly distinguishes MAI on the ground that Netcom did not take any affirmative action that directly resulted in copying plaintiffs' works other than by installing and maintaining a system whereby software automatically forwards messages received from subscribers onto the Usenet, and temporarily stores copies on its system. Netcom's actions, to the extent that they created a copy of plaintiffs' works, are necessary to having a working system for transmitting Usenet postings to and from the Internet. Unlike the defendants in MAI, neither Netcom nor Klemesrud initiated the copying. The defendants in MAI turned on their customers' computers thereby creating temporary copies of the operating system, whereas Netcom's and Klemesrud's systems can operate without any human intervention. The court believes that Netcom's act of designing or implementing a system that automatically and uniformly creates temporary copies of all data sent through it is not unlike that of the owner of a copying machine who lets the public make copies with it. . . . Although copyright is a strict liability statute, there should still be some element of volition or causation which is lacking where a defendant's system is merely used to create a copy by a third party.[36]

Accordingly, there is some support for the proposition that replication may not in every case constitute direct infringement. However, one of the most significant implications of such replication is that the Web site owner whose site has been replicated will not receive an accurate count of "hits" to its site.[37] The undercounting will equal the number of users who actually view the site owner's material as stored on the server which replicates the page.

---

[34] Religious Technology Ctr. v. Netcom On-Line Communication Servs., Inc., 907 F. Supp. 1361 (N.D. Cal. 1995), discussed in § **6.11.**

[35] 991 F.2d 511 (9th Cir. 1993).

[36] 907 F. Supp. at 1368.

[37] Another issue relates to potential staleness of content. If the replication server does not refresh the replicated material on a very regular basis, it may contain material which has been updated by the site owner on its site.

§ 6.13 —Misconceptions about Copyright on the World Wide Web

The following list is presented to correct the most common misconceptions about copyright law and the Internet.

10 Rules to Remember for Copyright in Cyberspace

1. Copyright law *does* extend to the Internet—albeit tough questions regarding which country's copyright laws apply will arise.

2. Do not assume that any material posted is public domain, particularly since the 1989 amendment to the Copyright Act makes clear that lack of a copyright notice does not affect whether copyright subsists in a work.

3. Fair use remains a consideration, but it does not make any use permissible merely by virtue of posting material on the Net.

4. When a person forwards material to others, such conduct *may* be viewed as a distribution, reproduction, publication, public display, or performance, or even an importation.

5. The transmission of audio files may involve the rights of both the author of the underlying musical work and the recording company (this latter twist is due to the Digital Performance Right in Sound Recordings Act of 1995).[38]

6. Before simply accessing and reproducing data from a site, consider both any potential compilation copyright under U.S. law, as well as the source of the data—current United Kingdom law provides for database protection, and the European Community (EC) Database Directive requires member states to implement national law by January 1, 1998 (even if a database is not protectable under United States law as an original expression under the *Feist* decision).[39]

7. In addition to copyright, take note of any restrictions which may purport to limit use of material or data on a site. The significance of such restrictions should be read with an appreciation of the Seventh Circuit's decision in *ProCD*.[40]

8. Even if you are merely an Internet access provider or online service provider acting solely as a retransmitter, take note that at least one court, albeit

---

[38] Pub. L. No. 104-39 (1995), discussed in § **6.9.**

[39] Feist Publications, Inc. v. Rural Tel. Serv. Co., 499 U.S. 340 (1991), discussed in § **6.23.** So, beware of European equivalents to the white pages online (and check on the current state of United States law on database protection).

[40] ProCD, Inc. v. Zeidenberg, No. 96-1139, 1996 U.S. App. LEXIS 14951 (7th Cir. 1996), discussed in § **6.24.**

most likely in an aberrant decision, has held a BBS liable as a direct—as contrasted with indirect—infringer.[41] At a minimum, consider adopting procedures for addressing scenarios where you are given notice of potentially infringing material. The current procedures of Netcom are an example, and they are a direct result of the suit by the Church of Scientology against Netcom relating to material transmitted by a Netcom subscriber, a former Scientologist, over the Netcom system.[42]

9.   Review carefully whether content suppliers have the necessary rights (either as owner or licensee) to permit you to post or transmit the content.[43]

10.   Do not assume that use for one purpose equates with use for any purpose. One use may be covered by a license or be a permissible fair use, and another, seemingly similar, use may be infringement. Accordingly, each use should be analyzed in its context to determine if the use is lawful.

§ 6.14   Trademark

A *trademark* is any word, name, symbol, or device (including sounds) used by a person to identify and distinguish the source of that party's goods or services from the goods or services of another party.[44]

Trademark rights are generally accorded on a national basis.[45] In addition, unlike copyright and patent law, state trademark rights coexist with federal rights. Under United States law, priority stems from use of a mark—commonly referred to as "common law rights"—whereas in most countries all rights stem from registration.[46]

---

[41] Playboy Enters. Inc. v. Frena, 839 F. Supp. 1552 (M.D. Fla. 1993), discussed in **§ 6.11.** Stay tuned to possible law reform relating to online service provider liability. This is an area in which content owners are pitted against the parties involved in transmission, such as telephone companies, Internet access providers, and online service providers such as America Online.

[42] Religious Technology Ctr. v. Netcom On-Line Communication Servs., Inc., 907 F. Supp. 1361 (N.D. Cal. 1995), discussed in **§ 6.11.**

[43] Although beyond the scope of this chapter, publicity rights are often overlooked. The practitioner should make sure that the distinct rights of the copyright holder and any distinct publicity rights are evaluated. Also, practitioners should be wary of the trap of advising that a photo of a person does not violate the right of publicity and fail to note that there may still be a need to license the copyright in the photograph.

[44] 15 U.S.C. § 1127. A *service mark* is a mark which is used to identify services rather than goods. The term *trademark* is often used to cover both types of marks, and that is how the term is used herein unless specifically noted.

[45] The new community trademark is an exception. A successful community trademark registrant will have rights throughout the European Community based upon a single application.

[46] Generally, the United Kingdom and its commonwealths and former colonies follow the common law principle, whereas civil code countries recognize registration-based trademark rights.

§ 6.15 —Scope of Right

A trademark owner has the right to prevent another party from using any word, name, symbol, or device that is *likely to cause confusion* with the trademark owner's mark.[47] The test does not require actual confusion, but rather that confusion is likely.

§ 6.16 —Dilution

In addition to trademark infringement, federal[48] and certain state laws protect certain well-known or famous marks from dilution. The federal statute protects against the dilution of the "distinctive quality" of a "famous" mark. In contrast to trademark infringement, dilution does not require likelihood of confusion. Thus, whereas the classic case of infringement occurs when a competitor adopts a trademark owner's mark, competition between the parties is not required for a dilution claim. It is worth noting that the federal statute does not expressly mention "tarnishment" as a form of dilution,[49] whereas a number of state statutes include tarnishment.[50] As such, if a party uses a famous mark in a manner which might be viewed as disparaging, this use might form a basis for a state law dilution claim, but not necessarily a federal claim. Under the federal statute, injunctive relief is available in any case of dilution, but damages, attorneys' fees, and destruction orders are available only if the defendant's conduct was willful. This statute has been the basis for district court orders requiring a domain name reservant to transfer domain names to a federal trademark registrant of a famous trademark.[51]

§ 6.17 —Difference in Infringement for Trademark and Copyright

The trademark infringement test differs from that under copyright for reproduction. The essence of trademark infringement is confusion, whereas in copyright the issue is substantial similarity of two works based upon copying. Thus, it is irrelevant to a copyright claim that consumers are likely to be confused, yet it is

---

[47] 15 U.S.C. § 1114(1).

[48] Federal Trademark Dilution Act of 1995, Pub. L. No. 104-98, 110 Stat. 985 (1995).

[49] However, as noted in Intermatic Inc. v. Toeppen, 40 U.S.P.Q.2d 1412 (N.D. Ill. 1996), discussed in § **6.21,** the legislative history to the federal statute states, "The definition is defined to encompass all forms of dilution recognized by the courts, including dilution by blurring, by tarnishment and disparagement, and by diminishment."

[50] *See, e.g.,* Minn. Stat. Ann. § 325 D. 165 (1994).

[51] See § **6.21.**

essential to a trademark claim.[52] Further, it is unnecessary to a trademark claim that the defendant copied the plaintiff's mark,[53] yet copying is essential to a copyright claim.

§ 6.18 —Intent-to-Use Trademark Applications

The Trademark Law Reform Act of 1988 established that a party could file a United States application for registration based upon a bona fide intent to use a mark, as an alternative to an application based upon actual use of a trademark in interstate or foreign commerce.[54] The Act provides that upon registration (which requires evidence of use of the mark in interstate commerce), federal trademark rights will vest in an intent-to-use applicant according priority from the date of filing the intent-to-use application, rather than the subsequent date of first use. In the online world, this is very significant because it enables a party to file an application prior to announcing its plans and thus establish priority based upon the federal filing date.

§ 6.19 —Transforming the Nature of Use of a Trademark or Service Mark

One of the fascinating aspects of the Internet is that in some instances parties who had used their trademarks solely to identify their goods are now providing services online. For example, a software publisher of a multimedia CD-ROM program may now provide access to information based upon the content of the CD-ROM product. Although the use of a mark on the packaging for the product was trademark use, use of that same mark in the online world may constitute service mark use. Similarly, many traditional hard copy news and entertainment publishers (whether newspapers or periodicals) may now find themselves using their trademarks online in connection with provision of information services. Accordingly, trademark owners should carefully evaluate whether they need to supplement their portfolios with service mark filings to cover their online use. In evaluating this issue, it is useful to consider whether the Internet is being used solely to market products or also as a distribution method. If the Internet is used for distribution, then you should scrutinize whether the distribution is best characterized as product distribution or service provision.

---

[52] Confusion is not required for a dilution claim.

[53] Copying of a trademark may lead a court to conclude that confusion is likely. In addition, copying is considered in determining whether willful trademark infringement has occurred.

[54] 15 U.S.C. § 1051(b) (1988).

§ 6.20   —Foreign Clearance and Protection

The international nature of the Internet should lead trademark owners to take a more careful look—both for purposes of clearance as well as protection—at international markets. Unfortunately, it will most likely be years before the law of particular jurisdictions resolves whether the mere fact that a Web site is accessible in a jurisdiction constitutes use of a trademark in the jurisdiction for purposes of infringement analysis. Accordingly, it is prudent to take a broad territorial approach both to clearance and protection for use of a mark on the Internet.

§ 6.21   —Trademark and Domain Name Interplay

A major issue that has arisen in the online context is the interplay of trademark rights and Internet domain names. Although the law remains unsettled, it appears that courts are recognizing that trademark owners have the same ability to take action against a domain name reservant as does a trade name or corporate name reservant—that is, if the use of the domain name is likely to cause confusion with the common law or registered trademark, an infringement action will lie. Furthermore, in the case of a famous mark, an action will lie against use of a domain name which incorporates the famous trademark if it can be shown that inclusion of the identical mark in a domain name will dilute the famous trademark.[55] In fact, the legislative history of the Trademark Law Reform Act of 1988 suggests that one of the Act's purposes was to address the conduct of individuals reserving domain names incorporating the famous marks of third parties.[56]

An area where one can expect continued fallout is the scope and enforceability of domain name dispute resolution procedures. The focus has been on the Network Solutions, Inc. (NSI) rules governing ".com" domain names. However, one should expect that similar conflicts will arise in international jurisdictions in connection with other country domain names. The most recent NSI rules provide that a United States or foreign trademark registrant can contact NSI to

---

[55] Hasbro, Inc. v. Internet Entertainment Group, Ltd., 1996 WL 84853 (W.D. Wash. 1996) (preliminary injunction against defendant's use of "candyland.com" to identify sexually explicit Internet site, pursuant to federal and Washington state antidilution statutes); Intermatic Inc. v. Toeppen, 40 U.S.P.Q.2d 1412 (N.D. Ill. 1996) (summary judgment granted in favor of plaintiff, the federal registrant of famous mark Intermatic, against defendant's reservation of "intermatic.com" under federal and Illinois state antidilution statutes).

[56] Senator Patrick J. Leahy (D-Vermont) stated: "[I]t is my hope that this anti-dilution statute can help stem the use of deceptive Internet addresses taken by those who are choosing marks that are associated with the products and reputations of others." Remarks of Sen. Leahy in the U.S. Senate, Dec. 29, 1995, Cong. Rec. S. 19312 (104th Cong. 1995) (quoted in *Intermatic,* 1996 U.S. Dist. LEXIS 14878, p. 12).

seek cancellation of a domain with a name identical to a previously issued United States or foreign trademark registration. NSI will then contact the domain reservant, and if the reservant does not present evidence of a prior United States or foreign trademark registration, NSI will give the reservant notice that the domain will be withdrawn. If a dispute arises between the trademark registrant and the domain reservant, NSI will "freeze" the domain until it receives a court ruling resolving the dispute.

As a practical matter, companies should consider reserving both .com and any foreign domains which may be pertinent to a company's business plan. If a company has a large number of marks, it may be prudent to reserve the domain for the company name, and then rely primarily upon trademark rights. Different rules apply for domain reservation in individual country domain registries.[57] Also, there are now proposals for additional registries operated by private entities which would result, potentially, in different parties having the same prefix to distinct domains established by different registries (for example, "fixit.com" versus "fixit.xyz"). Conceptually, this would permit coexistence of distinct yet similar domain names provided that: (1) the prefix is not a famous trademark; and (2) the domains are not used by parties operating in the same field of activity (unless the prefix is either generic or descriptive of (without secondary meaning attaching) the field of activity).

§ 6.22 Database Protection

The rules which govern protection of data collections on Internet sites is another area which is likely to receive increasing attention and which should not be overlooked. Four bodies of law should be analyzed: (1) copyright; (2) contract; (3) state misappropriation of property or unfair competition; and (4) sui generis database protection

§ 6.23 —Copyright

Databases are protected under the Copyright Act as compilations.

> A "compilation" is a work formed by the collection and assembling of preexisting materials or of data that are selected, coordinated, or arranged in such a way that the resulting work as a whole constitutes an original work of authorship. The term "compilation" includes collective works.[58]

The Copyright Office has issued rules governing registration of databases.[59]

---

[57] For instance, in France there is currently a limit of five domains which any given company may reserve.

[58] 17 U.S.C. § 101.

[59] *See* Circular 65 of the Copyright Office, Copyright Registration for Automated Databases.

The Supreme Court's decision in *Feist Publications, Inc. v. Rural Telephone Service Co.*[60] is the leading case on the issue of when collections of data are copyrightable. In *Feist,* the Court held that a telephone company's white pages were not copyrightable because the data contained in the listings was not arranged in an original manner and lacked the minimal degree of creativity needed for copyright protection. In reaching its decision, the Court rejected the "sweat of the brow" theory for protection of collections of data.

Since *Feist,* various circuit court decisions do not provide any clear sense of what will be needed to have a copyrightable collection of data.[61] As a result, a party seeking to use the data from a Web site should take care to ensure that use of that data does not risk infringement of copyright.

§ 6.24 —Contract

Aside from copyright, contract law may provide a basis for database protection. In the recent decision in *ProCD, Inc. v. Zeidenberg*[62] the Seventh Circuit held that contract law can protect databases even when the database is not copyrightable. In *ProCD,* the defendant sought to use the plaintiff's CD-ROM software which contained white pages directory information. The plaintiff's shrink-wrap license restricted use of the product and data contained in the software. The court held that the contract terms were enforceable. Accordingly, parties should undertake a careful analysis of any purported notices or contract terms on a Web site and assess whether they may be construed as forming part of a contract for use of the data on the site. If that is possible, then there may be a risk of a breach of contract claim in use of the data, *even if the data is not copyrightable,* or the nature of use does not implicate a right protected by the Copyright Act.

§ 6.25 —Misappropriation

State misappropriation or unfair competition law should also be considered before a party uses data from another Web site. In *NBA v. STATS,*[63] the district

---

[60] 499 U.S. 340 (1991).

[61] *Compare* CCC Info. Servs., Inc. v. MacLean Hunter Mkt. Reports, Inc., 44 F.3d 61 (2d Cir. 1994) (automobile "Red Book" containing used car valuations was copyrightable, and valuations were original creations dependent upon selection and presentation of various factors, such as car options, miles, and used car region) *with* BellSouth Advertising & Publishing Corp. v. Donnelly Info. Publishing, Inc., 999 F.2d 1436 (11th Cir. 1993), *cert. denied,* 114 S. Ct. 943 (1994) (headings for yellow pages held not copyrightable expression because idea merged with expression since headings were viewed as practically inevitable).

[62] No. 96-1139, 1996 U.S. App. LEXIS 14951 (7th Cir. 1996).

[63] 96 Civ. 1615, 1996 U.S. Dist. LEXIS 10262 (S.D.N.Y. 1996). This case is currently on appeal to the Second Circuit. Numerous amicii briefs have been filed because of the potential implications of the rationale.

court applied New York state law misappropriation theory to find the defendants liable for the transmission of real-time sports game data during the game. Although the holding is very likely limited to the unique facts, the case is likely to lead to questions about the scope of data which may be protected against use and transmission.

§ 6.26 —Sui Generis Protection

Aside from the above theories, sui generis protection of databases has been given increasing attention outside the United States. Current United Kingdom law protects databases, even when the data collection would not qualify for copyright protection under United States law. In addition, a 1996 EC Directive on Database Protection provides that all member states must afford national protection to databases by February 1, 1998. The EC Directive provides that the database owner shall have the exclusive right to control extraction and re-utilization. As in the case of United Kingdom law, the EC Directive would cover databases which would not be protected under United States copyright law. Finally, there is currently some prospect that United States legislation for sui generis protection of databases may be enacted in the upcoming years.[64] One of the key challenges in adopting a sui generis approach to databases is whether doctrine akin to fair use as well as First Amendment principles will be sufficiently articulated or developed to address competing needs for use of data.

§ 6.27 —Practice Pointers for Use of Data on a Web Site

In view of the factors discussed in §§ 6.22 through 6.26, the following steps should be taken in considering use of data:

1. Determine if the data collection is copyrightable, and if so, whether the proposed extraction or use would constitute copyright infringement.
2. Regardless of copyright, any terms or notices on the Web site should be evaluated.
3. The nature of the data—particularly if real-time game statistics or equivalent data is involved—should be evaluated from a misappropriation theory as applied in the *NBA v. STATS*[65] case.

---

[64] As evidenced by the tabling of action on a database treaty at the WIPO negotiations in Geneva in December 1996, this will be a hotly debated area. In May 1996, House Judiciary Chairman Carlos J. Moorehead introduced H.R. 3531, the Database Investment and Intellectual Property Antipiracy Act of 1996. No action was taken on the proposed legislation, and it is unclear if the bill will be reintroduced.

[65] 939 F. Supp. 1071 (S.D.N.Y. 1996), discussed in § 6.25.

4. Consider the national source of the data. If it is from Europe, determine whether the proposed extraction or re-use may be covered by local sui generis database protection law.

§ 6.28 Conclusion

As with many Internet issues, the law relating to copyright, trademark, and database protection is largely unchartered. It will likely take years for many issues to be resolved, either through legislation or judge-made law. The careful practitioner will critically assess traditional legal principles, with particular regard for the medium and the specific characteristics of the technology in use.

CHAPTER 7

STANDARDS

Dan Crouse

§ 7.1   Introduction

Standards are a cornerstone of Internet technical development and evolution.[1] The existence of a common networking protocol[2] makes it practical to interconnect the myriad networks that collectively form the Internet. Similar roles are played by standards regarding documents,[3] security,[4] and a host of other subject

---

[1] The views expressed in this chapter are solely those of the contributor, and may reflect positions not subscribed to by the editor or other contributors. The bulk of the research for this chapter was conducted on the World Wide Web. As a result, it is possible that some of the cited source materials may be relatively transitory and short-lived. In addition, many of the issues and organizations addressed are in flux. Before counseling clients, the reader is strongly encouraged to obtain and independently assess up-to-date source materials.

[2] The Transmission Control Protocol/Internet Protocol (TCP/IP) is the basic protocol for the networks that are connected to form the Internet. It is, however, only one portion of the suite of protocols upon which the Internet is based. Other such protocols include Simple Mail Transfer Protocol (SMTP) for e-mail, File Transfer Protocol (FTP) for file transfer, and Simple Network Management Protocol (SNMP) for network management. Networks that are not based upon TCP/IP may also be connected to the Internet by gateways, although they are not always considered part of the Internet. *See* E. Krol, The Whole Internet 15 (2d ed. 1994). For the purpose of this discussion, the term *Internet* will be understood to include both the broadest internetwork of networks and the individual networks protected from intrusion by firewalls and referred to as *intranets*. *See* the Institute for Academic Technology root site, *Intranets: Readings and Resources* at
    http://www.iat.unc.edu/guides/irg-34.html.

[3] For example, the Standard Generalized Markup Language (SGML) was adopted by the International Standards Organization (ISO) in 1986 as a standard for providing platform-independent and application-independent documents, while preserving the document's formatting information, as well as linked information. The Hypertext Markup Language (HTML) is a markup language for hypertext documents used in World Wide Web clients and supported by SGML.

[4] Examples relating to the security field include Secure Sockets Layer (SSL) and Private Communication Technology (PCT). See **§ 7.18** for a description of some of the additional subject matter areas that the Information Infrastructure Standards Panel (IISP) has identified as requiring standards to support the National Information Infrastructure (NII) and Global Information Infrastructure (GII).

matter areas. The support of "Internet standards" is a hallmark of most new products being developed for the Internet.[5]

Although various meanings are ascribed to the term *standard,*[6] for the purposes of this chapter, a standard will be defined as any specification of technology that has been approved or adopted for widespread use. A thorough understanding of such standards is made difficult by the sheer breadth of technologies involved,[7] the different ways in which standards arise,[8] and the multitude of organizations[9] involved in standards efforts. Still, a business person participating in standards work should have some familiarity with these issues. Similarly, an attorney representing standards bodies and consortia, as well as their members and participants, must sort through this complexity.

The goal of this chapter is to introduce the role played by standards in the evolving Internet and to describe some of the key organizations and legal issues involved in the standards process.[10] To that end, the chapter begins with general background information regarding standards,[11] followed by a comparison of *de facto* and *de jure* standards.[12] Next, the role of standards organizations is

---

[5] For example, Microsoft and Netscape have both expressed commitments to the support of Internet-related standards. *See* the Microsoft root site, *Microsoft Pledge on HTML Standards* at
    http://www.microsoft.com/internet/html
    and the Netscape root site, *Frequently Asked Questions About Netscape and Open Standards* at
    http://home.netscape.com/newref/std/standards_qa.html.

[6] For example, *standards* may be relatively broadly defined as "agreed upon specifications for the production of functionally compatible goods and services." R. Urowsky, *Market Definition and Standards,* in ALI-ABA, Antitrust/Intellectual Property Claims in High Technology Markets 19 (1995). Note that this definition does not describe (and is not limited by) the way in which such standards are "agreed upon." For a discussion of the distinction between standards reached by formal and informal agreement, see **§ 7.3.**

[7] The number of individuals, organizations, and technologies involved in *de jure* standards work is staggering. For example, the work of one organization, the ISO, has resulted in nearly 10,000 different standards covering a range of industries and technologies. Fortunately, the complexity of this topic can be reduced somewhat by restricting our field of interest to information technology and, more specifically, the Internet.

[8] See **§ 7.3** for a discussion of *de facto* versus *de jure* standards.

[9] See **§§ 7.12–7.24** for a discussion of some of the different organizations that play a role in the development and approval of Internet-related standards.

[10] As used herein, the *standards process* is broadly intended to encompass (a) the private development of technologies and their widespread adoption and practical acceptance as a standard, (b) the development or approval of technologies by consortia and formal standards organizations, and (c) various alternative approaches in between these two extremes. For additional general background information regarding standards work, *see* C. Cargill, Information Technology Standardization: Theory, Process, and Organizations (1989). The Association of Computing Machinery (ACM) periodical, *StandardView,* first published in 1993, also addresses computer-related standardization issues.

[11] **Section 7.2.**

[12] **Section 7.3.**

considered, including a discussion of the importance of such organizations,[13] how standards organizations differ,[14] and the challenges that the Internet presents for such organizations.[15] The chapter continues with a discussion of some recurring legal issues experienced by standards organizations and participants,[16] along with some strategies for addressing these issues. Next, some of the more important organizations associated with Internet standards development and approval are considered.[17] Finally, some recent trends in standards process and policy are outlined.[18]

§ 7.2 Background of Standards

The desire to provide standards as common frameworks for the implementation of technology is not a recent phenomenon. The International Telegraph Union (ITU)[19] was formed in 1865 to address technical, development, and policy issues relating to the nascent telecommunications industry. A similar organization was formed in 1906 to address international standardization issues relating to electrical products and systems.[20]

In contrast, the attention devoted to Internet standards is a more recent phenomenon.[21] Unlike the global telecommunications industry, the information technology (IT) industry was traditionally composed of standalone systems from individual vendors. The interconnection of system components was primarily a matter of interest to each vendor individually and of little interest to the broader community. As the networking of IT systems became increasingly important, however, the integration of systems from multiple vendors became essential.

---

[13] **Section 7.5.**

[14] **Section 7.6.**

[15] **Section 7.7.**

[16] **Sections 7.8–7.11.**

[17] **Sections 7.12–7.31.**

[18] **Sections 7.32–7.34.**

[19] See **§ 7.26.**

[20] For more information regarding the International Electrotechnical Commission (IEC), see **§ 7.15.**

[21] Additional factors that eventually lead to the demand for standards in the information technology industry are discussed in The Telecommunications Technology Committee, *Survey Report on Telecommunication-Related Forum's Activities* 5 (Mar. 1995) [hereinafter *Survey Report*], which states:

> [D]ue to the development of network globalization, increased downsizing in the environment with progress in decentralized processing technology, and development of various services utilizing advanced software technology, system integration in a multivendor environment became essential. Now, it has advanced into the world of open systems, such as OSI and UNIX.

(Footnotes omitted.)

Hence, the industry's growing interest in the development and implementation of standards.

The recent attention paid to standards by a broader community is perhaps also a function of the way in which the Internet evolved. Borne out of a research effort sponsored by the U.S. Defense Advanced Research Project Agency (DARPA) in the late 1960s, DARPA originally provided some central oversight over the system.[22] As the Internet has developed into a global network connecting many disparate organizations and individuals, however, DARPA's role gradually decreased and many management functions are now the responsibility of the Internet Society (ISOC).[23] Further technical evolution of such a vast enterprise under these conditions obviously requires considerable coordination, some of which is provided by the development of, and reliance upon, standards.[24]

§ 7.3   Types of Standards

Throughout history, standards have typically resulted through one of two processes: (1) widespread industry adoption of a technology; or (2) organizational proclamation of a particular technology as a "standard." Standards resulting from the former process are referred to as *de facto* standards, while standards produced by the latter process are typically known as *de jure* standards.[25]

---

[22] The original network based upon this work was the Arpanet. *See* the Department of Computer Science and Engineering—University of Nebraska-Lincoln root site, *History of Internet (DARPA)* at

   http://kolkata.unl.edu/~sarit/courses/cs452-862/tcp-ip/node4.html

and the National University of Singapore Student's Union root site, *A Brief History of the Internet and Related Networks* at

   http://www.nussu.nus.sg/nussu/faq/history.txt.

   For a lengthier discussion of the history of evolution of the Internet, see the Universidade Federal de Santa Catarina root site, H. Hardy, The History of the Net (1993), at

   http://www.inf.ufsc.br/ufsc/docs/nethist8.html.

[23] In 1986, the Internet Engineering Task Force (IETF) was formed as a forum for technical coordination by contractors for DARPA, working on the Arpanet, the United States Defense Data Network (DDN), and the Internet core gateway system. For more information regarding ISOC's role, see **§ 7.20.**

[24] *See* the ISOC root site at

   http://www.isoc.org

and the Internet Mail Consortium root site, D. Crocker, *Making Standards the IETF Way* at

   http://www.imc.org/making-standards

(reprinted from 1 StandardView (1993)).

[25] *De facto* means "[i]n fact, in deed, actually," while *de jure* means "[d]escriptive of a condition in which there has been total compliance with all requirements of law." Black's Law Dictionary (5th ed. 1979). The "law" that a *de jure* standard complies with may be the legal obligations applied by the organization promulgating the standard. So, for example, the ISO defines standards as "documented agreements containing technical specifications or other precise criteria to be used consistently as rules, guidelines, or definitions of characteristics, to

In the realm of the Internet, *de facto* standards are associated with a variety of technologies including security and graphics.[26] *De jure* standards for the Internet commonly result from the work of organizations such as the Internet Engineering Task Force (IETF) and include technologies such as document formatting and various data transfer protocols.[27]

In many respects, *de facto* standards present relatively traditional intellectual property challenges to the business community. A company's protection of its own intellectual property, as well as its relationship to competitors holding intellectual property, is often much the same regardless of whether either companies' technology has achieved the status of *de facto* standard. As a result, greater emphasis will be placed on issues arising out of the development, approval, licensing, and implementation of *de jure* standards produced by collaborative organizations.

§ 7.4   The Role of Standards Organizations

Before discussing the impact of standards work on intellectual property strategies, it may be helpful to review why standards organizations are important to

---

ensure that materials, products, processes and services are fit for their purpose." Griffith University root site, *Introduction to ISO* at

  http://www.gu.edu.au/gwis/repro/QA-ISO.html [hereinafter *Introduction to ISO*].

In other instances, the organization may be established by public law or treaty, making its work product even more deserving of the *de jure* moniker. The ultimate form of *de jure* standard is perhaps one with which compliance is mandated by law. *De facto* and *de jure* standards are also sometimes referred to as informal and formal standards, respectively. *See* Nimmer, *Standards, Antitrust and Intellectual Property,* Intellectual Property Antitrust 1996 (PLI Pats., Copyrights, Trademarks, and Literary Prop. Course Handbook Series No. G4-3968) [hereinafter *Nimmer*].

[26] For example, in the area of security, the Rivest-Shamir-Adleman (RSA) algorithm for public key cryptography is a *de facto* standard. For a complete discussion of the RSA algorithm and associated U.S. Patent No. 4,405,829, see B. Schneier, Applied Cryptography: Protocols, Algorithms, and Source Code in C 281–88 (1994). In the graphics area, another *de facto* standard relates to the Graphics Interchange Format (GIF) approach to image compression and decompression, which Unisys has asserted is covered by U.S. Patent No. 4,558,302. For a discussion of the controversy associated with Unisys's efforts to enforce and license its patent, see the links at the World Wide Web Consortium (W3C) root site, *Graphics Formats for the World Wide Web* at

  http:www.w3.org/pub/WWW/Graphics.

Many technologies (such as TCP/IP and HTML) may be fairly described as both *de facto* and *de jure*.

[27] For example, the SGML format for storing documents together with their logical structure, and perhaps layout information, is covered by ISO 8879. As for data transfer protocols, the IETF's specifications for FTP, SMTP, and SNMP are provided at Requests for Comments (RFCs) 959, 821, and 1157, respectively. A more complete list of standard protocols for the Internet is provided at the Information Sciences Institute of the University of Southern California root site, *Internet Official Protocol Standards* at

  http://info.internet.isi.edu/in-notes/rfc/files/rfc1500.txt.

clients, as well as the roles played by such organizations and clients in the overall standards process.

§ 7.5 —Standards Organizations' Importance to Clients

Clients have a variety of reasons for participating in standards work. For counsel to assist a client in assessing the relative costs and benefits of this work, as well as the potential implications of the work on intellectual property matters, counsel must have some sense of the objectives of the work and the standards' importance to the client's business.[28]

Eligibility for government contracts. Many governments require contracts to be fulfilled with standard-compliant technology.[29] There are various reasons for such a requirement: including the assurance of interoperability and the availability of multiple vendors. In the Internet environment, the United States Federal Internetworking Requirements Panel (FIRP) recently reevaluated the United States government's requirement for open systems networks and recommended a policy concerning the government's use of networking standards. Although the government had, at one time, identified Government OSI Profile (GOSIP)[30] as the official network protocol for all United States government use, use of other network protocols, especially TCP/IP, continued to grow. FIRP concluded that IETF standards (that is, TCP/IP) should be acceptable for government procurement since they are open, international, and voluntary standards.[31]

---

[28] In addition to those benefits discussed in greater detail in the text, which inure primarily to the benefit of the standards participants, the standards process benefits society in a variety of ways. For example, enhanced product quality and reliability, reduced numbers of different product models and product cost, simplification for increased usability, increased distribution efficiency, and ease of maintenance all may be achieved by standards. *See Introduction to ISO. See also* Anderson, *The Customer is Last, or How to Wreck a Perfectly Good Business,* Strategic News Service (Oct. 2, 1996) for a discussion of how standards actually harm customers in the personal computer industry, and Nimmer for a discussion of some of the costs and benefits of the standards process.

[29] The interface between standards and procurement in Europe is discussed in § 7.27. For a broader discussion of intellectual property issues relating to government procurement, *see* L. Hopkins, *Federal Government Intellectual Property Guide,* Licensing Law Handbook (1994-95 ed.), and for a review of factors influencing government procurement in the post-GATT era, *see* the McCarthy Tetrault root site, *Government Procurement* at
http://www.mccarthy.ca/mt-igove.html.

[30] For additional background information regarding GOSIP, *see* various links in the Computer Science and Mathematics Division—Oak Ridge National Laboratory root site, *OSI/GOISP Protocols* at
http://www.epm.ornl.gov/~sgb/GOSIP.html.

[31] *See* the draft FIRP report at National Institute of Standards and Technology (NIST) root site, *SNAD Activity: Federal Internetworking Requirements Panel (FIRP)* at
http://osi.ncsl.nist.gov/firp/firp.html.

Enhance compatibility and interoperability. Standards organizations bring together various members of the industrial sector, including vendors and customers, in an effort to establish consensus regarding the specifications and criteria to be applied to the development of products and provision of services. Because the specifications and criteria are designed to ensure the interoperability of compliant products and services, the offerings of different vendors are compatible. Byproducts of the resultant interoperability include the promotion of trade liberalization, the interpenetration of various market sectors, and the enabling of worldwide communications systems.[32]

Foster emerging technologies. In areas of emerging technology, such as the Internet, the availability of standards, whether *de jure* or *de facto,* may be an important catalyst to the emergence of the technology.[33] Rather than having industry participants work on opposing and conflicting solutions, the common framework provided by the standard allows industry members to work together in a symbiotic way in which the combined effort is greater than the sum of its component parts.

Initiate change in stable technologies. At times, it may be difficult for a single individual or company to spark the technical progress needed in an industry. For example, progress may be inhibited by industry investment in legacy systems, the cost of developing and deploying new technology, and the risk of a misdirection. At other times, technical change will be practical only if adopted by a substantial portion of industry. By collaborating, industry members may be able to overcome these obstacles and initiate the needed changes.

Education and the interchange of ideas. Standards organizations also provide an educational forum, allowing companies to understand each other's needs, as well as the needs of their customers. By involving a broad segment of an industry's technical community in the discussion of problems and opportunities, the organization's solutions may also be technically and practically superior to those that would be produced by a single developer.[34]

---

[32] *See Introduction to ISO.*

[33] *Id.*

[34] It should be noted that many of the foregoing benefits are also achieved by the open system development process. Microsoft's open system approach to software development involves "fostering broad industry participation and innovation; providing the best possible connectivity, compatibility and interoperability across multiple platforms; incorporating standards in a pragmatic, customer-focused way; ensuring smooth transitions to new technologies." Microsoft Corporation, *White Paper: Open Systems and the Role of Standards* 17 (1996) [hereinafter Microsoft White Paper].

§ 7.6 —The World of Standards Organizations

Myriad organizations[35] are involved in standards work. The relative roles and responsibilities of these organizations also vary considerably. Taken as a whole, the milieu of standards organizations is exceedingly complex. Fortunately, for the purposes of this discussion, only those organizations that are actively involved in Internet-related technology are of interest. Before discussing the structure and process of some of these entities, a few of the important distinctions in standards organizations are discussed.

Geographic jurisdiction. Organizations may sometimes be distinguished by their geographic jurisdiction. A number of organizations are responsible for standards at the international level. Examples include treaty-based organizations like the International Telecommunications Union (ITU),[36] as well as federations of national standards bodies like the International Organization for Standardization (ISO)[37] and entities like the International Electrotechnical Commission (IEC).[38] Other organizations are regional in their responsibility, including the European Standards Committee (CEN)[39] and the European Telecommunications Standards Institute (ETSI).[40] Still other organizations are national in jurisdiction. Examples of such organizations include the American National Standards Institute (ANSI)[41] and the Japanese Standards Association (JSA).[42]

Subject matter jurisdiction. Another way in which standards organizations are differentiated is based upon the technical subject matter for which they are

---

[35] These organizations are variously referred to by the terms organizations, bodies, consortia, and forums. A *consortium* is formally defined as "a group (as of companies) formed to undertake an enterprise beyond the resources of any one member," while a *forum* is defined as "a public meeting place for open discussion" Webster's Ninth New Collegiate Dictionary (1991). These designations, however, appear to be used relatively interchangeably in the standards world. A consortium or forum may, however, be generally distinguished from a formal standards organization such as the International Organization for Standardization (ISO) in a number of respects. For example, consortia tend to (a) focus on short-term issues, often using technology developed by one or more members as a foundation, (b) have a greater product focus, (c) employ less rigorous requirements on consensus, which may enable shorter production schedules, and (d) operate directly at international level (for example, through international corporations) avoiding the need to develop national and then international consensus.

[36] See § **7.26.**

[37] See § **7.14.**

[38] See § **7.15.**

[39] See § **7.28.**

[40] See § **7.29.**

[41] See § **7.17.**

[42] See § **7.31.**

responsible. For example, some organizations such as ISO[43] and ANSI[44] are responsible for virtually the entirety of modern technology. Other organizations, such as the Video Electronics Standards Association (VESA)[45] and the Internet Engineering Task Force (IETF),[46] have more limited technical jurisdictions.

Role played in standards process.   Another means of distinguishing standards bodies is the role they play in the standards process. Some organizations are actively involved in the *development* of technology and corresponding standards. For example, the ATM Forum is responsible, in part, for standards development relating to Asynchronous Transfer Mode products and services.[47] Similarly, the World Wide Web Consortium (W3C)[48] has responsibility for the World Wide Web of the Internet. Other organizations, such as ISO and ANSI, do not focus on technology development. Instead, these organizations establish consensus among disparate technical and business interests and *approve* standards based upon technical solutions developed outside the auspices of their organization.[49]

Openness to membership and participation.   Standards organizations can also be differentiated based upon the opportunities that third parties have to participate in the standards process. For example, some organizations such as the Internet Society (ISOC) and Internet Engineering Task Force (IETF) are extremely open to both public membership and participation.[50] Other organizations, such as ISO, have limited membership but offer relatively widespread opportunities for indirect public participation.[51]

---

[43] See § **7.14.**

[44] See § **7.17.**

[45] VESA addresses standards issues of interest to the video electronics industry. The home page for VESA is at
   http://www.vesa.org.

[46] See § **7.20.**

[47] The ATM Forum's home page is at
   http://www.atmforum.com.
   For a list of additional organizations involved in standards development in the information and communications industry, see the Information Market Europe root site, *The OII Standards and Specifications Fora List* at
   http://www2.echo.lu/oii/en/fora.html.

[48] See § **7.24.**

[49] In one survey, the role played by over 60 standards-related bodies was classified in the following manner: 27% of the organizations were involved in market research, information diffusion, and education; 16% were involved in the creation of substantial *de facto* standards; 41% desired to create specifications and guidelines for implementation and interconnectivity; and a final 16% intended to create prestandards. *See Survey Report* at 11–12.

[50] See § **7.20.**

[51] The structure and operation of ISO are discussed in § **7.14.** Another organization having limited membership is the Virtual Reality Modeling Language (VRML) Architecture Group,

Agility. One additional way in which to distinguish standards organizations is their relative agility. Several of the large international organizations, such as ISO and IEC,[52] face considerable hurdles in trying to respond quickly to the needs of industry. For example, the size, formality, and political nature of these organizations limit their agility. In contrast, other organizations, such as IETF,[53] pride themselves on their relative responsiveness to the changing demands of industry and technology. The structure and process of such organizations may be specially tailored to enable the standard development or approval process to proceed more quickly.

§ 7.7 —The Internet: A Challenge to Traditional Standards Organizations

Despite the various benefits derived from standards development and approval, the work of standards organizations is not universally acclaimed.[54] This is particularly true with respect to rapidly evolving technologies of the form typified by the Internet.[55]

Although the consensus established via the standards process is the foundation upon which many of the benefits of standards are built, it is also the basis of a serious limitation of the process. Consensus takes time. If a technology is evolving slowly, this may not be a problem. On the other hand, if the standards development process takes several years, it may never keep abreast of the demands of the technology being addressed. Few technologies have evolved as rapidly as the Internet during the last few years.

---

known as VAG. VAG is composed of eight technical experts who funnel the thoughts of the VRML community to foster the development of a scaleable, fully interactive standard. The VAG's home page is at

http://vag.vrml.org.

A mailing list is used to keep the broader VRML community apprised of VAG work.

[52] See § **7.15.**

[53] See § **7.20.**

[54] In addition to the problem of delay discussed in the text, problems sometimes associated with the work of formal standards associations include: (a) if the consensus of disparate participants is required, a suboptimal or unpopular technical solution may be produced; (b) complexity may lead to cost increases; and (c) despite the breadth of their undertakings, standards organizations are not practically able to address all technologies and problems. *See* Microsoft White Paper at 11. For example, the price of an Open System Interconnection (OSI) deployment has been estimated to be four times that of a TCP/IP installation due primarily to the development complexity and cost. *See* Wood, *European Standardization Policy,* 3 StandardView 112 (Sept. 1995).

[55] For another perspective on the challenges faced by formal standards organizations in a dynamic environment and relation to *de facto* standards, *see Survey Report* at 6.

As a result, a good deal of Internet technology is based upon *de facto* standards.[56] However, consortia and more agile organizations, such as IETF,[57] have been playing an increasingly large role in the development of standards for the IT industry. Traditionally, consortia developed solutions that would then be taken to the appropriate international standards organization for approval. Recently, however, the number of consortia has grown rapidly and they are increasingly publishing their specifications outside the ISO process.[58]

§ 7.8   Legal Issues Relating to the Standards Process

Participation in standards work raises a number of legal issues to be considered by business people and their counsel.[59] The purpose of §§ **7.9** through **7.11** is to summarize some of those issues. Where relevant, an effort is made to identify the different perspectives that the organization and its members may have.

§ 7.9   —General Issues for the Organization

Standards organizations and counsel for such organizations face a variety of legal issues which must be addressed not only at the time the organization is

---

[56] With the rapid pace of technical development associated with the Internet, even *de jure* standards are continually being extended to create new *de facto* standards. *See* the PCWeek On Line root site, B. Machrone, *'TANTSAAFL' Takes on a New Meaning* at
http://www.pcweek.com/opinion/0527/27mach.html.

[57] *See* § **7.20.** For a favorable comparison of the less formal, more responsive, process of the IETF to traditional organizations such as ISO, *see* S. Bradner, *There is No Success Like Failure,* Network World, Sept. 18, 1995, and the Internet Mail Consortium root site, D. Crocker, *Making Standards the IETF Way* at
http://www.imc.org/making-standards
(reprinted from 1 StandardView (1993)) [hereinafter Crocker].

[58] *See Survey Report.*

[59] For additional background regarding legal issues involving standards organizations, processes, and participants, *see* E. Yoches & K. Frankel, *Legal Implications of Standards in the Computer and Software Industries* 1995 (PLI Pats., Copyrights, Trademarks, and Literary Prop. Course Handbook Series No. G4-3942) [hereinafter Yoches]; M. Epstein, *Standards and Intellectual Property* 1993 (PLI Pats., Copyrights, Trademarks, and Literary Prop. Course Handbook Series No. G4-3903) [hereinafter Epstein]; Nimmer; the Lucash, Gesmer & Updegrove root sites, A. Updegrove, *Standard Setting and Consortium Structures* (1996) [hereinafter Standard Setting] and A. Updegrove, *Forming and Representing High-Technology Consortia: Legal and Strategic Issues* (1994) [hereinafter *Forming and Representing*], both located at
http://www.lgu.com;
and the Niigata University root site, K. Narwa, *Technical Standards and Intellectual Property,* Law in Cyberspace: Niigata University located at
http://www.hle.niigata-u.ac.jp/members/teachers/K-Nawa/law-in-cyberspace/TS_and_IP.html

formed but also as part of the day-to-day operation of the organization.[60] These issues include several matters that are likely to require contractual expression.[61] Among these issues are: organizational form; membership qualifications, obligations, and rights; and organizational governance (for example, board of directors and officers), process, and dissolution.

Of particular importance are those legal issues that the organization must address relative to intellectual property rights (IPR). IPR issues are discussed in greater detail in § 7.10. Counselors to standards organizations should also make sure that their clients are mindful of antitrust issues.[62]

Generally, members of standards organizations must address most of the same issues that the organization itself faces, albeit from a different perspective. Members often have less direct control over the legal framework of rights

---

[60] For a more detailed discussion of legal issues confronting the counselor to a standards organization *see Standard Setting* and *Forming and Representing*.

[61] An example of a membership agreement is provided at the W3C root site, *International World Wide Web Consortium Participation Agreement* at
   http://www.w3.org/pub/WWW/Consortium/Agreement/Full.html.
Membership information for additional organizations is provided at, for example, the Internet Society root site, *Join the Internet Society!* at
   http://info.isoc.org/membership/index.html
and The Open Group root site, *Become a Member* at
   http://www.osf.org/membership.htm.

[62] Potential bases for antitrust liability include §§ 1 and 2 of the Sherman Act (which prohibit contracts, combinations, and conspiracies in restraint of trade, as well as unlawful attempts to monopolize) and § 5 of the Federal Trade Commission Act (which prohibits unfair methods of competition). Agreements between competitors involving standards may run afoul of the antitrust laws if: (a) the agreement, or the resultant activity, unreasonably discriminates against competitors that are not members of the group; or (b) the standards produced under such an agreement have the effect of unjustifiably excluding competitors from activities that are necessary or important to their business. *See, e.g.,* Allied Tube & Conduit Corp. v. Indian Head, Inc., 486 U.S. 492 (1988).
The Federal Trade Commission Advisory Opinion No. 713 7002, 78 F.T.C. 1628 (Mar. 8, 1971), provides a list of factors that may be useful in assessing the legality of a standards program under the antitrust laws. For example, standardization must not be used to fix prices, lessen competition, exclude competitors, or withhold or control production. The standards promulgated should be kept up-to-date and any fees charged for participation should be reasonably related to the costs involved. Membership should be open to all competitors, and due process must be accorded all interested parties. *See also* Antitrust Guidelines for the Licensing of Intellectual Property (DoJ and FTC, Apr. 6, 1995).
With respect to Europe, the 1968 Communication on Agreements, 1968 O.J. (C75) 3, and the Communication from the Commission to the Council and the Parliament on *Standardization and the Global Information Society: The European Approach* 5 indicate that the consortia's existence should be made public; interested parties should be given an opportunity to participate, including genuine participation by less favored partners; a "transparent" decision-making process should be adopted; and competition should be allowed within the framework provided by the technical solutions being discussed.
For additional discussion of antitrust in the standards arena, *see* Nimmer.

and obligations imposed by the organization. As a result, much of the legal focus applied by members is on the proper interpretation and observance of membership obligations, as well as the appropriate exercise of membership rights.[63]

§ 7.10 —Intellectual Property Rights Ownership and Licensing

It is perhaps ironic, but despite the importance of intellectual property rights (IPR)[64] issues they are often overlooked or inadequately addressed by standards organizations.[65] Even organizations that have relatively simple, well-publicized, and mature policies governing IPR may find that members and the public are confused about those policies.[66] As a result, long after a particular project is completed, the standards organization and its participants may still encounter some misunderstandings or complications regarding the intellectual property rights associated with a standard.[67]

---

[63] It may also be useful to counsel participants regarding the full range of their involvement in organizational work including joining, participation in meetings and discussions, submissions and contributions, signing of documents, and so forth.

[64] For the purposes of this discussion, IPR will be understood to include rights in patent applications and patents, copyright, trade secret, and trademark. As discussed in § 7.11, trade secret is perhaps the only of these rights to be generally incompatible with standards work.

[65] Of the 63 forums surveyed by the Telecommunications Technology Committee (TTC) in its June 1996 report, only 17 indicated they have rules for handling IPR. *See Survey Report* at 19 n.66. For a summary of the way IPRs are handled by different organizations, *see id.* at 44–45 n.21.

[66] One such organization is ANSI. See § 7.17 for a general discussion of ANSI and § 7.19 for a review of ANSI patent policy.

[67] One example of such a technology is the video encoding standard produced by the Moving Picture Experts Group (MPEG) under the auspices of ISO/IEC JTC 1/SC29. *See* the MPEG root site, *MPEG Pointers and Resources* at
    http://www.mpeg.org/index.html
and CSELT site, *ISO/IEC JTC 1/SC 29 WG 11 MPEG* at
    http://www.cselt.stet.it/ufv/leonardo/mpeg/index.html.
Despite the technical success of this standard, implementation of MPEG II has been clouded by questions over the availability, terms, and conditions of licenses from a variety of companies claiming patent rights in the standard. For more details *see* the Interactive Multimedia Association root site, P. Dodds, *MPEG II: Are You Licensed to Drive? Open Standards Are Not Necessarily Free Standards* at
    http://www.ima.org/hot-top/newslet/010195-5.html.
In contrast, implementation of the Joint Photographic Experts Group's (JPEG) standard for a powerful, lossy compression technique for high-quality photographic images has occurred more smoothly. As described at the W3C root site, *Graphics formats for the World Wide Web* at
    http://www.w3.org/pub/WWW/Graphics,
the basic JPEG algorithm is free from patent issues, but a number of enhancements to JPEG are not and are, therefore, seldom practiced on the World Wide Web.

This section discusses some of the specific IPR issues confronting the organization.

Ownership of IPRs. Typically, a standards organization will want to consider the ownership of any IPR resulting from the organization's work, as well as any effect that membership is to have on the ownership of the member's preexisting IPRs. In most instances, ownership of a preexisting IPR is left intact although, in many instances, ownership of an IPR in technology and documentation produced by or for the organization will be owned by the organization.

It is particularly important that organizations that are chartered to *develop* technology for establishment as a standard address the ownership of that technology. Because most organizations also publish specifications or other documents describing the standard, ownership of the copyright in those documents should also be addressed.

Ownership of IPR is, however, only part of the equation. It is also important to consider what, if any, rights the various IPR owners will grant to others.

Licensing of IPRs. Since the organization's goal is almost certainly the widespread adoption of any standards produced by the organization, it is not surprising that licensing would be important to the work of most organizations. If the organization's ownership provisions contemplate the possibility of IPR ownership by the organization and its members, the organization should establish the licensing obligations between all such parties.

For a licensing program to be effective, some consideration must be given to how the existence of relevant IPRs is to be determined and called to the organization's attention. As shown by the discussion of various specific organizations' IPR policies in §§ **7.12** through **7.24,** organizations often require a party submitting a standards proposal to identify any IPR it owns that might be required to implement the standard. The contributor of a specification may also be required to identify any IPRs of third parties thought to cover the submission. These same obligations may be imposed on other, noncontributing, members of the organization. The organization itself, however, will typically disclaim any responsibility for identifying or assessing such IPR.

Organization policy regarding the identification of IPRs can be complicated by a variety of factors. For example, the organization should decide how comprehensive and conclusive such an identification must be. Some organizations require the identification of only those IPRs that are reasonably and personally known to the contributor. Other organizations specifically state that contributors and members are not required to actively search their IPR portfolios, for example, for relevant patents. In many instances, however, the level of awareness required to trigger the obligation to identify IPRs is unclear.[68] The identification of IPRs

---

[68] See § **7.11.** A careful resolution of this question may involve issues of agency, knowledge, and substance of the assertion being made.

may be further complicated by questions regarding the requisite substance, form, and timing of the notice.[69]

Next, organization policy should address the process by which owners of identified IPRs will license such IPRs, including the terms and conditions of such licenses. Without a predetermined licensing structure offering some restrictions on license terms and conditions, the efficiency of the standards process and viability of the standard may be at issue.[70] Most organizations require the IPR owner to provide an assurance that it will offer any licenses required to implement the standard on reasonable, nondiscriminatory terms and conditions. Some organizations extend this obligation by requiring the IPR owner to submit a copy of the proposed license agreement to the organization for public inspection and to report the experience of licensees that have contracted with the IPR holder.

One final issue that the organization should consider in connection with its handling of licensing issues is the implications of an IPR owner's refusal to grant any licenses required by organization policy. Frequently, the outcome of such a refusal is the organization's inability to approve or maintain the standard.

Obviously, organizations and members should have clear contractual understandings regarding their relative rights and obligations with respect to IPR licensing. In addition to contractual obligations between the member and organization, however, licensing obligations (or restrictions on the enforcement of IPR) may arise through equitable estoppel and regulatory action.

Equitable estoppel. It is possible that the owner of a patent application or patent that includes claims allegedly covering a standard may be precluded from enforcing those rights under a theory of equitable estoppel.[71] The basic elements of equitable estoppel are misleading conduct by the party to be estopped and the

---

[69] The "substance" of the notice may vary depending upon whether the participant is required to announce both the *existence* of IPRs and their *identity*. The "form" of the required notice may be written or verbal. The notice may be solicited by a formal request from the organization to the member or may be "automatically" required of the participant at some predefined point in the process. As for "timing," notice is typically encouraged early in the process to allow the existence of IPRs to be considered during the organization's approval of the standard.

[70] *See* Epstein for a discussion of the difficulty of maintaining an industrywide standard that is also proprietary and subject to licensing obligations.

[71] For additional discussion of the equitable estoppel theory applied to standards work, *see* Yoches. Yoches and Frankel also argue that Stryker Corp. v. Zimmer, Inc., 741 F. Supp. 509 (D.N.J. 1990), illustrates a situation in which a patent holder covering a *de facto* standard was estopped from enforcing its right. In *Stryker,* the court granted Stryker's motion for partial summary judgment against patent holder Zimmer on the grounds that the patent infringement claim was barred under the doctrines of laches (which bars recovery of damages for infringements that occurred prior to the filing of the suit) and equitable estoppel (which bars injunctive relief and the recovery of damages). The court stated that "from at least as early as 1974 to 1984—ten years—the '699 patent was being openly and widely used in the industry with Zimmer's acquiescence, certainly permitting Stryker to conclude, as it did, that Zimmer had abandoned any rights in the patent."

reasonable and detrimental reliance upon that conduct by the party asserting the estoppel.[72]

Courts have considered at least two cases in which a company failed to disclose the existence of patent rights covering a standard developed by ANSI.[73]

---

[72] A.C. Aukerman Co. v. R.L. Chaides Constr. Co., 960 F.2d 1020 (Fed. Cir. 1992).

[73] In Stambler v. Diebold, Inc., 11 U.S.P.Q.2d (BNA) 1709 (E.D.N.Y. 1988), *aff'd,* 878 F.2d 1445 (Fed. Cir. 1989) (unpublished) the court granted summary judgment in favor of Diebold, concluding that Stambler's patent infringement action against Diebold was barred by the doctrines of laches and estoppel. In 1974, Stambler wrote Diebold asking whether Diebold would be interested in a license. Diebold declined the offer and no further correspondence was conducted until the lawsuit was filed in 1985. The court said:

> [I]t appears that plaintiff's silence was intentionally misleading. Ten years before this suit was filed, plaintiff concluded that the proposed Thrift or MINTS standard infringed his patent. It was well known to plaintiff and throughout the industry that the same provisions the plaintiff is relying on for infringement were being contemplated as national and international standards. Moreover, in the mid-1970's plaintiff sat on an American National Standards Institute standards committee after concluding that the proposed thrift and MINTS standards [relating to Automatic Teller Machine technology] infringed his patent. Plaintiff subsequently left the committee without notifying it of the alleged infringement of his patent. Under these circumstances, plaintiff had a duty to speak out and call attention to his patent. Plaintiff contacted defendant only once, ten years before this suit was filed. In 1975, plaintiff testified that he believed defendant [was] infringing his patent. However, plaintiff failed to bring suit until ten years later. Plaintiff had a duty to speak out and his silence was affirmatively misleading. Plaintiff could not remain silent while an entire industry implemented the proposed standard and then when the standards were adopted assert that his patent covered what manufacturers believed to be an open and available standard. Furthermore, plaintiff's silence could reasonably be interpreted as an indication that plaintiff had abandoned its patent claims."

Id. at 1715.

In Potter v. Storage Technology, 207 U.S.P.Q. (BNA) 763, (E.D. Va. 1980), *aff'd,* 641 F.2d 190 (4th Cir.), *cert. denied,* 454 U.S. 832 (1981) (affirmed on ground of laches), the district court dismissed Potter's suit against Storage Technology and others, finding that Potter was barred from recovery by the doctrines of laches and equitable estoppel. Potter was asserting two patents, one of which allegedly covered a technique for information recording and storage (GCR). After Storage Technology's 1973 announcement of its plans to release a GCR product, Potter wrote to Storage Technology, stating that Potter's patent covered GCR and offering a license to Storage Technology. Storage Technology did not hear from Potter again until the suit was filed in 1979. Also, in 1973, IBM (one of Potter's licensees) proposed that ANSI adopt GCR as an industry standard. Potter representatives attended at least one meeting of the ANSI subcommittee responsible for the project, but failed to disclose the existence of the Potter patents. GCR was approved as an ANSI standard in 1976. Under the circumstances, the court concluded that Potter's delay in bringing suit was unreasonable. The court also stated:

> Potter actively participated with the ANSI Subcommittee in developing GCR as the industry standard—it intentionally failed to bring its ownership of the '685 patent to the committee's attention notwithstanding the committee's policy to the contrary. By so doing, Potter has gained a monopoly on the GCR industry standard without any obligation to make its use available on reasonable terms to competitors in the industry.

In both instances, the companies participated in the work of the committee responsible for the standard. ANSI's patent policy requires the disclosure of patent rights.[74] The companies did not, however, comply with the ANSI policy and it appears that the companies' actions were intentional rather than inadvertent. As a result, the companies were estopped from enforcing their patent rights. Both cases also involved fact patterns that allowed the court to find that the company was further barred from recovery under the theory of laches.

Regulatory Action.   It is also possible that the owner of a patent that allegedly covers a standard may be precluded from enforcing those rights by regulatory action. In 1996, the Federal Trade Commission (FTC) gave its final approval to a consent decree entered into with Dell Computer Corporation[75] prohibiting Dell from enforcing patent rights covering a standard adopted by VESA.

In the summer of 1992, Dell employees participated in the work of the Local Bus Committee of VESA, which approved a VL-bus design standard. As part of VESA's approval of the standard, a Dell representative twice certified in writing that "to the best of my knowledge" the proposal does not infringe on any Dell

---

Id. at 769.

In addition, in Wang Lab. Inc. v. Mitsubishi Elecs. Am. Inc., 29 U.S.P.Q.2d (BNA) 1481 (C.D. Cal. 1983), Mitsubishi asserted an equitable estoppel defense to Wang's claim of patent infringement relating to Single In-line Memory Modules (SIMMs). Wang agreed to make its patents available to the public on a reasonable basis and licensed approximately 40 companies. A few suppliers, including Mitsubishi, refused to enter into license agreements. A prior action by Wang against Toshiba resulted in a jury verdict in favor of Wang. Mitsubishi claimed that Wang was estopped from enforcing the SIMMs patents on three grounds, one of which involved Wang's efforts to promote the patented SIMMs as the industry standard.

> From 1983 through 1986, Wang allegedly promoted the now-patented SIMMs as an official industry standard through the Electronic Industries Association's standardization group know[n] as JEDEC. [Mitsubishi] participated as a member of JEDEC . . . . JEDEC's rules require disclosure of patent rights. . . . [Mitsubishi] contends that Wang persuaded JEDEC to adopt its memory "30-pin" module configuration as the industry standard, without disclosing the pending patent application on said module. Thus Wang successfully fueled market demand for a particular SIMM product, and then unexpectedly demanded royalties. . . . Third, [Mitsubishi] argues that Wang is estopped from enforcing the SIMM patents because such enforcement is illegal under the antitrust laws. [Mitsubishi] contends that Wang's enforcement of its patents constitutes patent misuse because (i) Wang abused the JEDEC standard-setting procedure . . . .

Id. at 1495. The court concluded that "[Mitsubishi] has adduced some persuasive evidence that Wang is estopped from enforcing its patents, and may have unclean hands." *Id.* at 1496.

[74] See § **7.19.**

[75] *See* Complaint, Decision and Order, Statement of the Federal Trade Commission, and Dissenting Statement of Commissioner Mary L. Azcuenga, *In the Matter of* Dell Computer Corp., FTC Docket No. C-3658 (1996). By eliminating the element of reliance required to support a cause of action based upon equitable estoppel, the § 5 action brought by the FTC potentially provides broader relief to the public. *See also* R. Skitol, *When Intellectual Property and Antitrust Law Collide: FTC Must Tread Lightly,* Wash. Legal Found. Critical Legal Issues: Working Paper Series (1996) and the FTC root site, *Antitrust and Intellectual Property in the Year 2000: Remarks of Commissioner Mary L. Azcuenga* at
http://www.ftc.gov/opa/speeches/intelp.htm.

patents.[76] In fact, Dell had been granted a patent in July 1991, which Dell later asserted gave it exclusive rights to technology required to implement the VESA standard. After the VESA bus design standard had been implemented in more than 1.4 million computers in about eight months, Dell demanded that other companies meet with its representatives to "determine . . . the manner in which Dell's exclusive rights will be recognized . . . ."[77] The FTC stepped in and, via a consent agreement, prohibited Dell from enforcing its patent rights against computer manufacturers using the bus standard.

The FTC action was not without controversy. One of the commissioners dissented, raising concerns about the lack of a finding that Dell had intentionally and knowingly misled VESA.[78] The FTC invited public comment and heard testimony from organizations such as ANSI. ANSI suggested that the FTC's action should not be interpreted to apply to an unintentional failure to disclose the existence of a patent and should not obligate companies to research their patent portfolios or risk losing their right to seek royalties.[79]

IPR Representations and Warranties. An important objective of most standards organizations is the avoidance of liability should the implementation of a standard, or some other organization activity, result in the infringement of third-party IPRs. As a result, the organization may choose to expressly disclaim any liability to its members or the public should such an event occur. Some organizations go even further and seek assurances from participants in the standards process that any resultant standard is, to a degree, free from (or not known to be covered by) the IPR of third parties. Additional steps that are sometimes taken include the requirement that legends be applied to all published specifications of the organization identifying any known IPR rights and disclaiming any other representations.

§ 7.11 —Intellectual Property Rights Procurement

The elements of an IPR procurement plan for Internet businesses are discussed in other chapters.[80] A party that is contemplating the contribution of its technology

---

[76] FTC Docket No. C-3658 at 2 (Dissenting Statement). The FTC stated that "Dell failed to act in good faith to identify and disclose patent conflicts . . . ." *id.* at 2 (Statement of the Federal Trade Commission). In a published bulletin, the FTC stated that "there is no reason to believe that Dell's failure to disclose the patent was not inadvertent," which can be found at the FTC root site, *For Your Information: June 17, 1996* 2 at

http://www.ftc.gov/opa/9606/dell2.htm.

[77] FTC Docket No. C-3658 at 2 (Complaint).

[78] *Id.* at 2 (Dissenting Statement). Commissioner Azcuenga, the dissenter, also noted the lack of any allegation that Dell had obtained market power as a result of the misstatement at issue.

[79] *See* the FTC root site, *Testimony by Amy A. Marasco, Vice President and General Counsel, American National Standards Institute before the Federal Trade Commission, December 1, 1995* at

http://www.ftc.gov/opp/global/marasco/htm.

[80] See **Chs. 2–6.**

to a standards organization may well wish to consider a number of additional factors. This section addresses some of these factors associated with each of the major forms of intellectual property.[81]

Patents. Patents are perhaps the most viable form of intellectual property available to protect technology that is the subject of a standard. Although, at first blush, patents and standards may seem at odds, it is not necessarily inconsistent for technology that is the subject of a standard also to be covered by a patent.[82] Having said that, the author is aware of no situations in which a formal standards organization routinely pursues patent protection for the standards it is developing. Some organizations do, however, expressly reserve ownership of patent rights to technology invented by organization employees during the standards development process.

Patent rights most commonly arise out of the procurement work done by members of the organizations participating in the standards process.[83] If the member's development work and patent filings occur *before* its involvement in a standards project, the standardization of the technology probably has little effect on the member's procurement decisions.

On the other hand, a participant weighing whether or not to pursue patent protection for a technology that is in the process of being standardized must consider a number of issues. Among the factors to be considered are: the expense of pursuing patent protection; the uncertain scope of any protection to be received; the IPR provisions of the organization involved (for example, the nature of a patent holder's obligation to license its IPR to other members and the public); the likelihood that a standard will be adopted despite the existence of patent rights; and the relative benefits of secured patent rights vis-à-vis the benefits of the standard to the patent holder. The balancing of these factors is perhaps least likely to weigh in favor of filing when the expense and deadlines associated with foreign prosecution are considered.

In many instances, the costs of patent procurement will outweigh the limited benefit of pursuing protection for technology being proposed as a standard. On the other hand, once a standard has been established, a company's implementation of the standard may involve improvements that could be protected by patent. The decision to pursue patent protection for a unique implementation generally

---

[81] Because *de facto* standards traditionally evolve over time, the procurement strategy for such technology in many instances may simply involve the same considerations governing the individual's or organization's broader IPR procurement strategy. As a result, this section focuses on procurement strategies relevant to *de jure* standards.

[82] See § **7.19.**

[83] If the member's development efforts and patent filings precede the member's involvement in standards work, the patent process is naturally unaffected by the standards participation. On the other hand, when patent protection is pursued at the same time the standards work is being conducted, the issues discussed in the text should be considered. See § **7.10** for a discussion of the MPEG II video encoding standard, which is allegedly covered by numerous patents and is still embroiled in licensing difficulties.

involves the same decision-making process associated with a company's broader patent procurement program.

Copyright. Copyrights are perhaps less useful than patents for protecting the *technology* that is the subject of most standards. There is a great deal of commentary discussing the bounds of copyright and the relative roles played by patent and copyright.[84] Several articles also specifically address the role of copyright in protecting standard technology.[85] It seems clear that, like patent, the existence of copyright is not inconsistent with the idea of a standard.[86]

Copyright often plays a significant role in protecting the published *specifications* upon which most standards are built. Because some organizations wish to control the publication of standards to preserve the integrity of the standard and to generate revenue,[87] they may choose to preserve copyright exclusively to themselves. An organization pursuing this course of action will want to ensure ownership of the copyright, or at least a sufficiently broad license in favor of the organization. In those situations where the organization does own the copyright, members are usually still allowed to retain copyright ownership of any material incorporated into a specification published as a standard.[88]

Of greater importance with respect to standards that may be implemented in software, copyright may also protect a particular company's implementation of the standard. In some instances, the standards development and approval process may require the standard to be demonstrated by one or more reference implementations. The contributor of such a reference implementation may also need to consider whether use of the implementation will be licensed to the organization, its members, and the public and, if so, the terms and conditions of such licenses.

One advantage of copyright vis-à-vis patent is the relatively minimal investment in, and actions required to preserve, copyright. As a result, relatively little

---

[84] *See* M. Nimmer & D. Nimmer, Nimmer on Copyright (1996) and D. Bender, Computer Law: Software Protection (1996).

[85] *See* Yoches and Epstein.

[86] One district court has said:

> By arguing that [Lotus] 1-2-3 was so innovative that it occupied the field and set a *de facto* standard, and that, therefore, defendants were free to copy plaintiff's expression, defendants have flipped copyright on its head. Copyright protection would be perverse if it only protected mundane increments while leaving unprotected as part of the public domain those advancements that are strikingly innovative.

Lotus Dev. Corp. v. Paperback Software Int'l, 740 F. Supp. 37, 79 (D. Mass. 1990).

[87] Compare the operation of the IETF, whose Internet Standards are posted to the Internet as Requests for Comments (RFCs) freely available to anyone, with the International Standards approved by ISO and available for a fee as described at the ISO root site, *How to Place Your Order* at

http://www.iso.ch/infoe/order.html.

[88] Such ownership would likely be subject to an appropriately broad license grant in favor of the organization.

strategic planning may be necessary to determine the appropriate policy with respect to copyright.

Trade secret.   The author is aware of no literature discussing the merits of pursuing trade secret protection in the context of standards work. Because the objectives of the standards process is usually the broad dissemination of information, it seems unlikely that reliance upon trade secret protection by either the organization or its members would be consistent with organizational goals. As with copyright protection for a software reference implementation, however, it is possible that a company might decide to pursue trade secret protection for a particular implementation of a standard.

Trademark.   Some organizations license the use of the organization's mark or marks to indicate to the public that products of licensees are in technical compliance with the organization's standards.[89] The determination of the proper form of a mark to be employed in such a program (for example, trademark, certification mark, collective mark) is a relatively complex task.[90] A certification program may involve a number of trademark procurement functions including mark selection, clearance, and registration, as well as downstream activities such as licensing, quality control, and enforcement.[91]

As for the individual members of an organization, the pursuit of trademark protection in connection with the member's marketing of its particular implementation of a standard is relatively unaffected by the standards process. Use of a member brand, perhaps in conjunction with the mark of the organization, is relatively widespread.[92]

§ 7.12   Internet-Related Organizations

The preceding sections discuss some of the reasons for participating in standards organizations, as well as the legal issues associated with such work. The objective of §§ 7.13 through 7.24 is to familiarize the reader with some of the standards organizations that may be of interest to Internet companies. To the extent

---

[89] For example, X/Open (which recently joined with the Open Software Foundation (OSF) to form The Open Group) offers such a branding program, the details of which are discussed at the X/Open root site, *The Brand & Procurement* at
    http://www.xopen.org/branding.htm.

[90] *See Forming and Representing* for a discussion of the complexities of whether or not to seek registration, and if so whether to register a trademark, service mark, collective membership mark, or certification mark.

[91] For a more general discussion of trademark practice, see **Ch. 1** and J. McCarthy, McCarthy on Trademarks and Unfair Competition (3rd ed. 1996).

[92] *See* Yoches for a discussion of the practice of computer industry manufacturers referring to each other's trademarks to make claims of compatibility, which is acceptable as long as such uses do not result in confusion.

practical, a brief synopsis of each organization's charter, structure, process, and IPR policy is provided.[93]

§ 7.13 —ISO/IEC, JTC 1, and ANSI

A first set of standards organizations are bonded by a common relationship involving information technology (IT). Specifically, the International Organization for Standardization (ISO) and the International Electrotechnical Commission (IEC) collaborate on IT through a Joint Technical Committee known as JTC 1. The United States' representative to both ISO and IEC is the American National Standards Institute (ANSI). Each of these organizations addresses issues of interest to the Internet communities.

§ 7.14 —International Organization for Standardization (ISO)

The International Organization for Standardization (ISO)[94] was formed in 1947. A nongovernmental organization, ISO includes one national standards body from each of more than 100 countries.[95] Each national body is the one deemed most representative of standardization in that country, and the United States' member body is ANSI.[96] ISO's mission is to "promote the development of standardization and related activities in the world with a view to facilitating the international exchange of goods and services, and to developing cooperation in the spheres of intellectual, scientific, technological and economic activity."[97] ISO collaborates with the International Electrotechnical Commission on standards issues relating to the Internet.

As noted above, ISO membership includes a representative national standards body from each member country. A Technical Management Board manages the

---

[93] A wider survey of various telecommunications-related forums is provided in The Telecommunications Technology Committee, *Survey Report on Telecommunications-Related Forum's Activities* (June 1996).

[94] For a wealth of information regarding ISO, *see* ISO's home page at
http://www.iso.ch.

[95] ISO's membership lists (including subscriber and correspondent members) are available at the ISO root site, *ISO Members Worldwide* at
http://www.iso.ch/addresse/address.html.

[96] *See* the ISOC root site, *Welcome to the Internet Society, Internauts!* at
http://info.isoc.org/index.html.
ISOC offers Regular, Associate, Contributor, and Start-up organizational memberships, with a price break being offered to nonprofit organizations. ISOC is currently composed of 40 network access providers, 30 vendors, 35 bodies like ITU and NIST, and 5000 private members.

[97] *See Introduction to ISO.*

technical work performed by a variety of technical committees and joint technical committees. National members' involvement in the work of a particular committee is designated by their status as either a P-member (participating) or O-member (observing). Committee work is governed by a chair, and draft work is performed by an editing committee. Committee work may be delegated among a number of working groups.

The ISO technical committees and subcommittees follow a six-step process in the production of International Standards.[98] The process is voluntary, industry-wide, and based upon consensus. During the first stage of the process, referred to as the proposal stage, the committee determines the need for a new standard and members' commitment to participate actively in development of the standard. During the preparatory stage, the working group prepares working drafts of the standard until it is convinced that it has developed the best technical solution to the problem. At the committee stage, the committee prepares another draft that is registered with the ISO Central Secretariat. Once consensus is reached on the technical merit of the solution reflected in this draft, the text is finalized for submission as a Draft International Standard (DIS). Next, the DIS is circulated to all ISO member bodies during an enquiry stage which includes a five-month voting and comment period and may result in a Final DIS (FDIS). At the approval stage, the FDIS is circulated to ISO member bodies for a two-month, final "yes" or "no" vote on the International Standard. The process ends with the publication stage.

§ 7.15 —International Electrotechnical Commission (IEC)

The International Electrotechnical Commission (IEC)[99] was created in 1906 as a nontreaty organization having, as its charter, the promotion of international cooperation on questions relating to standardization in the fields of electricity, electronics, and related technologies. The United States representative on the IEC is ANSI. As described in **§ 7.16,** the IEC collaborates with ISO on standards issues of interest to the Internet community.

The IEC is governed by a council or general assembly composed of the president of the IEC, as well as the presidents of the national committees.[100] The council is responsible for determining matters relating to membership, finances,

---

[98] *See* the ISO root site, *Stages of the Development of International Standards* at
http://www.iso.ch/infoe/proc.html.

[99] For additional information regarding the IEC, *see* its home page at
http://www.iec.ch.

[100] *See* the IEC root site, *IEC Structure and Operations* at
http://www.iec.ch/pig003-e.html.

and other administrative matters. The council has delegated responsibility for the management of the IEC's technical work to a committee of action. The committee of action establishes the Technical Committees (TCs) that do the actual standards work. These TCs may, themselves, be further divided into subcommittees (SCs).

§ 7.16   —ISO/IEC Joint Technical Committee 1 (JTC 1)

The relative responsibilities of ISO and IEC were agreed upon in 1976, providing the IEC with jurisdiction over the field of electrical and electronic engineering, while all other areas are the responsibility of ISO.[101] Subject matter of interest to both organizations is assigned to joint technical bodies. One such body is the JTC 1, responsible for IT.[102]

Structurally, the JTC 1 is composed of a Secretariat, a Chairman, a Special Working Group (SWG) on Functional Standardization, an SWG on Registration Authorities, and an SWG on Conformity Assessment, as well as a number of subcommittees (SCs), which are responsible for the technical work of JTC 1.[103]

Each SC is responsible for a particular area of technology.[104] For example, SC 6 deals with telecommunications and information exchange between systems, SC 18 is responsible for document processing and related communication, and SC 29 handles coding of audio, picture, multimedia, and hypermedia information. Many of these SCs are further divided into Working Groups (WGs). For example, SC 29 includes WG 1 (coding of still pictures (JPEG)[105]), WG 11 (coding of motion pictures and associated audio (MPEG)[106]), and WG 12 (coding of multimedia and hypermedia information (MHEG)).[107]

A WG typically includes a convenor, one or more project editors, and a number of individual participants. The convenor and project editors are appointed by the parent SC and are responsible for general administration and the production of

---

[101] *See Introduction to ISO.*

[102] For discussion of JTC 1, *see* the Accredited Standards Committee X3 root site, *Welcome to the ISO/IEC JTC 1 U.S. TAG Home Page* at
  http://www.x3.org/jtc1.

[103] *See* the ISO root site, *Procedures for the Technical Work of ISO/IEC JTC 1 on Information Technology* at
  http://www.iso.ch/dire/jtc1/directires.html.

[104] *See* the ISO root site, *JTC 1 Information Technology* at
  http://www.iso.ch/meme/JTC1.html.

[105] Joint Photographic Experts Group.

[106] Moving Picture Experts Group.

[107] Multimedia and Hypermedia Experts Group.

the WG's documents, respectively. The individual participants provide technical support and are nominated to the WG by the JTC 1's national member bodies. The standards process employed by JTC 1 is discussed in § **7.33.**

In 1988, ANSI, as the United States' national member body of JTC 1, formed the United States Technical Advisory Group (US TAG)[108] to JTC 1. The US TAG's ultimate charter is to maintain the United States' leadership in the arena of global standards. As part of that responsibility, US TAG coordinates the development of the United States' positions with respect to JTC 1 initiatives. To do this, US TAG must coordinate the disparate United States interests associated with the project and develop a consensus.

JTC 1 has recently been active in considering the standards necessary to support the Global Information infrastructure (GII). The G7[109] leaders recently asked the international standards organizations, including ISO/IEC JTC 1, to prepare a coordinated plan for the development of standards applicable to the GII.[110] US TAG responded by announcing the formation of a Special Working Group (SWG) on the GII.[111] The SWG will perform an advisory role to US TAG on GII issues and serve as the focal point for all US TAGs involved in standards-related activities involving technologies relevant to the GII. The SWG will also prepare preliminary contributions for use by the SWG-GII in producing a GII "standards roadmap."[112]

§ 7.17 —American National Standards Institute (ANSI)

The American National Standards Institute (ANSI)[113] is a private nonprofit institution formed in 1918 to coordinate the efforts of a wide range of private and

---

[108] *See* the JTC 1 US TAG's home page at

http://www.jtc1tag.org,

as well as the home page of the Information Technology Industry Council, administrator of US TAG, at

http://www.itic.org.

[109] The Group of Seven is composed of Canada, France, Germany, Italy, Japan, the United Kingdom, and the United States. For additional background regarding the G7, *see* the University of Toronto root site, *What is G7?* at

http://utl2.library.utoronto.ca/www/g7/what_is_g7.html.

[110] *See* the University of Torino root site, S. Perry, *Ministers Have Firmer Grip on Information Society Issues,* G7 Live at

http://di.unito.it/mail_archive/G7/0015.html.

[111] *See* the JTC 1 TAG root site, J. Emard, *Participants Sought for U.S. Special Working Group on Global Information Infrastructure* at

http://www.jtc1tag.org/jtgiipr.html.

[112] *Id.*

[113] ANSI's home page is at

http://www.ansi.org.

public sector organizations on voluntary standards. ANSI has approximately 1300 national and international corporate members, 40 federal state and government agencies, and more than 250 professional, educational, and consumer organizations.

ANSI does not actually develop standards but, instead, builds consensus among qualified development groups to enable the voluntary establishment and approval of such standards. ANSI's technical jurisdiction includes the full gamut of U.S. technology. As of 1995, ANSI had approved more than 11,500 standards.[114]

ANSI also plays an important role as the United States member body to ISO and IEC. ANSI is one of the five members of the governing council of ISO and is one of four permanent members of the ISO Technical Management Board. As for the IEC, the ANSI national committee is on the 12-member governing committee of action. In these roles, ANSI promotes the international adoption of United States standards and advocates the United States' policy and technical positions.

§ 7.18   —Information Infrastructure Standards Panel (IISP)

In 1994, ANSI established an independent body to identify critical standards needed to deliver products and services for the GII. This body, designated the Information Infrastructure Standards Panel (IISP),[115] is composed of, and funded by, more than 80 participants, including businesses, trade associations, standards organizations, and government agencies.[116] Membership is open to all directly and materially affected parties.

The IISP has prepared a detailed framework for identifying areas in which standards are needed. So far, the IISP has identified at least 40 standards necessary to implement the GII.[117] In addition to identifying needed standards, the

---

[114] *See* the ANSI root site, *An Introduction to ANSI the American National Standards Institute* at http://www.ansi.org/whatansi.html.

[115] The IISP's home page is at
http://www.ansi.org/iisp/iisphome.html
and includes a good deal of information.

[116] The IISP membership list is provided at the ANSI root site, *IISP Participants* at http://www.ansi.org/iisp/95-0063.html.
One particular member of interest is the Institute of Electrical & Electronics Engineers, Inc. (IEEE), which has formed its own standards coordinating committee to address information infrastructure standards issues. See the IEEE site, *IEEE Information Infrastructure Standards* at http://stdsbbs.ieee.org/groups/nii.gii/giiintro.html.

[117] Among the subject areas needing to be standardized are: reliability, network-to-network interfaces, application-to-application requirements, security, quality of service, survivability, protocol interactions, addressing, and directory services. *See* the ANSI root site, *IISP Identified Standards Needed to Implement the National and Global Information Infrastructures* at http://www.ansi.org/iisp/needlist.html.

IISP intends to take a number of actions to accelerate the development of such standards. For example, the IISP catalogs existing standards, obtains agreements from standards developers to fill the gaps, and promotes collaborative efforts between standards developing organizations, industries, and national, regional, and international standards efforts relating to information infrastructure.

§ 7.19 —ISO/IEC and ANSI Intellectual Property Rights Policies

One important product of the ISO/IEC and ANSI processes is the effect they may have on the rights of members and the public in related intellectual property. This section briefly discusses the policies of ISO and its United States national member, ANSI.

The ISO Policy. ISO has no objection in principle to an International Standard which includes technology covered by patent rights.[118] This is supposed to occur, however, only in exceptional circumstances when justified by technical reasons. In addition, the originator of the proposal for the International Standard must apprise the technical committee of any patent rights that the originator knows about and thinks may cover the proposal. Parties involved in the preparation of the standard must also notify the committee if they become aware of patent rights during development of the standard.

If a proposal is accepted on technical grounds, the proposal's originator must ask any known patent owners for a statement that they are willing to grant licenses under reasonable and nondiscriminatory terms and conditions. ISO is not involved in these discussions but keeps a record of the patent owner's statement. If a patent owner does not provide such a statement, ISO will not proceed with the International Standard without obtaining the approval of the ISO council or IEC council, as appropriate. In the event a license is not available after approval of an International Standard, the standard will be referred back to the technical committee.[119]

The ANSI Policy. ANSI has published *Guidelines for Implementation of the ANSI Patent Policy: An Aid to More Efficient and Effective Standards Development in Fields that May Involve Patented Technology.*[120] The stated purpose of

---

[118] ISO Directives Part 2, "Methodology for the Development of International Standards" (Jan. 29, 1995).

[119] A legend will also be applied to the specification to warn readers that patent rights have been identified as being claimed relevant to the specification.

[120] ANSI's patent policy is posted at the Accredited Standards Committee X3 root site, *American National Standards Institute Procedures for the Development and Coordination of American National Standards* at
   http://www.x3.org/help/ansi_sdo.html.

this document is to encourage "the early disclosure and identification of patents that may relate to standards under development, so as to thereby promote greater efficiency in standards development practices."[121]

To that end, during the standards development process, ANSI suggests that a standards developer may wish to periodically poll participants regarding the existence of patent rights required to implement the proposed standard. This process should not require participants to search for patents in their own portfolio or the portfolios of others, but should encourage the identification of patents early in the development process. The standards developer may also wish to encourage nonparticipants to indicate whether they have patents relevant to the standard being proposed.

When it appears that a candidate standard may require the use of a patented invention, the patent holder must provide: (1) a general disclaimer that the patent owner does not have, or plan to have, patent rights that would be required to comply with the proposed standard; or (2) a written assurance that a license will be available for the purpose of implementing the standard either on royalty-free terms or on reasonable terms and conditions that are demonstrably free of any unfair discrimination.[122]

The patent holder's statement will be kept on file by ANSI. If the patent holder wishes to apply some conditions to the license, the terms and conditions of the license must be submitted (in confidence) to ANSI along with a statement of the number of independent licensees that have accepted the patent owner's license terms.[123] ANSI's counsel verifies only that such statements have been provided. A determination of the acceptability of the statement is the sole province of the Board of Standards Review (BSR), with appeal to the ANSI Appeals Board.

Compliance with the patent policy is one of the factors considered by the BSR in determining whether to approve or withdraw approval of an ANSI standard.

§ 7.20   —Internet Society/Internet Engineering Task Force (ISOC/IETF)

Another conglomeration of Internet-related organizations is rooted in the Internet Society (ISOC).[124] The ISOC is a nongovernmental, professional organization

---

It may be of interest to note that this policy is currently confined to patents and not the broader field of other IPRs.

[121] *Id.*

[122] *Id.*

[123] It appears that these latter requirements are not applied in practice, and ANSI is currently considering their removal from the policy.

[124] ISOC's home page is at
http://www.isoc.org.

chartered to promote international cooperation on the evolution of the Internet. As part of this responsibility, the ISOC considers a range of social, political, and technical issues. ISOC's broad membership includes individuals, as well as network access providers, product vendors, information service and system management providers, major enterprise Internet operators, educational institutions, organizations for research, professions, industries, and standards, international treaty organizations, and government agencies.[125] The ISOC, through the work of several subsidiary organizations, plays a substantial role in the current development and approval of Internet-related standards.

§ 7.21 —ISOC/IETF Structure

The ISOC includes a number of organizations. A board of trustees, elected by the ISOC membership, governs the ISOC. Trustees approve appointments to the Internet Architecture Board (IAB) from nominees submitted by the IETF.[126]

The IAB is a technical advisory group within ISOC, appointed by the trustees from nominees submitted by the IETF. The IAB provides oversight of the overall architecture and growth of the Internet. The IAB also approves members of the Internet Engineering Steering Group (IESG), reviews and approves charters of new working groups, and provides an appellate body for decisions of the IESG.

The IESG is responsible for technical management of IETF activities, as well as the Internet standards process.[127] This process is governed by procedures that have been approved by the ISOC trustees, including the passage of specifications through a standards track process described in § 7.22. Members of the IESG are nominated by the IETF and approved by the IAB.

The IETF is a large group of network designers, operators, vendors, and researchers working together to ensure the sensible evolution of the Internet's

---

[125] Some of ISOC's relationships with other organizations are as follows. ISOC became a member of ITU-T in 1995. ISOC's Internet Standards have been proposed as ISO/IEC PAS. See § 7.33. ISOC is also associated with consortia including the W3C, ATM Forum, and ISODE Consortium.

[126] The home page for the IETF is at
     http://www.ietf.org,
and the IAB and IESG home pages are at
     http://www.iab.org/iab
and
     http://ietf.org/iesg.html,
respectively. In 1989, the IAB, which had previously been responsible for many Internet-related task forces, was restructured to govern only the IETF and the Internet Research Task Force (IRTF). In 1992, the IAB proposed its inclusion under the broader umbrella of ISOC.

[127] The IESG is composed of an IETF Executive Director, IESG Secretary, IAB Liaisons and the directors of the functional working group areas.

architecture, as well as its smooth operation.[128] There is no formal membership in the IETF, and management is handled by the IESG.

Some of the specific tasks performed by the IETF include: identifying technical and operational problems with the Internet, specifying protocol and architectural solutions to such problems, making standardization recommendations to the IESG, supporting the transfer of technology from the Internet Research Task Force (IRTF) to the Internet community, and providing a forum for the exchange of information among a wide range of parties interested in the evolution of the Internet.

The technical work of the IETF is done by a number of relatively small, focused working groups organized by subject matter into the following functional areas: Applications (APP); Internet Services (INT); IP: next generation (IPng); Network Management (MGT); Operational Requirements (OPS); Routing (RTG); Security (SEC); Transport Services (TSV); and User Services (USV).[129] Each area includes at least one area director, as well as an area directorate. A good deal of the working group's efforts are conducted through e-mail, although the IETF also meets several times a year. Decisions by the working group are based upon "rough consensus,"[130] rather than any kind of formal voting process. Once the working group's limited charter has been achieved, it is typically dissolved.

Individuals interested in forming a new working group may hold a Birds of a Feather (BOF) session to determine whether there is sufficient interest to warrant the formation of a group. If so, a chair is selected and the working group's description, goals, and milestones are drafted for approval by the area director and IESG/IAB.

The IRTF investigates the long-term research problems confronting the Internet. These problems are often too uncertain, too advanced, or not sufficiently well understood to be tackled by the IETF's working groups. The IRTF's work is overseen by an Internet Research Steering Group (IRSG).

Finally, the Internet Assigned Numbers Authority (IANA) includes the Internet Registry (IR) and the Internet Network Information Centers (InterNICs). The IR maintains the database of IP addresses and registered domains. The InterNICs post information from working groups and provide advice and assistance to users.

---

[128] The IETF first met in 1986, initially as a forum for technical coordination by contractors for the United States Department of Defense Advanced Research Projects Administration (DARPA). With the formation of ISOC in 1992, the IAB proposed that the IAB's and, hence, IETF's activities take place under the auspices of ISOC.

[129] By focusing the working group's charter narrowly on immediate problems, it is hoped that IETF can move quickly and provide solutions that do not arrive after their window of opportunity. See Crocker.

[130] "We reject kings, presidents, and voting. We believe in rough consensus and running code." IETF Credo, Dave Clark (1992).

§ 7.22 —ISOC/IETF Standards Process

The development of a standard under the auspices of the ISOC/IETF involves three stages: Proposed Standard, Draft Standard, and Internet Standard.[131]

The process begins with a Proposed Standard, which is a stable, well-understood specification that has no known technical flaws. A real implementation of the Proposed Standard is desirable but not necessary.

The next step in the process is the establishment of a Draft Standard. To qualify as a Draft Standard, at least two independent, interoperable implementations of the standard must have been established and successful operational experience gained. At this point, if intellectual property issues are known, the independent implementations must be based upon at least two separate exercises of the licensing process.[132] A Draft Standard is considered a relatively mature and final form of the specification.

The final stage in the process is the establishment of an Internet Standard. An Internet Standard occurs only after significant implementation of the specification and successful operational experience has been obtained.

At each stage, the working group first reviews the proposal for compliance, and then the entire IETF constituency is given an opportunity to comment via a "last call" process.[133] In addition to the criteria outlined above, there are constraints on the duration of each stage of the process.

The documents published by the IETF in connection with this process fit into one of two classes: Internet Drafts and Requests for Comments (RFCs). Internet Drafts are the working documents of the IETF. They are valid for limited durations of time, have no formal status, and are subject to change or deletion at any time. RFCs are the official vehicle for publication of IETF documents and, as such, are permanently archived. There are two series of RFCs: FYI (informational document produced by individuals, organizations, or other standards bodies) and STD (Internet Standard).

§ 7.23 —ISOC/IETF Intellectual Property Rights Policy

The IETF's IPR policy governing standards developed or approved by the IETF has undergone several changes in its short life. The current policy was approved in June 1996 and is set forth in RFC 2026,[134] replacing the 1994 policy set forth

---

[131] *See* the Information Sciences Institute of the University of Southern California site, *The Internet Standards Process—Revision 3: A Proposed Revision of Part of RFC 1602* at http://info.internet.isi.edu/0/in-drafts/files/draft-ietf-poised95-std-proc-3-06.txt.

[132] *Id.* at § 4.1.2.

[133] *Id.* at § 6.1.2.

[134] The new policy is published at the Information Sciences Institute of the University of Southern California root site, *The Internet Standards Process—Revision 3* at http://info.internet.isi.edu/in-notes/rfc/files/rfc2026.txt.

in RFC 1602.[135] RFC 1602, in turn, rendered obsolete the provisions in the 1992 policy published as RFC 1310.[136]

Rules governing contributions.   Under current IETF policy, each person actually submitting a contribution to the IETF is treated as making a number of representations on behalf of himself, any organization he represents, and any known owner of any property rights in the contribution.[137] Specifically, the contributor:

---

[135] RFC 1602 was published in March 1994 and is available at the Information Sciences Institute of the University of Southern California root site, *The Internet Standards Process— Revision 2* at

  http://info.internet.isi.edu/in-notes/rfc/files/rfc1602.txt.

IPR issues are addressed in § 5 of the RFC. RFC 1602 provided that a contributor of information or ideas, whether orally or in writing, (a) granted ISOC a nonexclusive, royalty-free license under any copyrights in the contribution, (b) warranted that other entities that helped prepare the contribution were informed of the rights granted to ISOC and that authorization to grant such rights had been obtained, and (c) warranted that the contribution does not violate the rights of others. Participants in standards work are also responsible for informing the IETF of any proprietary rights claimed in a contribution.

A technology that was subject to known IPRs could not be included in a Standards Track document without the prior written authorization of the IPR owner that: (a) ISOC was free to implement technology in its standards work, (b) upon adoption of an Internet Standard, any party will be able to obtain such rights under specified, reasonable, and nondiscriminatory terms, and (c) the IPR owner has the right to grant such licenses and knows of no other IPR that would prevent others from implementing the standard.

For a discussion of some of the perceived problems with the policy reflected in RFC 1602, *see* T. Abate, Internet Infighting, Upside 84 (Oct. 1995) (discussing concerns over the IETF's legal liability and "headaches" associated with Motorola's claimed patent rights in a point-to-point protocol (PPP) compression standard under development by the IETF, as well as IBM's claimed patent rights in a proposed standard for mobile Internet connections), and *Internet Task Force Wakes Up To Reality of Intellectual Property,* Information Law Alert 5 (Feb. 9, 1996).

[136] RFC 1310 was published in March 1992 and is available at the Information Sciences Institute of the University of Southern California root site, *The Internet Standards Process* at
  http://info.internet.isi.edu/in-notes/rfc/files/rfc1310.txt.

The intellectual property provisions of RFC 1310 are found in §§ 5 (Intellectual Property Rights) and 6 (Patent Policy). Section 5 provided that "[p]rior to the approval of a specification as a Proposed Standard, all interested parties are required to disclose to the IAB the existence of any intellectual property right claims known to them that might apply to any aspect of the Proposed Standard." Section 6 (which was tentatively proposed but awaiting legal review) further elaborated upon the disclosure requirements with respect to patent rights. Specifically, a holder of a patent right that the holder believed would be infringed by conformance to the proposed IS was to provide the IAB with an assurance that a license would be available for implementing the standard either (a) without compensation, or (b) under "specified reasonable terms and conditions that are, to the satisfaction of the IAB, demonstrably free of any unfair discrimination." The patent holder was also required to provide assurances that it had the right to grant the license and "notification of any other patent licenses that are required, or else assurance that no other licenses are required."

[137] RTC 2026 at § 10.3.1.

1. Grants an unlimited, perpetual, nonexclusive, royalty-free license to the ISOC and IETF under any copyrights in the contribution, including the right to prepare, copy, publish, and distribute derivative works of the contribution

2. Represents that all "major" contributors are properly acknowledged

3. Represents that no contributed information is confidential and that the information may be freely disclosed by others

4. Represents that the contributor has disclosed the existence of any proprietary or intellectual property rights in the contribution that are reasonably and personally known to the contributor[138]

5. Warrants that other named contributors were (a) made aware of *and* (b) agreed to accept the above terms and conditions on behalf of themselves, their organizations, and any known owner of proprietary rights in the contribution.

Rules governing standards track documents. An additional set of rules applies to documents that are on the IETF standards track.[139] Specifically, if any patent, patent application, or other proprietary right is known or claimed in any specification on the standards track, the IETF will attempt to obtain a written assurance from the claimant. This assurance provides that, upon approval of the specification, "any party will be able to obtain the right to implement, use and distribute the technology or works when implementing, using or distributing technology based upon the specific specification(s) under openly specified, reasonable, non-discriminatory terms."[140] The IETF will not, however, determine whether this assurance has been satisfied but will assume that it has when (a) the two unrelated implementations of the specification, required to advance from Proposed Standard to Draft Standard, were produced by different organizations, or (b) the "significant implementation and successful operational experience" required to advance from Draft Standard to Standard have been achieved.[141] In addition, the implementations required to advance a proposal through the standards process will be considered adequate only if the implementer provides a statement that it has appropriately addressed any identified IPRs (or claimed rights), for example, by licensing. Any specification advanced under these circumstances will bear a note indicating the existence of a right or claimed right.

---

[138] The IETF acknowledges that the contributor does not represent that he knows about all IPRs of any organization he represents, or of third parties.

[139] RTC 2026 at § 10.3.2.

[140] *Id*. at § 10.3.2(C).

[141] *Id*. at § 10.3.3.

§ 7.24   —World Wide Web Consortium (W3C)

Created in 1994, the World Wide Web Consortium (W3C)[142] is a nonprofit organization based at the Laboratory for Computer Science (LCS) of the Massachusetts Institute of Technology (MIT) and the French National Information Processing/Automation Laboratory (INRIA). Membership in W3C is open to any organization or corporation,[143] and more than 100 companies are currently members.

The W3C performs a number of functions. W3C teams develop standards required to support the continuing evolution of nearly all aspects of the WWW and also demonstrate sample applications of new technology.[144] The W3C maintains a repository of information about the WWW, including specifications relating to the WWW. The W3C further provides reference code implementations of standard technology.

As part of its work, the W3C cooperates with the IETF, as well as the European Laboratory for Particle Physics (CERN) and the National Center for Supercomputing Applications (NCSA).[145] Although W3C team members often participate in IETF working groups, the W3C teams are primarily responsible for *developing* technology standards, which may be submitted to the IETF standards track.

The W3C process is as follows.[146] Any member of the W3C can initiate a proposal for new work by preparing a complete draft specification of interfaces and functionality. The proposal then goes through a four-stage process. A trial review by an advisory committee is performed to determine whether a technical

---

[142] The W3C's home page is at
http://www.w3.org.

[143] There are two types of memberships: Full Members ($150,000 annual membership fee; for companies with gross revenues over $50 million) and Affiliate Members ($15,000 annual membership fee). Unlike membership in the ISOC, membership in the W3C is not generally open to individuals.

[144] For example, the W3C is working to standardize the ongoing extensions to HTML.

[145] CERN was the originator of the World Wide Web, and its home page is at
http://www.cern.ch.
For a discussion of CERN's role in the birth and evolution of the Web, *see* the ITU root site, *CERN: Birthplace of the World Wide Web* at
http://www3.itu.ch/MISSIONS/US/bb/cern.html#www.
NCSA is located at the University of Illinois in Champagne-Urbana and developed Mosaic, the initial graphic Web browser. NCSA's home page is at
http://www.ncsa.uiuc.edu.
Other organizations of interest include Enterprise Integration Technologies (EIT) and Commerce Net, a consortium of companies established to develop a pilot project for Web-based commerce.

[146] For more background, *see* the W3C root site, *W3C Process* at
http://www.w3.org/pub/WWW/Consortium/Process.

review is merited. If so, all W3C members are given the opportunity to participate in a three-month technical review. Upon successful completion of the technical review, the proposal enters a three-month public review period, during
which public comment is solicited via the World Wide Web. At the same time,
an implementation of the specification is pursued to demonstrate the specification's practical utility or "proof of concept." The final stage in the proposal's
journey is approval.

Software developed by the W3C is available to members during development.
One month after formal internal release, however, code developed by (or officially contributed to) the W3C is available for commercial use by the general
public.

Some of the IPR issues considered by the W3C are addressed in § 7 of the
Full Member Participation Agreement,[147] which sets forth members' obligations
regarding IPRs. For example, members agree that MIT, INRIA, and W3C members are all free to use information developed under the auspices of the W3C.
Software, documentation, and inventions developed for the W3C by MIT (or
visitors working at MIT) are owned by MIT. If developed by INRIA (or visitors
working at INRIA), such software, documentation, and inventions are owned by
INRIA. Inventions and copyrighted materials developed jointly by MIT, INRIA,
and a member are jointly owned, and MIT and INRIA agree to make such
inventions and copyrights available to the general public for "unrestricted use."
MIT and INRIA grant members a royalty-free, irrevocable license to all computer software and documentation. MIT and INRIA also indicate their intent to
grant similar rights to the general public.

In a separate draft document published for discussion,[148] the W3C also suggests additional steps that should be taken by a member submitting a technical
specification to the W3C. The member should submit a statement regarding the
IPRs associated with the specification, as well as a statement concerning the
terms of any proprietary technology known to the submitter and required to
implement the specification.

§ 7.25   Other Organizations

Along with the pivotal organizations already discussed, a number of additional
organizations have a stake in the evolving standards of the Internet. A few of
these organizations are discussed in §§ 7.26 through 7.31.

---

[147] The full membership agreement can be found at the W3C root site, *International World
Wide Web Consortium Participation Agreement: Full Member Agreement* at
http://www.w3.org/pub/WWW/Consortium/Agreement/Full.html.
The affiliate membership agreement can be found at the W3C root site, *International World
Wide Web Consortium Participation Agreement: Affiliate Member Agreement* at
http://www.w3.org/pub/WWW/Consortium/Agreement/Affiliate.html.

[148] *See* W3C root site, *Submission to the W3C* at
http://www.w3.org/pub/WWW/Consortium/Process/Submission.

§ 7.26 —International Telecommunications Union (ITU)

The International Telecommunications Union (ITU)[149] was originally formed in 1865 as the International Telegraph Union and, in 1947, became one of the specialized agencies of the United Nations.[150] The ITU has three areas of responsibility with respect to telecommunications: technical, development, and policy. In its technical capacity, the ITU attempts to ensure that international telecommunications are interoperable on a worldwide basis, in part through the development and approval of standards. The ITU is also responsible for supporting the establishment of telecommunications infrastructure in developing countries. Finally, the ITU addresses virtually all aspects of telecommunications policy at the global level.

The ITU is composed of more than 180 member states (that is, countries, like the United States), as well as roughly 360 member companies and organizations (for example, corporations such as Microsoft). The ITU maintains technical liaisons with ISO and IEC.[151] Given its emphasis on telecommunications, the work of the ITU Telecommunication Standardization Sector (ITU-T) has obvious implications for the Internet. In late 1995, roughly 400 delegates of ITU-T Study Group 15 met to discuss new standards and future workplans relevant to the development of the global information highway.[152] At that meeting, various recommendations were approved, and others proposed, regarding a variety of technical subjects including transport networks, audiovisual systems, Asynchronous Transfer Mode (ATM) equipment, and audio-video encoding for cellular and wireless telephony.

ITU Structure.   The ITU is directed by a Plenipotentiary Conference (PC) of member states. The PC is convened every four years and is responsible for long-term policy issues regarding the ITU and international telecommunications. Given the relatively infrequent occurrence of PCs, an ITU council provides interim direction to the ITU. The council is composed of 46 members and

---

[149] The ITU's home page is at
   http://www.itu.ch.
   For more background information regarding the ITU, *see* the ITU root site, *About the ITU* at
   http://www.itu.ch/aboutitu.

[150] Other United Nations special agencies include the World Intellectual Property Organization (WIPO) and the International Computing Centre, as well as universally recognized organizations such as the World Bank, the World Health Organization, and the United Nations International Children's Emergency Fund (UNICEF).

[151] For example, in the area of connection protocols, ITU and ISO/IEC collaboration resulted in the issuance of ITU-T Recommendations x.227 and x.247, corresponding to ISO/IEC Standards 8650-1 and 8650-2, respectively.

[152] *See* Jan. 5, 1996, ITU-T Press Release entitled *New Standards for the Global Information Highway* at the ITU root site
   http://www.itu.ch/press/1996/itu-03e.htm.

provides some fiscal oversight for the ITU. The daily administration and operation of the ITU is handled by the ITU General Secretariat.

The technical work of the ITU is done by several different sectors. The sector of greatest interest to Internet-related issues is the ITU-T.[153] The ITU-T was formed in 1992 as part of a structural reorganization of the ITU, replacing the earlier International Telegraph and Telephone Consultative Committee (CCITT).

The ITU-T activities are performed by World Telecommunications Standardization Conferences, a Telecommunications Standardization Advisory Group (TSAG), a Standardization Bureau, and a number of study groups. Conferences are held every four years to approve, reject, and modify recommendations. The administration of the ITU-T is the responsibility of the Standardization Bureau, which benefits from the advice and support of TSAG. Study groups are responsible for the technical work.

The United States Department of State is the United States' member body of the ITU. In that regard, the Department of State's role in the ITU is similar to ANSI's role in ISO and IEC.

ITU Process. The standards work of the ITU is done primarily through study groups.[154] These groups are organized to address areas of possible improvement in international telecommunications identified by a PC. Each group includes technical experts from various member organizations. These experts work together to develop and adopt the nonbinding technical standards of the ITU, referred to as recommendations.

Recommendations are published by the ITU in various "series." For example, the "v" series of recommendations (including, for example, v.32 and v.42) deals with data communications over telephone networks (using, modems), and the "x" series of recommendations (including x.25 for packet switching networks and x.400 for e-mail) relates to data networks and open systems communications.[155]

ITU Patent Policy. The ITU's policy regarding intellectual property issues specifically addresses only patents.[156] Given the ITU's ultimate goal of achieving compatibility in international communications, the ITU's policy is generally

---

[153] Other sectors include, for example, the Radiocommunication Sector (ITU-R) and Telecommunications Development Sector (ITU-D). The ITU-R was formed by the merger of the International Radio Consultative Committee (CCIR) and the International Frequency Registration Board (IFBR). The ITU-D replaces the earlier Telecommunications Development Bureau.

[154] For more details regarding ITU process, *see* the ITU root site, *What is ITU?* at
http://www.itu.int/aboutitu/whatitu.html#structure.

[155] A complete list of the ITU-T's recommendations is available at the ITU site, *List of ITU-T Recommendations* at
http://www.itu.ch/publications/itu-t/itutrec/htm.

[156] The ITU policy is set forth in *Statement of TSB Patent Policy,* Annex 2 (to TSB Circular 125). The TSB is the Telecommunications Standards Bureau.

intended to ensure that everyone has access to, and the freedom to use, the ITU's recommendations.

Some of the key elements of the ITU's patent policy are as follows. Any ITU-T member organization proposing a standard should, from the outset, advise the Telecommunications Standards Bureau (TSB) of any known patent or pending application, regardless of who owns the patent or application. If an ITU-T recommendation is developed, the patent holder must file a written statement with the TSB stating that: (a) the patent holder waives her rights and that the recommendation is accessible to everyone under no particular conditions, including no obligation of royalty; (b) the patent holder does not waive her rights but is willing to negotiate licenses with other parties on a "nondiscriminatory basis on reasonable terms and conditions;" or (c) the patent holder is not willing to do either of the above, in which case the recommendation cannot be established.

The ITU-T does not, however, involve itself in any licensing negotiations, royalty collections, or other details that may arise out of the organizations' compliance with the above policy.

§ 7.27 —Europe

Standardization in Europe has gone through several different stages in the last quarter century. Before the 1970s, standards were a national affair, often conducted with little regard for corresponding initiatives under way in other countries. Gradually, the barriers created by such a national focus were breached by directives, including technical specifications that were applicable to the entire European Community (EC).

In 1985, the EC shifted primary responsibility for the development of technical specifications required to implement directives to European standards organizations, such as the Joint European Standards Institution (CEN/CENELEC).[157] One member state's determination that a product complied with such a specification was all that was required.

Another transition in European standards policy occurred in the mid-1990s. The European Union traditionally required government contracts to be based upon European or International Standards.[158] A workshop on Information and Communication Technology Standardization, held by the European Commission in

---

[157] Council Resolution a New Approach to Technical Harmonization and Standards, No. 85/C136/01, 1985 O.J. (C 136).

[158] Council Decision on Standardization in the Field of Information Technology and Telecommunications, No. 87/95/EEC, 1986 O.J. (L 36/31). *See also* R.M. O'Connor, A Guide to the Requirements of the IT Standards Decision and the Revised Supplies Directive (2d ed. 1991). For information and communications technology, public purchases of a value of ECU 100,000 or more should include technical specifications in the tender documents that refer to applicable European Standards (ENs), European Pre-Standards (ENVs), or International Standards (IS) relating to information exchange and systems interoperability.

November 1994, resulted in recommendations opening government procurement and paralleling the FIRP's recommendations concerning the United States government's GOSIP.[159] The Director General of the Directorate General III (DGIII) concluded that "the concept of open systems has gained universal acceptance. We have also learned, however, that 'openness' does not necessarily require officially sanctioned or formalized standards. Indeed, the emergence of *de facto* standardization appears to have created a cheaper alternative to publicly promoted formal standardization exercises."[160]

As for the European view of standards in the Global Information Society (GIS), the 1994 Bangemann Report[161] provided recommendations to the European Council. Although acknowledging the traditional importance of formal standards organizations, the report noted that the standards process "raises a number of concerns about fitness for purpose, lack of interoperability, and priority setting that is not sufficiently market-driven."

The Bangemann Report went on to make a number of recommendations. For example, the report concluded that standards efforts should focus upon those interfaces where standardization is required to enable global interoperability, leaving the marketplace to develop solutions in other areas. Further, the standards process should be kept more closely in tune with marketplace concerns. Not surprisingly, the report stated that standards should be driven at the European level, not the national level. Other recommendations included increased support for Publicly Available Specifications (PAS), greater integration of community-funded research and development with standards work, and increased availability of free reference implementations of standard specifications.

European policy regarding the role of standards in the GIS was further addressed in a 1996 communication.[162] This document outlines various objectives and initiatives intended to ensure that standards work. The standards should improve global competitiveness, promote technical solutions, protect the public interest, and reinforce international cooperation with respect to the GIS.

One outcome of this work is the proposed organization of a worldwide conference on the GII to be convened in 1997. This conference will follow up on the conclusions of the 1995 G7 summit in Brussels, which generally proposed the identification and resolution of standards issues required to facilitate the timely development of the GIS.[163] Specifically, the conference is intended to provide an

---

[159] See § **7.5.**

[160] S. Micossi, Director General, DGIII, Introductory Speech to IT Standardization Policy Workshop (Nov. 28, 1994).

[161] Europe and the Global Information Society: Recommendations to the European Council (May 26, 1994). For a general discussion of the evolving European policy relating to standards, *see* Wood, *European Standardization Policy,* 3 StandardView 112 (Sept. 1995).

[162] Communication from the Commission to the Council and the Parliament on "Standardization and the Global Information Society: The European Approach," COM(96) 359 (July 24, 1996).

[163] Conference on Standardization for GIS, Preparatory Working Group Paper (August 20, 1996).

open forum for GIS market players to discuss applications for the GIS, impediments to these applications, standards issues, and related technical and legal regulations.

The European Organizations.   A 1986 European Council decision requires European IT and telecommunications standards work to be performed primarily at the regional level.[164] The European standards bodies responsible for this work include: CEN, CENELEC, and ETSI. The work of these organizations in the field of Information and Communications Technology (ICT) is coordinated by the ICT Standards Board. These organizations are discussed in §§ **7.28** through **7.30.**

§ 7.28   —Joint European Standards Institution (CEN/CENELEC)

The Joint European Standards Institution, CEN/CENELEC, is composed of the European Standards Committee (CEN) and the European Electrotechnical Standards Committee (CENELEC). CEN/CENELEC is based in Brussels and includes the national standards bodies and the electrotechnical committees of the following countries: Austria, Belgium, Denmark, Finland, France, Germany, Greece, Iceland, Ireland, Italy, Luxembourg, the Netherlands, Norway, Portugal, Sweden, Switzerland, Spain, and the United Kingdom. Although European Standards (EN and ETS) are usually based on ISO, IEC, or ITU standards, standards may also be created specifically for Europe when international standards are not available. This factor, in combination with the emphasis of European (rather than national) standards, has left organizations such as the German Institute for Standardization (Duetsches Institut für Normung, DIN) doing almost all of their work on European Standards.[165]

CEN/CENELEC publishes several types of documents including European Standards (ENs), European Pre-Standards (ENVs), and Harmonisation Documents (HDs). The standards bodies of the CEN/CENELEC members vote for acceptance of CEN/CENELEC draft technical specifications as ENs on a majority basis. Adopted standards must be implemented in their entirety as national standards, regardless of the way in which the national member voted. Any conflicting national standards must be withdrawn.

In rapidly evolving areas requiring some direction, an ENV may be prepared as a prospective standard. As a result, the preparation time is reduced and, once adopted, an ENV is subject to an experimental period of up to three years, with the ultimate goal of being transformed to an EN.

---

[164] Council Decision on Standardization in the Field of Information Technology and Telecommunications, No. 87/95/EEC, 1986 O.J. (L 36/31).

[165] *See* the DIN root site, *Standardization in Europe* at
http://www.din.de/en/din/DIN-Portrait/Europe.html,
where it is estimated that DIN is doing only 20% national standards work.

An HD is drafted and adopted in the same manner as an EN but need not be so rigidly applied as a national standard in each member country. Instead, technical conditions peculiar to individual member countries may be taken into account.

§ 7.29 —European Telecommunications Standards Institute (ETSI)

The European Telecommunications Standards Institute (ETSI)[166] has been recognized as a European standards-making body by the European Council of Ministers.[167] ETSI has subject matter jurisdiction over the field of European telecommunications and shares responsibility for IT and broadcasting with CEN/CENELEC and the European Broadcasting Union (EBU), respectively.[168] ETSI is actively involved in development of the European Information Infrastructure Standardization policy (EPIIS).[169]

Membership in ETSI is open to a variety of entities including network operators, vendors, service providers, administrators, users, and the research community. ETSI enables this community to determine the market requirements for standardization and then attempts to build the consensus required to successfully establish and deploy such standards.

Structurally, ETSI is composed of a General Assembly (GA), a board, technical committees, and special task forces and special committees.[170] The GA determines ETSI policy and has ultimate responsibility for the management of ETSI. The GA has delegated the operation of ETSI's Technical Organization to a board, which also supervises the day-to-day operations of ETSI. The Technical Organization is designed to offer technical experts an opportunity to work together on technical committees to provide market-driven, technologically oriented standards solutions.

ETSI's policy on IPR issues has been unsettled. In 1990, the EC issued a Green Paper on the Development of European Standardization.[171] The commission suggested that contributions to a standard should be given serious consideration

---

[166] ETSI's home page is found at
http://www.etsi.fr.

[167] Council Directive No. 83/189/EEC, O.J.L. 109/8.

[168] For a more complete discussion of ETSI's relationship with other organizations, *see* the ETSI site, *ETSI Presentation: ETSI and the World Around* at
http://www.etsi.fr/dir/about/present/around.htm.

[169] *See* the ETSI root site, *Building the Information Communications Technologies Highway* at
http://www.etsi.fr/ecs/reports/wip.htm,
and *ETSI EPIISG on European Information Infrastructure* at
http://www2.echo.lu/oii/en/epiisg.html.

[170] *See* the ETSI root site, *About ETSI* at
http://www.etsi.fr/dir/about/about.htm.

[171] For a more detailed discussion, *see* Epstein.

only if "sufficient information including, when appropriate, the applicable licensing provisions" is made available regarding any IPRs associated with the contribution. It also recognized that some solution needed to be found for those exceptional cases in which it is difficult to reconcile the need for effective standards and the legitimate interests of IPR owners.

ETSI responded with a proposal that involved compulsory, worldwide licensing. In the midst of industry opposition to that proposal, the commission came out with another communication indicating that agreements with IPR holders must be fair, reasonable, and nondiscriminatory, reasoning that without such agreements, it would be inadvisable to continue with a standard. Procedural fairness to the IPR holder was important.

Then, in 1994, ETSI's general assembly approved an interim IPR policy.[172] Some of the key provisions of that policy are as follows. Members shall use reasonable efforts to timely inform ETSI of "essential" IPRs (that is, if a standard can be implemented only by technical solutions that would infringe the IPR, the IPR is essential), although members shall have no obligation to search for such IPR. The European Commission may also request ETSI to have a search conducted for essential IPRs.

In the event an essential IPR is identified, the director of ETSI shall request the owner to provide a written assurance that it will grant irrevocable licenses on fair, reasonable, and nondiscriminatory terms and conditions. This license grant can, however, be conditioned upon the licensee's agreement to grant reciprocal licenses.

Should an IPR owner be unwilling to grant a license, ETSI will investigate the availability of a viable alternative technology. If none is found, ETSI will refer the matter to the director of ETSI and the ETSI counselors for consideration, which may result in nonrecognition of the standard.

Any IPRs owned by ETSI are licensed to members free of charge and to nonmembers on fair and reasonable terms and conditions.

§ 7.30   —Information and Communications Technology (ICT) Standards Board

In 1995, CEN, CENELEC, and ETSI formed the ICT Standards Board[173] to address common issues relating to ICT standards, to evaluate the need for standards, and to establish projects to address those needs. In addition to the three members, the board includes a variety of Publicly Available Specifications (PAS)

---

[172] *See* the ETSI root site, *Rules of Procedure of the European Telecommunications Standards Institute: Annex 6 ETSI Interim Intellectual Property Rights Policy* at
http://www.etsi.fr/dis/infocentre/RoP/RoP2.html.
See also Epstein for additional background regarding the history of ETSI's IPR policy.

[173] The ICT Standards Board home page is at
http://www.ict.etsi.fr/base.htm.
The ICT Standards Board replaces the Information Technology Steering Committee.

providers, such as ATM Forum, Network Management Forum (NMF), and X/Open. Among the initiatives under consideration by the board's High-Level Strategy Group (HLSG) are electronic commerce, interoperability of broadband networks, and city-level information infrastructures.

§ 7.31 —East Asia

In contrast to Europe, less effort appears to have been made to centralize standards work in East Asia. Certainly, individual countries are represented in the international standards organizations by their national member organizations.[174] Some organizations are also chartered specifically to address the needs of the IT industry.[175] Given the general decentralization of this work across East Asia, however, even a brief discussion of the organizations involved is beyond the scope of this article.

§ 7.32 Recent Developments

As noted in § 7.7, the standards world has been grappling with a number of challenges presented by the dynamic environment associated with IT. Organizations have responded to these challenges in a variety of ways, some of which are discussed in §§ 7.33 and 7.34 as recent developments in standards processes and policies.

§ 7.33 —Publicly Available Specifications (PAS)

One of the primary difficulties that IT presents to traditional standards organizations is the rapid rate of technological change. In many instances, it is simply not

---

[174] For example, national members (excluding correspondent and subscribing members) in ISO/IEC include Standards Australia (SAA), China State Bureau of Technical Supervision (CSBTS), Dewan Standarisasi Nasional (Standardization Council of Indonesia), Japanese Industrial Standards Committee (JISC), Committee for Standardization of the Democratic People's Republic of Korea (CSK), Korean National Institute of Technology and Quality (KNITQ), Department of Standards of Malaysia (DSM), Mongolian National Institute for Standardization and Metrology (MNISM), Standards New Zealand (SNZ), Philippines Bureau of Product Standards (BPS), Singapore Productivity and Standards Board (PSB), Thai Industrial Standards Institute (TISI), and Viet Nam Directorate for Standards and Quality (TCVN). Looking at one East Asian country in particular, in addition to the work of the JISC, a number of other organizations pursue standards work in Japan including: Japanese Standards Association (JSA), Telecommunication Technology Committee (TTC), and Japan Electronic Industry Development Association (JEIDA).

[175] Two such organizations include the Interoperability Technology Association for Information Processing (INTAP) and Information Processing Society of Japan/Information Technology Standards Commission of Japan (IPSJ/ITSCJ).

practical for the deliberate consensus building of traditional standards processes to keep abreast with the needs of such an industry. The JTC 1 recently defined and implemented a policy intended to address this problem by encouraging the transposition of technical specifications developed by sources outside the JTC 1 into international standards.[176] These specifications are referred to as Publicly Available Specifications (PAS).

To better understand the significance of PAS, it may first be helpful to discuss the traditional JTC 1 process. Normally, the process begins when one of the JTC 1's technical bodies establishes a proposal developed over an open-ended and potentially lengthy period of time. The establishment of consensus for the proposal is followed by a four-month ballot of JTC 1 national bodies to approve promotion of the specification to an International Standard (IS). As part of its fast-track process, a national body (or a liaison organization) is able to submit a standard from any source directly to a final JTC 1 ballot, which may become an IS at the end of a six-month ballot.[177]

The PAS process differs in several ways. First, a PAS and its originator generally (although not necessarily) must satisfy a number of criteria. The *specification* is evaluated to determine its quality,[178] support or consensus,[179] and alignment.[180] The *organization* is, in turn, evaluated to determine its cooperative stance,[181] characteristics,[182] and position on IPRs.[183] For example, the organization's willingness to comply with the ISO/IEC patent policy and to grant needed

---

[176] *The Transposition of Publicly Available Specifications into International Standards—A Management Guide,* ISO/IEC JTC 1 N 3582 [hereinafter Management Guide]. A trial process for PAS extended through January 1997.

[177] Also, an International Standardized Profile (ISP), which brings together elements of ISs, may be submitted to the JTC 1's Special Group on Functional Standardization (SGFS) along with an accompanying explanatory report. The SGFS then submits the ISP to the national bodies with a review report for a four-month ballot.

[178] Management Guide § 4.1: the completeness of the description of the functionality required to implement the PAS, as well as the clarity, testability, stability, and availability of the specification.

[179] *Id.* § 4.2: development process, user involvement, market acceptance, credibility.

[180] *Id.* § 4.3: relationship to existing standards, adaptability.

[181] *Id.* § 3.1. X/Open was the first recognized submitter of PAS.

[182] *Id.* § 3.2.

[183] The IPR section of the Management Guide is as follows:

Section 3.3 Intellectual Property Rights: (M)

The organization is requested to make known their position on the items listed below. In particular, there shall be a written statement of willingness of the organisation and its members, if applicable, to comply with the ISO/IEC patent policy in reference to the PAS under consideration.

Note: Each JTC 1 National Body should investigate and report the legal implications of this section.

3.3.1) Patents:

a) How willing are the organization and its members to meet the ISO/IEC policy on these matters?

copyrights are factors influencing the acceptability of an organization as a PAS submitter.

The transposition process itself involves three key phases: recognition, submission, and ballot. During the *recognition* phase, an organization wishing to submit a specification must submit statements regarding its organizational qualifications and an identification of the PAS to be submitted. A three-month ballot of the JTC 1 national bodies is then held to approve the organization as a PAS submitter, which status remains valid for two years.

During the *submission* phase, the document is submitted to the JTC 1 Secretariat, along with an explanatory report that contains statements regarding the document-related criteria, as well as any statements regarding the submitter's unwillingness to have the PAS changed through transposition. The explanatory report is critical to successful transposition, and various JTC 1 organizations are available to assist the PAS submitter in preparing the report. The JTC 1 Secretariat checks the recognition status of the submitter and forwards the specification and explanatory report to either (a) the ISO/IEC Information Technology Task Force (ITTF) to initiate the appropriate ballot process among JTC 1 national bodies, or (b) JTC 1/SGFS if it is intended for transposition into an International Standardized Profile (ISP).

The *ballot* process follows normal JTC 1 rules. The PAS is submitted to the national bodies along with the explanatory report. The national bodies may suggest changes. The balloting process takes anywhere from five to eleven months. If the ballot fails, the submitter will be notified of the reasons for the failure and have the option of resubmitting. If the specification is being transposed into an IS, balloting follows the fast-track process. If the specification is

---

3.3.2) Copyrights:

a)   What copyrights have been granted relevant to the subject specification(s)?

b)   What copyrights is the PAS originator willing to grant?

c)   What conditions, if any, apply (e.g., copyright statements, electronic labels, logos)?

3.3.3) Distribution Rights:

a)   What distribution rights exist and what are the terms of use?

b)   What degree of flexibility exists relative to modifying distribution rights; before the transposition process is complete, after transposition completion?

3.3.4) Trademark Rights:

a)   What trademarks apply to the subject specification?

b)   What are the conditions for use and are they to be transferred to ISO/IEC in part or in their entirety?

3.3.5) Original Contributions:

a)   What original contributions (outside the above IPR categories) (e.g., documents, plans, research, papers, tests, proposals) need consideration in terms of ownership and recognition?

b)   What financial considerations are there?

c)   What legal considerations are there?

being transposed into an ISP, balloting follows the ISP process. The final step in the process is publication.

As a result, the PAS is intended to allow an IS to be established more rapidly than through the conventional normal and fast-track processes.

§ 7.34 —Normative Referencing

Another approach being considered by the JTC 1 to allow more rapid adoption of standard technology is normative referencing.[184] Normative referencing would allow a specification from some source other than ISO, IEC, or ITU to be referenced within an International Standard (IS), without actually becoming an IS. It should be noted, however, that JTC 1 prefers PAS over normative referencing.

The normative referencing process is initiated when a JTC 1 technical subcommittee (SC) determines the need for a normative reference. The SC then selects and evaluates the appropriate proposed Referenced Specification (RS). Guidelines help the SC decide whether and how to incorporate an RS into a JTC 1 IS.

For example, the RS must comply with JTC 1 rules concerning conformity and interoperability and must include a Referencing Explanatory Report (RER). The RER describes the rationale for the referencing, the extent of market acceptance of the RS, the reasons why transposition is an inappropriate or impractical alternative, and the compliance of the RS with various criteria. These criteria (which guide, rather than restrict, the SC) include the existence of a written statement from the RS originator that it agrees to the referencing of a specific document in a JTC 1 standard. The criteria also address responsibility for maintenance of the RS, the originator's receptiveness to any changes requested during balloting on the referencing standard, public availability of the RS on "fair, reasonable and non-discriminatory terms and conditions," and the originator's willingness to notify the JTC 1 of any intention to terminate the availability of the RS. The SC must also obtain from the originator a written statement concerning IPR. This statement must include the RS position on ISO/IEC patent policy, the existence of copyrights and the originator's willingness to grant rights throughout the evaluation and publication cycle, and the existence and conditions of trademarks applying to the RS.

The SC's work is ultimately subject to balloting by the national bodies. The material submitted for ballot includes a copy of the proposed RS, as well as a copy of the referencing standard. The RS does not have to be published or distributed with the referencing standard.

---

[184] *The Normative Referencing of Specifications other than International Standards in JTC1 International Standards,* JTC1/WG-RS DC 5. This proposal is not as advanced as the PAS process discussed in **§ 7.33.** Normative referencing is to be contrasted to informative referencing covered in ISO/IEC Directives Part 3.

§ 7.35 Conclusion

As this chapter demonstrates, the interplay between standards and the Internet covers a wide range of organizations and issues. In the confines of this chapter, it has not been possible to do more than expose the reader to some of the issues and, it is hoped, raise the reader's awareness of the complexity and uncertainty associated with some of these issues. With that background and the requisite research, business participants in standards organizations may be better equipped to serve the organizations and their interests. Similarly, counselors may be better able to advise their clients involved in standards work, regardless of whether those clients are standards organizations, members, participants, or simply members of the public wishing to employ standard technology.

CHAPTER 8

LITIGATION AND JURISDICTION

Katie Sako

§ 8.1   Introduction

Much discussion in earlier chapters concerns the technologies, old and new, that make up the Internet. With respect to intellectual property rights, there is some expectation that the Internet community can pick and choose the forms of rights and enforcement that will apply to the Internet. However, it is abundantly clear that the old forms will not simply die off, but that much of the debate will be taken up in legislative efforts and in the courts. This chapter briefly addresses a few issues relating to litigation and jurisdiction that may arise because of the wide-ranging use of the Internet.

One topic at the forefront of any discussion of Internet-related litigation is whether our understanding of jurisdiction will be completely confused by the international, unbounded nature of the Internet. On the national level, these issues can be resolved with application of existing rules. Some early cases deciding jurisdiction, particularly in trademark and copyright cases, refuse to consider the Internet the sole reason for subjecting a person to wide-ranging jurisdiction. However, there are also cases that suggest that use of the Internet may subject a person to personal jurisdiction in numerous forums simply because of "potential" contact with the forum. Another looming question concerns how likely it is that a foreign defendant will be subject to jurisdiction in the United States based in whole or in part on the defendant's contact over the Internet.

In **Chapter 6,** copyright and trademark issues, including the key substantive litigation topics, are discussed in detail. In summary, copyright law must be viewed in light of the increased ease of reproduction and transmission, and trademark law is running head-on into possible conflict with domain naming practices. Conflict in these two areas has arisen quickly and is being dealt with on judicial, regulatory, and legislative fronts. In the area of patents and trade secret, the immediate conflicts are not so apparent. Issues particularly related to patents are discussed in § 8.3. Trade secret practice issues are not greatly affected by the Internet other than the fact that it is easier to disseminate an ill-gotten secret, and an entity may want to beef up its network security to ensure that external access to trade secrets is not accidentally provided.

§ 8.2   Jurisdiction

The Internet communication network crosses territorial boundaries, leaving behind momentarily traditional notions of jurisdiction and local law. The connections are easy to achieve, and the path of communications is generally nondeterministic. The architecture of the Internet may make the physical placement of information at a given time difficult. Although computers and users can still be located, any act that might be "infringing" may not be readily associated with a physical location, which in turn would be associated with a set of laws and regulations.

For intellectual property rights, the personal jurisdiction issues arise in the "usual" fashion. In copyright disputes, an infringement action might be brought against a service provider who provides copyrighted material at its site, a user who downloads the software, and maybe a network operator who allows transmission of the materials over its system. Trademark disputes may arise when a domain name conflicts with a trademarked name. In this case, the providers of each marked service or product will be in conflict. In patent cases, similar to copyright cases, an action may be brought against a service provider who provides patented material at its site, a user who downloads the software, and maybe a network operator who is operating a network using patented components. Finally, trade secret claims will arise when materials otherwise protected are delivered over the Internet and "found" at an Internet site. In each case, the players can be identified, but the ease of their connection and disconnection may make the physical relationship rather tenuous.

There are countless scenarios that illustrate the complex relationships between parties and activities that may arise on the Internet. A few examples are:

Scenario 1: A user in Seattle accesses a computer in Oregon via the URL (Uniform Resource Locator) www.HappyPlace.com. The Oregon computer stores software that might infringe a United States patent. The software might also represent infringement of a copyrighted work. The software is downloaded (in part or in whole) to the Seattle site. Alternatively, the user can cause the software to run and receive the results over the network.

Scenario 2: The same network is used as in **Scenario 1,** but software components are downloaded to the Seattle site and the components are combined with components already on the Seattle computer to create an infringing program. The user visited the site casually and downloaded the software only after it was offered, for free, by the provider.

In these scenarios, it is likely the user never knows that HappyPlace is located in Oregon, or that the service that maintains HappyPlace is located in California. It might also be the case that the service that maintains HappyPlace does not know that the particular user has accessed the site and downloaded the software, and does not know the infringing nature of that activity. Thus, in each case, the user is remote from the server being accessed, the service provider is unaware of the particular user's access, and the user is unaware of the location of the server, the operation of the system, and the existence of the infringement.

The focus of a jurisdictional question raised in the Internet environment may be more on individuals and their relationships rather than the physical connections between the parties or activities. Communications over the Internet are often anonymous, either purposefully or incidentally. A person can access a service (or server) without identifying himself or possibly by forging an identification. This may not be the case if access is restricted either to registered users or to users who are willing to provide some initial identification for access. Currently, a "hit" on a Web site may be counted but a server cannot ascertain any further information about the user, except possibly to determine what service, such as Prodigy, was used to make the connection. On the flip side, a person can access a service without knowledge of the physical location of the service or of who is controlling the service.

Some URLs include an indication of the physical location of the Web page or at least the location with which the Web page author has some relationship. A few examples include:

1. www.Seattle.com: a site entitled "Rendeszous Online," which provides information about the Seattle, Washington area

2. www.Hawaii.org: a site for Hawaii Research + Technology, maintained by the University of Hawaii

3. www.Washington.org: a site devoted to activities in and around Washington, D.C. (might someone accessing this site be looking for information related to Washington, the state?)

In the United States, Web sites are identified as .org (organization), .com (commercial), .gov (government), or .edu (education). In contrast, in Europe and other countries, the site is identified with a country location such as .fr (France) or .uk (United Kingdom). In international questions, these delimiters may play a role in determining what the defendant knew and her expectations regarding a relationship with a particular country.

It may also be the case that a Web site is so popular that its "location" is presumed to be known by all or at least by someone who regularly accesses the site. However, it is usually not the case that a URL clearly points to a physical location and, even if it appears to, the actual physical location of the server may not be the same as that suggested by the URL. An example illustrates that a Web site can disclose a variety of information, both clarifying and confusing, about its location. At the Netscape Corporation home page (www.Netscape.com), there is no indication that Netscape is located in California, unless the user is familiar with the area code that appears with a telephone number at the bottom of the home page. A section of the home page dealing with code downloadable in a variety of languages is much more prominent than the area code. The question is what impression is left on a user regarding the internationalized code—that the code is available from one site or from a variety of international sites? Netscape's engineers are probably the only people who know the answer.

To further potentially complicate matters, the Internet is rapidly evolving from a "passive" system, one in which no communication takes place unless a query is initiated by a user, to a system wherein service providers may "push" data to users. An example of a pushed service is an advertising service that sends out unsolicited e-mail advertisements to users who meet a certain demographic profile. This is very similar to services that deliver hard copy junk mail. Thus, although many jurisdictional questions will center around a defendant's explicit activities to query a Web site or establish a connection, questions will also be raised by services that can be more proactive and initialize unsolicited contact with a large number of users.

Finally, the scenarios presented can be easily complicated by placing either end of the communication outside of the United States, or even placing both ends outside of the United States but having information flow through servers in the United States. International issues are beyond the scope of this chapter other than to note that they should be considered whenever a strategy to avoid or reduce exposure is developed.

The question to be answered is: what is the right forum for adjudicating a claim of infringement, whether by the user, the service provider, or a third party? The classic test requires consideration of the relationship between the desired forum state and the defendant. That approach does not change for cases involving the Internet, although it may take some extra work to determine what the defendant knew or understood his relationship to be with the forum.

§ 8.3 Jurisdiction Basics

For those of us who do not deal with litigation issues on a daily basis, a brief refresher on jurisdiction is provided. These same principles will be applied to Internet-related intellectual property disputes.

A court may exercise jurisdiction over a defendant if the defendant is physically present in the forum (general jurisdiction), or if the defendant has sufficient contacts with the forum (specific jurisdiction). With general jurisdiction, the defendant's presence in the forum makes the defendant subject to jurisdiction in relation to any cause of action that arises anywhere in the world. The forum does not have to have an interest in or relationship to the cause of action. Thus, it is likely that a defendant, accused of a violation of intellectual property rights, will be subject to general jurisdiction in the forum in which he or she is present.

The interesting question for Internet-related litigation is whether specific jurisdiction can be exercised, given the often uncertain physical relationships between people and forums established by communication over the Internet. It is unlikely that the law will be applied such that a simple contact in a forum state represented by a user or service provider being resident in the state will itself subject a person to personal jurisdiction in that forum. Thus, the inquiry will generally focus on circumstances in addition to simple contact over the Internet.

The inquiry into whether jurisdiction is proper asks whether a state has the power over the defendant and whether it is reasonable to subject the defendant to litigation in the forum.[1] The first part of the test is usually delineated by a state's long-arm statute, and the second part of the test reflects the due process inquiry under the Fifth or Fourteenth Amendment. Another way of stating the first part of the test is whether the defendant has had minimum contact with the forum—for example, whether the defendant has purposefully availed herself of the privileges of conducting activities within the forum, such that it was reasonably foreseeable that she would not only be able to claim the benefits and protections under its laws but might have to defend her conduct in the forum.[2] When a defendant initiates the contact on which the jurisdiction is asserted, this question is often then answered in the affirmative. This particular pattern may be key in cases involving jurisdiction disputes and certain conduct related to the Internet.

The second part of the jurisdiction test, whether it is reasonable to subject the defendant to the laws of the forum, calls for a balancing of the defendant's, the public's, and the plaintiff's interests. This part of the test has been further refined by the Supreme Court. The five elements to consider are:

---

[1] International Shoe Co. v. Washington, 326 U.S. 310 (1945).

[2] Core-Vent v. Nobel Indus. AB, 11 F.3d 1482, 1485 (9th Cir. 1993).

1. The relative burden on the defendant
2. The forum state's interest in adjudicating the dispute
3. The plaintiff's interest in obtaining convenient and effective relief
4. The interstate judicial system's interest in obtaining the most efficient resolution to the controversy
5. The shared interests the several states have in furthering fundamental substantive social policies.[3]

Although the balancing of interests is required, the key focus is on whether it would be fundamentally unreasonable to subject the defendant to jurisdiction given the defendant's activities.

Federal courts presented with a federal question will decide jurisdiction according to their federal circuit's interpretation of the due process clause of the Fifth Amendment.[4] In patent cases, issues of personal jurisdiction are analyzed in accordance with the examples set by the Court of Appeals for the Federal Circuit.[5] Although the analyses are at least similar, the interpretation followed by each court should be considered.

A type of federal long-arm jurisdiction statute was created in 1993 by Rule 4(k)(2) of the Federal Rules of Civil Procedure. The rule slightly broadens the few exceptions to jurisdiction a federal court can exercise beyond the limits imposed by the long-arm statute of the state in which the federal court sits. Rule 4(k)(2) allows a court to assert jurisdiction in a federal question case when the defendant has sufficient minimum contacts with the nation as a whole but insufficient contacts with any given state. This rule may be used when activities related to the Internet make clear that an individual is carrying out activities within the United States, but it is unclear if any specific state is the intended target of the activity. It appears that if any one state could properly exercise jurisdiction over the defendant, then jurisdiction under this rule would not be allowed. In defending against jurisdiction under Rule 4(k)(2), the defendant would have to argue that there is a total lack of minimum contact with the United States or that a particular state could exercise jurisdiction. There are obvious problems with the latter argument.[6]

In a case involving a plaintiff incorporated in the Netherlands, an Italian defendant, and a Minnesota codefendant, the federal district court in Massachusetts found that it had personal jurisdiction over the Italian defendant under Rule 4(k)(2).[7] The Italian defendant was the nominal title holder of a set of patents

---

[3] Burger King Corp. v. Rudzewicz, 471 U.S. 462, 467–77 (1985).

[4] Akro Corp. v. Luker, 45 F.3d 1541, 1544 (Fed. Cir. 1995).

[5] Pharmachemie B.V. v. Pharmacia S.p.A., 934 F. Supp. 484 (D. Mass. 1996).

[6] David D. Seigel, Supplemental Practice Commentaries, *reprinted in* 28 U.S.C.A. Fed. R. Civ. P. 4, 83 (West Supp. 1993).

[7] Pharmachemie B.V. v. Pharmacia S.p.A., 934 F. Supp. 484 (D. Mass. 1996).

against which the plaintiff filed a declaratory judgment action. The Italian defendant had literally no contacts with the United States except to ship unpatented raw materials to Ohio and New Mexico, and the assignment of the patent rights to the Minnesota defendant. The Italian defendant argued that it was not subject to jurisdiction in Massachusetts under Rule 4(k)(2) because it was subject to jurisdiction in Ohio, New Mexico, or the District of Columbia. The court found that the Ohio and New Mexico long-arm statutes would not confer jurisdiction in those states because of a lack of relationship between the Italian defendant's activities and the cause of action.

The Italian defendant pointed to the patent statute which provides that any foreign patent owner is subject to personal jurisdiction and service of process for lawsuits related to its patent in the District of Columbia.[8] The court found that because the District Court for the District of Columbia is a court of limited jurisdiction, it did not meet the requirement of the rule that personal jurisdiction be available in a court of general jurisdiction. The court agreed with the defendant that this application of the rule was somewhat outside of the intended scope of Rule 4(k)(2). However, the literal reading of the rule conferred jurisdiction. Under the analysis of this rule, there was no due process analysis.

Our discussion is mainly focused on personal jurisdiction questions rather than venue. However, one should consider whether broad ranging activity over the Internet, by companies such as Prodigy and America Online, will subject them to personal jurisdiction in each state. If so, venue may become a critical factor in deciding whether the defendant will be tried in any particular court. The *Inset* case[9] illustrates a situation in which change of venue might be the defendant's only way to avoid jurisdiction in the plaintiff's chosen forum.

§ 8.4 Useful Analogies

As noted in § 8.3, jurisdictional questions related to the Internet will turn on determining the defendant's understanding of her contact with a given locale and the extent to which the contact was substantial enough to warrant the exercise of jurisdiction. There are several lines of cases dealing with the same types of circumstances that are presented by the Internet. Cases dealing with defamation, advertising, and telephone contacts address some of the same issues regarding focus of contact and relationship to the forum.

Defamation cases often involve plaintiffs and defendants who have had little, if any, physical relationship. The jurisdiction questions in these cases turn on the defendant's acts and what effect they had or may have had in a given forum. In

---

[8] 35 U.S.C. § 293.

[9] Inset Sys., Inc. v. Instruction Set Inc., 937 F. Supp. 161 (D. Conn. 1996), discussed in §§ 8.5 and 8.6.

one defamation case, in which defendants had actual knowledge that the likely location of the effects of their conduct would be in California, the Supreme Court found that personal jurisdiction in California was justified.[10] The Court reasoned that the defendants had focused their activities at a certain person and understood where the impact of their activities would occur. A contrasting case involved an unsolicited telephone interview that resulted in an allegedly defamatory publication.[11] No personal jurisdiction existed in the forum of the publication (and interviewing reporter) over the remote defendant who had provided the information for the publication. The court had difficulty analyzing the long-arm statute as well as the "purposeful availment" aspect of the due process clause. The court went on to make its decision by balancing all of the factors with the reasonableness of exercising jurisdiction. The reasoning in these cases may be applied to the provision of Internet services or access to Web sites, or the provision of information over the Internet that may cause "harm" at a particular location. Because Internet services will be able to "automatically" target individuals or geographic areas with certain information, the defamation analogy may prove helpful.

With respect to advertising and sales, generally when a defendant advertises in media located in or that reaches a forum state, jurisdiction may be predicated on a "doing business" theory. However, if there is nothing more to the contact, minimum contacts might not be established. In each case, the character of the advertising contact in relation to the cause of action should be considered. Generally, simply receiving business as a result of the advertising is not adequate. The courts tend to look at volume of sales resulting from the advertising, likely requiring substantial sales, before this type of activity will satisfy the minimum contacts requirement. Advertising and sales cases may be analogized to commercial e-mail or Web-based advertising.[12]

A toll-free telephone number that is accessible from many, if not all, states may be analogous to the operation of a bulletin board or Web site. The existence and distribution of a telephone number alone, even if some calls are made to the number, may not confer jurisdiction at the site from which the call was made.[13] This would probably not meet the purposeful availment test. However, if the contact with the site is two-way, such as being used to negotiate an agreement or enter into a substantial business relationship, the jurisdiction may be exercised over the telephone service operator.

Other possible analogies are cases involving the exchange of letters (possibly legal demand letters). In the case of telephone calls, letters, and advertising, if these activities have a significant connection to the cause of action—for example,

---

[10] Calder v. Jones, 456 U.S. 783 (1984).

[11] Ticketmaster v. Aliotto, 26 F.3d 201 (1st Cir. 1994).

[12] Discussed further in Richard Zembek, *Jurisdiction and the Internet: Fundamental Fairness in the Networked World of Cyberspace,* Alb. L. J. Sci. & Tech. 339, 368–70 (1996).

[13] *See* Far West Capital, Inc. v. Towne, 46 F.3d 1071 (10th Cir. 1995).

they resulted in a contract which is being adjudicated—they will likely contribute to a finding of minimum contacts. However, if the activities are unrelated to or not connected with the cause of action, they will be given less weight in the overall analysis.

§ 8.5   Early Cases

In the few cases discussing jurisdiction and the Internet, the decisions reflect a more traditional analysis than might be expected given the nature of the technology. The courts have grasped both the expansiveness and limitations of the technology and are able to analyze the facts of the communication or business transaction that is at the heart of the dispute. The fact that the jurisdiction question is embedded in Internet technology simply means that the surrounding facts may be a bit more complex (more opportunities for ready communication) and more uncertain (the players do not necessarily know each other) than in other scenarios. A few courts have explicitly addressed the issue of personal jurisdiction being premised on "normal" Internet activities. Most courts note that jurisdiction will be too easily established if Internet activities, or even possible Internet connections, are all that is necessary to establish power over a defendant. Only one court has seemingly premised its power over the defendant based mainly on the possibility of contact with the forum via the Internet and a toll-free telephone service.[14] A review of a few cases provides a starting point for analyzing Internet contacts for jurisdiction questions.

§ 8.6   —United States Parties

In a case involving CompuServe,[15] jurisdiction was exercised over a defendant who used an Internet service in the forum state to distribute his software. CompuServe filed a declaratory judgment action against a software developer named Patterson who had used CompuServe's online service to distribute his own software. Patterson was a Texas resident who had signed CompuServe's shareware registration agreement, under which his software would be distributed by CompuServe. The agreement was completed electronically, from Texas. The agreement stated it was being entered into in Ohio and that interpretation of the agreement would be governed by and construed in accordance with Ohio law. Patterson began sending complaints of common law trademark infringement to CompuServe via e-mail and regular mail when CompuServe began selling a similar program.

---

[14] Inset Sys., Inc. v. Instruction Set Inc., 937 F. Supp. 161 (D. Conn. 1996).

[15] CompuServe Inc. v. Patterson, 89 F.3d 1257 (6th Cir. 1996), *reh'g denied,* 1996 U.S. App. LEXIS 24796 (1996).

Patterson moved to dismiss CompuServe's complaint based in part on a lack of personal jurisdiction. The district court dismissed the action, but the circuit court reversed. To determine whether there was adequate minimum contact with Ohio, the appeals court considered Patterson's initiation and ongoing contacts with Ohio in his relationship with CompuServe. The court found that minimum contact and, therefore, purposeful availment followed from these activities. The appeals court then determined that the cause of action—the trademark infringement claim—arose from the same facts supporting minimum contact. The appeals court found that the marketing and sale of the product solely on CompuServe meant that any trademark rights would originate and be violated in Ohio at the location of the CompuServe site. Finally, the appeals court concluded it was reasonable for a software vendor, selling through a service provider such as CompuServe, to expect that disputes with the service provider would result in a lawsuit brought in the service provider's home state.

The court also identified, but did not resolve, several other jurisdictional questions. First, it was not decided that the defendant could be subject to jurisdiction in any state in which his software was sold. Rather, a pattern of sales in a forum or active solicitation by the defendant might be enough to support jurisdiction. Second, the court did not decide whether another party from a third state could sue the defendant in Ohio for problems related to the sale of the software via the Ohio service provider. Ohio might be considered the point of sale, which, for torts causing economic injuries, may be able to exercise jurisdiction. This question may be more difficult if the software is licensed for no fee or a low fee. Finally, the court did not decide whether it would exercise jurisdiction over a subscriber who does nothing more than access a site in Ohio.

CompuServe, in both its holding and dicta, suggests that passive use of an online service will not confer jurisdiction in the service provider's home state without more, but that activities such as soliciting and advertising products and services will increase the likelihood that jurisdiction will be found, and that the quantity and geographic focus of the activities will be critical.

Another trademark case illustrates that maintaining a Web site that can be and is accessed from another state may not in itself be enough to confer jurisdiction on the state in which the access takes place.[16] In this case, the owner of New York's Blue Note jazz club brought a claim in New York against the owner of a Missouri club, named The Blue Note. The claim was for trademark infringement and dilution, and unfair competition based on a Web page advertising tickets for the Missouri club. The district court dismissed the case for lack of jurisdiction.

The Web site, operated from a server in Missouri, described the Missouri club, its calendar of events, and ticketing information. The site is accessible to anyone; no subscription or authorization is required. Initially, the site also referenced the New York club and specifically disclaimed relationship between the two entities. It also included a hyperlink to the plaintiff's Web site. After the plaintiff complained, the defendant removed the hyperlink along with other text.

---

[16] Bensusan Restaurant Corp. v. King, 1996 U.S. Dist. LEXIS 13035 (S.D.N.Y. Sept. 9, 1996).

The district court dismissed the case because the activities were not directed towards New York specifically—for example, tickets were sold and shows were performed in Missouri only.

The court found that the New York long-arm statute, requiring a tortious act to be committed within the state, was not satisfied. The court attempted to analogize the existence of the Web site to an offer for sale of a product in New York, which would meet the requirement. It determined that the mere operation of a Web site that could be accessed by a New York resident did not amount to advertising, promoting, selling, or otherwise targeting a product or activity towards New York. The court also found that under an alternative section of the long-arm statute, the defendant, among other things, did not necessarily expect that its acts would have consequences in New York. The court stated:

> [The plaintiff's] primary argument in support of both statutory bases for personal jurisdiction is that, because defendant's Web site is accessible in New York, defendant could have foreseen that the site was able to be viewed in New York and taken steps to restrict access to his site only to users in a certain geographic region, presumably Missouri. Regardless of the technical feasibility of such a procedure, . . . mere foreseeability of an in-state consequence and a failure to avert that consequence is not sufficient to establish personal jurisdiction.[17]

The court noted that the due process clause would also not be satisfied in this case since the defendant's operation of a Web site was not a purposeful act directed towards New York. The court supported its position by noting:

> There are no allegations that King actively sought to encourage New Yorkers to access his site, or that he conducted any business—let alone a continuous and systematic part of its business—in New York. . . . [The plaintiff's] argument that King should have foreseen that users could access the site in New York and be confused as to the relationship of the two Blue Note clubs is insufficient to satisfy due process.[18]

In contrast, in a trademark case dealing with a conflict between a domain name and a registered trademark, the court found the defendant's operation of a Web site and toll-free telephone number was adequate to establish minimum contact and thus a basis for personal jurisdiction.[19] The court was not influenced by the fact that the defendant had not engaged in conduct specifically directed towards the state. The court held:

> In the present case, [defendant] has directed its advertising activities via the Internet and its toll-free number toward not only the state of Connecticut, but to all states. The Internet as well as toll-free numbers are designed to communicate with people and their business in every state. Advertisements on the Internet can reach

---

[17] *Id.* at 13041–12.

[18] *Id.* at 13051.

[19] Inset Sys., Inc. v. Instruction Set Inc., 937 F. Supp. 161 (D. Conn. 1996).

as many as 10,000 Internet users within Connecticut alone. Further, once posted on the Internet, unlike television and radio advertising, the advertisement is available continuously to any Internet user. ISI has therefore, purposefully availed itself of the privilege of doing business within Connecticut.[20]

Although the Connecticut case suggests that some courts will give great weight to Internet-related activities, it is unlikely that a defendant's Internet activity unrelated to the claim before the court will confer general jurisdiction on a court.

In a case involving a Minnesota defendant sued for copyright infringement in a California court, the court refused to find personal jurisdiction.[21] The plaintiff argued, in part, that the court had jurisdiction because the defendant maintained a Web site, but there was no allegation that the copyrighted material was distributed over the Web or accessible from the Web site. The court stated:

> Because the Web enables easy world-wide access, allowing computer interaction via the Web, to supply sufficient contact to establish jurisdiction would eviscerate the personal jurisdiction requirement as it currently exists; the Court is not willing to take this step. Thus, the fact that Fallon has a Web site used by Californians cannot establish jurisdiction by itself.[22]

Although the Connecticut case is unique in this set of cases, it reflects a reasonable balance between the commercial benefits available because of the Internet's relatively unlimited audience and the possibility of being called into a jurisdiction in which the defendant does not do any "traditional" business. Courts should look more closely at the expanded commercial opportunities provided by the Internet. Defendants who take advantage of those opportunities in an intentional fashion should be prepared to face a commensurate increase in the possibility of being called into court in many jurisdictions.

§ 8.7 —International Issues

One case provides a glimmer of international Internet jurisdiction issues.[23] The question that was discussed was whether a United States court can and will exercise jurisdiction over a foreign defendant in relation to the operation of a foreign-based Web site accessible from the United States. Although the case is not directly on point, it provides pointers to future cases that will turn on this issue. Briefly, the plaintiff, Playboy Enterprises, brought a claim for contempt against an Italian defendant based on the publication of a "Playmen" Web site in

---

[20] *Id.* at 165.

[21] McDonough v. Fallon McElligott, Inc., 1996 U.S. Dist. LEXIS 15139 (S.D. Cal. 1996).

[22] *Id.* at 15145.

[23] Playboy Enters., Inc. v. Chuckleberry Publishing, Inc., 39 U.S.P.Q.2d (BNA) 1746 (S.D.N.Y. 1996).

Italy, which publication was a breach of an earlier injunction. The court had retained jurisdiction from the previous case[24] and thus did not discuss jurisdiction. However, it did discuss whether defendant distributed or sold Playmen magazines in the United States when it established an Internet site containing pictorial images under the Playmen name. This was just one element that needed to be satisfied to find the defendant in contempt. This is similar to an analysis a court might perform to determine whether the defendant had adequate minimum contact with the forum state for personal jurisdiction. The court found that:

> Defendant actively invites [downloading and storage of images]: the Internet site allows the user to decide between viewing and downloading images. Thus this use of Defendant's Internet constitutes a distribution. . . . Defendant actively solicited United Sates customers to its Internet site, and in doing so has distributed its product within the United States. When a potential subscriber faxes the required form to [defendant], he receives back via e-mail a password and user name By this process, [defendant] distributes its product within the United States.[25]

The court did not give much weight to the defendant's argument that the access by the user, in Italy, is the critical activity. It may be that such an argument might be given more weight if jurisdiction were being decided. This case is also interesting because it purports to order a limited restriction on the Internet site so that only United States subscribers are prevented from access. When it is difficult to identify a forum which can exercise personal jurisdiction over a foreign defendant whose Internet activities are related to the cause of action, the reasoning of this case should be combined with the cases dealing with Federal Rule of Procedure 4(k)(2).[26]

§ 8.8 Regulatory Considerations

The extent to which a state regulates certain activities, and does so successfully based on the impact on local citizens, may further enlighten the jurisdiction discussion. For example, the Attorney General of Minnesota has asserted the right to regulate gambling that occurs on a foreign Web page that was accessed and brought into the state by a local resident, and the New Jersey securities regulatory agency has asserted the right to shut down any offending Web page accessible from within the state.[27]

---

[24] 687 F.2d 563 (2d Cir. 1982).

[25] 39 U.S.P.Q.2d (BNA) at 1746.

[26] See § 8.3.

[27] Discussed in David R. Johnson & David G. Post, *Law and Borders—The Rise of Law in Cyberspace,*
www.cli.org/X0026_LBFINFN.

§ 8.9   Practical Considerations

Rather than sitting back and enjoying the free and fast exchange of information over the Internet, a user or service provider should think about the information regarding jurisdiction that is exchanged during substantive interactions. It should be possible to avoid situations where the defendant can disclaim knowledge of the relationship of the exchange to a specific location. A service provider might also wish to keep track of contacts with users to establish a rough guess of "actual" contact with a forum to rebut a plaintiff's argument that the number of possible connections in a forum represents the likely connections that occurred. Finally, in drastic situations, steps can be taken to lock out users from particular forums to prevent the establishment of personal jurisdiction in those forums.

At a Web site, establish on the front page the location of the server or at least the business responsible for the service. Alternatively, if there is a logical section of the site that provides information regarding the service, be sure to include physical location information. When software or other information is down-loaded, include an indication of the physical location of the source or owner of the material. Although this is somewhat counter to some practices of being unobtrusive to the user, it may be a useful means to establish the user's knowl-edge of relevant facts of the transaction.

When there is a formal relationship established between a user and a service provider such as by electronic contract, a choice of law and jurisdiction clause should be used. These will likely be upheld as long as they are related to the subject matter and do not somehow offend public policy.

If a user registers for a service or provides some identification to obtain access, include an exchange of location information. Because it is not currently possible for a Web site to automatically identify a user who accesses the site, explicit steps must be taken to gather that information.

Following the court's suggestion in *Playboy,*[28] it may be possible to lock out users from a particular jurisdiction. This will work only if the users or something about their user names identify their origin. If this information is available, the Web site can be set up to prevent access to all or some of the information at the site.

Finally, when the Internet is used for advertising or marketing, if possible retain good records regarding when the information was available, how many hits occur at the site, and whether there was any specific focus of the information dissemination.

---

[28] Playboy Enters., Inc. v. Chuckleberry Publishing, Inc., 39 U.S.P.Q.2d (BNA) 1746 (S.D.N.Y. 1996), discussed in § 8.7.

EUROPEAN PROTECTION STRATEGIES FOR THE INTERNET

Dr. Heinz Goddar

Dr. Axel Nordemann*

* The authors acknowledge the assistance of Marion Tönhardt and Christian Czychowski in preparing this chapter.

§ 9.1   Introduction

This chapter explores the European response to Internet technologies and the manners in which the European community and its Member States are protecting intellectual property rights in Internet technologies.

§ 9.2   Significance of the Internet in Europe

In Europe, as in America, the ongoing digitalization of the media has produced many new questions.[1] In addition to sociological aspects, such as the increasing information flow, and political effects, such as the abolition of national barriers, massive legal problems will also soon begin to show in Europe. The center of

---

[1] *See* Dreier, *Authorship and New Technologies from the Viewpoint of Civil Law Traditions,* 26 IIC 989 (1995), with important references to the actual effects of digitalization.

attention is now the so-called Internet, a concept encountered almost daily in the media. Like no other media phenomenon, this network incorporates the new world of the information age and science-society. The Internet is being used increasingly in Europe.[2] Although groups of experts in the United States have concerned themselves with legal protection on the Internet for some time, this legal area has so far received scant attention in Europe. Only the European Union (EU) Commission has put forward a paper.[3] European legal experts have so far come forward only with the outlines of solutions.[4] Although legal science has concentrated itself chiefly on slogans such as "multimedia," "information superhighway," or "online,"[5] the internal debate on the law and the Internet is clearly heating up. This is evident from the reactions to the first attempts to place the Net in a legal framework.[6]

There are at present no special legal solutions in Europe regarding the Internet.

§ 9.3 Legal Position in Europe and the Harmonization of Laws in the European Union

The European Union (EU) is so far no more than an association of states based on an economic community. There is therefore no watertight European legal system. Instead, the EU is aiming for harmonization of laws. The old national

---

[2] The number of users increase in Europe is above average, Frankfurter Allgemeine Zeitung [hereinafter FAZ], 9 July 1996, at 22.

[3] Copyright and Related Rights in the Information Society: Green Paper by the EU Commission, COM (95) 382.

[4] *Cf.* Woebke & Wilske, *The Law of Cyberspace,* (CoR (forthcoming).

For Germany: Bothe & Kilian, *Rechtsfragen grenzüberschreitender Datenflüsse,* Heidelberg 1996; Ackermann, *Ausgewählte Rechtsprobleme der Mailboxkommunikation* (1995) at http://gaius.jura.uni-sb.de/Dissertationen/Ackermann/;

Kreile & Becker, *Multimedia und die Praxis der Lizenzvergabe von Urheberrechten,* Gewerblicher Rechtsschutz und Urheberrecht Int. [hereinafter GRUR] 1996, at 677; Müller-Hengstenberg, *Nationale und Internationale Rechtsprobleme im Internet,* Neue Juristische Wochenschrift [hereinafter NJW] 1996, at 1777; Nordemann et al., *Gewerblicher Rechtsschutz und Urheberrecht in Internet,* Computer und Recht [hereinafter CR] 645 (1996).

See generally WIPO (Publ.), WIPO World-Wide Symposium on the Impact of Digital Technology on Copyright and Neighbouring Rights, Geneva, 1993; WIPO (Publ.), WIPO World-Wide Symposium on the Future of Copyright and Neighbouring Rights, Geneva, 1994; WIPO (Publ.) WIPO World-Wide Symposium on Copyright in the Global Information Infrastructure, Mexico 1995 (Conference Report to be issued shortly); WIPO (Publ.) WIPO World Forum on the Protection of Intellectual Creations in the Information Society, Naples, 1995 (Conference Report to be issued shortly).

[5] *See* Fromme, *Online und im Internet hinken Rechtsprechung und Gesetzgebung der rasanten Entwicklung hinterher,* FAZ, 13 May 1996, at 5 ("As to whether we had all this under our control, the specialists [the participants at the 79th Conference of the Study Circle on Press Law] all replied: No, for God's sake, No.").

[6] *Cf.* Rheingold, *Eine Frage der Macht, nicht der Moral,* pl@net 3+4/96, at 34, which reduces questions regarding legal protection on the Internet to the formula: "not morality but power motivates those who wish to censor the Internet."

legal systems will continue to exist until a Europe-wide solution is found in the area concerned. This approximation is proceeding mainly through so-called regulations and directives which are enacted by the European Council (EC) on the basis of the EC Treaty.[7] There is a whole series of directives and regulations concerning competition law, trademark law, patent law, and copyright, but a uniform system will be slow in coming.

The EU has for years been discussing the problems of digitalization. However, no special European legal rules exist as yet for the Internet. Nonetheless, certain European authorities can also be applied to legal questions concerning the Internet.

For example, Member States are required to translate the Database Directive[8] into national law by January 2, 1998. The directive is aimed at protecting the compilation of data and offers protection under copyright and competition law. Exclusive rights are to be vested in any person who compiles data creatively or by working on them.[9] In addition, the Council is at present considering a remote inputs directive, which is also to apply to contractual arrangements for online services.

Finally, the EU in its Green Paper on *Copyright and Related Rights in the Information Society*[10] has put the subject out for thorough discussion by experts from the copyright aspect. Concrete results of the discussion are awaited.[11] The Green Paper is concerned specifically with copyright questions. After general comments on the reasons underlying the challenges and national legal framework and the opportunities open to the EU (Chapter 1), Chapter 2 raises so-called "horizontal" questions as to choice of law, questions concerning the rights affected, and, finally, questions concerning law enforcement.

§ 9.4   Status of Legal Harmonization

In §§ **9.5** through **9.8,** the process of European harmonization in the areas of patent law, copyright law, trademark law, and competition law are discussed.

---

[7] EC Treaty, art. 189.

[8] Council Directive 96/9/EEC, 1996 O.J. (L 77).

[9] For the United Kingdom, see Berkvens, *Will the Data Protection Directive Prevent a Global Information Infrastructure?*, 11 Computer L. & Prac. 38 (1995).

[10] COM (95) 382.

[11] For Germany, see Lewinski, *Multimedia und Urheberrecht,* GRUR 1995, at 831; Wachter, *Multimedia und Recht,* GRUR 1995, at 860; the follow-up paper at the EU Commission on the Green Paper (Brussels 1996).

§ 9.5   —Patent Law

Patent law is playing an exemplary pioneering role in the process of European harmonization. Ever since the European Patent Convention came into force in 1978, the European Patent Office has dealt with a steadily growing number of applications. In 1995, approximately 78,300 patent applications were submitted to the European Patent Office, an increase of 5.5 percent from the previous year.[12] The European Patent Office is a "functional" European agency with a large fund of legal precedents from the Objections Division. The European Patent Office may therefore serve as an example for other fields of the law in relation to international organization, legislation, and precedent.

The particular quality of international cooperation in the field of patent law is not least attributable to its immense interest both publicly and privately on account of the great economic importance of patents, and strict requirements are therefore being made of both statute law and precedent.

Sixteen nations[13] have now signed the European Patent Convention. An appropriate petition will further enable a European patent application to be extended to all noncontracting states[14] with whom "extension agreements" exist at the date of their submission.

With the exception of Norway and Iceland, recourse can therefore be made to a uniform patent law for the whole of Western Europe, while far-reaching national provisions also apply in Eastern Europe.

§ 9.6   —Copyright

No mention of copyright appears in the EC founding treaties. However, the EU Commission was quick to enter this field of the law[15] even though the Maastricht Treaty did not explicitly incorporate copyright into EC primary law. The European Court of Justice has consistently assumed that copyright and related rights are subject to the free movement of goods under Articles 30 and 36 of the Treaty, freedom of services under Articles 59 and 66 of the Treaty, the antitrust provisions of Articles 85 and 86 of the Treaty, and finally the general ban on discrimination under Article 6.

---

[12] EPO press release, Feb. 1996.

[13] Belgium, Denmark, Germany, Finland, France, Greece, Great Britain, Ireland, Italy, Luxembourg, Monaco, the Netherlands, Austria, Portugal, Sweden, Spain, and Switzerland/Liechtenstein (status 30 June 1996).

[14] Albania, Latvia, Lithuania, and Slovenia (Status 30 June 1996).

[15] *See* Kreile & Becker, *Neuordnung des Urheberrechts in der Europäischen Union,* GRUR 1994, at 901.

Building on this basis, the EU has enacted several laws concerning copyright. They are chiefly directives, which are intended to harmonize legal systems. They include the directives protecting computer programs,[16] on leasing and lending law,[17] the time limits for protection,[18] satellite and cable TV,[19] and databases.[20]

The computer program directive extends copyright protection to computer programs, where this was not already done under national legislation. Protection for computer programs is accordingly stated to presuppose only "individuality" without additional qualitative aspects, as was previously necessary, for example, in Germany. Although, in the tradition of Continental European copyright, the directive recognizes the programmer as author, it nonetheless vests full exploitation rights in the employer where the programmer is an employed person.

For all copyrighted works, protection under the period of protection directive extends for 70 years following the author's death.[21] Related rights, such as those of performing artists or manufacturers of sound recordings, are protected for 50 years from the performance or publication.[22]

The leasing and lending directive grants authors, performing artists, and film and sound recording manufacturers an exclusive right to lease or lend originals or copies of the work. Finally, the satellite radio and cable directive is concerned with cross-border broadcasting and is preparing the way for the creation of a uniform audio-visual area within the EU. In addition, the Commission is preparing a directive on the law of succession and protection of moral rights.

This "harmonisation bundle"[23] is being supplemented by the EU's Decision of May 14, 1992, as a result of which all Member States were required to accede to the latest version of the Revised Berne Convention and the Rome Convention as of January 1, 1995.

§ 9.7   —Trademark Law

The European Union has used two different instruments to harmonize trademark law. First, the Trade Mark Directive[24] has extensively harmonized national

---

[16] Council Directive 91/250/EEC, 1991 O.J. (L 122) (legal protection of computer programs).

[17] Council Directive 92/100/EEC, 1992 O.J. (L 236) (leasing and lending law, and certain rights related to copyright in the field of intellectual property).

[18] Council Directive 93/98/EEC, 1993 O.J. (L 290) (harmonizing the period of protection by copyright and certain related rights).

[19] Council Directive 89/552/EEC, 1989 O.J. (L 298/23) (coordinating certain provisions of copyright and related rights regarding satellite radio and cable distribution).

[20] Council Directive 96/9/EEC, 1996 O.J. (L 77) (protection of databases).

[21] Period of Protection Directive, art. 1.

[22] *Id.* art. 3.

[23] Kreile & Becker, *Neuordnung des Urheberrechts in der Europäischen Union,* GRUR 1994, at 901, 909 *et seq.*

[24] First Council Directive 89/104/EEC, 1988 O.J. (L 40/1) (harmonizing the legal provisions of member states concerning trademarks).

trademark laws of Member States. As the national parliaments had merely to convert the Trade Mark Directive into national law, the Trade Mark Directive has therefore continued the independent existence of the national Trade Mark laws.

However, a uniform, EU-wide trademark law also exists as a consequence of the community trademarks regulation.[25] When filing a Community mark with the Harmonisation Office for the Single Market at Alicante, Spain, the trademark proprietor therefore receives a unique right valid in all Member States of the European Union. However, the Community trademarks regulation applies only to the application and registration procedures; the elaboration of claims in the event of an infringement is expressly left to the national legal systems of Member States concerned. Unlike, for example, German national trademark law, according to which a mark is first registered after the formal application requirements and eligibility for protection have been verified, and is then published, and objection can be made only within three months subsequently, the Community trademark application is first only published and then registered only when any opposition proceedings have been successfully completed from the applicant's aspect. Objection can be laid against a Community trademark application not only in respect of registered national or international trademark rights but also of known older marks within the meaning of Article 6 of the Paris Convention and of older unregistered marks or other marking rights used in commercial dealings of more than local significance. A Community trademark application can therefore mean a high financial risk for the applicant not only because the losing party in opposition proceedings must within certain limits refund the costs of the winning party, but also because a successful objection under marking rights protected even in only one Member State prevents the registration of the Community mark in respect of the European Union as a whole. In this case, the applicant is still able to transform the Community trademark application into national applications; however, national conversion fees must then be again paid in each individual Member State.[26]

§ 9.8 —Competition Law

Even though the Internet has essentially developed into a sphere of competition and the European Union has become established as an economic community, competition law is the legal field in which the EU has so far achieved the lowest degree of harmonization.

The EU merely enacted a regulation against imitated goods, in 1986.[27] In addition, only one directive exists concerning confusing advertising, dating to

---

[25] Council Regulation (EC) No. 40/94, 1993 O.J. (L 11/1) (Community Trade Mark).

[26] For details of Community marks, see Nordemann, Wettbewerbs-und Markenrecht, ¶¶ 436 *et seq.* (8th ed. 1995) [hereinafter Nordemann].

[27] Council Regulation (EC) No. 3842/86, 1986 O.J. (L 357) (measures to prohibit circulation of imitated goods in free movement under customs law).

1984.[28] A further directive concerning comparative advertising is nearing completion.[29] With its nine articles, the confusing advertising directive is tightly drawn and is aimed at an initial approximation of competition law. It has not resulted in any appreciable stimulus towards the further development of German law. However, the directive must be taken into account, especially when interpreting the various national general clauses, such as § 3 of the German Unfair Competition Act (UWG).[30]

§ 9.9   Overview of Legal Problems on the Internet

When mention is made in Europe of data highways and the Internet, it is usually its enormous potential and future opportunities that are concerned.[31] Reports about hackers, computer fraud, and illegal copying show that the new transport paths for data are also throwing up quite a few legal problems in Europe. Weak spots appear particularly to be law enforcement and especially criminal prosecution. What interests the public most is computer crime in connection with the protection of data and young people. In fact, however, it is not only the criminal content that is concerned. Copyright, like trademark law, plays a major role. The Swiss courts, for example, are already hearing cases concerning protection for trade names in electronic addresses.[32] Many questions are also arising in competition law.[33] Finally, it is in the interests of each individual user to protect the copyrighted works that he inputs into the Net and the tradename that he uses for his homepage.

Unlike traditional data networks, the Internet links the whole world. A user can access every computer on the Net from every point on earth. Unlike TV or radio, questions and answers can in some parts of the Net be reciprocally and simultaneously exchanged as on a telephone. In view of the digital basis of all data on the Internet, items that are moved across the Internet can simply be changed by any user anywhere in the world and fed back into the Net. With digital technology, items can be compressed into the smallest space.

---

[28] Council Directive 84/450/EEC, 1984 O.J. (L 40) (approximation of legal and administrative provisions of member states concerning misleading advertising).

[29] Amended proposal for a Directive by the European Parliament and Council concerning comparative advertising and amending Directive 84/450/EEC concerning misleading advertising (91/C 180/15), COM(19)147 final; prevailing updated version: Council Document 4340/96 (1996).

[30] *See* Baumbach & Hefermehl, Wettbewerbsrecht ¶ 612 (18th ed. 1995).

[31] The economic importance, especially the location advantages of modern legislation, should in no way be underestimated. *See* Vogel, *Ohne Schutz der Urheber keine Datenautobahn,* 68 Blick durch die Wirtschaft 9 (1996) [hereinafter Vogel].

[32] *See* Auf der Maur, *Das Ende für den Selbstbedienungsladen Internet?,* 39 Neue Züricher Zeitung [hereinafter NZZ] 25 (1996) [hereinafter Auf der Maur].

[33] For Switzerland, see *Von der Datenbank zum elektronischen Kiosk,* 35 NZZ 20 (1995) (legal aspects of advertising on the Internet).

The view has hitherto prevailed in Europe that there are gaps in protection for use of international networks.[34] Whether this statement is implicitly correct or to what extent it might apply remains to be examined. To do so, the most varied uses must be analyzed and assigned to the European legal position. Only then will it be possible to see where gaps exist and what laws are affected. Typical problems in using the Internet at the places where they technically arise are examined in this section:

1. E-mail
2. Homepage
3. Newsgroup
4. Database.

E-mail is the electronic counterpart of the traditional letter post. Here, no particular questions of copyright, trademark law, or competition law arise. However, problems may result in connection with questions of evidence. They include, for example, whether submissions made to the courts meet the requirements of procedural law.

Homepages are a kind of video screen on which information is made available about one's company or about oneself. Of interest here are the name of the homepage, where chiefly questions of trademark law arise, access to the contents, which falls primarily under copyright, and lastly the contents themselves, which may affect copyright but especially competition law.

Some examples: Does an American museum shop encroach on the rights of a German painter if it uses a picture of the painter to advertise on the Internet? If so, what exploitation rights under copyright law are concerned and of which country is the law to be applied to this process? How should one deal with the person who in Cambodia scans the latest novel by a French writer and retains it on the Internet for calling up at a fee? Is it permissible in competition law to make a Coca-Cola homepage accessible to Spanish consumers, on which it is alleged that Coca-Cola tastes much better than Pepsi?

The position with the part of the Internet known as the "Usenet" is rather different. The Usenet contains the *newsgroups*. News put forward in these forums circulates the globe to all hosts that access the forums concerned and are stored locally there. A breach of rights in data transfer could be dealt with similarly as for the situation with homepages.

Various suppliers provide *databases* online with information concerning science, art, politics, and society. The press uses this area of the Internet in particular in order to make newspapers and journals available online.[35] The number of

---

[34] For Germany: Dreier, *Harmonisierung des Urheberrechts in der Informationsgesellschaft,* Zeitschrift für Urheber und Medienrecht [hereinafter ZUM] 1996, 69, 70–71. For the United Kingdom: Berkvens, *Will the Data Protection Directive Prevent a Global Information Infrastructure?,* 11 Computer L. & Prac. 38 (1995).

[35] *See* Weber & Mager, *Werkstatt,* Medium Magazin, Mar. 1996, at 2–15 (with the most varied examples).

newspapers on the Net tripled to 175 in 1995. A further doubling is forecast for 1996.[36] Data can be polled from the Net as from a card index. In the course of this, works protected by copyright may be transferred, but unlawfully so. Here, the same copyright queries arise regarding the exploitation of works as with homepages. However, competition law may again be concerned. What, for example, is the position with the despatch of mail-shots that are unlawful under German competition law from France following an order in a database, and how would one proceed on a title possibly obtained?

§ 9.10   Security

Security matters on the Internet can be divided into three areas: the availability of data, the confidentiality of data, and security of handling. No generally applicable standards have as yet been adopted in Europe regarding these three goals of security on the Internet. However, so-called firewall concepts are favored, with which network transition to the local area network (LAN) or personal computer (PC) concerned can be controlled.

In addition, more and more users are coding their data without, however, any hint of a discussion of their legal acceptability. In Germany, the independent testing body is the Federal Office for the Security of Information Technology. So far, Deutsche Telekom's TCOS (Telesec chipcard operating system) linked with DOKRYPT or SFile software modules has proven especially effective.

§ 9.11   —Data Protection on the Internet

Data protection on the Internet is one of the most urgent tasks. However, so far only a start has been made on it in Europe.

The EU Commission is preparing a directive.[37] The directive is about to be published in the Official Journal. It harmonizes all the elements of a modern data protection system, but in doing so departs appreciably from the German Federal Data Protection Act. It is aligned on the protection of newly developing data processes and therefore also offers potential application to the Internet. Independently of the field of operations, of the information technologies used, and of the place of processing, the directive harmonizes the hitherto very different national laws in the Member States. It introduces entitlements to information and reporting, but also specific new rights which could be relevant to the Internet. They include, for example, the right to know the origin of data.

---

[36] *Id.* at 3.

[37] From the United Kingdom's view, see Davies, *Law and the Internet,* 11 Computer L. & Prac. 106, 108 (1995). From the EU Commission's view, see Brühann, *EU-Datenschutzrichtlinie— Umsetzung in einem vernetzen Europa,* Recht der Datenverarbeitung [hereinafter RDV], Jan. 1996, at 12.

The person responsible in terms of the directive is she who decides on processing. This is, for example, the sender of e-mail. On the other hand, the network operator is responsible for the processing of access data.[38] For certain data processing operations, the express consent of the person concerned is necessary. However, the directive regards clicking onto an appropriate icon on the instruction panel as sufficient for express consent.[39] This first impression shows that a good deal of discussion is still required. Apart from this, the German government is preparing a law on information and communication services.[40] There will be changes in the national law on data protection.

§ 9.12 —Protection under Criminal Law

The hitherto most intensively discussed area of legal protection on the Internet is protection under criminal law. As an example, one need mention only neo-Nazi propaganda or child pornography.

The debate in Europe has shown that there is general agreement that the existing criminal law is adequate for action on the Internet.[41] However, the question of choice of law is in no way clear. In Germany, the commentators appear to make the place of performance of actions on the Internet dependent on the final interests of the person acting.[42] However, they also stress that there is no question of the service provider being liable in criminal law.

§ 9.13 —Protection Against Computer Viruses and Hackers

Hackers means persons who procure unauthorized access to other persons' computers through a data network. In this case, it therefore means intentional encroachment on the intellectual and, sometimes, also the material property of others. The problem affects the Internet greatly because it is an "open" system, where contact is possible with partners who were previously unknown. Ascertaining the identity and trustworthiness of the partner is therefore all the more important. Even if an internationally operative legal system were available, capable of sanctioning unlawful access by a hacker, it would still undoubtedly be difficult to enforce legal claims.

A solution to the problem must therefore lie on the technical side. It is already customary in many branches of the economy to legitimate oneself to a computer

---

[38] Brühann, RDV, Jan. 1996, at 12, 15.

[39] *Id.*

[40] Government draft on law of information and communication services (Bonn, Nov. 1996).

[41] For Germany: Collardin, *Strafrecht im Internet*, CR 1995, at 618.

[42] *Id.;* Sieber, *Strafrechtliche Verantwortlichkeit für den Datenverkehr in internationalen Computernetzen*, Juristen-Zeitung [hereinafter JZ] 1996, at 429, 494.

by means of a password or identity card, sometimes also in combination with a secret code. Under network conditions, such legitimation is impracticable as the user would be exposed to illegal access to the data path, with the legitimation data being copied.

A network securing system has recently been developed[43] which works with an authentication hierarchy precisely imitated from the tree-type name structure on the Internet. The trustworthiness of a partner is then certified by a superimposed central unit which if necessary must again identify itself to a unit superior to itself. In effect, when a "pass" is checked, the checker would still have to know only a relatively small number of digital signatures, namely those up to the lowest common superior of the two communicating partners.

The Internet user faces a further problem which may well be insoluble by legal means, in connection with computer viruses. *Computer viruses* are programs which are fed into the computer system, frequently in connection with unrequested programs, and do great damage by, for example, destroying existing data. They are often able to reproduce themselves, so that the impression that the computer system has been invaded by a virus is all the greater. Viruses are especially pernicious because it is practically impossible to detect their introduction into the system.

The technical solution to this seems to lie in a programming language called JAVA[44] developed by Sun Microsystems, which is said to make the writing of harmful programs—and these include computer viruses—impossible. Every potentially dangerous instruction would thereby be reduced to a grammatical error in the syntax of the programming language. A formal check for grammatical correctness—made by a compiler or an interpreter—could then immediately indicate whether a program was harmless.

§ 9.14   Server Protection

The discussion in §§ **9.15** through **9.20** concerns protection of the server, including issues of intellectual property in both the hardware and the software.

§ 9.15   —Hardware Patents

Technically and commercially viable hardware components for computers would be eligible for patent protection in principle, provided they are new and are based on inventive work. This would also apply to any special components required to operate a server.

---

[43] Thomas Beth, *Secure Open Data Networks,* Spektrum der Wissenschaft, May 1995, at 46.

[44] Christoph Pöppe, *Blitzkarriere in World Wide Web—Die Programmiersprache JAVA,* Spektrum der Wissenschaft, July 1996, at 17.

However, the opportunities for patenting hardware on the Internet would be altogether limited because the components used are for the most part already known from other computer applications. According to the consistent precedents of both the Federal Court of Justice as the Supreme Court of the Federal Republic of Germany and the Appeal Chambers of the European Patent Office, the reference to a new method of application of a known facility does not establish its novelty.[45] Using hardware of a known type unchanged to process a new program does not therefore make it new. The position may be different if the hardware is adapted to suit the program.[46]

§ 9.16 —Hardware Patented Designs

In addition to patent law as technical protective law, protective laws also exist in ornamental designs laws which were created expressly to protect aesthetic design. The design of hardware components for computers can therefore be protected under the law on ornamental designs. In this case, server components again form no exception. Famous designers have devoted themselves for years to designing computer hardware components.

Unfortunately, the same sophisticated international concepts as under patent law by no means exist under the law on ornamental designs. It is true that an international ornamental design application can be made with effect for 16 Western and Eastern European states,[47] but important European states, such as the United Kingdom and Sweden, are not included. There are, therefore, no uniform possibilities in Europe to achieve protection for an ornamental design. Although the procedure for the international filing of ornamental designs is purely a registration process, other countries check for novelty and specific character. These countries include Finland, Sweden, and the Russian Federation.

Aesthetic designs can also be protected by patent, if features exist that adequately define a technical object. In particular, the article to be patented must be aimed at the solving of a technical problem and cannot be limited to achieving aesthetic effect.[48] The Federal Court of Justice also takes this view.[49]

---

[45] *See* BGH, *Sitoteryglycoside,* GRUR 1982, at 548.

[46] *See* T 208/84, Official Journal of the European Patent Office, 1987, at 14.

[47] Belgium, Germany, France, Italy, Yugoslavia, Liechtenstein, Luxembourg, Monaco, the Republic of Moldavia, the Netherlands, Rumania, Switzerland, Slovenia, Spain, Hungary, and the Vatican City.

[48] T 962/91, *cited in* European Patent Office, Precedents of the Appeals Chambers of the European Patent Office, 1996, at 32.

[49] Rauhreifkerze, Mitteilungen der Deutschen Patentanwählte 235 (1972); Kennungsscheibe, GRUR 1977, at 152.

§ 9.17 —Hardware Semiconductor Protection

According to the "Act concerning Protection of Topographies of Micro-electronic Semi-Conductor Products" applying in Germany, three-dimensional structures of microelectronic semiconductor products may be protected if they have specific character. The material prerequisites are therefore the same as those for an ornamental design. However, protection does not extend to the designs, process, systems, or techniques underlying their three-dimensional structure or to the information stored in them. This is probably the reason why the number of applications for semiconductor protection has remained small. The law cannot prevent possible "reverse engineering."

The Technical Appeals Chamber of the European Patent Office has also considered the extent to which semiconductor components can be protected. In Case T 453/91[50] a product claim concerning a very large scale integration (VLSI) chip was considered new and inventive, as were procedural claims not aimed just at the design steps for the chip—which were not regarded as patentable—but also included the feature "material production of the chip so designed."

§ 9.18 —Software Patents

In the eyes of the information technologists, the development of software is a field of technology and the view is now taken generally that "computer programs are technical products which must be assessed according to technical criteria."[51] However, certain prerequisites must be met if software components are to be protected by a patent. Both the German Patents Act[52] and the European Patent Convention (EPC)[53] exclude computer programs as such from patent protection.

However, the nonpatentability of computer programs as such does not prevent computer-related inventions from being patented. However, consideration must then be given to the technical contribution that the article concerned actually makes as a whole to the state of the art.[54]

The European Patent Office investigated the patentability of computer-related inventions in a comparative study in 1989.[55] The Technical Appeals Chambers

---

[50] European Patent Office, Precedents of the Appeals Chambers of the European Patent Office, 1996, at 34.

[51] Broy & Lehmann, GRUR 1992, at 423.

[52] PatG § 1 (2) 3.

[53] EPC art. 52 (2) c.

[54] European Patent Office, Precedents of the Appeals Chambers of the European Patent Office, 1996, at 23.

[55] European Patent Office, *Patentability of Computer-Related Inventions* (Project 12.5), Comparative Study, Trilateral Cooperation EPO-JPO-USPTO (Sept. 1989).

have in the meantime developed principles according to which software components can also be patented.

Decision T6/83[56] must be stressed in connection with the Internet, where the Chamber decided that:

> [A]n invention relating to the coordination and control of international communication between programs and data files, which are kept in various processors in a data processing system with a multiplicity of processors interlinked in a telecommunications network, and the features of which are not aligned on the nature of the data or the way in which a particular applications program influences them, must be regarded as a solution to an essentially technical problem. It must therefore be considered an invention within the meaning of article 52 (1) of the Convention.[57]

The precedents of the Technical Appeals Chambers of the European Patent Office regarding the patenting of software were developed further in subsequent years. In particular, Decision T158/88[58] qualifies Decision T6/83 in that a computer program would not become part of a technical operating process if the doctrine resorted to is limited to changes in data and initiates no effect in excess of simple information processing. In its Decision T769/92[59] the Appeals Chamber agreed with the view of software developers regarding the technical nature of software programs. The decision states that an invention which comprises functional features achieved through software does not run afoul of the patentability exclusion under Article 52 (2) and (3) if details of the solution to the problem according to the invention necessitates technical considerations if the invention is to be implemented. Decision T59/93[60] states that processes that comprise features which fall within the patenting exclusion but nonetheless solved a technical problem and produced technical effects that must be regarded as a contribution to the state of the art.

The Federal Court of Justice, which already addressed the question of the technical character of computer programs at a very early date,[61] similarly confirmed in its "Submerged computer" decision[62] that programs are technical by nature if they possess a technical character as a whole and make a technical contribution.

The comments in this section are also relevant to the patentability framework for special software components for servers.

---

[56] Official Journal of the European Patent Office, 1990, at 5.

[57] *Id.* (principle underlying decision).

[58] Official Journal of the European Patent Office, 1991, at 566.

[59] Official Journal of the European Patent Office, 1995, at 525.

[60] European Patent Office, Precedents of the Appeals Chambers of the European Patent Office, 1993, at 25.

[61] Straken, GRUR 1977, at 657; *Anti-blocking System,* GRUR 1980, at 849.

[62] GRUR 1992, at 430.

§ 9.19 —Software Copyrights

Since the EC issued a directive protecting computer programs,[63] computer programs in Europe have been subject to copyright. However, as already illustrated, patent protection may also apply in specific cases. Certain countries (for example, Germany since 1985 under § 2 (1) 1 of the German Copyright Act) had extended copyright protection to computer programs previously. As a prerequisite for protection, the directive requires only individuality without additional qualitative aspects and so makes fewer requirements of the protectability of programs than the German Federal Court of Justice, in particular, did.[64] This could result in all software for the Internet being normally protected by copyright, whether in a relational database or in an interrogation system.

Contrary to the otherwise customary arrangement for works created in a service or working situation, § 69b of the German Copyright Act, which goes back to the EC Computer Directive, vests all property rights legally in the employer.

According to the period of protection directive,[65] software is protected for 70 years following the death of the author, who under European law cannot be a corporate body but is always the programmer.

§ 9.20 —Standards versus Patents

It might be said that Microsoft Corporation may be building a virtual monopoly with its software. It is proceeding with its own online service MSN—the Microsoft Network—to transfer a standard created through its Windows software package onto the Internet as well. If monopoly status is achieved, there is a question as to what extent further developments are possible. At least, there seem to be no problems with other companies for Microsoft Corporation with regard to the further development of the software itself.[66]

The development of industrial technology should not be obstructed or damaged by the monopoly of the holder of protected rights, especially in a field as important to public interests as telecommunications. A compulsory license might seriously be considered in cases where a third party cannot exploit a dependent earlier invention or development. However, compulsory licenses are awarded in only very small numbers. If, in particular, the patent holder can point to further improvements of his own and argue that he is therefore himself able to offer

---

[63] Council Directive 96/9/EEC, 1996 O.J. (L 77), discussed in § **9.3.**

[64] *See* BGH GRUR 1991, at 449, "Operating System."

[65] See § **9.6.**

[66] *See, e.g.,* Microsoft Corporation Windows 3.1 User Manual, inside cover, with list of cooperating software developers.

something similar to the general public, the license seeker must be able to prove that, compared with the patentholder's improvement patents, she is in a position to produce something that is technically superior, or even that she can proceed along a completely new path.[67]

An effective method of undermining a standard is to create a new standard. The programming language JAVA has created a basis. JAVA permits object-oriented programming, whereby individual programs can be made available for certain applications. A person can therefore compile his own programs from specific individual programs as required, without having to purchase the entire, expensive package.

These individual programs are similarly transmitted through the Internet, at present still free of charge. Should charges become necessary—and this question also arises with the reproduction of other, possibly protected works—they could probably be collected most easily through an electronic licensing mechanism in which computer online services would participate, undertaking the transfer of the protected works. It further appears that the difficulties with electronic licensing mechanisms are both technical and legal. Progress in this direction is expected in the near future.[68]

§ 9.21   User Protection

The discussion in §§ **9.22** and **9.23** concerns protection for computer programs and graphical designs that are employed on the user's computer.

§ 9.22   —Applications Software

Browsers and the like are computer programs that enjoy copyright protection, their individuality being assumed. The law in Europe makes no distinction at this point between software on a server computer and software on the end user's computer. Like all computer programs, applications software is exposed to illegal copying.

Software licensing contracts are predominantly regarded as purchase contracts although, at least in Germany, they should be regarded as mixed contracts with leasing and copyright aspects.[69] On the other hand, the processing and probatory force of software licensing contracts on the Internet is still an open question.

---

[67] Entscheidungen des Reichsgerichts in Zivilsachen [hereinafter RGZ] 130, 360, 366.

[68] *US comparison with computer on-line services,* GRUR 1996, at 78; R. Kreile & J. Becker, *Multimedia und die Praxis der Lizenzierung von Urheberrechten,* GRUR 1996, at 677.

[69] Nordemann, *CPU Klauseln in Software-Überlassungsverträgen,* CR 1996, at 5, 6–7.

§ 9.23 —Screen Layouts

Protection for screen layouts and graphics has so far received scant attention. Layouts may be covered by copyright. However, in Germany, this presupposes a "personal intellectual creation," which will seldom be the case as chiefly "Everyman" creations will be concerned. Also conceivable is protection under the Patented Designs Act. For this, layouts must be new and possess particular character.[70] However, such protection assumes an application to the German Patent Office. The period of protection in Germany is a maximum of 20 years.

On the other hand, where a personal intellectual creation exists in a specific case, no application is required. Copyright protection commences with the creation and in Europe lasts for a uniform 70 years following the creator's death. Apart from this type of protection, one may also draw on the Unfair Competition Act as a means to protect illegally duplicated screen layouts.

§ 9.24   The Internet as a Place for Competition

Sections 9.25 through **9.32** discuss the Internet as a forum for competition.

§ 9.25   —Protection for the Homepage

The use of homepages will open up a new type of advertising. Apart from the traditional mix of print, radio, and television, the importance of homepages will increase on the Internet in the future. They will be increasingly used to offer and advertise products as well. In addition, the Internet is a services platform. Information can be obtained, details called up, and advice requested.

Persons are proceeding to reserve names for themselves for homepages, in order to sell these names to the firms they belong to. The same applies to companies who are having their names registered as homepage names so that they might contact other companies laying claim to these names. Here the actual problem arises of trademark rights on the Internet.[71] The Community Trade Marks Regulation reserves settlement of trade mark claims to the national legal systems in the event of a breach,[72] and therefore solutions to the problems must be found in national law.

---

[70] *See* German Ornamental Designs Act § 1.

[71] This problem is very pertinent at the present time in the United States, where there are hundreds of cases. In particular, the limits to national trademark protection are becoming clear. *See Names Writ in Water,* Economist, July 8, 1996, at 79, 80.

[72] Community Trade Marks Regulation, art. 14 (2).

§ 9.26 —Protection for the Homepage Name

Homepages on the Internet are found and called up by an address or domain under the Domain Name Service (DNS). The homepage "name" is usually included in the domain. For example, the Italian automobile manufacturer Fiat uses the address "http://www.fiat.com" for its homepage, and the German communications magazine *Focus* uses the address "http://www.focus.de." There is an issue of whether Internet addresses constitute the use of a name, trade name, or trademark in legal terms or whether they must be regarded simply as file references. In our opinion, there can really be no doubt that this must be regarded as name, trade name, or trademark use, because precisely on the Internet, many users search somewhat aimlessly and will in first instance be guided by marks or trade names or other names familiar to them.[73] In addition, an Internet user who chances upon "Fiat.com" on the homepage will of course suspect that an Italian automobile manufacturer is behind it; similarly, a person coming upon "Focus.de" on a Homepage will expect to find the latest products or news from the German communications magazine. Just like any letterbox designation, any address quoted in an advertisement or any visiting card incorporates a reference to the person named, the DNS on the Internet also serves to point the user to the highlights on the homepage or its creator. Without the DNS, the World Wide Web could not function. After all, the DNS was created because the simple digit-based TCP/IP address was insufficient to direct the user to the homepage. In particular, the argument that the appropriate Internet page would in any event be selected only through links and not by entering an address does not match the facts. In that case, there would be fewer references to Web pages in print advertisements, on letterheads, or in television advertising.

At least, there seems to be a growing trend on the part of the courts in Germany to protect beneficiaries from third parties with more or less malicious intent. For example, the Mannheim Regional Court found for the city of Heidelberg when it sought an interim injunction against a private entrepreneur who had reserved the domain "Heidelberg.de" for himself, and ordered him to cease using it because the domain "Heidelberg" had a naming function and was consequently reserved to the city.[74]

In cases such as that of the city of Heidelberg, the courts may also possibly have a rather easier job because quite obviously someone was trying to obtain an advantage by unfairly using a well-known city name. Likely to be far more difficult are cases where two companies wish to adopt identical or confusing

---

[73] Nordemann et al., *Protection of Industrial Property and Copyright in the Internet,* CR 645 (1996); Kur, *Internet Domain Names,* CR 325 (1996).

[74] Mannheim Regional Court, Judgment of 8.3.1996-7 0 60/96; see
    http://www.focus.de/DD/DDA/dda.htm;
    CR 353 (1996).

company names or marks in absolutely different industries. The scope of an identical name is particularly problematical in this case because once a company has set up a homepage under its name, another company with an identical style is technically prevented under the DNS system from similarly setting up a homepage. There can consequently be no *de facto* right to equal names on the Internet. In a dispute, the courts will have little left in the case of simple use of a company's own name or own style than to decide on the principle of priority.

Cases of use of only similar homepage addresses, which introduce the risk of "spelling mistakes" or similar confusion, may well normally be a problem when similar or identical goods, services, or areas of business are concerned. In trademark law, a decision can be based here under the established principles under which the trademark or trade name proprietor with earlier priority will win. However, in a case in which two trademarks or trade names that have already coexisted outside the Internet for years or even decades collide on the Internet and have become open to confusion because of the special technical peculiarities of use of Internet addresses, the principles of same name rights will be applied and the companies concerned may be expected to add distinguishing suffixes to their Internet addresses as far as technically possible. Otherwise, equal name rights will have reached their limits.

§ 9.27 —Homepage Protection for Trademarks and Trade Names

Not only Internet addresses but homepages themselves usually contain a multiplicity of trademarks and trade names. However, no special features seem likely to arise here through use of these marks and names on the Internet because either advertising appears on a homepage or goods or services are offered. The use of marks and names on a homepage therefore implicitly means use in commercial dealings so that infringements can be solved without problem through the entitlements and remedies offered by the national trademark laws.

§ 9.28 —Liability; Applicable Law

The question arises of who may be sued. The answer could be found by reference to trademark law and competition law.[75] This means that a claim may be filed against not only the homepage proprietor but also the service provider. This is not fully discussed in Europe and the EU Commission is preparing a paper on this issue.

---

[75] See § **9.30.**

On the other hand, the question of applicable law presents a new problem which could also be discussed under copyright, but which becomes particularly acute in trademark law. If the concept of market effect is applied to cross-border infringement of marks, it must be possible, for example, for a German plaintiff to impugn the homepage of a company in France. However, in view of the territoriality of trademark rights, that can hardly provide a solution. Possibly, the mark protected in Germany does not exist in France at all. Because dissemination cannot be nationally restricted on the Internet, a claim lodged against the host in France would have direct global effects. Commercial online services at present protect themselves against such global effects by building clauses into their contracts whereby the user will in the worst case agree to a global solution—although the act is prohibited in one country only.

§ 9.29 —General Law of Contract

The distribution of databases or online interrogation for which payment is due presupposes a contract between the supplier and user. However, it is quite unclear at present how concluded contracts and "supplies" can be technically proven.[76]

Electronic data exchange is proceeding increasingly according to the technical standards of the UN/EDIFACT rules. In Western Europe, harmonization of the EDIFACT-BOARD (WEEB), is being continued, with the support of the EU Commission in connection with the Trade Electronic Data Interchange System (TEDIS). The legal basis for applying this technology is an outline agreement that contracting parties make before use.

The EU Commission has proposed a so-called electronic data interchange (EDI) agreement.[77] However, individual contracts for specific transactions are required to complete this proposal, which may be regarded as more of an outline. The EDI agreement in this case particularly governs the conclusion of individual contracts (place, time, access, challenge), the requirements for proof and documentation, the parties' liability, and the services concerned. Apart from this, the German government shows some notion to introduce a digital signature with its new law on information services.[78] The question of applicable law can be answered generally at this point for all types of contract. Within the framework of the special areas of law, only points relating the applicable law of tort will be discussed.

---

[76] *See* Wuermeling, *Besserer Schutz for Produktpiraterie,* 98 Handelsblatt 29 (1996).

[77] Commission Decision of 28 Dec. 1994, 1994 O.J. (L 383/98). *See* Davies, *Law and the Internet,* 11 Computer L. & Prac. 106, 108 (1995).

[78] Draft law on information and communication services, Art. 2.

Contracts concluded in connection with the Internet can be divided into three categories:

1. Database contracts (for example, concerning interrogation of databases)
2. Communications contracts (for example, concerning data exchange)
3. Service contracts (for example, concerning network use).

In every day use on the Internet, these types of contract will never occur in pure form. Instead, the types appear in combination with each other.

In Germany, international contract law is governed by Article 27 of the German Civil Code Enabling Act (EGBGB). This permits a free choice of law, with Article 28 of the Enabling Act setting up certain presumptions in the absence of agreement.[79] This includes, in particular Article 28 (2), which in case of doubt declares applicable the law of the country where the party rendering the characteristic service is established. Article 34 lays down a limit where the mandatory provisions of German law cannot be circumvented.

Both under database contracts and service contracts, the law of the country in which the service provider is established should therefore be applied. Under communications contracts, the question of applicable law depends more on the specific case, depending on who makes the service available. However, should a purchase contract concerning the supply of goods be concluded outside the Internet together with the communications contract, uniform United Nations purchase law could apply[80] which has not yet been ratified by all Member States of the EU.

§ 9.30 —Competition Law

The further that the Internet extends into consumer circles, the more traditional-style competition will take place online, with more and more advertising being conducted through homepages and more and more databases making their services available and presumably also increasingly selling products, such as with an electronic mail order catalogue. Matters that could be relevant in competition law are traditional advertising, Internet shopping, and service piracy. However, these processes do not amount to more in competition law than traditional competition and commercial dealings, because the Internet is merely a new medium by which this information is presented to the market.[81]

---

[79] For further comment on private international law in contract law from the German perspective, see Fromm & Nordemann, *Urheberrecht,* Commentary (8th ed. 1995) [hereinafter Fromm & Nordemann]; Schricker-Katzenberger, *Urheberrecht,* Commentary, Munich (1988).

[80] U.N. Convention concerning contracts for the international purchase of goods of 11 April 1980, effective in Germany as of 1 Jan. 1991, BGBl. 1989 II at 588, reports 1990 II at 1699.

[81] Davies, *Law and the Internet,* 11 Computer L. & Prac. 106 (1995).

§ 9.31 —Liability

Under German law, which offers solutions comparable to those in other European states, the person answerable is first of all the perpetrator of the illegal competitive act.[82] However, this strict liability has been extended in competition law to the sole importer of a journal or its publisher.[83] In addition, instigators and assistants are also liable under the same principles.[84] This means that the service provider who maintains a homepage and shares the income from interrogation with the proprietor may therefore be regarded as the responsible person in addition to the owner of the trade name. The draft law on information services in Germany contains an article dealing with the liability.[85] It states a liability for any service provider that even transfers data as far as it has knowledge of the content.

§ 9.32 —Applicable Law

Exploitation processes on the Internet are often cross-border. The question then arises what law is applicable to tortious actions. The problem of cross-border actions has been covered by competition law,[86] which has developed its own solutions. The problem is partly discussed under the heading of "Multistate" crime.[87] However, the situation is anything but clear.[88]

Under German law, three actions can be distinguished:[89] competition abroad with effect on German offers, cross-border competition, and foreign competition with effects for German ownership. Exploitation processes on the Internet may for the most part be assigned to the second group. Because the Internet has a global effect and no national limitation can be introduced we are not concerned here with the usual question of the extent to which a competitive action may to some extent also influence another country as a side-effect[90]), it is more a question of the intended effect in all states of the world.

From the aspect of traditional private international law, the place of commission is essentially both that of contract and that of effect (loci delicti commissi).

---

[82] For Germany, see Nordemann, *Indizienkette,* GRUR 1995, at 693, 695.

[83] *See id.,* with further references.

[84] BGB § 830(2).

[85] Draft law on information and communication services, Art. 1, § 5.

[86] *See* Paefgen, *Unlauterer Wettbewerb im Ausland,* GRUR 1994, at 99.

[87] Kort, *Zur "multistate" Problematik grenzüberschreitender Fernsehwerburg,* GRUR 1994, at 594.

[88] *See* Staudinger-von Hoffmann, BGB (12th ed. 1992). Art. 38, EGBGB ¶ 544 describes the problem as "largely unclarified."

[89] Hoth, *Ausländische Werbung mit Inlandswirkung,* GRUR 1972, at 449.

[90] *See* Schricker, *Die Bekämpfung der irreführenden Werbung in den Mitgliedstaaten der EG,* GRUR 1990, at 112.

According to Kegel, therefore, there can be more than one place of effect.[91] If these places lie in different states, according to German precedent, the state with the law most favorable to the injured party will apply.[92] This results in a call on a multiplicity of legal systems and to an extension to the applicable law extremely problematical to the courts.[93]

If the user, host, and homepage company are established in Germany, German law is undoubtedly applicable. However, even if the company is established abroad, German law will apply if exploitation originates with the terminal server of the host in Germany. The real problem arises when both the host with terminal server and the company are located abroad. Then, according to established opinion, the law of the country will apply where the host is established. This could have dire consequences if the host is established in a country without adequate competition law.

However, the idea of a "market order law" is being increasingly accepted in competition law. According to this, the market that the competitive act influences or may influence is decisive; the place of commission is consequently unimportant. The problem then arising lies in the boundless extent of the sales market effects regarded as the key concept.[94]

To be able to proceed effectively against such infringers who act from abroad, either account must be taken of the sales market effect, or a solution must be found based on the broadcasting of Internet data, by analogy with the so-called Bogsch Theory dismissed by EC law.[95] The proposed directive concerning confusing advertising[96] has opted, consequently also in its Article 3 (c), for a procedure different from that of the Television Directive. It proceeds implicitly from the applicable law of conflict and leaves it at that. According to the Bogsch theory, an infringer who unlawfully—in terms of German competition law—makes material available in Germany would be judged under German law irrespective of whether the data was kept in Germany. Otherwise, terminal servers in countries with little or no legal protection against competition would be preprogrammed for "flagging out." The German Federal Court of Justice is also relying increasingly on the place of market effect.[97]

---

[91] Kegel, Internationales Privatrecht, § 18 IV a. bb (7th ed. 1995).

[92] BGH, NJW 1964, at 2012; 1981, at 1606, 1606–07.

[93] *See* Nordemann ¶¶ 19 *et seq.* on the development of private international law in competition law.

[94] *See* Paefgen, GRUR 1994, at 99, 102.

[95] Council Directive 89/552/EEC, 1989 O.J. (L 298/23), which coordinated certain provisions of copyright and protection of industrial property rights concerning satellite broadcasting and cable relaying, dismissed the Bogsch Theory and introduced the transmission country theory. For details, see Kreile & Becker, *Neuordnung des Urheberrechts in der Europäischen Union,* GRUR 1994, at 901, 909.

[96] Council Directive 84/450/EEC, 1994 O.J. (L 250/20), on the approximation of legal and administrative provisions of Member States concerning confusing advertising.

[97] *Purchases abroad,* BGHZ 113, at 1. For details, see Paefgen, *Unlauterer Wettbewerb im Ausland,* GRUR 1994, at 99.

§ 9.33 Data Transfer on the Internet

The transfer of data is based essentially on copyright. At this point, the EU Green Paper and the follow-up paper mentioned in § 9.2 is important.[98]

§ 9.34 —Protected Works, Proprietors, and Prerequisites for Protection

Protected works of art include literary works such as printed matter, speeches, computer programs, musical works, pantomime works, works of graphic art, photographic works (photography), film, and achievements of a technical or scientific nature such as databases.

A special problem, which has a bearing not merely on the Internet, are multimedia works. For example, an encyclopaedia article on Beethoven with text, graphics, and sound on a compact disc, interactive (CD-I) raises the question of how such a multimedia work should be described. Without going into detail at this point,[99] it might also be possible to regard multimedia works as a database. This would have direct effects on the rights then available since the EU Directive on database protection will be binding as of 1998.

In principle, the creator principle applies in Europe, with the exception of the Netherlands, where contracts of employment are concerned, and the United Kingdom, with its common law basis. The proprietor of copyright is always the creator of the work, never the employer. However, the EU Green Paper discussed in § 9.2 lists new creative forms where the contribution of the individual creator can be distinguished only with difficulty. It points to multimedia producers also being regarded as proprietors of copyright.

Unlike the former legal position under common law, there is neither a need nor a possibility in Europe for entering works on a copyright role, nor is a copyright reference mandatory. However, individual national legal systems in Europe have provisions like § 10 of the German Copyright Act, whereby the person described as the author on the reproduced copies of a published work or on the original of a work of graphic art in the usual way is regarded as the author until proven to the contrary. Other European states have similar positions for performing artists, so that affixing a © or entering "P" is always to be recommended because this facilitates law enforcement.

---

[98] *But see* the results of the panel discussion the Commission held in May 1996: *DGXV, Copyright and Related Rights on the Threshold of the 21st Century,* Florence 1996 (still unpublished).

[99] For the United Kingdom: Turner, *Do the Old Legal Categories Fit the New Multimedia Products?,* 3 EIPR 107 (1995); Henry, *Multimedia: Mythology, Metaphor and Reality,* 1 Ent. L. Rev. 79 (1995); Sherwood-Edward, *It's Cruel to Be Clear: Clearing Rights in a Multimedia World,* 1 Ent. L. Rev. 3 (1995). For France: Muenchinger, *French Law and Practice Concerning Multimedia and Telecommunications,* 4 EIPR 186 (1996). For Germany: Vogel at 9 (sees no new kind of work in multimedia works).

§ 9.35 —Exploitation Rights on the Internet

There has been lively discussion to date as to whether use on the Internet should be regarded as distribution, reproduction, broadcasting, or a new user right. These questions arise especially with homepages and with use of a database. Data for the homepage or a database is saved in a computer. Consequently, to take the sequence of events, first uploading and then storage can be analysed.

Uploading

Uploading comprises the reproduction of a work, a right which is reserved to the author.[100] This applies similarly to browsing—even if this takes only a few seconds—whereby a work enters a PC's main storage. However, one might wonder whether buffering in a so-called router should necessarily be regarded as reproduction. On careful consideration, this seems unlikely as a router receives no benefit at all from the work.

In addition, digitalization of data on the way into the PC, such as during scanning, could be regarded as processing. However, this is questionable because typesetting a handwritten manuscript cannot be regarded as processing, and digitalization, although potentially involving enormous practical consequences, does not change the substance of the work. It is therefore reproduction that consequently requires reproduction rights, but not processing authorization under § 23 of the German Copyright Act.

Retention

It does not seem likely that retaining data would constitute copyright infringement. However, it may be a starting point for liability of the service provider, if keeping the data available facilitates subsequent infringement by a third party.

Data Transfer

Questions concerning data transfer[101] have been discussed intensively by commentators.[102] It is open to doubt, however, whether a transfer is a new type of exploitation[103] or whether transfer should be regarded as processing, reproduction, or transmission.[104]

---

[100] Council Directive 91/250/EEC 1991 O.J. (L 122), art. 4.

[101] The process of transferring data into the network is described in this discussion by the term "transfer" or "transferring" in order to prevent any misunderstanding regarding transmission rights and the concept of transfer of rights.

[102] *See, e.g.,* Christie, *Reconceptualising Copyright in the Digital Era,* 11 EIPR 522, 526 (1995) (demands a new "right to prevent access to a work").

[103] For the separate question of new type of use, see § **9.37.**

[104] For the various solutions offered in Germany, see Vogel at 9.

The United Kingdom could not detect any of the traditional modes of exploitation in data transfer. It has therefore introduced a new section into its laws. Special protection has existed in the United Kingdom since March 18, 1995, against unlawful reception of data transfer.[105] English law therefore latches onto reception and guarantees the author a kind of "right to award a receiving licence."

The EU Commission and the United States take a different view. President Clinton's task force describes the temporary copying of a document from the Internet into a PC working storage as reproduction, while it regards keeping data available as dissemination.[106] The EU Green Paper discussed in § **9.2,** on the other hand, adopts no final position that lets it be known that it advocates a "right to digital distribution."[107]

The EU Database Directive has opted for special protection.[108] It prefers a specific kind of right against unlawful expropriation from databases. This should apply both to traditional databases and to the Internet. However, there are also people who are taking this debate as an excuse for doing away with copyright altogether on the Internet.[109] However, copyright has always adapted itself to technological changes as film, radio, and computers indicate.

Section 15 of the German Copyright Act allows for certain corporeal and incorporeal exploitation. However, the rights listed are not exhaustive. Rather, an author has a comprehensive right to exploit her work.[110]

The reproduction as a typical form of *physical exploitation* presupposes further items for reproduction under the traditional view of supply. However, on the Internet, a data record broadcast with an IP address is always the original. Some advocate reproduction rights with the interesting comment that not only the recipient but also the supplier undertakes a certain kind of "remote reproduction."[111] However, data transfer proceeds without a direct physical wrapping. This view could therefore be countered with there being no physical exploitation, even though the process is more like reproduction.[112]

Incorporeal disposal according to § 15 (2) of the German Copyright Act is protected only on public playback. The necessary public element, according to § 15 (3) of the German Copyright Act, arises if the playback is intended for a

---

[105] *See* Copyright, Design and Patents Act §§ 297–299 (1988).

[106] U.S. Information Infrastructure Task Force, at 30; Intellectual Property and the National Information Infrastructure—The Report 30 (Washington, D.C., 1995).

[107] Copyright and Related Rights in the Information Society: Green Paper by the EU Commission, COM(95)382, at 56–57.

[108] Council Directive 96/9/EEC, 1996 O.J. (L 77).

[109] For the United Kingdom: Christie, *Reconceptualising Copyright in the Digital Era,* 11 EIPR 522, 526 (1995); *see also ZENSIERT: Der Staat vs. The Net,* the provocative approach in the journal pl@net 3+4/96.

[110] Fromm & Nordemann § 15, ¶ 1.

[111] *See* paper by Schwartz at the 1996 GRUR Annual Conference in Hamburg, Annual Meeting of German Soc'y for Protection of Industrial Property and Copyright, so far unpublished [hereinafter Schwartz].

[112] Nordemann, *Das Urheberrecht in der Informationsflut: Felseiland oder Sandbank, in* Auf der Medienautobahn 33, 35 (1995) [hereinafter Nordemann, *Das Urheberrecht*].

number of persons, unless the circle of such persons is specifically delimited and they are linked personally to each other through mutual relations or through a relationship with the organizer. That is precisely the case on the Internet. The circle of persons who potentially have the use of a homepage is quite unlimited. There is no medium on this earth which achieves a similar density of distribution.[113]

However, public playback requires simultaneous reception by several persons. However, even this may arise if we consider the technical situation involved with the Internet. The data packages pass through the Net like radio waves in traditional broadcasting and can be received simultaneously—at least potentially—so that to some extent artificial "successive publication" is unnecessary. The host is the originator and organizer of all conduct by the user. Without the host making the data permanently available on the telephone line, the user could simply not become active. If, finally, we compare the homepage with a video screen which runs permanently, playback is even more clear. If we accept the parallels with the gist of the Bogsch Theory, there is every reason for regarding use on the Internet as a broadcast.[114] However, it must be credited to the opponents of this view that data packages on the Internet are called up by the user and the latter is not passive, as in the case of a traditional broadcast.

If broadcasting rights under § 20 of the German Copyright Act were involved on the Internet,[115] the decisive aspects of private international law would be more satisfactorily and essentially more conclusively solved for the author. Nevertheless, the solution of reproduction, at least in Schwartz's variant of "remote reproduction," also offers satisfactory solutions at this point.[116]

However, we must also recognise that categorization as a broadcast has its disadvantages. On the one hand, under § 49 of the German Copyright Act, electronic press reviews would be permitted, which would compete appreciably with the traditional media, while on the other hand, performing artists and record manufacturers would have no prohibitory rights, but only a claim to remuneration under § 86 of the German Copyright Act. The most serious objection, however, would be that mentioned by Vogel, that under Article 11 a. (2) of the Revised Berne Convention, the prohibitory rights in certain cases can be traced back to a compulsory licence and not applying at all to works of graphic art.

Data transfer may be classified as reproduction, as broadcasting, or even as a right of a specific nature. The fact remains that copyright offers adequate protective mechanisms.

---

[113] The novel *Le Grand Secret* by President Mitterand's personal doctor, which was offered by an Internet Cafe in Besançon, was called up over 50,000 times within a few days. *See* NZZ of 27.1.1996, No. 22, at 20.

[114] *But see* Vogel at 9 (legal consequences should be determinative).

[115] *Id.* (advocates new "digital transmission rights" in Germany as a kind of public playback not so far expressly regulated).

[116] Schwartz.

Downloading

Downloading includes reproduction of a work.[117] This procedure can be regarded the same as the uploading procedure.

Limits to Exploitation

Private copying is the second problem point. Downloading is regarded as the production of copies by third parties. Private reproduction assumes a new dimension on the Internet.[118] Reproduction for private or other own use is permitted by § 53 of the German Copyright Act. This provision would have to be restricted[119] to adapt the privilege to the new circumstances. In view of the possibilities for copying works on private computers, reprocessing them, and printing them out without any loss of quality, such use should no longer be covered by the now existing reprography levy.[120]

Commentators have suggested in the past that the free use in the private area of works protected by copyright should be limited to those uses that can no longer be verified on practical and technical grounds.[121] The EU's Green Paper discussed in **§ 9.2** assumes that in the future every use, however significant, in digital media will be recordable on computer and a royalty charged for it. Private use free of charge would thereby be practically reduced to cases where no "digital footprint" was left.

§ 9.36 —Moral Rights on the Internet

Moral rights present particular difficulties. Because works can quite simply be altered without any loss of quality, digital use on the Internet threatens the integrity of works fed into the Internet.[122] In addition to the rights of the creator of the work to integrity,[123] his right to have his name mentioned is particularly under threat.[124] Infringements based on photographs that enter the Internet without

---

[117] Council Directive 91/250/EEC 1991 O.J. (L 122), art. 4.

[118] For Germany: Vogel, *Multimedia und weltweite Vernetzung,* 67 Blick durch die Wirtschaft 9 (1996).

[119] Nordemann, *Das Urheberrecht,* at 33 (36).

[120] *See* Vogel, *Elektronischer Pressespiegel und Wissensdatenbank,* 70 Blick durch die Wirtschaft 9 (1996).

[121] Auf der Maur.

[122] Copyright and Related Rights in the Information Society: Green Paper by the EU Commission, COM(95)382, at 65.

[123] *E.g.,* German Copyright Act § 14.

[124] *E.g., id.* § 13.

any name mentioned can hardly be prevented in practical terms. It is a fact that German law offers sufficient protection against such infringements (exceptions are performing artists, in whom only limited personal rights are vested).

The actual question of possible prosecution remains open, however. It is not clear how action can be taken against infringements of moral rights if there are no means of verifying them. Vogel advocates a solution under the law of copyright.[125] However, this would have the disadvantage of further advancing the progressive disposability of moral rights. Even if it may seem meaningful in the area of law concerning the press[126] to speak of such disposability, we can see no immediate need for this in the original area of copyright. A solution should rather be found on the law enforcement side.

Until new solutions are found to this problem, the author is dependent on the existing resources of copyright which, although legally extensive, technically leave problems of evidence unclarified.

§ 9.37 —Copyright Law: A Use Not Yet Known?

A self-contained problem of copyright is the exploitation of "old" (but not yet protected) works for which exploitation contracts exist only in respect of old types of use. This question is dealt with by provisions comparable to those of § 31(4) of the German Copyright Act. It is decisive that not only is the technical potential of the type of use contemplated, but also that it is recognized as economically significant and exploitable.[127] The Internet has existed since the 1970s, and universities and technicians have been using the Net for quite some time.

On the one hand, the question whether a type of use is known cannot be objectively answered in terms of the protective aims of § 31(4) of the German Copyright Act, but must be decided from the author's perspective.[128] The possibility of using the Net on one's own as a private person has existed only a short while. Only the triumphal progress of personal computers with ever-easier means of operation has permitted private individuals to join the circle of Internet users. This was possible hitherto only through large computers, but only on such private utility as the Internet boomed.

On the other hand, the Net has become interesting to companies through its increased use in recent months, which is clear from the currently increasing number of applications. However, the Internet is thereby only now achieving

---

[125] Vogel, *Elektronischer Pressespiegel und Wissensdatenbank,* 70 Blick durch die Wirtschaft 9 (1996).

[126] *See* Götting, *Persönlichkeitsrechte als Vermögensrechte,* Tübingen 1995, at 142.

[127] *See* BGHZ 95, at 274, 284 (GEMA presumption I); BGH GRUR 1988, at 296, 298 (GEMA presumption IV); BGH GRUR 1991, at 133, 136 (Videozweitauswertung); BGH NJW 1995, at 1496, 1497 (Videozweitauswertung III); Fromm & Nordemann §§ 31/32, ¶¶ 9–10.

[128] Fromm & Nordemann §§ 31/32, ¶ 10; left open in BGH GRUR 1991, at 133, 136 (Videozweitauswertung).

economic importance. This is also clear from the figures regarding host computers linked to the Internet worldwide. Although in July 1991 there were only 535,000, by 1993 there were already 1.3 million, and in 1994 3.8 million. The figure increased in 1995 to almost 7.0 million. Finally, at the start of 1996, there were already 9.4 million connections.[129] Use on the Internet[130]—whether by e-mail, homepage, or database—must accordingly be regarded as an unknown type of use in terms of § 31(4) of the German Copyright Act.[131]

One proposal indicates a desire to see this outcome restricted in the interests of the information requirements of the general public and enumerates possible solutions—such as a statutory license, mandatory exploitation company, and obligation to make an offer—with an argument in favor of the second of these.[132]

§ 9.38 —Liability

The question of liability concerns the technical prerequisites described in § 9.37 and the scenarios developed from them. Liability is borne first of all by those who are themselves in breach of the law. The only prerequisite is that an adequate causal connection exists between the behavior complained of and the breach of the law.[133] However, the person who has instigated the breach of a legal right may also be liable.[134] That person is the proprietor of the homepage, the company on the Internet.

Other persons may be liable as well. For example, the organizer of a musical event is liable even if she herself plays no music.[135] Any person who makes software available for a homepage on the Net and also stores the data available on the homepage may be regarded as an instigator. This applies all the more so if the service provider sets up the homepage for gain and divides up the income, keeps data ready, and looks after the installations.

The service provider will certainly attempt to evade responsibility by arguing that she is doing no more than facilitating a transfer and cannot be liable for the content. However, an argument of this kind will not prevail over the organizer's liability for a performance,[136] nor can the service provider prevail by pointing to

---

[129] FAZ, 11 July 1996, at 21.

[130] Endter, *Internet—(K)ein urheberrechtsfreier Raum,* NJW 1996, at 975 (speaks imprecisely of the Internet itself as a type of use).

[131] *See id.* at 976; Vogel, *Was sind noch nicht bekannte Nutzungsarten,* 72 Blick durch die Wirtschaft 10 (1996).

[132] Vogel, *Was sind noch nicht bekannte Nutzungsarten,* 72 Blick durch die Wirtschaft 10 (1996).

[133] *See* BGHZ 42, at 118, 124 (Personalausweise beim Tonbandgerätekauf).

[134] *See* BGHZ 15, at 338; BGH GRUR 1987, at 37, 39 (Videolizenzvertrag).

[135] *See* BGH GRUR 1956, at 515, 516 (Tanzkurse).

[136] For the United Kingdom: Davies, *Law and the Internet,* 11 Computer L. & Prac. 106, 107 (1995) (restricted only by certain considerations of practicability).

postal or telecommunications secrecy.[137] The purpose of this guarantee of basic rights is secrecy of communication as against the state, not as against private persons.[138] Postal and telecommunications secrecy may therefore certainly play a role in criminal law but not in trademark, copyright, or competition law, as aspects of civil law. We cannot discern any indirect third-party effect—from whatever perspective this might be considered—because homepages or databases made available to the public can hardly be treated as other than video screens.

In the United Kingdom, the Lord Chancellor's Department is preparing a statutory amendment whereby service providers are expressly declared responsible. However, the bill also provides for clearly defined, tightly drawn exceptions to such liability on grounds of practicability.[139]

§ 9.39 —Choice of Law

The question of what law should apply to exploitation processes on the Internet remains open and disputed.[140] Article 38 of the German Civil Code Enabling Act (EGBGB) states that the only claims that can be made against a German in respect of an unlawful act perpetrated abroad are those that would be actionable under German law. This article proceeds from the general principle that the legal consequences of a tort must be considered under the law of the place of commission.[141] This presents no problem in traditional cases of local infringement. Difficulties arise, however, if the actions are transnational—as on the Internet. The traditional view of the place of commission as the place of contract and the place of effect is discussed in **§ 9.32.** The law of the country where the data is uploaded and also that of the country where it is downloaded will therefore apply without any problem.

Claims in respect of unlawful acts in copyright are pursued in Germany under the law of the place of perpetration.[142] However, under the protective country principle, this is only the place of contract.[143] This means that if exploitation of a work were categorized on the Internet as reproduction, the law of the country of origin would apply.[144] Only Schwartz's view, whereby "remote reproduction"

---

[137] German Constitution, art. 10.

[138] Pieroth & Schlink, *Grundrechte,* Heidelberg ¶¶ 856 *et seq.* (6th ed. 1993).

[139] Davies, *Law and the Internet,* 11 Computer L. & Prac. 106, 107–08 (1995).

[140] For Germany, see Dreier, *Harmonisierung des Urheberrechts in der Informationsgesellschaft,* ZUM 1996, 69, 71 *et seq.* For Switzerland, see Auf der Maur.

[141] For Germany: 96 RGZ 94, 96; 57 BGHZ 264, 265; 87 BGHZ 95, 97.

[142] Fromm & Nordemann.

[143] Schricker-Katzenberger, *Urheberrect,* Commentary, Munich (1988).

[144] *Id.*

arises, would point to a different solution.[145] Against this, one could possibly in the case of broadcasting apply the law of the country of effect.

Competition law is also increasingly going by the place of effect, so that arguments in respect of copyright can also be drawn from this premise. The country from which exploitation actually proceeds should not therefore always be regarded as the country of origin in terms of copyright law. For legal certainty on the Internet, new solutions must be found. Because the new TRIPs Convention[146] offers no more far-reaching solutions in this respect, suitable solutions must be found by recourse to the appropriate provisions of the law of conflict.[147] The actual problem also arises in copyright when both the host with the terminal server and the company are located abroad. Then, the law of the country in which the host is established will apply under traditional private international copyright law. This can have serious consequences if the host has moved its registered office to a country like Cambodia, where no copyright law exists.

To proceed effectively against such infringers who act from abroad, a solution must be found that is based on the dissemination of Internet data.[148] According to this theory, an infringer who unlawfully in terms of German law makes data available in Germany must be judged by German law irrespective of whether the data is kept in Germany. Otherwise, "flagging out" (that is, leaving countries with high copyright standards) of terminal servers in countries with little or no copyright protection would be preprogrammed. There is, therefore a concrete need for discussion here. The solution in the literature of competition law, of proceeding according to the effect, also corresponds to the function of the law of liability, which is to control behavior and make good the loss.

It appears that the EU Commission wants to follow a "country of origin" principle.[149] However, it stresses that the question is one of practicable solutions. Nonetheless, the trend seems to be to proceed in the direction of the Satellite Directive solution.[150] This approach should be resisted especially because of its impracticability.[151]

---

[145] *See* Schwartz.

[146] Agreement on Trade-Related Aspects of Intellectual Property Rights of 1993, GATT Document MTN.TNC/W/FA, BGBl. 1994 II at 1565 (English) and 1730 (German).

[147] *See* Dreier, *Harmonisierung des Urheberrechts in der Informationsgesellschaft,* ZUM 1996, 69, 72 (regards this as only one of various solutions).

[148] This approach also affects the question of method of exploitation. See § **9.37.**

[149] Copyright and Related Rights in the Information Society, Green Paper by the EU Commission, COM(95)382, at 38.

[150] *Id.* at 41.

[151] For further details from the German point of view, see von Lewinski, GRUR 1995, at 831, 833–34.

§ 9.40   Interactive Media

The legal position in Europe regarding interactive television and home shopping offers falls within the major legal area of the law of the media. The European debate on this has only just been ignited. In Germany, a statute is at present in preparation on this subject.[152] Especially unclear is the extent to which online services form part of radio[153] and are therefore subject to the restrictions of state registration.

Just recently there has been a law drafted by the states[154] and one drafted by the federal government.[155] Each entity argues that it has the competence to regulate this field of law. Both drafts contain rules on how to set up a service provider, how to manage a service, and who is liable for any problems.

§ 9.41   Standards and Regulatory Law

So far there are no special features in Europe regarding legal protection for Internet matters nor any regulatory laws that contain provisions specifically for the Net.

§ 9.42   Future Protection Strategies

The application of the law to user infringements on the Internet essentially presents no special difficulties either in the competition and trademark area or in copyright—provided the existing laws are interpreted sensibly in accordance with the new situation. Problems arise in all legal fields with the question of applicable law. It must therefore be clearly understood that this outcome is diametrically opposed to usage on the Internet. So-called Netiquette is a view of a certain anarchy on the Net.[156]

§ 9.43   Law Enforcement

The real problem on the Internet is law enforcement. Who keeps what information on what computer has so far been untraceable and unprovable, let alone

---

[152] Federal Minister of Education, Science, Research and Technology, Outline legal conditions for new information and communications services, Bonn/Berlin, May 1996
     http://www.bmbf.de/.

[153] The German debate and the concept are discussed in Hermann, Fernsehen und Hörfunk mit neuen Medien ¶¶ 11–12 (1995).

[154] Draft law on information and communication services (Bonn, Nov. 1996).

[155] Draft of state treaty between the federal government and the states concerning media services (Koblenz, Oct. 1996).

[156] See § 9.44.

enforceable.[157] It has also been said that the Internet is evading attack because it is so designed that it will survive even the worst possible attack, namely a nuclear disaster.[158]

Various technical outline solutions are at present under discussion.[159] The technical prerequisites must be created to ascertain what data exists in what host and who is disseminating and calling it up. The latest technical innovation of copyright importance—computer programs—has already shown that nothing of importance can be achieved by new laws alone.

Despite protection under the Revised Berne Convention and the TRIPs Agreement, despite the EC Directive and conversion into § 69a *et seq.* of the German Copyright Act, the phenomenon of computer program piracy has not changed significantly. What will therefore be decisive is whether technical solutions can be found that make infringements on the Internet effectively prosecutable. This is a challenge especially to the exploitation companies.[160] They could be given the role of a so-called one-stop shop, with the possibility of acquiring all rights from an institution.[161] In addition, evasion of one-stop shops could be prevented by so-called digital footprints, which would indicate in respect of each data set who holds the rights thereto, whether the data set has been modified, and where it was outputted. However, we must be aware that any prosecution of such infringements on the Internet would presuppose penetrating the computers linked to it. The constitutional problems that would result have only been hinted at. Any such penetration could affect the sacrosanctity of the home or encroach on the user's personal rights. However, the major firms in the industry are already working on programs—so the rumor goes—which can recognize on the Internet whether a computer contains a pirated program and can immediately transmit a killer virus which will paralyze the whole computer.

If the company feeding unlawful data into the Internet is located on a South Sea Island, there is at present no chance of an injured author or company getting at the infringer. It may "sell" umpteen thousand scanned copies of a book protected by copyright without being called to account for it. Or it can provide its homepage with the name of a major firm and "extort" a blackmail payment from it. In any event, despite the unwieldiness of their commissions, the International Conventions, especially the particularly relevant TRIPs Convention, should be adapted.

---

[157] Munich Public Prosecutor v. AP, SZ No. 281 of 6 Dec. 1995, at 12.

[158] Borchers, *Alles unter Kontrolle,* pl@net 3+4/96, at 38.

[159] Copyright and Related Rights in the Information Society, Green Paper by the EU Commission, COM(95)382, at 79 *et seq.;* Interactive Multimedia Association, Technological Strategies for Protecting Intellectual Property in the Networked Multimedia Environment, (1994); Vogel, *Was sind noch nicht bekannte Nutzungsarten,* 72 Blick durch die Wirtschaft 10 (1996).

[160] *See also* Vogel, *Was sind noch nicht bekannte Nutzungsarten,* 72 Blick durch die Wirtschaft at 10.

[161] *Id.*

Insofar as contractual solutions are concerned, the European exploitation companies, and the German exploitation company GEMA above all, are making an effort to find a user-friendly solution. They would like to set up a clearing house which will operate as a "one-stop shop" and so award all rights for multimedia products. In the initial stage, this house would begin by collecting information only and pass it on to the exploitation companies concerned. At a further stage, it should also be able to award licenses itself.

§ 9.44 —Netiquette

Like every developing society, the Internet has its own protective system, so-called Netiquette.[162] With news groups, in particular, a moderator ensures that participants remain true to their subject. Breaches are sanctioned by killfiles or mailbombs.[163] Nonetheless, comment on this self-protection hitherto has shown that no viable system exists. Such situations are unacceptable in view of the expansion of the Internet and the associated mass legal infringements of copyright or trademark law. We cannot wait until the Internet society regulates itself.

It would at least be expedient for Netiquette to be regarded as a phenomenon equivalent to a set of ethical rules at those places where it is already sufficiently established and in general circulation, and thereby enter into the concept of public policy under § 1 of the German Unfair Competition Act (UWG).

---

[162] *See*

http://www.screen.com/understand/Netiquette.html.

[163] Borchers, *Alles unter Kontrolle,* pl@net 3+4/96, at 39. On the specific law of the Internet, see

ftp://parcftp.xerox.com/pub/MOO/papers/VillageVoice.html.

CHAPTER 10

ASIAN PROTECTION STRATEGIES FOR THE INTERNET

Joon Kook Park

§ 10.1   Information Technology and Intellectual Property Law

Information technology (IT) is a general categorization used to describe the various technologies of processing, storing, and transmitting information, in the form of voice, data, sound, or image, by electronic means. This can encompass everything from computer hardware, software, and networking systems to new forms of telephony and broadcasting and even new forms of information content, such as multimedia. With Korea's 1995 enactment of the Basic Act for the Promotion of Information and Communication, the legal protection of IT will play an important role in the success of Korea's informatization projects.

IT can be protected under intellectual property (IP) laws upon satisfying the statutory threshold requirements for eligibility. Some of these technologies, however, pose problems in the application and enforcement of intellectual property rights.

Digital technology, the common denominator of all IT, permits the compression of large amounts of information without distortion. Digitalization coupled with high-capacity telecommunications network systems, such as B-ISDN (Broadband Integrated Services Digital Network), will enable the transmission of more data at faster speeds with better quality. It will also raise challenging new questions about copyright laws: How can copyrights be enforced when software and other works of authorship can be copied and transmitted over personal computer (PC) networks with no degradation of copy quality and no means of tracking where or how many copies have been made? With the advent of computer networks and PC communication systems, traditional intellectual property rights (IPR) concepts of "public disclosure," "publication," and "reproduction" will seem archaic unless they are reexamined and redefined.

As seen on the Internet's World Wide Web, multimedia applications are made possible by a wide variety of technologies, such as software and integrated circuits, in order to bundle into one package various formats of text, audio, graphics, and interactive capabilities. Such creations would traditionally be covered by different IP principles, such as copyrights for the creative works of authorship, including the software, and patents for the computer hardware. In Korea and Japan, patent protection is exclusively limited to highly advanced technical creations utilizing the laws of nature, most commonly in the form of a manufactured product or a process. Computer programs per se are not eligible for patent protection because they are considered to be a type of algorithm or mathematical formula, which fails to satisfy the utilization-of-a-law-of-nature requirement. However, with the ever-growing importance, and market value, of software necessary to integrate the various elements of computer hardware found in multimedia applications and network systems, computer programs—incorporated into an apparatus or system to perform a predetermined function—have gained some patent recognition.

In Korea, the Computer Program Protection Act grants rights to owners of computer programs that differ little from those of copyright. The problem with copyright protection is that it is very narrowly tailored to fit only the exact expression of the work of authorship, so that an owner of a copyright can prohibit someone only from copying the work as it is fixed, but not the stealing of the main idea of the work. Patent protection, on the other hand, grants to owners the broader right to prohibit the infringement of the idea, as well as the copying or misappropriation of the tangible expression of the idea. This comes from patent's requirement for novelty. Patent protection extends to prohibit the making or using of similar inventions even if they were independently created.

§ 10.2 —Intellectual Property Rights in Korea and Japan

In Korea and Japan, IPR laws are set forth in various statutes. Each country has a Patent Act, a Copyright Act, a Trademark Act, an Unfair Competition Prevention Act recognizing the protection of trade secrets, and a Semiconductor Chip Layout Design Protection Law (called the Act Concerning the Circuit Layout of a Semiconductor Integrated Circuit, in Japan). An invention may qualify for more than one form of IPR protection.

A major difference in the laws of the two nations is that Korea protects computer programs under the Computer Program Protection Act (the CPPA, effective July 1, 1987), whereas Japan recognizes protection of computer programs through its copyright law, amended in 1986. Both laws are designed to protect foreign computer program copyrights and to allow the import and licensing of such programs. Both laws also provide for moral rights and economic rights of ownership and are closely related in that the rights granted under the CPPA are nearly the same as those for copyrights.

Many provisions of these IPR laws have been newly enacted or substantially amended within the past 10 years to tighten enforcement. As much as by the need to keep pace with Korean's growing technology output, these new IPR laws were enacted in response to foreign criticism of Korean industry practices, especially in the areas of copyright infringement and unauthorized copying of computer software programs. Patent laws were amended to meet the standards for reciprocity in the treatment of Korean IPR overseas under international treaties such as the Paris Convention and the Patent Cooperation Treaty (PCT), and by the coordinative efforts of organizations such as the World Intellectual Property Organization and the World Trade Organization.

§ 10.3 Information Technology and Patents

Patents provide the most significant form of IPR protection for IT because it protects the broad concept of the invention, as well as its physical embodiment.

For inventions relating to IT, a patent can be granted as long as an invention falls within the definition of "highly advanced" technical creation "utilizing laws of nature" and meets the criteria of novelty, industrial usefulness, and nonobviousness.

Any physical, electrical, or mechanical device or combination of devices, such as computer hardware, electrical circuits, or data storage devices, and also any electrical, mechanical, or chemical process, such as the manufacturing process for a semiconductor device or a computer-performed process, can be patented.

Computer software where the program is implemented in a computer application for the performance of a particular predetermined function, such as a computerized data processing system, can be granted patent rights. As a general rule, however, a computer program per se is copyrightable, but not patentable. The courts in Korea have not been able to expound on this issue because there has been no case precedent on software patents in Korea, and despite the existence of the *Standards of Examination for Computer Software-related Inventions,* used by the Korean Industrial Property Office (KIPO) to examine applications incorporating computer software, there is still uncertainty in this area of patent law.

To understand the patenting of IT-related inventions in Korea and Japan, the patent laws and procedures must be carefully studied.

§ 10.4 —Administration of the Patent Act

In Korea, the administrative decrees adopted by the President, (known as Enforcement Decrees), ordinances promulgated by the Ministry of Trade and Industry, and the administrative regulations of KIPO together make up the patent laws.

The patent laws in Korea are administered by KIPO. Its counterpart in Japan is the Japan Patent Office (JPO), which is an agency of the Ministry of International Trade and Industry. The JPO's statutory directive, similar to that of KIPO, is "to encourage inventions by promoting their protection and utilization and thereby to contribute to the development of industry."[1]

§ 10.5 —Priority and the First-to-File Rule

Both Korea and Japan follow the "first-to-file" rule of priority. Regardless of who made the invention or when, patent rights are granted to the party who was the first to file an application. Protection and the right to enforce patent rights, either by injunction or damages, begins upon registration of the patent.

Both Korea and Japan are members of the Paris Convention and the Patent Cooperation Treaty (PCT). Each country recognizes the priority filing date of an application filed for the same invention in a foreign Paris Convention or PCT member nation. Such priority claimants must strictly adhere to the procedural filing requirements set forth in the Japan and Korea Patent Acts.

For PCT applications, the Korean filing date is deemed to be the international filing date, provided that the PCT application was filed within 20 months of the Korean application filing date.

As for cases filed under the Paris Convention, the filing date of the earliest corresponding foreign application is deemed to constitute the Korean filing date as long as the Korean application is filed within one year of the relevant foreign filing. Foreign applicants (of countries which are members of the Paris Convention) may claim priority in Korea if their countries extend to Korean nationals the reciprocal right of claiming priority.

---

[1] Japanese Patent Act (JPA) art. 1.

If a PCT application claims as a priority date an earlier filing made in Korea, a request must be submitted to KIPO setting forth the following information within 20 months of the priority date as defined in Article 2(xi) of the PCT:

1. Name and address of the applicant
2. Date of the filing in Korea
3. Title of the invention
4. Name and address of the inventor
5. Priority date, if priority is being claimed
6. International filing date and number
7. Name and address of applicant's Korean patent agent.

§ 10.6   —Standards for Patentability

Unless stated otherwise, the discussion below pertains equally to both Japanese and Korean patent laws.

An IT-related invention can be patented if it is "a highly advanced creation of technical ideas utilizing laws of nature."[2] In addition, the invention must have industrial utility, novelty, and nonobviousness. The Patent Act does not explain what level of creativity is intended by the term *highly advanced,* or what is meant by *laws of nature.* In practice, however, patents are granted to products or processes that satisfy the requirements of industrial utility, novelty, and non-obviousness (the inventive step requirement). These threshold requirements of utility, nonobviousness, and novelty are interpreted by, and subject to the discretion of, the KIPO examiner.

The novelty requirement under the Patent Act cannot be satisfied if an invention was publicly known or worked in Korea prior to the date of the application for patent. Similarly, such requirement would not be met if an invention was described in a publication distributed in or outside Korea prior to the date of the application for patent. Judicial precedents in Korea have indicated that it is sufficient to prove that the matter in question was actually known by, or available to, many unspecified persons in order to establish that there was public knowledge of such matter and that it was distributed. According to such precedents, actual public knowledge and actual distribution need not be proven. The mere existence of a publication describing the invention, without proof of actual distribution, however, may or may not be sufficient proof of loss of novelty.

The patent laws provide three exceptions to the novelty requirement. These exceptions apply when a disclosure of the invention is made unintentionally, or

---

[2] Korea Patent Act (KPA) art. 1; JPA art. 1.

such disclosure results from a government-sponsored exhibition or by a scientific publication. However, an application claiming such exception must file the application for patent for the disclosed invention within six months of the disclosure event. Further, the applicant must submit documents, within 30 days of the filing of the request, which prove that the prior disclosure constitutes one of the recognized exceptions to the novelty requirement.

Both Korea and Japan afford patent protection to foods, chemical products, medicines, and agrochemicals, which can be produced chemically. A new and distinctive variety of plant can be patented as long as it can be reproduced asexually, that is, without seeds (for example, grafting or cutting) in order to show that the inventor can duplicate the plant. As of July 1, 1995, Japan recognizes the patentability of an invention of a substance manufactured by the transformation of the atom. Korea will soon enact a similar amendment.[3]

§ 10.7   —Patents and Utility Models

Both Japan and Korea have laws for utility model protection, which has a less stringent creativity requirement than that for patents, but the requirements for usefulness, novelty, and nonobviousness remain the same. The laws provide that an invention be merely "a creation of a technical idea utilizing the laws of nature."

Although very similar in definition and in practice, utility model protection differs from patent protection most notably in the subject matter: utility model rights extend only to specific devices, not to processes. Therefore, computer programs would not be eligible for utility model protection under a process theory.

The term of protection also differs for the two. Utility model protection lasts for 10 years from the date of publication, with no right of extension, and patent protection lasts for 15 years from the date of publication, with a right of extension (but not to exceed more than 20 years from the date of filing).[4]

For patents, an invention is nonobvious if it could not have been "easily conceived" by one skilled in the art. The utility model definition modifies the wording to read "very easily conceived."

In Korea, an application for patent protection can readily be converted to one for utility model protection, and vice versa. This occurs most commonly when the KIPO examiner finds fault with the level of nonobviousness of the invention in question.

---

[3] Ahn, Kwang-Koo, Commissioner, KIPO, in a paper, *The Korean Government's IPR Protection Policies,* presented at the 1995 AIPPI Symposium, Nov. 8, 1995.

[4] Recent proposed amendments to the KPA will make the term of the patent 20 years from the date of filing the application, as discussed in **§ 10.9.**

§ 10.8 —Procedures for Obtaining and
Maintaining Patent Rights

This section explores the procedures involved in obtaining and maintaining patent rights, from application to registration.

Application

In order to obtain a patent for an invention in Korea, an application for patent must first be filed with KIPO. A priority document must also be filed within sixteen months of the priority filing date. A power of attorney must be filed within two months after the filing date, with a 30-day extension available upon request. Although the provisions of the patent laws do not require a submission of a nationality certificate, KIPO sometimes requests that such certificate be submitted with respect to the applicant.

In Japan, however, only a Japanese inventor who is a resident can file his own application. A nonresident must hire a patent administrator, with a domicile in Japan, to file the application on behalf of the inventor and represent her in the proceedings before the JPO.

Korean applications and all supporting documents must be in the Korean language. In Japan, as of July 1, 1995, the application and all other documents filed at the JPO may be done in English, as long as a Japanese translation is filed within two months after the filing date. Moreover, any corrections of translator's errors can be made at any time until the end of the term for filing a response to the first action by the JPO. Such corrections may include the introduction of any matter omitted in the translation but included in the English version of the application earlier filed. Translations must not include the introduction of new matter, which can be grounds for rejection, opposition, or invalidation.

The formal application for a patent consists of submitting a request and a specification, in a form dictated by KIPO or JPO. The request must contain the following information:

1. The name and address of the applicant, including, for juridical persons, the name of an executive or other qualified representative
2. The date of the filing
3. The name and address of any designated agent [in Korea]
4. The title of the invention
5. The country where the corresponding foreign application was filed and the date of such filing if priority is being claimed [in Korea]
6. The names and addresses of the inventors.

The specification must state:

1. The title of the invention
2. A description of drawings if drawings form a part of the application
3. A detailed explanation of the invention
4. The claims and, if appropriate, drawings
5. An abstract of the disclosure [in Korea]
6. A certified copy of the priority document if priority is being claimed [in Korea]
7. A power of attorney [in Korea]
8. In cases relating to microorganisms, a deposit of same or other prescribed proof of the microorganism's availability [in Korea].

Specification

The specification of the invention must describe the invention in such a manner as to enable a person with ordinary skill in the art, to which the invention pertains, to easily perform, construct, or use the invention for its intended purpose.[5] The patent laws do not require that the applicant reduce the invention to practice. In the process of the application, however, KIPO will usually insist that the claims be entirely supported by the working examples of the specification.

The scope of the patent is determined by the claims. As the practice in Korea is to interpret claims narrowly, the drafting of the claims language for an application is of primary importance for an applicant.

In Japan, prior to July 1, 1995, the patent laws dictated that only those features indispensable for the constitution of the invention and necessary to prove its superiority over the prior art be contained in the claim.[6] After July 1, 1995, however, this restriction was eased to permit the clear and concise statement of all matters necessary to define the invention.

In Korea, the acceptable format for the claims is set forth in the Enforcement Decrees, to which the specification should closely adhere. Because the Korean application must be submitted in the Korean language, if an application was originally filed in a foreign jurisdiction, and a priority claim is sought, then accurate and technically correct translations must be made for the purpose of the Korean application.[7]

---

[5] KPA art. 42(2) and (3).

[6] JPA art. 36.

[7] KPA art. 54 refers to Priority Claims under Treaty, by which the filing date for the application can be substituted with a prior filing date in a foreign jurisdiction of a country which recognizes reciprocal rights for the filings of Korean nationals.

In Japan, the JPO, in its *Manual of Examination Standards,* issues examples of proper claim format setting forth the construction, degree of specificity, and even the number of examples needed to support a given type of claim.

Claim

The application must relate to only a single invention. An application may, however, cover a group of related inventions, which form a single general concept. This "unity-of-invention" rule is reflected in the Enforcement Decrees, which specify the type of claims to which an application shall relate:

1. One or more independent claims for either a product or a process
2. One independent claim for a given product, and one additional independent claim for one process specifically adapted for the manufacture or use of the said product
3. One independent claim for a given process, and one additional independent claim for one apparatus (including machinery and instruments) specifically designed for carrying out the said process
4. One independent claim for a given product, one independent claim for one process specifically adapted for the manufacture or use of the said product, and one independent claim for one apparatus specifically designed for carrying out the said process.

Method of Filing

The JPO permits the filing of the application by (1) online transmission directly to the computer at the JPO, (2) mailing a diskette to the JPO, or (3) physically delivering the paper documents to the JPO. Electronic filing has the advantages of immediate verification by the JPO to the filing applicant.

KIPO is presently working on a computerized processing system for its entire operations, including filings, but the only means of filing an application to date is to physically submit the paper documents at the offices of KIPO.

Deposit of Microorganisms

In Korea, the deposit of microorganisms prior to the filing of an application for an invention incorporating microorganisms is not required for applications filed on or after March 28, 1988, as long as a prior deposit has been made with an international depository recognized under the Budapest Treaty. For most IT technologies, this requirement is not relevant.

Laying Open of Application

In Korea, the pending patent application is laid open in an official gazette 18 months after the filing date, unless such publication is deemed not proper for national security reasons.[8] The procedure is the same in Japan. Upon laying open the application, the invention can be used by anyone in the public for research or even commercial purposes. Although the rights of ownership adhere to the applicant who was first to file, these are not enforceable until the invention prevails in the examination and a patent is issued. This laying open period can also be used by opponents to submit prior art pertaining to the application, which can be used in the examination proceedings.

Request for Examination

In Korea and Japan, a patent cannot be granted unless the application is scrutinized in an examination proceeding. Applications are not examined until a request for examination is separately made by the applicant or anyone else. In Japan, the examination process takes approximately three years. Recent amendments to the Japanese Patent Act (JPA) have been aimed at reducing the amount of time required for the examination process.[9]

In Korea, a request for examination must be made within five years from the date of filing; otherwise, the application will lapse irrevocably. In Japan, the period is seven years. In the case of an application converted from utility model to patent, or vice versa, or a divided application, the original filing date controls for the purpose of determining the request period rather than the date of the conversion or division. Some applications are intentionally permitted to lapse by the applicant, especially when the application was filed merely as a defensive ploy (whereby the laid-open application, from its filing date, is considered prior art) to block the priority application of a competitor in the field.

Under the theory of the patent laws, the patent applications were to be examined in the order of their filing dates. In practice, however, this is not necessarily the order for examinations. Due to the way the examination policy evolved and the fact that the examination groups within KIPO follow different practices, some groups examine applications in the order of their request dates, while other groups designate priority by the filing date. Because of the backlog of pending

---

[8] In Paris Convention cases, the 18-month period is measured from the priority date. In PCT cases, the period is 20 months after the defined priority date. If PCT applicants wait the full 20 months before applying for a patent in Korea, laying open occurs directly after the Korean filing.

[9] The Law Partially Amending the Patent Act, enacted on April 23, 1993, restricts the types of amendments possible to an application (for example, no "new matter" shall be introduced in an amendment) and sets forth a new no-examination procedure for utility model applications.

applications, it may take two to three years to even commence the examination proceedings.

Accelerated examination can be requested if (1) the invention is being worked in Korea by an unauthorized third party, or (2) KIPO determines that the urgent disposition of the application is necessary. In Japan, "preferential examination" can be requested if the applicant can show that the claim is presently being infringed. An "accelerated examination" can be requested where an applicant or a licensee can demonstrate that the claim is presently being worked, or will be worked in Japan, within six months of the request date. The accelerated examination requires a prior art search and a statement as to its relevance.[10]

Examiner's Response

If the examiners find that an application is not satisfactory, they will issue a notice of preliminary rejection. A notice of amendment might be issued requiring the applicant to submit additional documents or satisfy certain formalities. For example, such notices might require that an applicant submit a power of attorney or a nationality certificate. A notice of preliminary rejection will contain the description of any matter which is found to be objectionable and the time within which the applicant must respond to such notice. Usually the period for responding to the preliminary rejection is 60 days from the date of notice. In Japan, the applicant may submit written arguments or amendments in response to the JPO notice, within 60 days for applicants residing in Japan or three months for foreign applicants. An extension to respond may be requested for a period of up to 30 days. As many as five extensions can be requested on separate occasions.

If the applicant does not adequately respond to the preliminary rejection, the examiners will issue a notice of final rejection. If the response is satisfactory, the examiners may then issue a decision for publication. It is possible, however, that even if the applicant responds satisfactorily to the first preliminary rejection, the examiners may discover another ground for rejecting the application. In such event, the examiners will issue another notice of preliminary rejection, and the applicant will need to respond to such notice.

If final rejection is issued with respect to an application, the applicant may then appeal to KIPO's appellate trial board within 30 days of the issuance.[11] The

---

[10] Unlike in the United States, there is no requirement that an application filed in Japan or Korea contain any citations or references to relevant prior art. There is, however, a requirement that a paragraph stating the meritorious effects and the benefits over the prior art be placed at the end of the specifications.

[11] At the time of such appeal, the applicant may also file an amendment to the application. This is the last opportunity to file an amendment to an application. If such amendment is filed, the trial board will delay a hearing on the application until the examiners have had the opportunity to reconsider the application in light of the amendment. The applicant also has one final opportunity to convert the patent application to a utility model application before filing an appeal with the trial board. Such opportunity lapses upon the filing of an appeal with the trial board.

request for appeal may be extended up to two additional months. If the trial board finds for the applicant, the application will be remanded to the examiners for reexamination. If the trial board upholds the rejection, the applicant may appeal to the Supreme Court of Korea.

If the examiners render a decision for publication, the notice of such decision is delivered to the applicant or a designated agent of the applicant. The complete application is thereupon published for opposition in the official gazette. In both Korea and Japan, the applicant may then commercially exploit the invention claimed in the application, but the exclusive rights will be contingent upon the granting of the patent. Usually, the courts will defer enforcement of such rights until the patent grant has actually issued. Otherwise, the applicant will be liable for the enjoinder of an "infringer" of a patent that fails to be granted.[12]

Opposition

In Japan, effective January 1, 1996, the pregrant opposition procedure was abolished, replaced with a postgrant procedure. This applied to all pending applications at the end of 1995, so that these were patented without publication for opposition. In turn, anyone can file opposition to a patent within six months of the date it was granted. The postgrant oppositions are to be examined by appeals judges, not by the JPO examiners.

In Korea, once an application is published, any person may file an opposition within two months from the date of its publication. An opposing party must file a notice of opposition within that period. Complete supporting materials must then be submitted within 30 days. Once opposition is initiated, both the applicant and the opposing party are free to submit arguments and counterarguments until the examiners reach a decision. The applicant may even amend the specification and claims in order to counter the arguments of the opposition.

If the examiners dismiss the opposition, the patent will be issued. The opposing party does not have a right to appeal from the examiner's decision to dismiss. If the opposing party wishes to continue to block the patent, it will be necessary for such party to file a separate action with KIPO to invalidate the issued patent.[13] If the examiner upholds the opposition and issues a final rejection, the

---

[12] JPA art. 52(3), (4).

[13] The grounds for an invalidation action are:

1. obtainment by a person who is not entitled to the patent
2. The patent covers statutorily unpatentable subject matter
3. The patented invention lacks the requisite inventive step or novelty
4. The application for the patent fails to provide sufficient description to be worked by a person skilled in the art
5. The patent was applied for after the filing date of a similar application
6. The patent was granted to a foreign applicant whose country denies to Korean nationals similar patent protection.

Generally, there is no bar for filing an invalidation action. Invalidation actions are usually filed in response to an action for infringement.

applicant may appeal to KIPO's appellate trial board through the procedure discussed earlier in this section.

Registration and Maintenance

Once the patent is granted for an invention, the applicant must register the patent by paying the publication fee and the annuities for the first three years. Unless the patent is registered, the applicant cannot pursue any remedies to enforce its patent rights. The annuities are based on the number of claims in the patented invention. Such payment must be made within three months of the notice of patent grant. There is a six-month grace period for the payments, although a penalty doubling the original fee will be assessed for late payment. Upon payment of these fees, the next payments the applicant must make are three-year annuities starting from the fourth year from when the patent was granted.

§ 10.9 —Patent Term

In Japan, the patent term is 20 years from the date of filing the application. In Korea, the term is generally 15 years from when the application was published for opposition. Such term shall not exceed 20 years from the filing date of the application. Recent pending amendments to the Korean Patent Act (KPA) will reflect the changes of the GATT Uruguay Round TRIPs Agreement, making the term of patent protection 20 years from the date of filing the application. Because of the length of time it takes to reach the publication stage, whether the term is measured from the filing date or the publication for opposition date, the effect of the new term on the life of present patents will not be very substantial (an increase of about 2 years).

In Korea, for pharmaceuticals or agrochemicals requiring governmental review and approval pursuant to the Pharmaceutical Affairs Act and the Agrochemicals Administration Act, the term may be extended up to five more years, but (1) the extension may not exceed the time that was actually required to obtain government approval to work the invention, (2) in no event shall the term exceed beyond 12 years from the date of the final government approval to work the invention, and (3) the recognized delay forming the basis of the extension of the terms cannot include the time during which the applicant unjustifiably failed to take the steps necessary to obtain the approval or the time involved in delays in the approval process attributable to the applicant's lack of diligence. If fewer than all of the claims in an application are subject to government approval prior to being worked in Korea, only those claims subject to government approval are entitled to the patent term extension.

§ 10.10 —Scope of Patent Rights

Once the patent is granted, the patentee has the exclusive right to work the invention for business purposes. The working of an invention means:

1. For the invention of a product, acts of manufacturing, using, assigning, leasing, importing, displaying, or offering for the purposes of assignment or lease the product
2. For the invention of a process, acts of using such process
3. For the invention of a process of manufacturing a product, acts of using, assigning, leasing, displaying, or offering for the purposes of assignment or lease, or importing the article produced by such process.[14]

This exclusive right, however, does not prohibit others from using the invention solely for experimentation or research purposes. Also not subject to the exclusionary rights of the patentee are inventions aboard vessels, aircraft, or vehicles merely in transit through Korea. The patentee's rights are limited by the scope of another's earlier filed patent, utility model, or design. Further, the patentee may not interfere with the making, selling, and using of any products identical to the patented product if such product already existed in Korea on the filing date of the application for the patent in question.

§ 10.11 —Infringement

Any unauthorized working of the patented invention is an infringement of the patent. Indirect infringement is set forth in both the Japanese and Korean Patent Acts.

If the patent concerns a product invention, infringement consists of manufacturing, assigning, leasing, displaying for the purpose of assigning or leasing, or importing in business anything used exclusively for the production of such patented product. If the patent concerns a process invention, infringement consists of acts of manufacturing, assigning, leasing, displaying for the purpose of assigning or leasing, or importing in business anything used exclusively for the practicing the patented process.[15]

In Korea, willful infringement is a criminal offense under the patent laws. The penalty for committing such an offense is a prison term of up to five years and a fine of up to 20 million Korean won. Criminal proceedings are not usually

---

[14] JPA art. 2(3); KPA art. 2(3).

[15] JPA art. 101; KPA art. 127.

undertaken unless the plaintiff instigates a criminal action against the alleged infringer.

Only infringement committed knowingly or negligently can be the grounds for awarding damages. In both Korea and Japan, however, the burden of proof is on the defendant, who is presumed to have acted negligently in committing the infringing act.[16]

§ 10.12   —Enforcement and Remedies

In the event of an infringement, the patent owner may bring an action in a court of law seeking:

1. An injunction
2. Damages
3. Measures to restore business reputation.

In Korea, in addition to these remedies, the aggrieved party may seek return of profits made by the alleged infringer or lost by the owner due to the infringement activities.[17] In Japan, in addition to the patent owner, an exclusive licensee may have standing to sue as long as the license has been registered, but a nonexclusive licensee may not sue without joining the patent owner.[18]

Under the KPA, both temporary and permanent injunctions are available as remedies. It should be noted, however, that an action for temporary injunctive relief is regarded as a separate remedy distinct from the permanent injunction, and entirely separate procedures govern the obtainment of such relief. The time in obtaining a preliminary injunction is often as long as the proceeding for a permanent injunction, so some plaintiffs forgo the separate action for preliminary relief and pursue a permanent injunction from the beginning.

The statute of limitations in an action for damages is three years from the time an aggrieved party became aware of the infringement. An absolute bar exists for any such action brought more than ten years after the infringement.

In Japan, damages are calculated by statutory presumption in a case where the patentee is working the invention through a license. Then, the damages may be measured as the profit by reason of infringement and the amount of reasonable royalty, which the court can adjust upward or downward, at its discretion, based on the willfulness or gross negligence of the infringement.

Commencement of an infringement action is usually met with an administrative action for invalidation of the patent brought on by the alleged infringer. In such instances, the civil court will defer to the outcome of the administrative

---

[16] JPA art. 90; KPA art. 130.

[17] KPA arts. 126, 128, 131.

[18] JPA art. 100.

hearing by staying the infringement action. Therefore, if the patent is found to be invalid by the KIPO (or JPO) tribunal, the court will most likely dismiss the infringement proceedings. In Korea, however, if the invalidation action is based on public knowledge of the invention at the time of the filing of the patent application for an invention, the courts will not defer to KIPO on such an issue. Therefore, there is no advantage to bringing a separate KIPO action for invalidation on such grounds.

A KIPO action normally takes about eight to ten months to conclude. If an appeal is sought at the KIPO appellate trial board, the proceeding can take an additional twelve to eighteen months to conclude. In Japan, the JPO has primary jurisdiction over invalidation of a patent. Normally, the action will take three years or more, but where an infringement case is pending, the procedure can be accelerated and a decision rendered within one or two years. The losing party can then take an appeal to the Tokyo High Court and then to the Supreme Court. A decision to invalidate a patent can be appealed before the Tokyo High Court.

In Korea, the confirmation-of-scope action is also available to the patentee and to third parties. As its name implies, this action is to show that a particular product or process is either covered by (positive scope) or excluded from (negative scope) the scope of a given patent. Though this action offers merely declaratory relief, it can influence the civil court's determination of the pending infringement action. In some cases, if there is doubt as to the infringement, it is advisable that the plaintiff commence a confirmation-of-scope action prior to bringing the more lengthy and costly infringement suit.

§ 10.13   —Licensing

Both Korea and Japan favor policies for licensing inventions between the owner of the patented invention and a user of the invention. Compulsory nonexclusive licensing is even statutorily mandated in certain cases. In Japan, when someone makes an improvement to the main invention of the patent, then a patent can be granted for the improvement as well as a nonexclusive license for the underlying patent. In addition, if the owner of a patent fails to use the invention continuously for three years, or if use of the invention is deemed necessary for the public interest, a compulsory nonexclusive license will be granted upon request. The JPO, however, has never issued a compulsory license; rather, parties have opted to negotiate a voluntary license between themselves.

In Korea, compulsory nonexclusive licensing is granted for patented inventions by operation of law in the following circumstances:

1. An employer is given a nonexclusive license (without any requirement for the employer to pay a reasonable royalty) when an employee makes an invention (in the course of employment) applicable to the employer's line of business

2. A third party who was already working the same invention is given such license if the invention was being worked on in good faith at the time the patent application was filed (no compensation required)

3. An owner of a patented invention is given such license if the owner was working such invention in good faith when a successful invalidation action against the owner's patent is filed on the ground that a previously filed application exists (reasonable royalty must be paid)

4. An owner of a design right is given such license if the patent term for such design has expired and the product conflicts with a later filed patent right, to the extent necessary to continue using the design (with payment of a reasonable royalty)

5. The original patentee may continue to work the patent after the patent's rights are auctioned off in execution of a lien placed upon such patent (reasonable royalty to be paid)

6. A third party who had begun working the invention is given such license if such work was begun in good faith reliance on the original decision regarding invalidation, limitation, rejection, or grant of license, and such original decision is subsequently reversed in a special action for reconsideration of a trial or appellate judgment (depending on circumstances, a reasonable royalty may be required from the statutory licensee).

The amount of royalty must be agreed to between the parties or, in the absence of such agreement, an action must be brought in a court to determine the amount of such royalty.

In addition to these statutory licenses, a person may petition to KIPO for the right to use the patented invention. In such a case, KIPO may grant a license for such invention to the petitioner after considering the merits of such petition. If a license is to be granted, KIPO determines the amount of compensation to be paid by such petitioner to the patentee based on prevailing market conditions.

In the following circumstances, KIPO has the authority to grant a license notwithstanding the objections of the patentee to the granting of such license:

1. The patented invention has not been continuously worked in Korea for a three-year period without justifiable reason, or the extent of use in Korea of such invention is insufficient to meet domestic demand, or working a patent is in the public interest

2. The use of the patented invention is necessary to work another invention, and the patentee of the earlier invention will not, or is unable to, grant a license

3. The use of the patented invention is necessary for national defense.

It should be noted that in the circumstances described in the first item of the list, the petition for license will not be accepted until at least four years have elapsed since the date of the registration of the patent in question. In the circumstances described in the second item of the list, the petitioner for the license must demonstrate that the subsequent invention represents an outstanding technical advance over the basic invention, and the use of such earlier invention will be limited in scope to only that which is necessary to work the subsequent invention. Notwithstanding the foregoing, KIPO has not yet granted a compulsory license to any person.

§ 10.14   —Extinguishment of Patent

A patent right may be extinguished upon the occurrence of any of the following circumstances:

1. Unless extended, the patent will become extinguished at the end of its term.
2. If a patentee fails to pay required annuities, the patent will become extinguished.
3. When a patentee who is an individual dies without leaving an heir, the patent will become extinguished.
4. A patentee may abandon the patent by submitting a written declaration of abandonment. A patent may be abandoned in whole or partially only with respect to certain claims.
5. The Korean government may cancel a patent if such cancellation is necessary for national security or if the patented invention is nonworking even after a compulsory license is granted.
6. The patent may be extinguished by an invalidation action brought before KIPO. Only an "interested party" or KIPO may bring such an action.[19]

§ 10.15   Information Technology and Copyright

Any creation of IT that fits copyright's statutory definition of a *work* and meets the requirements for publication can be eligible for copyright protection. In Japan, software is expressly protected by copyright following Japan's amendment of its copyright law in 1985. Korea enacted the Computer Program Protection Act (CPPA) in 1987. Though Korea has this separate law for computer programs, the rights granted to the creator of a program are essentially the same rights as those under the copyright law.

Copyright requires that a work express some intrinsically creative element of the creator that will somehow contribute to the development of a cultural aspect

---

[19] An *interested party* is defined in a Supreme Court decision as a person who suffers damage to his business or one who is likely to suffer because of the patent in question.

of literature, science, or the arts. This is the minimum level of creativity necessary for a work to be worthy of protection. In the case of IT, the utilitarian aspect of the creation will not preclude its copyright as long as this requisite level of creativity is satisfied. Unfortunately, copyright laws are inadequate protection against the stealing of this utilitarian conceptual element in that the laws prohibit only the copying of the fixed expression of the created work.

§ 10.16 —Conditions for Copyright Protection

Copyright law protects only *works,* defined under the Copyright Act as "an original literary, scientific or artistic work." IT can be protected in whole or in part by copyright if it comprises a work of authorship, a performance, a phonogram, a broadcast, or a wire transmission.

The Copyright Act gives some examples of protected works:

1. Oral or written literary works (lectures, narrations, novels, poems, scripts, theses, and the like)
2. Musical works
3. Theatrical works (choreographs, dramas, pantomimes, and the like)
4. Works of fine and applied art (calligraphy, designs, handicrafts, paintings, sculptures, and the like)
5. Architectural works (architectures, architectural models and drawings, and the like)
6. Photographic works
7. Visual or cinematographic works (motion pictures, films, videos, and the like)
8. Maps and diagrammatic works (blueprints, charts, design drawings, models, sketches, and the like)
9. Computer program works (in Korea, governed by relevant sections of the Copyright Act if no applicable law exists under the CPPA).

The key factor in determining whether a work qualifies for protection is the level of creativity inherent in the work to warrant copyright protection.

Works falling into any of the following six categories are not protected under the Copyright Act:

1. Legislation
2. Public announcements or administrative guidelines issued by the State or a local public entity
3. Decisions, judgments, or orders of judicial courts or decisions or resolutions issued in administrative trial procedures and other similar procedures

4. Collections or translations of those mentioned in the preceding three items made by the State or a local public entity
5. News reports conveying only facts
6. Speeches delivered in an open court, at a local council, or the National Assembly.

A *derivative work* is an alteration of an original work by means of arrangement, adaptation, modification, translation, visualization, or other means. It is recognized as being a separate and independent work from the original work and is protected without prejudice to the rights of the creator of the original work. Collections of works also have the same protection rights without prejudice to the rights of each of the original authors of the works as long as the selection and arrangement of the collection shows creative originality.

§ 10.17   —Foreign Works

The works of foreigners are protected in Korea if the foreigner is a permanent resident of Korea, or if Korea is the first place to publish the work or the work is published in Korea within a 30-day grace period from the date it was first published abroad.

Otherwise, foreigners's copyrights are protected pursuant to any treaties that Korea has joined. The same applies for Japan's Copyright Act, but the applicant must have a principal place of business in Japan, not merely a permanent residence, in order to be considered a Japanese national.[20] Under the Berne Convention, Japan is obligated to afford copyright protection to nationals of other convention members.

Works published prior to Korea's joining the Universal Copyright Convention and the Geneva Phonogram Convention in October 1987 are not entitled to protection in Korea. New amendments to the Korean Copyright Act, effective July 1, 1996, however, retroactively grant protection to foreign works originally created abroad between 1957 and 1987, the year Korea joined the Universal Copyright Convention and the Geneva Convention.

§ 10.18   —Administration of the Copyright Act

Rights under copyright vest in the creator automatically upon the creation of an artistic, literary, or scientific work. No formalities are required, such as registration. Registration is advisable, but not necessary to establish copyright. Copyright recognizes the "work-for-hire" rule, whereby an employer can claim ownership of the work of an employee.

---

[20] JPA art. 6(i).

In Korea, the registering of copyrights is administered by the Ministry of Culture and Information (MCI), which also issues the license that is required for the management of copyrights in Korea. However, the Ministry of Information and Communications now registers programs under the CPPA in Korea. In Japan, copyrights are registered with the Culture Department of the Ministry of Education.

§ 10.19 —Ownership of Copyright

Copyright is attained upon creation of a work by the "person who has created the work." Copyright is, however, subject to the work-for-hire rule. In the event that the work is created while the creator is acting as an employee, the employer is entitled to the copyright ownership, unless an arrangement has been made between the employer and the employee. Otherwise, one may assume that the author of the work is the person whose real name or well-known alias is listed on the original work or on the reproduction thereof or listed in the public performance or broadcast or indicated as the publisher or performer.

Joint ownership of a work is recognized under the act for works that have been created by the joint contribution of two or more persons, but the law prohibits transference of any shares of ownership without the consent of all joint owners.

§ 10.20 —Rights Granted under Copyright

The rights granted under the copyright law can be divided into two categories: moral rights and economic rights. Under moral rights, the creator has the right to govern release of the work, to be identified as the creator of the work, and to dictate any alteration in content of the work. Moral rights are not assignable, and therefore expire upon the death of the creator. However, the reputation of the creator and the work is protected long after the creator's death.

Economic rights are not restricted like that of moral rights. As long as the work is registered with the Ministry of Culture and Sports (in Korea, for computer programs, under the CPPA, registration must be done with the Ministry of Information and Communication), it is common practice to assign, exercise, pledge, and transfer economic rights.

§ 10.21 —Duration of Rights

The economic rights of the creator remain effective for a period of 50 years after the death of the creator. In the case of joint ownership of a work, the economic rights stay effective for 50 years after the death of the last survivor. Economic rights for anonymous works, or works under aliases not well-known and the real names of the authors are not registered with the MCI, the terms end 50 years after the divulgence of the works.

In Japan, for any copyright granted under the Berne Convention, when the copyright protection expires in the country of origin, the work is no longer entitled to protection in Japan.[21]

Under the CPPA, computer programs are protected for a term of 50 years from the date of the program's creation.

§ 10.22   —Scope of Rights

The creator of a work may prevent unauthorized copying of the work (economic rights), as well as prevent another from using the work in a manner that injures the author's honor or reputation (moral rights). The creator's economic rights also include the right to perform, broadcast, recite, exhibit, or translate the work. However, these rights are limited when the work is used:

1. In judicial, legislative, or administrative proceedings
2. For reporting news
3. By broadcasters for temporary sound or visual recordings
4. For quotations for criticism, research, reporting, and so forth
5. For educational purposes
6. For reproduction for public libraries
7. For reproduction for nonprofit examinations
8. For reproduction in braille
9. For nonprofit public performances and broadcasts
10. For reproduction for personal home use
11. As an exhibition or reproduction by the owner of the work.

§ 10.23   —Compulsory Licenses

Under certain circumstances, copyrighted works may be used without any permission of the copyright owner. The Copyright Deliberation and Conciliation Committee authorizes and grants licenses for the use of the works. However, compensation is required, as determined by the committee.

In Japan, several copyright clearing houses perform the task of collecting royalty for the use of certain copyrighted materials, including IT-related software. Such clearing houses are the Japanese Society of Rights of Authors and

---

[21] Japanese Copyright Act (JCA) art. 58.

Composers (JASRAC), the Japan Copyright Center, and the Photographic Copyright Center of Japan. This method of tracking and enforcing copyrights is proving to be difficult, however, in light of the growing variety of IT incorporating digitalization techniques.[22]

Compulsory licenses are granted if: (1) seven years have passed since the date of publication and if there are no Korean translations in print or if the publications are no longer available; and (2) negotiations with the owner of the work have failed or if the owner of the work cannot be located.

The seven-year grace period may be reduced to one year when translations are needed for the "purpose of education, study, or research." Compulsory licenses for phonographic recordings are also available as long as the recording has not been marketed for three years. Licenses for visual works can only be granted once every five years, unless otherwise agreed upon with the first licensee. The rights to adapt the work for production, to reproduce and distribute, to publicly screen, to broadcast, and to use a translation of the visual work must all be included in the agreement.

§ 10.24   —Publishing Right

The right to publish a work is different from the right to reproduce and distribute the work. The publishing right may be assigned, pledged, and granted only with the approval of the holder of the right to reproduce and distribute. The publishing right holder, once licensed, must publish the work within nine months of receiving the work, acknowledge the reproduction right of the owner on all publications, and "publish the work continuously according to customary practice."[23] Unless otherwise stated, publication rights are effective for three years after the first publication date. New editions may be published after consulting with the original author of the work for possible revisions.

§ 10.25   —Neighboring Rights

Under the Korean Copyright Act, neighboring rights are protected for performers (the right to record, videotape, or to photograph the performance and receive compensation for broadcast thereof) , phonograph producers (the right to reproduce or distribute the phonograph record and receive compensation for broadcast thereof), and broadcasters (the right to reproduce or simulcast by means of recording, videotaping, photographing, or other similar means, as well as the right to broadcast live).[24]

---

[22] Furuta, Osamu, *An Overview of the Intellectual Property Aspects of Multimedia: Recent Discussions and Perspectives in Japan,* in Pacific Telecommunications Rev., June 1995.

[23] Korean Copyright Act (KCA) art. 55.

[24] KCA arts. 61–69.

The term of protection is 50 years from the year following the one in which the performance or broadcast was made and the phonograph or other recording was initially fixed.[25] Registration requirements are the same as those for copyright.

§ 10.26   —Copyright Deliberation and Conciliation

Japan offers mediation of disputes concerning copyright matters through the Department of Culture of the Ministry of Education. Alternatively, parties may bring suit in the civil court.

In Korea, the Copyright Deliberation and Conciliation Committee (CDCC) was established by the Minister of Culture and Information in order to "mediate any dispute over rights protected pursuant to" the Copyright Act, including issues concerning compensation, rates, and fees of copyright agents, and so forth. The MCI appoints 15 to 20 members to serve on this committee for a three-year term, electing one chairperson and two deputy chairpersons. The term may be renewed.

Within the CDCC, a Mediation Board is formed composed of three members, one of whom must be a lawyer. The Mediation Board's responsibility is to mediate disputes by making recommendations before going to court, and when a recommendation is put into effect, it becomes an out-of-court settlement. However, where the parties cannot reach an agreement over a dispute, or the dispute has not been resolved within three months, or the parties do not want to comply with the Mediation Board's recommendations, the Mediation Board cannot make further suggestions, resulting in the closing of the mediation proceedings. All expenses are the responsibility of the two parties or the petitioner of the proceedings if an agreement was not reached. The CDCC determines the expense amounts.

§ 10.27   —Enforcement

Protection against acts of infringement are covered in the Copyright Act. It also covers any act that infringes the author's moral rights such as "using a work in a manner [that] injures the author's reputation." Two injunction proceedings exist: provisional and permanent. Provisional proceedings are special proceedings for injunction claims and take less time to process than permanent proceedings.

Compensation may be claimed for infringements within three years of learning about the infringer, along with the "action necessary to restore his reputation" if it was an infringement of the author's moral right. If infringement occurs after the death of the author, a member of the author's surviving family or the author's testamentary executor may file the complaint charges.

---

[25] *Id.* art. 70.

Criminal sanctions are available when a person has infringed the author's moral or economic rights or has registered or recorded false information. A maximum penalty of either a three-year prison term or a 30 million Korean won fine will result. However, prosecution will take place only if a complaint is filed within six months of discovering the infringement. The courts also have the right to confiscate the infringing material, if necessary.

§ 10.28   Copyright and Computer Programs

Under the Copyright Act and the Computer Program Protection Act (CPPA), only the expression of the work is protected, not the concepts embodied in the work. As a result, programming languages (letters and symbols and their system for use), rules (a special rule on how to use a programming language), and algorithms (methods of combining instructions given to a program in a program) are excluded from protection. This is because these elements of the program are considered to lack the requisite creativity necessary to be afforded protection. They are considered to be merely the "flow of processing in the program itself."[26]

Of major concern to IT owners is the issue of whether, and how, copyright should apply to database and video game programs. Most IT incorporates some elements of database and multimedia applications. A database can be considered a compilation, protectable under the Copyright Act, but this will not protect the data elements of the work, only its collection and arrangement aspects; copyright protects only the fixed expression of the work, not the elemental concepts embodied in the work. Video games contain multimedia (audio, visual, interactive) aspects, which can change the expression of the program each time it is played. Courts in Japan and the United States have nonetheless recognized video games to be within the parameters of copyrightable subject matter. In Korea, the same trend is followed, and new legislation amending the CPPA will help clarify the various issues in these matters.[27]

§ 10.29   —Definition of Computer Program

Under the CPPA, a *computer program* is defined as a work expressed in the form of a series of instructions or orders that are used directly or indirectly to obtain a specific result in a computer or other device having information-processing

---

[26] Wineburg, Intellectual Property in Asia § 5.61, paraphrasing the court in System Science v. Tovo Soku Ki K.K., Tokyo District Court, Mar. 31, 1989, Tokyo High Court, June 20, 1989, Hanji No. 1322 at 138.

[27] Lee, Sung-Hae, Information and Communications Bureau of the Korean Ministry of Information and Communication, in a paper, *Ultra High-Speed Information and Communications Foundation Construction Plan and Multimedia Copyright,* presented at the International Seminar for Seoul Bookfair '95, May 18, 1995.

capability.[28] Protection is provided to programs that are considered to be creative expressions, but, as in Japan, not to the elements of the program that are considered as a means to create the expression. Thus, program languages, syntax, rules, and algorithms (which are used for arranging programs) are not protected because they are considered as a means to create an expression rather than a form of expression.[29] Korea's CPPA protects source codes (programs), object codes (programs), voice programs, and operational programs, but interface protocols and program solutions are excluded from protection for lack of creativity.

A cognate program that is derived from an original program is called a *derivative program* (like a derivative work in copyright law). The CPPA defines a derivative program as a program made from the original program by method of adaptation, or making use of all, or a substantial part of, the series of instructions or a command of the original program.[30] A derivative program does not share protection with its original program; it is protected as an independent program.[31]

The concept of derivative programs is troubling to IT-related software creators because the extent of modification to a prior work is not clear. Much controversy arises over issues of infringement, especially in the case of video games and software graphics.

§ 10.30 —Rights and Ownership of Computer Programs

Just as in copyright, both moral rights and economic rights are protected under the CPPA. Programs created by any nationals of World Trade Organization (WTO) member countries are protected retroactively for 50 years from the date of creation.[32]

The requirements for the protection of computer programs created by foreigners are the same as those under the Copyright Act, except that instead of a requirement for residence in Korea, there is a principal place of business in Korea requirement.

Under the CPPA, the 50-year term of protection for a program copyright is measured from the date of creation of the program, not from the death of the creator, as in copyright law.[33]

The title to a program created by an employee in the course of employment belongs to the employer, unless otherwise agreed between the parties.

---

[28] CPPA art. 2.

[29] Young S. Song, Intellectual Property Law 229 (1989).

[30] *Id.*

[31] CPPA art. 2.

[32] CPPA art. 3, addendum 2.

[33] *Id.* art. 8 (3).

The owner of a program, which has been released to the public, cannot refuse to provide the program to an enduser unless the terms and conditions for use are unreasonable.

§ 10.31 —Registration and Protection

As with copyrights, registration is not necessary for the protection of a program. However, if the creator of a program fails to register her program, she will be unable to register any transfer or pledge of the program copyright, which is required to give notice to third parties and make the transfer or pledge effective against bona fide purchasers.

The creator of a program has up to one year after its creation to register the program.[34] Program registration has another significant presumptive effect which is not related to the registration of other copyrighted works. Any infringement of a registered program is presumed solely to be the consequence of the violator's negligence. Therefore, due to this presumption, the alleged infringer has the burden of proving no negligence. This is significant to the plaintiff owner because the awarding of damages is contingent upon the defendant's negligence or willfulness. The profits made by the infringer can be presumed to be the damages resulting from the infringement, or actual lost profits of the owner resulting from the infringement can be claimed.

The registration of computer programs under the CPPA is administered by the Ministry of Information and Communication. The program register is a public record for the registering of a program and such other copyright-related matters, like licenses and pledges, which limit or transfer rights to the program.[35]

Acts of infringement are the same as those for copyright infringement. In addition, knowingly using a bootleg (unauthorized) program in one's business is considered to be an act of infringement.

§ 10.32 Information Technology and Trade
Secret Law

Owners of IT do not always pursue patent or copyright protection either because they do not want to disclose the IT to competitors or because the IT is not yet ready to meet the statutory requirements for IPR protection. For example, an owner of a copyright may not have yet published the work in Korea and Japan. In such instances, trade secret laws protect against unauthorized disclosure and use.

---

[34] *Id.* art. 21 (1).

[35] *Id.* art. 21 (3) and (4).

Japan has protected trade secrets since June 1991 under its Unfair Competition Prevention Law. In Korea, the Unfair Competition Prevention Act (UCPA), by amendment, effective December 1992, provides statutory protection for trade secrets. Until then, trade secrets were accorded limited protection under contract law (employer-employee) and under negligence law.

The amendment has no retroactive effect. According to a transitional provision, it does not apply to acts of infringement committed prior to the effective date. In addition, trade secrets acquired prior to the effective date are not covered even when they are used after the effective date.

§ 10.33   —Subject Matter Eligible for Protection

Trade secrets are broadly defined as any technical or business information, such as experimental data, know-how, drawings, manuals, customer information, and the like, which is used for commercial purposes and maintained in secret and not publicly known. Korea's revised UCPA defines *trade secrets* as:

1. technical or operational information useful for any production and sales methods and other business activities,
2. which is not known to the public,
3. which has an independent economic value, and
4. which has been kept secret through considerable efforts.[36]

§ 10.34   —Violations

The UCPA sets forth the following infringing acts, which are similar to Japan's trade secret law:

1. Acquiring a trade secret by theft, fraud, coercion, or other unlawful or dishonest acts (hereafter, the "unfair acquisition") or thereafter, using or revealing a trade secret so acquired;
2. Acquiring, using, or disclosing a trade secret with actual or constructive knowledge of its prior unfair acquisition;
3. Although innocently acquiring a trade secret, using it or disclosing it after learning of its earlier unfair acquisition; and
4. Using or disclosing a trade secret in breach of a contractual obligation to maintain confidentiality is an unfair acquisition.[37]

---

[36] UCPA art. 2-2.

[37] UCPA art. 2-3.

§ 10.35 —Remedies

Injunctive relief is available against actual infringement or likelihood of infringement. As part of the injunctive relief, the trade secret owner may request that the court order the destruction of products made by the infringing act or the equipment used to carry out the infringing act, to the extent necessary to prevent any further infringement.

Damages are available against those who have intentionally or negligently infringed a trade secret. In addition, the court may also order appropriate measures to restore the business reputation of the trade secret owner that has been damaged as a result of the intentional or negligent infringement of a trade secret.

In Japan, damages can be presumed to be the amount of profit gained by the misappropriator or the market value consideration for the use of the trade secret.

A criminal action is available against an officer or employee of an enterprise who disclosed to a third party a trade secret regarding a production technology peculiar to the enterprise in order to gain an unfair profit or injure the enterprise. Such violation may be subject either to imprisonment for a period of up to three years or a fine not exceeding 30 million Korean won.

In Japan, trade secret actions are tried in the civil court. This raises the spectre of public disclosure because the Japanese Constitution requires judgments to be released. Such a release would defeat the whole purpose of the trade secret law.

§ 10.36 Semiconductor Integrated Circuit Layout Design Act

One of the most central core technologies incorporated into all other IT is that of the semiconductor chip. Although this law was enacted in Japan and Korea in response to the United States' demand for reciprocity concerning the United States Semiconductor Chip Protection Act, it is a firm example of the responsiveness of law to the changing demands of the new information technologies.

§ 10.37 —Registration Requirement

Protection of the right in a semiconductor chip layout design is triggered once the layout design is registered with the Ministry of Trade and Industry. Registration must be filed within two years from the date that the work was first used for commercial purposes. Registration may be denied for any of the following reasons:

1.   The applicant is not the creator
2.   A joint application was not filed for more than one creator

3. The two-year grace period for the registration has expired
4. other Presidential Decree grounds were not upheld.

In addition, registration may be canceled under any of the following circumstances:

1. A person or a country is committing an act of infringement
2. The work has not been used in Korea for two or more consecutive years after establishing registration
3. The registration was established on false terms
4. The work is not a creation
5. The registration will violate the Act, the Presidential Decree, or other relevant regulations.

Registration of the work allows for the establishment, grant, transfer, modification, or expiration of an exclusive use right, of an ordinary use right, of a pledge, or the transfer or disposition thereof.

§ 10.38   —Rights and Remedies

The protection term is 10 years after establishing registration. Foreign works are protected under any treaties Korea has entered into, from a treaty's effective date. Works created in the course of employment shall be considered the works of the employer and not the actual creator unless the parties have agreed to a prior arrangement.

Acts of infringement will result in criminal proceedings with penalty of imprisonment not to exceed three years or a fine not to exceed 10 million Korean won. Compensation may be claimed by the copyright holder for any damages suffered as a result of the infringement. A person who registers under false indication, deceit, or other unlawful act, or divulges information regarding the program, will be prosecuted along with any representative of a juridical person who commits an offense.

§ 10.39   Korea's Statutory Protection of Information Technology

The laws discussed in §§ 10.40 through 10.43 reflect Korea's recognition of the importance of information technologies for national economic success. Though these various acts are directed at the promotion and development of their respective industries, they can also be viewed as a means of protecting IT.

§ 10.40 —Basic Act for the Promotion of Information and Communication

This Act broadly promulgates the promotion of information and communications industries and prioritizes the development of information and communication infrastructures, such as the building of a fiber optic network of transmission lines for high-speed telecommunications capabilities. Allocation of funding for such projects as well as special governmental considerations for businesses engaging in the research and development or transfer of such relevant technology is outlined in the Act.

§ 10.41 —Disc and Video Act

This law requires the registration of compact discs and videos with the Ministry of Sports and Culture. The review of content by the Performance and Ethic Committee is required for the importation or copying of any compact disc or video. Criminal penalties can be enforced against violators.

§ 10.42 —Computer Network and Networking Promotion Act

This law promotes the development of computer networks through the Ministry of Information and Communication (MIC). It establishes a National Computerization Agency and a Mediation Council of Computer Networks. Most importantly, the MIC must administer the standards for compatibility and connectivity of computer systems. The Act provides criminal sanctions against interference or unauthorized disclosure of information processed, stored, or transmitted by computer networks.

§ 10.43 —Software Development Promotion Act

This Act aims to promote the creation of software as well as increase public awareness and utilization of computer software. The Act establishes a Council for the Promotion of Software to administer software creations, as well as assist in the development of the software industry.

§ 10.44 Technology Development Promotion Act

The Technology Development Promotion Act is a Korean law that requires a report to be filed with the Ministry of Science and Technology when a domestic person intends to enter into a contract by which an industrial property right, technology service, or technology know-how is transferred, provided, or licensed to a foreign entity for more than US$100,000.

The report to the Ministry of Science and Technology shall include a plan and information regarding:

1. The particulars of the exported technology and the method of the transfer
2. The amount and the mode of payment for the transferred technology
3. The term of the contract
4. The expected impact of such technology transfer.

Upon receipt of the report, the Minister of Science and Technology may recommend the modification of the plan for the proposed technology transfer. In the event that the proposed technology transfer involves defense technology and industry, prior approval by the Minister of Defense is required in addition to that of the Minister of Science and Technology.

When the technology proposed to be transferred is a *strategic technology* (defined to be technology which, if misused or misplaced, may jeopardize or be harmful to world peace or international security), an approval of the Minister of Science and Technology upon the consultation with the Minister of Trade, Industry, and Energy is also required. The approval of the Minister of Science and Technology may be made with conditions to the technology transfer.

§ 10.45 Engineering Technology Promotion Act

Under the ETPA, any proposed export of engineering technology for more than US$300,000 must be reported to the Engineering Technology Promotion Association. The report shall be accompanied by the overall plan and the details for the proposed export of the engineering technology and the proposed export agreement or contract (along with a Korean translation). The Engineering Technology Promotion Association may, in its discretion, return the report and the plan for revision or modification.

§ 10.46 Contract Law

The law of contract embodied in the Civil Code of Korea governs technology transactions including technology license agreements. The basic task of the law is to give effect to the will of the parties involved in such agreements by providing a rational, unbiased, and speedy court system, or what can be termed a "transparent court system," and an effective means to enforce the agreement.

The obligations of the contracting parties will be measured by the true intention of the parties. The courts rely on the rule of good faith in interpreting obligations. A party is obliged to perform contractual obligations in good faith as agreed upon with the other party. The other party is bound to accept the performance in good faith pursuant to the contract. A party will be held responsible for a breach of an obligation unless he can prove that his nonperformance was not caused by any willful or negligent act.

When a party is in breach and the performance is still possible, the other party may demand a performance within a reasonable period of time. If the party in breach does not perform the obligation in time, the other party may rescind the contract or seek a compulsory performance. The aggrieved party may in any event seek damages caused by the breach. The damages may be awarded to the extent ordinarily arising out of the delayed performance or nonperformance. Consequential or special damages may also be awarded as long as they were foreseeable. When a contract provides for liquidated damages, the aggrieved party under the contract has only to prove the delay or nonperformance of the other party in order to recover damages. The party does not have to show the extent of damages actually sustained. A liquidated damages clause is enforceable as long as it is reasonable in light of the anticipated or actual harm caused by the breach.

§ 10.47   Unfair Trade Practices in Technology Transactions

The Fair Trade Committee of Korea (FTC) has released a revised notice on the types of unfair trade practices in international technology inducement agreements. The guidelines, which became effective in April 1995, will have a strong bearing on the drafting of IT-related agreements. The following is a list of various provisions deemed to be unfair trade practices:

1. Any provisions requiring a technology licensee or transferee to purchase from the technology supplier, or a person designated by the supplier, raw materials, components, equipments, and related products that are necessary to make the products (contract products) using the technology (contract technology) provided under the agreement.

2. Any provisions placing unreasonable restrictions on the sale or export of the contract products. However, prohibition from entering the territories where the technology supplier has registered the contract technology or has granted a third party an exclusive right to sell the contract products shall not be deemed unreasonable.

3. Any provisions requiring a licensee to sell the licensed products through the licensor or any person designated by the licensor, or to those designated

by the licensor; any provisions giving the licensor the power to set the maximum manufacture and sales quantity of the licensed products; or any provisions enabling the licensor to set the minimum manufacture and sales targets and to terminate the agreement unilaterally when the licensee fails to attain such targets.

4. Any provisions unreasonably restricting distribution, sales volume, or method of sales of the contract products or unreasonably fixing the sales price or resale price of the contract products.

5. Any provisions unreasonably restricting the technology supplier from dealing with products competitive with or similar to contract products or from using technologies competitive with or similar to contract technology after the expiration of the contract.

6. Any provisions restricting use of the technology or requiring payment of fees after the industrial property rights to the contract technology expires, or after the technology know-how is made public.

7. Any provisions imposing royalties upon products unrelated to the contract products, or requiring the technology licensee or transferee to take other technologies as a condition to the license or transfer of the contract technology.

8. Any provisions restricting the technology licensee or transferee from improving the contract technology.

9. Any provisions obligating the technology licensee or transferee to provide the technology supplier with such improvements.

10. Any provisions requiring the technology licensee or transferee to incur unreasonable amounts of sales promotion expenses, including advertising expenses.

11. Any provisions leaving the assessment of royalty payments only to the licensor's discretion. However, it is not considered unfair for the licensor to impose a minimum royalty amount on the licensee.

12. Any provisions unfairly disadvantageous to one party in termination of the contract or selection of an arbitration organization or designation of a governing law applicable to any possible disputes of the parties.

13. Any provisions giving the licensor the power to terminate the agreement in case a third party contests the validity or confidentiality of the licensed technology.

Any agreements incorporating such unfair trade practices can be sanctioned by the FTC, which can result in the nullification of specific violative provisions or the whole agreement.

§ 10.48   Special Considerations in the Development of Information Technology

There are particular concerns that arise in the development of IT and the protection of IPR in such technology, including the treatment of works made for hire and joint works.

Works Made for Hire

Most IT inventions are developed and created within the context of an employer-employee relationship or a commissioned work-for-hire, as with a subcontractor. This is because of the high costs and specialized skills needed for research and development in IT.

For patents, assignment of exclusive and nonexclusive rights is recognized in the laws. This is essential because patent theory does not recognize the work-for-hire doctrine, in which the owner of the invention is not necessarily the actual creator, but rather the employer or person who commissioned the work, in the course of which the invention resulted. In patent theory, therefore, the employee remains the owner. But most employment contracts require that all the rights in any creations made within the parameters of the employment be transferred to the employer. Nonetheless, both Korea and Japan recognize, by statute, the right of the employer to a nonexclusive license to use any employee invention.

For copyrights, including computer program copyrights, the employer, or one who commissioned the work, can be the owner of a work created by an employee under the work-for-hire doctrine.

Jointly Developed IT

Much of IT is jointly developed by consortiums of private business companies as well as public sector research facilities, such as universities or government-sponsored research institutes. Very often, these joint research partners are from different nations.

The arrangement of rights, interests, and obligations between joint research partners is largely up to the parties involved, subject to national security interests embodied in the regulations on the transfer of technology. The will of the parties will be determinative in the interpretation of agreements. The protection of IT must then be viewed from two perspectives: protection of interests as against joint partners and protection against infringement by third parties.

The intellectual property clause of the research agreement should clearly establish ownership of any new intellectual property as well as set forth prior intellectual property individually owned by each party and used in the course of research. A warranty of noninfringement should be included for such prior IP. The parties usually cross-license to each other the right to use or manufacture processes or products arising out of the research with certain territorial restrictions. Other aspects of the contract, such as choice of law, arbitration, and so forth, are the same as other international business agreements.

§ 10.49 International Standards of Protection

Through joint international efforts, both developed and developing nations must establish basic protection standards and guarantees of enforcement of IPR. Today's international business transactions embody at least some aspect of IPR. Harmonization of the relevant laws and standards of IPR protection will ensure the smooth and secure flow of technology across multinational borders.

Research and development of IT is a high-cost, collective effort. Korea is finally realizing that it can no longer hold onto the old belief that lax enforcement of IPR laws is a necessary means to "borrow" technology and thereby bridge the gap with developed nations. In today's highly competitive IT market, such practices will often produce the opposite effect of inhibiting the flow of valuable technology into its borders.

The main obstacle to the success of a globally unified system of IPR protection is jurisdiction. IPR protection laws can vary from country to country. Where a particular IT is developed jointly across many borders, the question is under which of the multinational owners, and in which jurisdiction, should the invention be registered? The common practice today is to register for IPR protection in all the jurisdictions where the invention is "worked," that is, anywhere it is used, sold, manufactured, or licensed. This is a very expensive procedure, however, with unsatisfactory results due to policing and enforcement problems.

The problem of setting international standards for the protection of IPR touches upon a more fundamental question of law and society. Laws reflect the culture and social attitudes of the people governed by the laws. Must universal legal standards be adapted to such different laws, or must the local laws be adapted to fit the universal standards?

Perhaps the way will become clear as nations of the world come to realize the important value of acknowledging creativity and inventiveness, regardless of borders and jurisdictions.

§ 10.50 Changing Policies and Changing Laws

Korea's various laws aimed at the promotion of IT show how laws can be shaped to implement important socioeconomic policies. Whether these specialized laws are effective remains to be seen. Changing the laws will not always result in the desired effect. Oftentimes, new laws will breed ignorance and chaos within its targeted social group. Then the question becomes: Should new laws be implemented to protect and promote IT or should traditional laws be extended to fit new applications of IT?

In Japan, recent amendments to the patent laws try to shorten the application time for the issuance of patents. For instance, the new amendments restrict the introduction of new matter once the first action by the JPO has been taken. These laws recognize the limited shelf life of today's IT, where in some cases, the three years of waiting for the patent to issue, during which time the invention is fully published and disclosed, will give competitors time to simply invent around the technology, thereby crippling its applicability. Or in other cases the competitors will simply have moved on beyond the technology in the application.

In Korea, by amendment to the patent law, effective March 1, 1998, the Trial Board and the Appellate Trial Board of the Korea Industrial Property Office will be merged to create the Patent Trial Tribunal, which will be the new forum for initial administrative trials relating to patent lawsuits. After exhausting this administrative remedy, a trial de novo can be had in the newly established Patent Court. The Patent Court is a court of law authorized under the powers of the Supreme Court. Appeal of final judgments can be heard before the Supreme Court.

The unique characteristic of the Patent Court is its specialization in the Patent Laws; the judges on its bench will be specially trained in the relevant laws, and technical advisors will assist judges in understanding highly technical materials.

All these reforms reflect the growing importance of IPR in today's litigation and acknowledge the ever-increasing complexity of today's technology. These are examples of the law's attempt to meet the changing needs of IPR protection. Such continued efforts should provide the necessary secure environment for the development and transfer of IT in Korea and Japan.

INDEX